CONSENTABILITY

Problems regarding the nature of consent are at the heart of many of today's most pressing issues. For example, the #MeToo movement has underscored the need to move beyond viewing consent as a simple matter of yes or no. Consent is complex because humans and their relationships are complicated. Humans, as a result of cognitive limitations and emotional and physical vulnerabilities, are susceptible to manipulation and mistakes. Given the potential for regret, are there some things to which one should not be permitted to consent? The consentability quandary becomes more urgent with techno-logical advances. Should we allow body hacking? Cryogenics? Consumer travel to Mars? Assisted suicide? In *Consentability: Consent and Its Limits*, Nancy Kim proposes a bold, original framework for evaluating consentability, which considers the complexities surrounding consent.

Nancy S. Kim is Professor of Law at California Western School of Law and Visiting Professor at the Rady School of Management, University of California, San Diego. She is an elected member of the American Law Institute and the author of numerous articles, essays and two books, *Wrap Contracts: Foundations and Ramifications* and *The Fundamentals of Contract Law and Clauses: A Practical Approach*.

Consentability

CONSENT AND ITS LIMITS

by

NANCY S. KIM

California Western School of Law

CAMBRIDGE
UNIVERSITY PRESS

CAMBRIDGE
UNIVERSITY PRESS

University Printing House, Cambridge CB2 8BS, United Kingdom

One Liberty Plaza, 20th Floor, New York, NY 10006, USA

477 Williamstown Road, Port Melbourne, VIC 3207, Australia

314– 321, 3rd Floor, Plot 3, Splendor Forum, Jasola District Centre,
New Delhi – 110025, India

79 Anson Road, #06–04/06, Singapore 079906

Cambridge University Press is part of the University of Cambridge.

It furthers the University's mission by disseminating knowledge in the pursuit of
education, learning, and research at the highest international levels of excellence.

www.cambridge.org
Information on this title: www.cambridge.org/9781107164918
DOI: 10.1017/9781316691311

First published 2019

Printed and bound in Great Britain by Clays Ltd, Elcograf S.p.A.

A catalogue record for this publication is available from the British Library.

Library of Congress Cataloging-in-Publication Data
NAMES: Kim, Nancy S., 1966– author.
TITLE: Consentability : consent and its limits / by Nancy S. Kim, California Western School
of Law.
DESCRIPTION: Cambridge, United Kingdom ; New York, NY, USA : Cambridge University
Press, 2019. | Includes bibliographical references and index.
IDENTIFIERS: LCCN 2018038863 | ISBN 9781107164918
SUBJECTS: LCSH: Consent (Law)
CLASSIFICATION: LCC K579.16 K56 2019 | DDC 344.04/12–dc23
LC record available at https://lccn.loc.gov/2018038863

ISBN 978-1-107-16491-8 Hardback
ISBN 978-1-316-61655-0 Paperback

Cambridge University Press has no responsibility for the persistence or accuracy of
URLs for external or third-party internet websites referred to in this publication
and does not guarantee that any content on such websites is, or will remain,
accurate or appropriate.

To S. B., M. B. and A. B., as always.

Contents

Contents

Figures

Acknowledgments

I am grateful to many people for their support during the process of writing this book. I thank William Aceves, Dan Barnhizer, Orit Gan, Danni Hart, Tom Joo, Chunlin Leonhard, Kaipo Matsumura, and Joanna Sax, all of whom read portions of this book at various stages and provided valuable comments. I presented portions of this book at KCon XII at Southwestern Law School, the Osher Institute at UC San Diego, and at a faculty workshop at California Western School of Law, and I thank the attendees at these presentations for helping me refine my ideas. For their careful research and diligent cite-checking assistance, I thank my wonderful research assistants, Heather Daiza, Vivian Lin, Ethan Shakoori, and Meagan Stevens. I thank my employer, California Western, for providing me with necessary resources, Heddy Rudd for much needed help preparing the bibliography, and the always amazing library reference desk staff for their efficiency and professionalism. I also thank my students at California Western and the University of California, San Diego, for their questions and their eagerness to learn which makes my job so rewarding.

Much thanks to my editor, Matt Gallaway, for shepherding me through the publication process a second time, and to the editorial and production team at Cambridge University Press for pulling it all together.

Finally, I am most grateful to my family, Seth, Mina, and Amelia. Thank you for your support, wisdom, encouragement, humor, and so much more. I really could not have done it without you.

Introduction

When Kim Suozzi, a twenty-one-year-old woman, was diagnosed with an aggressive brain cancer, she sought ways to save her life. With no cure on the horizon, she turned to cryogenics. Her parents were uneasy with the idea, but Suozzi forged ahead with her plans. She raised the $80,000 fee for cryopreservation from various donors, including the Society for Venturism. Shortly after she died at age twenty-three, a medical technician performed procedures to keep the blood vessels in her brain from collapsing, and she was placed into an ice bath and rushed to Alcor Life Extension Foundation, a U.S.-based cryonics organization. There, she was decapitated and cryoprotectant pumped through the main arteries in her brain. The hope was that one day, when technology had advanced enough, she would be revived with her brain largely intact, even though she would have no body. A CT scan later showed that the cryoprotectant had only reached part of her brain, leaving the rest vulnerable to damage.[1]

Advancements in science, technology and medicine have placed more ideas within the realm of possibility and created new situations which test societal norms and expectations. Yet, these ideas are fraught with unknown consequences. The pace of change surpasses the ability of lawmakers to respond. In some cases, new norms become established without consideration of their long-term societal implications. In other cases, laws quickly become outdated or obsolete.

At the center of many of these exciting innovations is the issue of consent. Should individuals be permitted to consent to participate in activities which are novel and dangerous? What does consent mean in situations which are replete with uncertainties? Should participants be permitted to withdraw from such activities – and if so, should there be constraints on their ability to do so?

---

[1] Amy Harmon, *A Dying Young Woman's Hope in Cryonics and a Future*, N.Y. TIMES (Sept. 12, 2015), www.nytimes.com/2015/09/13/us/cancer-immortality-cryogenics.html; *see also* George Dvorsky, *23-Year Old Kim Suozzi Undergoes Cryonic Preservation After Successful Fundraising Campaign*, 109 GIZMODO (Jan. 21, 2013), https://io9.gizmodo.com/5977640/23-year-old-kim-suozzi-undergoes-cryonic-preservation-after-successful-fundraising-campaign.

Consent both protects individual liberties and permits the exercise of them. Yet there are reasons to doubt the invincibility of consent. Choices – and the ability to refuse to consent – may be affected by personal circumstances, economic constraints, social pressures, time restrictions and cognitive limitations. Human beings are impulsive and susceptible to manipulation and deception. To err is human, and so is the inclination to make decisions that are short-sighted, irrational and regrettable.

The passage of time may degrade consent. Consent given at one time may no longer be valid at a later time. The perspective, motivations or feelings of the consenting party may have changed. Time may have altered the nature of the act itself, making it more or less difficult or affecting its desirability. Additional information might become available about the harms or benefits of a particular act or transaction. The emotionally gratifying short-term benefits may have waned or been fulfilled. The value of the long-term benefits may have been recalibrated due to changing circumstances or needs. The shifting nature of consent poses difficult and troubling issues, especially where performance involves the risk of serious physical injury.

Tough questions arise when individuals, with their human weaknesses and cognitive fallibilities, are given the power to make harmful and potentially life-threatening decisions. The government determines what activities are lawful and so may limit the scope and power of consent. Laws and regulations seek to balance the value of autonomy with the compromises necessary for living in a civilized society. Individual desires must be weighed against community needs and mores. Yet, this balancing act often lacks transparency or discernible parameters. Why do we permit individuals to enter into some transactions and not others? Why do we allow individuals to consent to perform in pornographic movies but not to be paid for sexual services? Why do we allow an individual to risk his or her life to serve in the military or to participate in mixed martial arts fighting, yet prohibit that individual from selling a kidney which will save the life of another? Why do we turn away in disgust at the sight of people who have implanted silicon chips into their hands, yet ogle at women who have implanted silicone into their breasts?

New technologies raise new legal and ethical questions regarding the nature, scope and boundaries of consent. Individuals have more options today regarding how they choose to live, die, procreate, conceive and interact with the world. Should we allow people to sell their body parts? Should we let them participate in early-stage drug trials or medical experiments? Should they be allowed to modify their bodies – and, if so, to what extent? Are there limits to consent – and if so, what are they?

Issues regarding whether someone should be permitted to consent to an act or activity – which this book refers to as "consentability" – are usually framed as issues of public policy. For example, in some states, surrogacy contracts are unenforceable because they are deemed to be against public policy.[2] In some cases, the public interest in prohibiting the act is deemed to be so strong that the act itself is criminalized.[3] But why are some acts considered inconsentable?

Consent in the law is typically viewed as a conclusion, an all-or-nothing concept where the actions of the parties are considered objectively and statically. This conception provides no guidance regarding which acts should be consentable. This book argues that consent is more complicated and should be understood as a dynamic which is context-dependent, incremental, variable and relative.[4] Decision-making does not occur in a vacuum, but is affected by what the consenting party knows, the available options and the consenting party's emotional state at the time consent is granted. It is also affected by the actions of the party seeking consent. Accordingly, while the requirement of consent recognizes the value of autonomous decision-making, the *validity* of consent hinges upon the context in which it is given and the dynamic unleashed by both parties.[5]

Consent is distinct from consentability. This book gives the term "consentability" two different meanings. The first involves possibility. An act which is consentable means that it is possible for there to be consent given the nature of the proposed activity. The second meaning of consentability involves legality. An act which is consentable is (or under the right circumstances, can be) legal. The possibility of valid consent is essential to consentability but it is not sufficient. Consentability is thus determined by assessing the effect of an activity upon both the individual and society.

This book proposes a framework for assessing consentability which is both normative and descriptive, meaning that it explains both what the state should do and what it often does. The descriptive account is only partially accurate because state action is often inconsistent or incoherent. The advantage of a framework is to render transparent the process by which decisions regarding consentability are made and in doing so, yield more consistent and predictable results. A structured way to think about consent and consentability may lead to better law and better policy; it may also

---

[2] See Kaiponanea T. Matsumura, *Public Policing of Intimate Agreements*, 25 YALE J. L. & FEMINISM 159, 162 (2013) ("Contracts between intimates governing decisions pertaining to the use of reproductive technologies are just the latest type of intimate agreements that many courts have shied away from enforcing on public policy grounds."); Deborah Zalesne, *The Intersection of Contract Law, Reproductive Technology, and the Market: Families in the Age of Art*, 51 U. RICH. L. REV. 419, 420 (2017) ("Ethical and legal questions persist regarding the enforceability of contracts that facilitate the formation of non-traditional families.").

[3] See, e.g., 42 U.S.C. § 274e (2012) (prohibiting organ purchases). This book discusses legal issues surrounding consent which are relevant in any jurisdiction where consent is part of the law. Please note, however, that unless otherwise indicated, references to specific legislation or rules assume U.S. law.

[4] See Kaiponanea T. Matsumura, *Consent to Intimate Regulation*, 96 N.C. L. REV. 1013, 1021 (2018) (stating that "[c]onsent is not a totemic concept that one must accept or reject wholesale, but rather a conclusion about the nexus between subjective will, conduct, and consequence.").

[5] While there may be more than two parties to a contract and more than two parties affected by an act of consent, for simplicity, this book generally assumes the model of two parties: the consenting party (the consenter) and the party seeking consent (the consent-seeker).

help improve decision-making on an individual level and provide a restraint against impulsivity and the social and visceral influences which often cloud our best judgment.

This book is organized in three parts. Part I analyzes the meaning of consent. This part also highlights some of the problematic cases involving consent and consentability. Part II introduces a consentability framework which assesses the validity of consent based upon the robustness of the consent conditions relative to the given act and the conduct of the parties. Part III suggests ways to improve the conditions of consent and reduce opportunism. Part III also revisits the hard cases using a consentability framework.

The Contours of Consent

We use the word "consent" in a variety of contexts. A person might be said to have consented to the terms on a company's website, to a search by a police officer, to having sexual relations, to undergoing surgery. But what does it mean to consent? The common understanding of consent is that it indicates a subjective state willing to accept or proceed with an act or activity. Another understanding of consent is that it is a conclusion which legally or morally justifies the commission of an act or activity. Under this second conception of consent, the subjective state is not determinative and may not even be relevant.

Part I provides an overview of the implications of these two interpretations of consent.[6] Chapter 1 examines the meaning of consent and the conditions necessary to establish its validity. It also introduces the concepts of consent construction and consent destruction. Chapter 2 presents three different types of situations which highlight the problems surrounding consent. They include cases of self-harm (such as suicide), self-improvement, contracts involving the body, and untested and novel technologies. These cases test societal norms, and prompt the question: Are there limits to consent?

---

[6] Selected passages in Chapter 1 and Chapter 4 are substantially similar to those previously published in Nancy S. Kim, *Relative Consent and Contract Law*, 18 NEV. L.J. 165 (2017) (hereinafter Kim, *Relative Consent*).

1

What Does it Mean to Consent?

In societies which value individual freedom, consent plays a singular role. Philosophers and scholars have pondered its meanings, as have lawyers and ethicists who wrestle with its implications. Consent by one party permits another to act in a way that might otherwise be illegal or immoral. Without consent, sex would be rape, and the exchange of property would be theft. Consent permits private ordering, which in turn allows individuals to allocate their rights in a way that suits them. There is consensus that consent is legally and ethically transformative. Franklin Miller and Alan Wertheimer have written that consent makes it permissible to act "in a way that would be impermissible absent valid consent."[7] Heidi Hurd has referred to consent as a "moral game-changer" and "morally magical."[8] John Kleinig refers to consent as a "transformative moral notion."[9]

Yet the moral authority of consent depends upon its authenticity or what we typically refer to as the "validity" of consent. It may seem nonsensical to refer to consent in terms of validity, because *invalid* consent is simply no-consent. Invalid consent *is* an oxymoron, yet it serves a useful purpose. To refer to consent in terms of validity is a way to separate out the act communicating consent (the "manifestation of consent") from the conditions under which that communicative act was made, and to distinguish instances of consent from those of no-consent.[10] As Margaret Jane Radin notes, "A system based on consent, as is our institution of contract, must also be based upon nonconsent. Why? Because the system must have the basic commitments and procedures that will enable a decision-maker to conclude that observed

---

[7] Franklin G. Miller & Alan Wertheimer, *Preface to A Theory of Consent Transactions: Beyond Valid Consent, in* THE ETHICS OF CONSENT: THEORY AND PRACTICE 79 (Franklin G. Miller & Alan Wertheimer eds., 2009).

[8] Heidi M. Hurd, *The Normative Force of Consent, in* THE ROUTLEDGE HANDBOOK OF THE ETHICS OF CONSENT 52 (Peter Schaber ed., 2018).

[9] John Kleinig, *The Nature of Consent, in* THE ETHICS OF CONSENT, *supra* note 7, at 5.

[10] I use the term "no-consent" to refer to instances where a party has expressed objection to the activity, and the term "non-consent" to refer to situations where the party did not validly consent, or changed her mind. Non-consent captures instances of no-consent as well as instances where consent was defective or was withdrawn.

physical and verbal behavior (or lack of such behavior) amounts to nonconsent rather than consent."[11] Referring to contractual consent, Brian Bix writes that the "gap between the assertion that there had (not) been consent and the conclusion that the agreement (should) not be binding is often hidden by use of terms like '*full consent*' or '*valid consent*,' which indicate, at the least, that there are different types or different extents of consent or, alternatively, that consent needs to be combined with other factors for it to transform the moral or legal effects of some action."[12]

Recognizing and distinguishing the various types of consent accounts for consent's contextual, incremental and variable nature. Chunlin Leonhard has referred to consent as a "spectrum" which runs from "informed consent to increasingly problematic consent."[13] To say "yes" means to agree, but the way that yes is said and the acts to which it grants permission may be subject to dispute. A reluctant acquiescence, even if voluntary, may not merit the same moral or legal deference as an enthusiastic engagement. Consent may be incremental, especially in situations where the activity is progressive or where the boundaries are ill-defined. Orit Gan has stated that consent is more than a "yes-or-no question," and can be "gradual and continuous."[14] It can also be abruptly discontinued. For example, in the context of physical relations, an individual may consent to kissing and then to sex – or to kissing but *not* to sex. In commercial settings, one may consent to certain responsibilities given certain circumstances, but not to those same responsibilities in other circumstances. An important issue then is whether consent to one activity includes consent to a progressive or more involved version of that activity, or whether another communicative act is required. The answer affects the burden between the parties – is it the burden of the party consenting (the "consenter") to communicate no-consent, or is it the burden of the party seeking consent (the "consent-seeker") to obtain a new communicative act which permits the expanded activity? An answer cannot fairly be given in the abstract, as it would depend upon the nature of the communicative act (meaning how specific and how definite) and the nature of the

[11] Margaret Jane Radin, Boilerplate: The Fine Print, Vanishing Rights, and the Rule of Law 20 (2013) (hereinafter Radin, Boilerplate).

[12] *See* Brian H. Bix, *Contracts, in* The Ethics of Consent, *supra* note 7, at 251; *see also* Radin, Boilerplate, *supra* note 11, at 19–32 (explaining that one way to consider consent is to consider what consent is *not* and to consider "varieties of non-consent" and "problematic consent" to explain the meaning of consent).

[13] Chunlin Leonhard, *The Unbearable Lightness of Consent in Contract Law*, 63 Case W. Res. L. Rev. 57, 69 (2012) (discussing "scenarios of consent" which "present a spectrum of consent, from informed consent to increasingly problematic consent"); *see also* Tom W. Bell, *Graduated Consent in Contract and Tort Law: Toward a Theory of Justification*, 61 Case W. Res. L. Rev. 1, 3 (2010) (stating that consent "varies by degrees").

[14] *See* Orit Gan, *The Many Faces of Contractual Consent*, 65 Drake L. Rev. 615, 616–17 (2017) ("consent is not simply a 'yes-or-no' question; consent is more complex than such an analysis suggests and can be both gradual and continuous . . . Factors of power, intimacy, trust, arm's length relations, and more all differently influence consent.").

expanded activity (meaning how serious the consequences to the consenter of continuing to the more involved activity).

Consent may be affected by new information or changes in circumstance. A party may consent only because that party had misinformation. For example, an employee may consent to working at a company because she believed her supervisor was reasonable. Consent may be valid only to a certain extent, beyond which it becomes invalid. The employee may consent to working with a supervisor until she discovers that he is abusive. The employee's consent to working with the supervisor does not extend to working with one with a bad temper and an abusive personality.

Assessing the validity of consent requires recognizing the dynamic nature of consent and understanding the different conditions which are constitutive of it. *Consent construction* refers to the conditions under which the manifestation of consent was made. *Consent destruction* refers to the effect of new information or circumstances upon the conditions of consent.

A. CONSENT CONSTRUCTION

Consent has a variety of meanings in the law, but it is typically a conclusion based upon the presence or absence of three conditions: an intentional manifestation of consent, knowledge, and volition/voluntariness. Knowledge requires both *under-standing* and *information* in light of the consenting party's *motive* for consenting. Consent must be *manifested* either through words or actions, meaning that the consenting party must express it in some way to the other party. This *manifestation of consent* must be *intentional*, meaning the reason or purpose for the manifestation of consent is to communicate consent to the act. Intentionality is closely related to the requirement of *voluntariness*. Voluntariness has two aspects. The first is that of volition or control, meaning that the manifestation of consent must have been intended rather than reflexive. The second is that of desire and is defined in relation to absence of undue pressure or coercion. Coercion is defined by context. An evaluation of coercion must consider the degree and likelihood of harm to the victim. A threat to cause physical harm is coercive provided that it is credible. Aside from credible physical threats, there is less certainty about what constitutes coercion.

My description of consent construction generally captures the basic requirements of consent put forth by other scholars. For example, John Kleinig states that where A consents to B, "consent is centrally and most appropriately a communicative act that serves to alter the moral relations in which A and B stand – and that for the moral relations to have been altered for B, a communicative act must have occurred."[15] In order for the communicative act to constitute consent for which A should be held responsible, Kleinig states that the conditions of competence, voluntariness, knowledge and intention must be met. Tom Beauchamp, focusing on informed consent,

---

[15]   *Id.* at 5.

argues that autonomous choice and voluntariness are the central features of consent.[16] His theory of autonomy features conditions of intentionality, understanding and voluntariness.

Thus, the normative account of consent requires that a person with legal capacity must intentionally and knowingly (with understanding, and properly informed) engage in a voluntary communicative act. Each of these conditions must be sufficiently established in order to show that the consenting party was acting autonomously, meaning the act consented to is an expression of that person's free will, and not the result of compulsion or coercion. The legal account of consent, however, does not always correspond to the normative one. Often, these consent conditions need only be sufficiently established, because perfect conditions rarely exist. An act of consent will rarely be free from external influence, and a decision-maker will almost never have perfect information. The difficult legal question involves whether a condition has been "sufficiently established" in a given case. As Margaret Jane Radin notes, there is a "large grey area" in the space between "full consent" and "nonconsent."[17] While there is general agreement that consent requires enough information to make an informed decision, what is the extent and quantity of that information? Similarly, at what point does a voluntary act become involuntary? How much pressure is too much pressure? What type of external circumstances warrant a conclusion that the consenting party has been deprived of free will? The answers require assessing each of the conditions of consent with a nuanced and realistic understanding of human nature.

1. Heuristics, Biases and the Limits of Human Cognition and Self-Control

Perhaps the most difficult and problematic consent condition to assess is the knowledge condition. The law typically requires only the provision of relevant information, and not evidence of understanding. The responsibility for providing that information depends upon the transaction and the relationship between the parties. For example, a surgeon should provide more information to a patient before an operation than a car seller provides to a buyer before a sale.

Yet, the mere provision of information is inadequate, given the limits of human cognition. Nobel Prize winner Herbert Simon coined the term "satisfice" to refer to the concept of bounded rationality. As he explained, because of limits on cognitive capacity, time, and access to information, human beings must settle for a certain level of information in order to make a decision.[18] Yet, to acknowledge that human

---

[16]   Tom L. Beauchamp, *Autonomy and Consent, in* THE ETHICS OF CONSENT, *supra* note 7, at 55.
[17]   RADIN, BOILERPLATE, *supra* note 11, at 161.
[18]   *See* Herbert A. Simon, *Rational Decision Making in Business Organizations*, 69 AMER. ECON. REV. 493, 503 (1979) (noting that as soon as a decision-maker finds an alternative which has certain desired attributes "he would terminate the search and choose that alternative," which Simon refers to as "satisficing"); *see also* Herbert A. Simon, *A Behavioral Model of Rational Choice*, 69 Q. J. ECON. 99 (1955).

beings satisfice when making decisions raises the question of when it is justifiable to hold a person to a decision which is based upon limited information.

Limited information is not the only factor which impedes decision-making. People may act irrationally and in ways contrary to their beliefs, desires and self-interest for a variety of reasons. Social scientists refer to human ways of thinking as being controlled by two "systems." System 1 is automatic, emotional and instinctive. System 2 is deliberative, rational and logical.[19] Traditional economics and much of contract law assume human beings use System 2, but it is System 1 which tends to be more frequently at work. In a groundbreaking 1974 article,[20] Amos Tversky and Daniel Kahneman examined three heuristics which people use to assess probabilities and predict values: representativeness, adjustment/anchoring, and availability. They argued that people use these heuristics when thinking under uncertainty, and that these lead to biases and "severe and systematic errors" in decision-making.[21] Representativeness is the heuristic where "probabilities are evaluated by the degree to which A is representative of B, that is, by the degree to which A resembles B."[22] This leads to cognitive biases which hinder people from accurately interpreting the reliability of evidence which they use to base their predictions.[23] The anchoring heuristic refers to the making of an estimate based upon the initial value, producing results which are biased toward the initial values. It may also create a bias in the evaluation of conjunctive and disjunctive events where people tend to overestimate the probability of a conjunctive event and underestimate the probability of a disjunctive event.[24] Tversky and Kahneman explain:

> Biases in the evaluation of compound events are particularly significant in the context of planning. The successful completion of an undertaking, such as the development of a new product, typically has a conjunctive character: for the undertaking to succeed, each of a series of events must occur. Even when each of these events is very likely, the overall probability of success can be quite low if the number of events is large. The general tendency to overestimate the probability of conjunctive events leads to unwarranted optimism in the evaluation of the likelihood that a plan will succeed or that a project will be completed on time. Conversely, disjunctive structures are typically encountered in the evaluation of risks. A complex system, such as a nuclear reactor or a human body, will malfunction if any of its essential components fails. Even when the likelihood of failure in each component is slight, the probability of an overall failure can be high if many

---

[19] DANIEL KAHNEMAN, THINKING, FAST AND SLOW 20–30 (2011) (explaining that the terms System 1 and System 2 were originally proposed by psychologists Keith Stanovich and Richard West).

[20] Amos Tversky & Daniel Kahneman, *Judgment Under Uncertainty: Heuristics and Biases*, 185 SCI. 1124 (1974).

[21] *Id.* at 1124.

[22] *Id.*

[23] *Id.* at 1125–26.

[24] *Id.* at 1128.

components are involved. Because of anchoring, people will tend to underestimate the probabilities of failure in complex systems.[25]

The availability heuristic refers to an individual's assessment of the probability of an event by the ease with which that individual can recall similar events.[26] For example, one might evaluate the probability of dying from ovarian cancer based upon the number of acquaintances one knows who died from it. Some recollections might be more salient because they leave a more emotional or sensorial impact. Tversky and Kahneman explained how seeing a house on fire would likely have a greater effect on one's assessment of the probability of such an event than would reading about a house fire in the newspaper.[27] The availability heuristic creates a bias of imaginability which may cause one to evaluate frequency or probability depending upon how readily the instance can be constructed, even though the ease of constructing instances does not reflect their actual frequency.[28]

The bias of imaginability makes evaluating the predictability of future events especially problematic where the future event is novel, unfamiliar or unprecedented. In these situations, the consenting party lacks the experience to make accurate predictions, including the ability to predict his own reactions to the anticipated outcome. In an unprecedented situation, such as one involving an experimental drug or technology, there is no information based upon *anyone's* experience. The novelty of the situation means there is no past experience upon which the consenting party can base a decision. Much of the information may be speculative. The dearth of information regarding the experience of others may lead an individual to optimistically discount or ignore the risks involved in a proposed novel situation.

The research by Herbert Simon, Daniel Kahneman and Amos Tversky unleashed an entire discipline, behavioral economics, which challenged the classical economics concept of the rational "economic man" and showed how irrational humans actually are. Studies demonstrated, for example, that humans were susceptible to "overconfidence bias," which causes them to overestimate their abilities and underestimate risks.[29] "Optimism bias" causes people to overestimate the probability

---

[25] *Id.* at 1129.
[26] *Id.* at 1127.
[27] *Id.*
[28] *Id.* at 1127–28. "Imaginability plays an important role in the evaluation of probabilities in real-life situations. The risk involved in an adventurous expedition, for example, is evaluated by imaging contingencies with which the expedition is not equipped to cope. If many such difficulties are vividly portrayed, the expedition can be made to appear exceedingly dangerous, although the ease with which disasters are imagined need not reflect their actual likelihood. Conversely, the risk involved in an undertaking may be grossly underestimated if some possible dangers are either difficult to conceive of, or simply do not come to mind." *Id* at 1128.
[29] Stefana DellaVigna, *Psychology and Economics: Evidence from the Field*, 47 J. Econ. Literature 315, 341–45 (2009) (discussing research finding overconfidence bias and implications for policy).

of a positive outcome and underestimate the probability of a negative one.[30] Humans are also prone to "confirmation bias," or a tendency to give greater weight to information that confirms their existing beliefs.[31] These biases may result in people according more weight to desired than to undesired information.

Other cognitive biases negatively affect an individual's ability to make optimal decisions, especially where there is a temporal disconnect between the intentional manifestation of consent and performance of the consented-to act. Some commentators refer to these faulty decisions as "internalities," or costs that the present self imposes upon the future self.[32] The more complex the process to the outcome, the greater the potential for misperception. The difficulty in accurately predicting one's feelings or actions becomes even greater with limited information and limited time. "Narrow framing," where a decision-maker considers each risk in isolation rather than with other sources of uncertainty, may result in decisions which underestimate the likelihood of a risk occurring.[33] More information may fail to improve and may even impair decision-making ability. Psychological studies show that for humans, attention is a scarce resource, and complex information may escape a decision-maker's notice.[34] Aggravating the problem of limited attention and complexity, information is less likely to be salient when it is further in the future.[35]

There may be "visceral factors" which result in sub-optimal decision-making and which may negatively affect behavior.[36] George Loewenstein noted that factors such as hunger, thirst, mood, emotions and sexual desire have a disproportionate effect on behavior and tend to overshadow other considerations; moreover, people discount or ignore how these visceral factors will influence their behavior.[37] Accordingly, individuals in a heated emotional or physical state tend to make decisions they never intended to make and which they later regret. Subjects in

---

[30] Neil D. Weinstein, *Unrealistic Optimism about Future Life Events*, 39 J. PERSONALITY & SOC. PSYCHOL. 806 (1980); TALI SHAROT, THE OPTIMISM BIAS: A TOUR OF THE IRRATIONALLY POSITIVE BRAIN (2011).

[31] Raymond S. Nickerson, *Confirmation Bias: A Ubiquitous Phenomenon in Many Guises*, 2 REV. GEN. PSYCHOL. 175, 177 (1998) ("A great deal of empirical evidence supports the idea that the confirmation bias is extensive and strong and that it appears in many guises.").

[32] *See* R. J. Hernstein et al., *Utility Maximization and Melioration: Internalities in Individual Choice*, 6 J. BEHAV. DECISION MAKING 149 (1993); *see also* CASS SUNSTEIN, WHY NUDGE: THE POLITICS OF LIBERTARIAN PATERNALISM 38 (Yale Univ. Press 2014) (hereinafter SUNSTEIN, WHY NUDGE) ("We can think of internalities as occurring when we make choices that injure our future selves.").

[33] Nicholas Barberis, Ming Huang & Richard H. Thaler, *Individual Preferences, Monetary Gambles, and Stock Market Participation: A Case of Narrow Framing*, 96 AM. ECON. REV. 1069 (2006).

[34] DellaVigna, *supra* note 29, at 341–45 (discussing research involving human inattention).

[35] *Id.* at 352 ("Holding constant the informativeness, information that is further into the future (or past) is less likely to be salient. In general, it is difficult to control for informativeness, since information that is further away is usually less relevant or less precisely estimated.").

[36] George Loewenstein, *Out of Control: Visceral Influences on Behavior*, 65 ORG. BEHAV. & HUM. DECISION PROCESSES 272 (1996) (explaining how visceral factors, including hunger, thirst and sexual desire, affect human behavior).

[37] *Id.*; *see also* DAN ARIELY, PREDICTABLY IRRATIONAL 89 (2008) (discussing the effect of arousal on behavior).

a sexually aroused state, for example, reported a higher willingness to engage in behavior associated with date rape than when they were in a non-aroused state.[38] Studies have demonstrated that even non-visceral factors significantly affect decision-making.[39] Sunny weather, for example, has been associated with higher levels of expressed happiness,[40] higher tips,[41] and higher stock returns.[42]

People may have motivations other than self-interest. They may be motivated by altruism, social pressure, concern for others, or a combination of these factors.[43] Although such "other"-focused motivations may be socially beneficial in some cases, they may be socially harmful in others. They may also harm the consenter's self-interest and cause her to make decisions that she regrets. Social psychologists have demonstrated that human beings are highly susceptible to external influences, which affect both their behavior and their beliefs. External influences vary in degree from outright commands to subtler forms of manipulation and persuasion. The way that external forces affect human behavior is often unexpected, even shocking. In an infamous experiment, Stanley Milgram told subjects to monitor the learning of another subject and to administer electric shocks when that subject made a mistake. Sixty-two percent of the subjects obeyed the experimenter's orders and escalated the electric shocks up to 450 volts, despite the subject's pained screams.[44] Yet, when a different group of subjects was provided with a description of the experiment, not a single one predicted that anyone would administer up to 450 volts of electric shocks.[45]

People are likely to underestimate the effect that external influences have upon human behavior. They are more likely to blame a person's behavior on his disposition and to underestimate or disregard the role of environmental or situational factors.[46] Moreover, human beings may fail to recognize that they are being manipulated and may neglect to take into account the incentives or self-interest of

---

[38]   Dan Ariely & George Loewenstein, *The Heat of the Moment: The Effect of Sexual Arousal on Sexual Decision Making*, 19 J. BEHAV. DECISION MAKING 87 (2006).

[39]   DellaVigna, *supra* note 29, at 359.

[40]   Norbert Schwarz & Gerlad L. Clore, *Mood, Misattribution, and Judgments of Well-Being: Informative and Directive Functions of Affective States*, 43 J. PERSONALITY & SOC. PSYCHOL. 513 (1983).

[41]   Bruce Rind, *Effect of Beliefs about Weather Conditions on Tipping*, 26 J. APPLIED SOC. PSYCHOL. 137 (1996).

[42]   Edward M. Saunders, Jr., *Stock Prices and Wall Street Weather*, 83 AM. ECON. REV. 1337 (1993); David A. Hirshleifer & Tyler Shumway, *Good Day Sunshine: Stock Returns and the Weather*, 58 J. FIN. 1009 (2003).

[43]   *See* DellaVigna, *supra* note 29, at 336–41 (summarizing and discussing research in the area of social preferences).

[44]   Stanley Milgram, *Behavioral Study of Obedience*, 67 J. ABNORMAL & SOC. PSCYHOL. 371 (1963).

[45]   *Id.*

[46]   Schwarz & Clore, *supra* note 40; LEE ROSS & RICHARD E. NISBETT, THE PERSON AND THE SITUATIONS: PERSPECTIVES OF SOCIAL PSYCHOLOGY, at 2 (1991) ("a half century of research" has revealed that in most novel situations "one cannot predict with any accuracy how particular people will respond. At least, one cannot do so using information about an individual's personal dispositions or even about that individual's past behavior."). *But see* John Sabini, Michael Siepmann & Julia Stein, *The Really Fundamental Attribution Error in Social Psychological Research*, 12 PSYCHOL. INQUIRY 1, 2 (2001) ("the

the party seeking consent.[47] In one study, researchers analyzed investor responses to analyst recommendations.[48] Analyst forecasts tend to be biased upward, and affiliated analysts tend to be even more biased. Large investors took into account this bias and discounted heavily positive recommendations by affiliated analysts. Small investors, however, followed recommendations without taking into account the positive bias, and failed to discount for analyst affiliation.

The vast body of social sciences research indicates that, contrary to what classical economists assume, there may be other motivating factors instead of, or in addition to, self-interest. These very human cognitive and behavioral limitations and fallibilities complicate assessments of consent because they impair the knowledge condition, undermine the ability of an individual to act in her best interests, and often result in the consenter regretting her decision.

B. CONSENT DESTRUCTION

Consent, once constructed, may be destroyed prior to performance. A party consents assuming certain conditions and circumstances. These implied assumptions may later prove to be false. Conditions or circumstances may change the consenting party's understanding – and invalidate consent. In some cases, newly acquired information may be corrective. For example, X agrees to buy Y's farm, believing that Y's farm is suitable for farming avocado trees. X later finds out that the soil on Y's farm contains an unusual chemical that makes it impossible to grow avocado trees. Although X had consented to purchase Y's farm, that consent was based upon misinformation.

Additional information may have to do with the circumstances surrounding the transaction, and not the transaction itself. This type of additional information is not a deficiency in the knowledge condition because it does not alter the information upon which consent was based. It does, however, affect the motives for the party's consent. For example, X again agrees to buy Y's farm, still believing that Y's farm is suitable for farming avocado trees. X finds out that he has an illness and that it is likely that he will die within the year. X decides that he does not want to spend his savings on the farm, but would rather travel the world while he can. X's consent is destroyed because X's motive for entering into the contract is undermined by the new information.

Consent should be distinguished from contract. In the second scenario above, X will still have an obligation to purchase Y's farm. But the reason for enforcing the

problem people have is not that they have a general tendency to attribute one way or another, but that they underestimate the importance of certain specific factors.").

47 Sabini, Siepmann & Stein, *supra* note 46, at 6 (noting that in various studies, people are "simply unaware of how certain motives . . . make us easy to manipulate.").

48 Ulrike Malmendier & Devin Shanthikumar, *Are Small Investors Naïve About Incentives?*, 85 J. FIN. ECON. 457 (2007); DellaVigna, *supra* note 29, at 357.

promise is not that X still consents; it is that X *at one time* consented. One might argue that the reason for enforcing X's promise to purchase the farm is because X agreed to do so; consequently, to bind X at a later time when X no longer wishes to purchase the farm honors X's autonomy. The argument expresses a preference for honoring the desires of an earlier stage X (X1) over a later stage X (X2). But the conditions necessary for consent no longer exist for X2 (the only X which exists at the time of performance). The argument then must be that one should be required to keep one's promises regardless of later circumstances. This, however, is not an argument in favor of autonomy; rather, it is an argument in favor of certainty.

One might argue that the value of autonomy is furthered by making decisions more certain. But that argument is convincing only if the initial decision was made under perfect consent conditions. Perfect consent conditions, however, rarely exist in reality. Before making a decision, an individual may not have all relevant information. Even if the consenter has access to all the information possessed by the consent-seeker, additional information may be discovered after contract formation. In many situations, time alters the reasons for consenting or the understanding of what doing so entails. Consent is specific to a given moment under certain conditions, and so consent is constructed within those limitations. The more time that elapses between the manifestation of consent/contract formation and contract performance, the greater the likelihood that the consenting party may change her mind.

To understand the problems with consent destruction requires recognizing the inherent contradiction of a *societal* interest in individual autonomy. The contradiction manifests itself in the potential conflict between the autonomy interests of individuals. A party who initially consented but who later changes her mind may nevertheless have an obligation to perform because her consent may have provoked a response in the other party. What happens where one individual's interests (to control her property rights) conflicts with another's interests to do the same? The contract between X and Y means that X has agreed to purchase Y's farm (thus exercising her right to do what she wants with her money), and that Y has agreed to sell it (thus exercising his right to do what he wants with his land). A contract requires *mutual* consent. Regardless of whether Y has taken steps in reliance upon the contract, Y has restricted his freedom over his property rights simply by agreeing to sell his property to X. His consent to sell his property was induced by X's consent. To permit X to change her mind without repercussion would disregard and devalue the fact of Y's consent.

The rights and liberties of individuals in any society are prone to conflict. The question is how to resolve the conflict when it arises. While a change of heart should not always allow someone to renege upon a promise, in some cases it should. But what rules and standards should be used to make such a determination?

Consent destruction may be caused by a deficient knowledge condition, but it may also be caused by a deficiency in the voluntariness condition. A business partner may threaten to leave the practice unless the other partner consents to a deal. Third parties, such as friends or family members, may exert pressure on the consenting party. This pressure may be conscious and deliberate, or it may be inadvertent and indirectly communicated. The removal of that pressure may result in consent destruction.

Consent destruction occurs because of the impossibility of predicting the future. The temporal nature of consent does not, however, necessarily mean that a consenting party's change of heart at a later date negates the initial granting of consent. Valid consent typically refers to consent construction or the fact that consent existed at one time and that it either (1) continues to exist at the time performance is required or (2) no longer exists (has been "destroyed") but should nevertheless be treated as though it still exists. To put it more precisely, in (2), the individual does *not* consent *at the time of performance*, but the other party's consent induced by the individual's past consent compels performance. Temporal disconnect is inherent in every contract because most contracts (with the exception of unilateral contracts) involve a notable period of time between formation and time for performance. Contracts involve mutual consent; therefore, the consenter generally should be required to perform in most situations despite consent destruction. In non-contract situations, however, consent is one-sided and consent destruction generally means that the consenter may revoke consent and terminate the activity.

2

The Hard Cases

This chapter introduces the hard cases regarding consentability. These hard cases illustrate the complexities of consent. They involve physically intrusive acts, exposure to grave bodily injury, or transgressions of custom and social norms. These acts elicit unease and often stronger reactions, such as shame, fear, anger, contempt or disgust. They generally fall under one of three categories.

The first category consists of "self-directed" activities, such as suicide or body modifications. The second category, "bodily integrity exchanges," consists of activities which involve the body on an intimate or personal level. They pose varying degrees of risk of harm but the risk is generally considered acceptable. The basis for the objection to the activity is not that the risk is unreasonably high, but that the commercialization of the exchange or activity is morally objectionable because it commodifies the body. This category includes surrogacy contracts and kidney sales. The third category encompasses activities which involve a high-risk of serious bodily injury or death. The purpose of the activity is not to harm oneself but to achieve some other objective through a dangerous or highly risky undertaking. Examples of these high-risk activities include participating in an experimental study or a dangerous maiden voyage or quest, such as a mission to Mars.

The bodily integrity transactions, in particular, have been the subject of much academic discussion.[49] The scholarship is extensive and daunting, and it is not my objective to simply retread well-covered territory. My objective is to provide a unified approach for all three types of "hard cases," and move the focus away from the issue of payment or "commodification." Specifically, this chapter explains that the issue common to hard cases is that consent seems improbable, ill-advised or otherwise suspect. This chapter concludes that, while the fact of payment may affect the conditions of consent, the fact of payment alone does not justify inconsentability.

---

[49] *See* MARGARET JANE RADIN, CONTESTED COMMODITIES: THE TROUBLE WITH TRADE IN SEX, CHILDREN AND OTHER THINGS (1996) [hereinafter RADIN, CONTESTED COMMODITIES]; DEBRA SATZ, WHY SOME THINGS SHOULD NOT BE FOR SALE: THE MORAL LIMITS OF MARKETS (2010); MICHAEL J. TREBILCOCK, THE LIMITS OF FREEDOM OF CONTRACTS (Harvard Univ. Press, 1996); RETHINKING COMMODIFICATION: CASES IN READINGS IN LAW AND CULTURE (Martha M. Ertman & Joan C. Williams eds., 2005).

A. SELF-DIRECTED ACTIVITIES

The category of self-directed activities consists of those which are undertaken by an individual upon his own initiative and control. This category is broad and encompasses all activities which affect an individual's health and pose a high risk of harm. It includes acts which have as their primary objective self-harm, such as suicide, as well as those which are intended to improve one's self in some way yet pose serious risks, such as cosmetic surgery. They also include activities in-between, such as smoking, drinking and taking drugs, which are undertaken neither to self-harm nor to self-improve, but which have harmful consequences for the individual.[50] This section focuses on suicide and body modifications because they raise particularly difficult issues of consent.

It may seem inapt to consider consent in the context of self-directed activities, because consent usually refers to permission granted by one person to another. But where an individual undertakes an act which has harmful and lasting effects on her body and impinges upon her ability to act independently, she is affecting the autonomy of her future self. Despite the persistent myth of the rational actor, science and history demonstrate that humans often fail to accurately predict their future emotions and desires. Furthermore, no human can predict future events and how they might affect one's personal circumstances and future needs.

In addition, even though an act may be entirely self-directed, other parties may be involved in its execution, or may influence the decision to act. The potential involvement of other parties complicates the issue of consent. For example, body modification is a self-directed act; however, it typically involves another person who may be benefitting in some way from the act. The benefit may be monetary. For example, an individual (X) may be paying someone else (Y) to perform the modification. If X decides to withdraw consent, Y may insist upon payment. The benefit to the other person may be non-monetary. X may seek breast implants at the urging of Y, for example.

1. *Self-Harm/Suicide*

Activities where the objective of the actor is to inflict self-harm involve the autonomy of the actor engaging in the self-harming activity, but may also involve the interests of others. The interdependence of members of society means that many self-harming acts have the potential to harm others, which justifies state prohibition or interference. John Stuart Mill distinguished between one's obligation to act in one's best interest, and one's obligation to act in the interests of others, the latter being more justifiably compelled than the former:

---

[50] I thank my colleague William Aceves for his insightful comments which helped me clarify the meaning of self-directed activities.

If any one does an act hurtful to others, there is a prima facie case for punishing him, by law, or, where legal penalties are not safely applicable, by general disapprobation. There are also many positive acts for the benefit of others, which he may rightfully be compelled to perform ... such as saving a fellow-creature's life, or interposing to protect the defenceless against ill-usage, things which whenever it is obviously a man's duty to do so, he may rightfully be made responsible to society for not doing. A person may cause evil to others not only by his actions but by his inaction, and in either case he is justly accountable to them for the injury. The latter case, it is true, requires a much more cautious exercise of compulsion than the former. To make any one answerable for doing evil to others, is the rule; to make him answerable for not preventing evils, is, comparatively speaking, the exception. Yet there are many cases clear enough and grave enough to justify that exception.[51]

Joel Feinberg observed "the public interest is always involved, at least to some small extent, when persons harm themselves" because society is deprived of the services provided by those individuals.[52] In the aggregate, these self-caused deaths and injuries "are a considerable public inconvenience, at the very least."[53] Understood in this way, self-harm also causes societal harm.

While the actor may have consented to the act, others who have been harmed have not. There are very few purely self-harming activities; even those which physically harm only the individual actor may impinge upon the rights of others. Certainly, the exercise of rights by one individual always has the potential to infringe upon or impair the interests of others. If, for example, I sell my house to someone who is very confrontational and noisy (assuming that I was a non-confrontational and quiet homeowner), my neighbor might feel I have diminished her interest in her property, as her enjoyment of her property is reduced. But my impairment of her property rights was indirect. The person encroaching upon my neighbor's enjoyment of her property is not me but the buyer of my property. Any claim that my neighbor may have is – and should be – against the buyer.

One could argue that, similarly, a person who commits a self-harming act, such as suicide, is not impinging upon anyone else's interest; he is exercising his own right of self-determination which leads to the reconfiguring of obligations. But this is an inaccurate description if considered from the standpoint of affected parties. The individual committing the act may have done so with fully constructed consent, but that act may impose burdens upon other parties who have not consented and who would not have consented if given the choice. The clearest example of a self-harming activity which implicates other parties is the suicide of a parent. Because parents have legal responsibilities to their children, their deaths transfer those responsibilities to others who may not want them but feel there is no option but to

---

51   JOHN STUART MILL, ON LIBERTY 11–12 (Charles W. Elliot ed., Barnes & Noble 2004).
52   JOEL FEINBERG, HARM TO SELF: THE MORAL LIMITS OF THE CRIMINAL LAW 22 (Oxford Univ. Press, 1986) [hereinafter JOEL FIENBERG, HARM TO SELF].
53   Id.

accept them. If there is another parent, she or he must accept the burdens of single parenting. If there is no other parent, relatives or friends may accept the task out of a sense of duty rather than real desire. The state may have to step in if there are no adults willing or able to take responsibility for the children. The children themselves are forced to accept a situation which they did not want. The affected parties did not consent to these new obligations, nor would they have consented to them if given a choice.

The right to autonomy is a negative right meaning that it protects an individual's right to live free from interference, but it is not an affirmative right in the sense that the individual may always exercise that right. An individual may only exercise autonomy rights if they are not outweighed by the autonomy rights of other individuals. In other words, the "freedom from" outweighs the equivalent "freedom to." For example, X's right to control his body does not give him the right to walk his body over Y's property or to rub his body against Z's body. X has a right to bodily integrity which means that X has a right to prevent others from touching him. It does not give him the right to use his body in any manner he pleases. His negative right to bodily integrity does not give him the right to infringe upon the autonomy interests held by others. In the words of John Stuart Mill, we are free to pursue our own good in our own way "so long as we do not attempt to deprive others of theirs, or impede their efforts to obtain it."[54]

Some may question the utility or advisability of criminalizing self-harming activities.[55] A person who successfully commits suicide is not able to be prosecuted, and it seems ill-advised to prosecute one who has failed in such an attempt. People who are contemplating suicide should be encouraged to seek help. If suicide were a crime, they might be deterred from doing so. Suicide seems to be one of the situations where, as Mill writes, societal attempts to control behavior would "produce other evils, greater than those which it would prevent."[56]

Yet, as most states have done, there are reasons to criminalize the conduct of those who encourage *others* to engage in self-harming activities or fail to prevent them.[57] Vulnerable people may be goaded or encouraged to commit suicide.[58] Technology has created new ways that people can be encouraged to self-harm. There have been

---

[54] MILL, *supra* note 51, at 13.

[55] *See, e.g.*, FEINBERG, HARM TO SELF, *supra* note 52, at 144 ("there is something moot in the philosophical debate over the propriety of suicide laws when a person with the resources and opportunities can kill himself if he is so determined, whatever the law says.").

[56] MILL, *supra* note 51, at 12.

[57] *See, e.g.*, MINN. STAT. § 609.215 (LEXIS through ch. 118 2018 Reg. Sess. (except ch. 103, 113, 115)), www .revisor.mn.gov/statutes/?id=609.215; CONN. GEN. STAT. § 53a-56(a) (LEXIS through Pub. Acts 18-1 2018), www.cga.ct.gov/2001/pub/Chap952.htm#sec53a-56.htm.

[58] *See* Monica Davey, *Online Talk, Suicides, and a Thorny Court Case*, N.Y. TIMES (May 13, 2010), www .nytimes.com/2010/05/14/us/14suicide.html?action=click&contentCollection=U.S.&module=RelatedCoverage&region=EndOfArticle&pgtype=article; Katharine Q. Seelye & Jess Bidgood, *Teenager Who Urged Friend to Kill Himself Is Guilty of Manslaughter*, N.Y. TIMES (June 16, 2017), www .nytimes.com/2017/06/16/us/suicide-texting-trial-michelle-carter-conrad-roy.html.

several disturbing cases where depressed or troubled people were manipulated into committing suicide by someone they met online who was masquerading as a therapist or other trustworthy figure.[59]

While it may be counterproductive to criminalize suicide, it makes sense to criminalize efforts to aid, abet, and (at least in some situations) fail to prevent it. The knowledge that failure to intervene is a *crime* may be empowering in the sense that it may prompt someone to take action without being unduly concerned about intruding into the private affairs of another. This does not mean that a failure to intervene in all situations where someone plans to engage in self-harm should be criminalized. It is worth noting, however, that there are laws which punish people for encouraging or failing to prevent some types of self-harming activity. One's duty to others may be higher or more inflexible than one's duty to oneself. A parent has a legal obligation to ensure that his child is properly cared for, meaning that she has nutritious food, a place to sleep and receives schooling. An obligation may arise from a formal relationship between the parties, but it may also arise from the situation itself. Although there is no "duty to rescue," there are laws that punish those who aid in the commission of a crime or fail to report it.

Another layer of complexity is added where an individual is terminally ill and in pain or facing the onset of severe dementia. The individual might decide that rather than enduring the ordeal that awaits her, she wants to terminate her life. In those circumstances, should it still be considered a crime to assist her in her decision – or should she be forced to find a more uncertain method which might be more painful and more unpredictable? A decision to end one's life in these situations should be viewed differently from suicide because it may enhance, rather than diminish, autonomy. Where control over one's life is substantially and rapidly diminishing, and death is imminent, the option of assistance in dying may reflect a society's mercy rather than its apathy or cruelty *provided that* stringent safeguards are implemented. The issue of assistance in dying is further discussed in Chapter 7.

2. Self-Improvement

The category of "body modifications" covers a wide range of acts, including cosmetic surgery, tattoos, and even voluntary amputation; however, the individual is not trying to self-harm but is seeking to improve or enhance that individual's mental, emotional or physical condition.

Technology has undoubtedly enhanced many of our abilities. Those who often forget birthdays and dentist appointments may be grateful for the ability to outsource these functions to an external memory, such as a smart phone with automated reminders. Technology has enabled us to swim faster, sleep more soundly and make better coffee. Companies have developed products that allow us to access

---

[59]   Davey, *supra* note 58.

the Internet or record images with the blink of an eye. Some of these technological aids are placed on a desk or counter; others are attached or worn on the body. Some "transhumanists," however, have gone even further and have implanted foreign devices in their body in a quest to improve their natural abilities.

Transhumanists believe that humans can harness the power of technology to surpass biological constraints and alter human evolution.[60] Their efforts are often referred to as "body hacking" or "biohacking" and encompass a wide variety of practices. Generally, they refer to extending, improving or altering natural abilities by implanting digital devices or technological tools into the human body. Rob Spence, a one-eyed filmmaker, embedded a wireless video camera into his prosthetic eye.[61] Another man, Neil Harbisson, found a way to overcome his inability to perceive color. He had a device, consisting of a fiber-optic sensor and microchip, implanted into his skull, which enables him to "see" colors by converting their frequencies into vibrations. This new ability gives him a "sixth sense" which enables him to detect ultraviolet rays.[62] At a convention in Texas, people lined up to have a radio-frequency identification or "RFID" chip implanted into their hands.[63] Some individuals have implanted objects or devices as part of artistic or political statements. A professor at New York University's Tisch School of the Arts had a small digital camera surgically implanted in the back of his cranium as part of an art project[64] so that he could "establish a dialogue about surveillance."[65] His art project implicates a different contemporary social issue – to what extent should we allow individuals to alter their bodies to surpass their human limitations?

Humans have long embedded foreign objects within their bodies to improve their performance, and insurance has even paid for it.[66] Pacemakers, for example, are surgically implanted within the human body. Artificial limbs enable mobility. IUDs prevent unwanted pregnancies. Metal and plastic replace knee and hip joints. But, some may argue, all those procedures are medically prescribed and regulated. They arguably don't improve the human body so much as repair or preserve it or facilitate

---

[60] *See* Francis Fukuyama, *Special Report: Transhumanism*, FOREIGN POL'Y (Oct. 23, 2009), http://foreignpolicy.com/2009/10/23/transhumanism/ (describing transhumanism as a "strange liberation movement" which seeks to "liberate the human race from its biological constraints" and "wrest [its] biological destiny from evolution's blind process of random variation and adaptation and move to the next stage as a species").

[61] *See* EYEBORG PROJECT, http://eyeborgproject.com/ (last visited May 23, 2018).

[62] D. T. Max, *Beyond Human*, NAT'L GEOGRAPHIC MAG., Apr. 2017, at 40–63.

[63] Eyder Peralta, *"Body Hacking" Movement Rises Ahead of Moral Answers*, NPR (Mar. 10, 2016), www.npr.org/sections/alltechconsidered/2016/03/10/468556420/body-hacking-movement-rises-ahead-of-moral-answers.

[64] *Artist Has Digital Camera Implanted in Head*, ASSOCIATED PRESS (Nov. 24, 2010), www.cbsnews.com/news/artist-has-digital-camera-implanted-in-head/.

[65] Laura Dolan, *New York Professor Installs Camera in Head*, CNN (Dec. 2, 2010), www.cnn.com/2010/US/12/02/new.york.camera.head/index.html.

[66] This observation has been shared by others. *See*, for example, Susan Butler, *Your Grandmother is a Bodyhacker*, BODYHACKING CON. (July 27, 2015), https://bodyhackingcon.com/blog/your-grand mother-is-a-bodyhacker.html.

a naturally occurring result that could be achieved in another less desirable or more cumbersome way. Under this view, there is something fundamentally different, even grotesque, about embedding foreign objects within the human body which are not medically advised. Some may worry that the line between humans and robots will fade, degrading what it means to be human.

Yet, the same argument could be made against cosmetic procedures, which are widespread and growing in popularity and range from minimally invasive laser treatments to surgical alterations of major body parts. According to a report issued by the American Society of Plastic Surgeons, in 2016 in the United States alone, a total of 17,192,816 cosmetic procedures were performed.[67] Of those, 1,780,987 were surgical procedures and 15,411,829 were minimally invasive procedures.[68] The shifting popularity of procedure types strongly correlates with changing – and more demanding – perceptions of what is considered beautiful, especially for women. For example, from 2000 to 2015, the number of upper arm lifts increased by 4,969 percent, lower body lifts increased by 3,973 percent, buttocks lifts increased by 252 percent and tummy tucks increased by 104 percent, while the number of liposuction surgeries decreased by 37 percent,[69] reflecting the changing ideal of female beauty as one that is muscular in addition to being slender.[70] The most popular type of surgery, however, is breast augmentation. In 2015, there were 279,143 breast augmentation procedures, which reflected a comparably modest increase of 31 percent, likely because large breasts have always been considered desirable on women.[71] The popularity of surgery types reflects cultural trends. According to a survey conducted by the American Academy of Facial Plastic and Reconstructive Surgery, one in three plastic surgeons reported seeing an increase in "selfie" surgeries, which are facial procedures to make the patient look better in online images.[72] The most popular cosmetic procedure is Botox injections, which increased 759 percent from 2000 to 2015 from 786,911 to 6,757,198. Also popular are soft tissue fillers (2,440,724 in 2015) and chemical peels (1,310,252 in 2015).[73]

---

[67] ASPS, 2016 PLASTIC SURGERY STATISTICS REPORT, at 10 (2017), www.plasticsurgery.org/documents/
       News/Statistics/2016/plastic-surgery-statistics-full-report-2016.pdf (this report represents a "universal
       and comprehensive" estimate of cosmetic and reconstructive procedures performed by members of
       the American Society of Plastic Surgeons).
[68] *Id.*
[69] ASPS, 2015 PLASTIC SURGERY STATISTICS REPORT, at 7 (2016), www.plasticsurgery.org/documents/
       News/Statistics/2015/plastic-surgery-statistics-full-report-2015.pdf [hereinafter 2015 PLASTIC SURGERY
       STATISTICS REPORT].
[70] A minority of the procedures were undertaken by men, but the vast majority of cosmetic procedures,
       including the ones mentioned above, are undertaken by women. *Id.* at 6.
[71] *Id.*
[72] Press Release, AAFPRS, *Selfie Trend Increases Demand for Facial Plastic Surgery: Annual AAFPRS
       Survey Finds "Selfie" Trend Increases Demand for Facial Plastic Surgery Influence on Elective Surgery*
       (Mar. 11, 2014), www.aafprs.org/media/press_release/20140311.html.
[73] 2015 PLASTIC SURGERY STATISTICS REPORT, *supra* note 69, at 7.

Cosmetic procedures have become more socially acceptable as celebrities, who in past years might have refused such procedures or lied about having them done, undergo them and publicly acknowledge having done so.[74] The visibility of celebrities with cosmetically enhanced features hastens their adoption by non-celebrities. A report commissioned by the United Kingdom Department of Health[75] found that "hearing about celebrities having cosmetic interventions, and the portrayal of this as everyday behavior, is itself highly influential" in normalizing them.[76]

There is likely a self-reinforcing loop between feelings of physical dissatisfaction and inadequacy and the prevalence of cosmetic procedures. The increase in the incidence of cosmetic procedures in ordinary people raises cultural standards of beauty, making more people feel that they don't measure up in terms of appearance. As celebrities and other public figures lead the charge in removing the stigma associated with having cosmetic procedures, the rate of such procedures will likely increase.

Studies indicate that women are more likely to undertake cosmetic interventions than men.[77] They undertook 98 percent of all upper arm lift procedures, 91 percent of all lower body lifts, 92 percent of buttock lifts and 88 percent of liposuction procedures. They undertake 100 percent of breast augmentation procedures.[78] Even women who have personal objections to cosmetic procedures may feel compelled to undergo them, given stringent societal expectations of female beauty. As Debora L. Spar, writes:

> [A]n entire generation of feminist and postfeminist women who stormed the barricades of the American work force, planned their reproductive destinies, and even got their partners to fold the laundry are now engaged in an odd sort of collective self-delusion. Everyone (at least in certain high-profile or professional circles) is doing it, and very few are confessing, a fact that in some ways is more disturbing than the surge in the surgeries themselves. Because not only are we

---

[74] *See* Michele Willens, *No More Stigma Against Plastic Surgery, Please,* ATLANTIC (July 1, 2013), www .theatlantic.com/sexes/archive/2013/07/no-more-stigma-against-plastic-surgery-please/277427/ (celebrities who have publicly acknowledged having had cosmetic procedures include former First Lady Betty Ford, and many actresses, including Jane Fonda, Jamie Lee Curtis and Nicole Kidman).

[75] CREATIVE RESEARCH, REGULATION OF COSMETIC INTERVENTIONS: RESEARCH AMONG THE GENERAL PUBLIC AND PRACTITIONERS (Mar. 28, 2013) Job. No. 618/Version 3, www.gov.uk/government/ uploads/system/uploads/attachment_data/file/192029/Regulation_of_Cosmetic_Interventions_Research_Report.pdf [hereinafter U K. DEPT. OF HEALTH REPORT]. The report was conducted by Creative Research Ltd. and commissioned by the U.K. Dept. of Health in the wake of a scandal involving defective breast implants. *Id.* at 9. The purpose of the report was to assess public understanding of issues relating to cosmetic interventions (both surgical and non-surgical), including their risks and whether they were regulated. *Id.* Notably, the study excluded those who were strongly opposed to cosmetic interventions. *Id.*

[76] *Id.* at 17.

[77] U.K. DEPT. OF HEALTH REPORT, *supra* note 75, at 11 (noting that based upon available statistics and earlier research, "patients and prospective patients are more likely to be female and aged 22–55 years.").

[78] 2015 PLASTIC SURGERY STATISTICS REPORT, *supra* note 69, at 7.

nipping, suctioning and using hormones, but we're also feeling embarrassed about it, and lying. Neither of which was really the point of women's liberation.[79]

While women undertake the vast majority of cosmetic procedures, men, too, are increasingly feeling the pressure.[80] According to one plastic surgeon:

Cosmetic procedures for men have doubled in the past ten years. There's a huge pressure to look more youthful for business. My male patients come in, because maybe they are looking for a new position in a very youth-dominated culture. They are competing with people a decade of two younger, and they feel a professional pressure to look youthful and relaxed and less angry.[81]

Older workers who can afford to undergo plastic surgery may be able to stave off irrelevance and unemployment for several more years, but older workers who are unable to afford the procedures may look even older by comparison and be viewed as less relevant and employable. Furthermore, the standard for what constitutes "youthful" becomes increasingly more unrealistic, as people in their thirties and even twenties start to have procedures to forestall any signs of aging.[82]

Conventional cosmetic surgeries tend to reflect and reinforce existing power dynamics, and beauty standards are traditionally driven by heterosexual reproductive drives. Cosmetic surgeon Dr. Steven Teitelbaum stated:

What women ask for the most is to look like a fertile, young woman. What does that mean? Higher, fuller breasts; narrower waist; a curve to the hips; a smaller, more diminutive nose; fuller, redder lips; cute little chin; high eyebrows.[83]

Cosmetic procedures narrow categories of beauty, normalizing perfection and stoking feelings of inadequacy. They harm society in an insidious way by altering society's perception of what is normal and natural. They encourage superficiality and, by reinforcing existing power dynamics and prejudices, promote ageism, sizeism, sexism and racism. Dr. Teitelbaum explained:

In the big picture, plastic surgery is about people aspiring to look like the dominant social class ... when you live in a white, European-dominated world, there is a tendency to want to emulate that. That's why for years you've seen some black people try to Caucasianize their nose, or you've see Asian women try to Europeanize their eyes. And now, because of the greater awareness of plastic surgery, because of the abundance of credit cards and everyone living in debt, a

---

[79]   Deborah L. Spar, *Aging and My Beauty Dilemma*, N.Y. TIMES (Sept. 24, 2016), www.nytimes.com/2016/09/25/fashion/aging-plastic-surgery-feminism.html.

[80]   U.K. DEPT. OF HEALTH REPORT, *supra* note 75, at 11 (stating that there is evidence of increased activity in men over 35 years of age).

[81]   LAUREN GREENFIELD, GENERATION WEALTH 189 (2017).

[82]   U.K. DEPT. OF HEALTH REPORT, *supra* note 75, at 11 ("There is also evidence of a growing interest in cosmetic procedures among teenagers and young adults, notably females.").

[83]   GREENFIELD, *supra* note 81, at 190.

greater number of different socio-economic groups are aware of plastic surgery and have the resources to get it.[84]

Unconventional body modifications, on the other hand, expand categories of attractiveness and reject what it means to be conventionally beautiful. While conventional body modifications reinforce existing cultural power structures, unconventional ones upend them. Society may find unconventional body modifications alarming and discomfiting because they betray traditional notions of beauty, but this is precisely why they are less insidious than cosmetic procedures. Unconventional body modifications do not perpetuate societal pathologies of age, physical appearance and gender to the extent that cosmetic procedures do. Instead, they challenge conventional notions of beauty and force society to address its values, standards – and its hypocrisy. Why, for example, does the idea of a glowing RFID chip implanted into a hand disgust, but not the idea of a paralyzing poison injected into a forehead? There seems to be no principled basis upon which to make lawful distinctions between conventional and unconventional body modifications. To the extent that a body modification introduces an additional functionality or utility for the human body, it may improve quality of life. Body hacks – dangerous and unusual as they might be – may have practical applications which enhance human capabilities. For example, they may provide insights which may help in the design of better medical devices or prosthetics.

The novelty and functionality of body hacking and its often-conspicuous melding of man and machine contrast with cosmetic procedures, which are typically intended to look "natural." Yet it is precisely the undetectability of cosmetic procedures which makes them so pernicious. Cosmetic surgeries gradually shift social expectations and normalize the abnormal by altering what aging looks like. Because cosmetic procedures present an improved version of reality, their spread has been insidious. Body hacks, on the other hand, are striking and often reported by media in a sensationalist manner. Their novelty threatens the social order. Yet, it is their tendency to shock which makes them less subversive and less socially harmful than cosmetic procedures.

The enforcement of social standards of beauty is not – or should not be – a fundamental societal value. Disgust is a response to the unfamiliar. Female genital mutilation is generally viewed as abhorrent by those outside of cultures that practice it, evoking outrage and disgust. Yet, labiaplasty, which involves surgery on a woman's genitals to make them more aesthetically pleasing, has been growing in popularity and even teenaged girls are reportedly seeking it.[85] There have been increasing requests by men for penis enlargement procedures, which require surgical operations on male genitalia. One review found these procedures to be ineffective, to have

---

[84] *Id.* (quoting Dr. Steven Teitelbaum).

[85] *Round Up: Cosmetic Surgery*, 18 REPROD. HEALTH MATTERS, no. 35, May 2010, at 179–81 (noting "clear signs that labia excision in the U.K. is increasing" and that "[m]ost women asking for surgery are in their late teens or early 20s, but some as young as 10 or 11 are requesting it.").

"unacceptably high" risks, and to often result in unwanted outcomes, such as deformity, scarring and sexual dysfunction.[86]

We can readily identify the harmfulness or barbarity of an act when it is outside of our cultural norm. Often, however, we fail to recognize the barbarity or harmfulness of practices which have become normalized within our own culture.[87] Female genital mutilation/circumcision is illegal in many jurisdictions even with the consent of the subject. In the state of Minnesota, for example, anyone who performs the act on another commits a felony and "[c]onsent to the procedure by a minor on whom it is performed or by the minor's parent is not a defense" to the crime.[88] But how does the scenario where a girl consents to a form of female circumcision/genital mutilation differ from one where a girl seeks to have a nose job, breast implants or labiaplasty? Neither situation presents an easy case for consent. Rather, they are examples of "adaptive preferences," which, as Serene Khader explains, are "self-depriving desires people form under unjust conditions."[89] Girls and women may feel inadequate in their bodies because they live in a society where they are bombarded by unrealistic images of what they should look like. Individual perceptions and beliefs are shaped by social conditioning and cultural norms. Societal pressures may not be as obvious as physical force, but they can be just as coercive. What does consent mean in a culture – any culture – where young women are so unhappy with the aesthetics of their perfectly normal and healthy face and body that they are willing to pay money and suffer the pain of surgery to have them altered? This is not to suggest that genital mutilation is the same in all respects as labiaplasty or that it should be treated identically. But it is too simplistic to say that in the first case, the girl was forced and in the second she was not. Individual perceptions and beliefs are shaped by cultural norms and values so that "free will" is never entirely free of social influence.

One approach would be to prohibit *all* non-medically advised body modifications. A law making any type of permanent, non-therapeutic "unnatural" alteration illegal would be facially neutral; more importantly, it is most respectful of the natural diversity and beauty of humanity. The performance of the procedures could be prohibited altogether, or they could be treated like self-harming activities. In most cases, the wisest and most defensible position is to leave a healthy, functioning human body alone. The current state of perpetual nipping and tucking to an elusive standard of perfection smacks of social pathology and further encourages it.

---

[86] *Id.* at 175–76.
[87] *See* Nancy Ehrenreich & Mark Barr, *Intersex Surgery, Female Genital Cutting, and the Selective Condemnation of Cultural Practices*, 40 Harv. Civ. Rights-Civ. Lib. L. Rev. 71, 75 (2005) (arguing that the refusal of opponents of female genital cutting to embrace the cause of those who oppose intersex cutting is based upon "a racially privileged North American exceptionalism" and that this "white privilege" prevents them from acknowledging the harm caused by intersex cutting).
[88] Minn. Stat. Ann. § 609.2245 (West Supp. 2016).
[89] Serene J. Khader, Adaptive Preferences and Women's Empowerment 4 (2011).

Unfortunately, such a ban would be impracticable. First, it would be difficult to implement and enforce. A significant amount of revenue is generated from cosmetic procedures. One report stated that over $16 billion was spent in 2016 on cosmetic procedures in the United States.[90] It is highly unlikely that there would be the political consensus required to ban cosmetic procedures. The economic value has already been established and the cultural norm is firmly entrenched.[91]

Furthermore, to categorically ban cosmetic procedures altogether raises troubling issues of social inequality. It is useful to remember that the first plastic surgeries were attempts to correct physical deformities, scars and damaged tissue caused by burns, tumors and birth defects so extreme that often ordinary human functions were severely restricted. Before the evolution of plastic surgery, people with these deformities were simply ostracized from society, and referred to as "monsters," with no employment or romantic prospects.[92] Their social isolation and physical pain were so great that they were even willing to undergo the torture of invasive and dangerous surgical procedures fully awake and without anesthesia in the hopes of improving their appearance.[93] Writer Cristina O'Keefe Aptowicz describes what it was like for those early patients:

> Patients of *les operations plastiques* . . . were often too aware of their lot in life: that of a monster. It was inescapable. They hid their faces when walking down the street. They took cover in back rooms, excused themselves when there were knocks at the door. They saw how children howled at the sight of them. They understood the half a life they were condemned to live and the envy they couldn't help but feel toward others – whole people who didn't realize how lucky there were to wear the label HUMAN.[94]

These people were willing to undergo these highly risky and extremely painful surgeries for a chance at a normal life:

> It was not uncommon for these patients to enter the surgical room fully prepared to die. Death was a risk they happily took for the chance to bring some level of peace and normality to their mangled faces or agonized bodies.[95]

One might argue that laws could distinguish between surgeries to correct a severe deformity from those intended merely to enhance an already "normal" appearance. The former help correct an abnormality while the latter help create one. If it is primarily the non-therapeutic "enhancing" surgeries which degrade the human

---

[90] 2016 Plastic Surgery Statistics Report, *supra* note 67, at 6.
[91] *See* U.K. Dept. of Health Report, *supra* note 75, at 39 (noting that there is "currently little counterpoint to the increasing normalization of and familiarity with the cosmetic intervention industry.").
[92] Cristin O'Keefe Aptowicz, Dr. Mutter's Marvels 19–20 (2014) (explaining how people with severe physical deformities were referred to as "monsters" for whom "death was often seen as a blessing").
[93] *Id.* at 19–21.
[94] *Id.* at 20.
[95] *Id.*

condition – and not the corrective or therapeutic ones – laws could prohibit purely cosmetic or aesthetic procedures but allow therapeutic, reconstructive or rehabilitative ones. In reality, this type of line drawing is difficult to put into application. Even the nineteenth-century surgeries performed on "monsters" were not typically necessary for survival.[96] As these extreme cases illustrate so well, the effects of cosmetic surgery are more than skin-deep. Self-image and physical appearance play a major role in life satisfaction. Many patients undergo cosmetic procedures to boost self-confidence and improve their mental health.[97]

Furthermore, the line between reconstructive and aesthetic procedures is porous and trying to distinguish between "normal" and "abnormal" raises the same concern about conformity as other types of conventional cosmetic surgeries. Some women, for example, are rejecting breast reconstruction after undergoing breast cancer surgery.[98] Their experiences reveal much about societal norms and expectations regarding beauty. Their decision to forgo the painful reconstructive process has sometimes elicited disturbing and objectionable reactions from others, including their doctors. Some physicians do not inform patients of the option to remain flat after breast surgery. They may assume that all women are willing to suffer the physical and psychic toll of reconstruction for the sake of aesthetics. Some women report being pressured by their physicians to get implants even after they have indicated they don't want them. One woman who had told her physician that she did not want reconstruction reported waking up after her mastectomy with "unsightly flaps of skin and tissue" that could be used if she later changed her mind.[99]

It might be that as more people engage in forms of unconventional body modification, these modifications – like cosmetic procedures – will become normalized. Widespread adoption of most unconventional body modification, such as silicone horns, is unlikely because they are too impractical for most people. Their purpose is not to gain popularity or even mainstream acceptance; on the contrary, they are intended to challenge conventional aesthetics and expectations. However, there may be certain types of body modifications which become popular. Some body hacks may prove useful, which might encourage others to adopt them. Other body modifications may become viewed as beautiful, at least to a segment of society. Tattoos, for example, used to be limited to the arms of sailors and the torsos of gangsters; now, a broad cross-section of society sports an array of colorful tattoos. As people become more comfortable with certain body modification practices, they

---

[96] *Id.* ("The surgeries weren't physically necessary to save their lives; rather, they were done so the patient might have the gift of living a better, normal life.").

[97] U.K. Dept. of Health Report, *supra* note 75, at 31 (finding that individuals receptive to cosmetic interventions "talked about increasing self-esteem, confidence and wanting to feel better about some aspect of themselves" as the primary reason for having a cosmetic procedure).

[98] Roni Caryn Rabin, *"Going Flat" After Breast Cancer*, N.Y. Times (Oct. 31, 2016), www.nytimes.com/2016/11/01/well/live/going-flat-after-breast-cancer.html.

[99] *Id.*

may start to adopt them and make them more conventional. This type of normalization, through conscious and deliberate adoption, rather than unconscious and adaptive social conformity, may reflect social change in its ideal form.

If an individual's desires are shaped by socio-cultural forces, are they any less valid or worthy of respect? For example, is "gender identity disorder" the product of a rigid and closed-minded society, and dysphoria a reaction to it, rather than a condition that requires "fixing"? Do gender reassignment surgeries[100] merely validate and reinforce the gender binary norm – the either/or of being male or female instead of encouraging us to celebrate gender diversity, the range of the spectrum and its various shadings? Will we view gender reassignment surgeries performed on minors as compassionate and humane, or as well-intentioned but misguided, in the same way that we are starting to view intersex surgeries on infants and children? Similarly, will we view conventional cosmetic surgeries as ways to help people feel good about themselves – or will we see them as exploiting the vulnerable, encouraging body dysmorphia and promoting superficiality? Will we understand – too late for some – that it was our cultural norms and expectations that needed to change rather than the perfectly healthy body of the individual undergoing the risky surgery? By permitting surgeries to "correct" functioning bodies, are we simply reinforcing cultural expectations of what it means to be a woman or a man, or what it means to be attractive, healthy and *normal*?

Even the questions presume a duality that may not exist, an either/or dichotomy that suggests there is a right and wrong reason for a right and wrong kind of modification. The answers are unknowable in the abstract because they depend upon the individual, the situation, and the societal context. The social acceptability of a particular type of bodily modification may justify it and perpetuate it – but it should not determine its consentability. Most of the time, for most of us, we make decisions for our lifetime and for our present realities. An individual may feel trapped in the wrong body or may feel her body is inadequate because today's society is unable to accommodate a more varied conception of gender or beauty; that doesn't mean, however, that the individual should bear the burden of transcending existing social norms at the cost of personal happiness. It does mean that we should question and challenge the cultural expectations which compel individuals to undergo painful surgical procedures in order to feel complete or valuable. A woman may get breast implants and liposuction after a divorce in order to attract more dates. A man may get a face lift in order to increase his chances of getting a new job after a layoff. In each case, the individual may be reacting to societal rejection, and that rejection may be viewed in retrospect as a mark of shame on society, but the solution is not to take decision-making power away from the individual. The individual is adapting to societal expectations in a way that he or she has determined

---

[100]   I use the term "gender reassignment" and "sex reassignment" surgery because these are the commonly accepted terms used by medical professionals. I suspect that, as society evolves, the terminology will also evolve to replace the term with "gender confirmation."

is best. Societal expectations and cultural norms may be the problem, but it is the individual who is suffering from them. Should we forsake that individual and that individual's needs?

If the idea of replacing a healthy body part – any body part – repels us, we can refrain from the procedure ourselves, try to dissuade others who are contemplating the procedure, and work to change or broaden the cultural definitions and expectations which motivate an individual to undergo such procedures. A free society does not mean an uncaring and uncompassionate one. But we should not allow our personal preferences to prevent others from determining for themselves what they need to do to survive and perhaps even find some measure of personal happiness.

B. BODILY INTEGRITY EXCHANGES

Contracts enable people to reallocate their property rights in a manner that promotes their self-interest. But contracts can involve more than the transfer of property rights. They may involve the transfer of other rights or interests, unless there is a law prohibiting their transfer. Certain exchanges are prohibited[101] or highly controversial because they involve monetary payment for the use or possession of a part of the human body. These exchanges include sex work/prostitution,[102] the selling of kidneys, and reproductive services. These exchanges are sometimes referred to as "noxious" or "repugnant" transactions.

There are two types of argument in favor of permitting these transactions. The first uses the language of freedom and choice and argues that people should be allowed to do what they want with their bodies and their money. The second type of argument is utilitarian and focuses on the net benefit to society of permitting these transactions. This argument typically adopts the language of economics and supply and demand by, for example, arguing that organ sales will save lives and redistribute resources in a more efficient manner, benefitting both parties to the transaction.[103]

Bodily integrity exchanges are controversial not because they involve an act which itself is objectionable, but because of the context in which the act is performed. Child-bearing, for example, is not particularly controversial, but paid surrogacy is. Sometimes, the act is highly valued, even noble. A kidney donor is often viewed as brave, generous and compassionate. The objection is also not based upon the act being extremely or unreasonably risky. Although there may be risk associated with

---

[101]   See 42 U.S.C. § 274e(a), (b) (2012).

[102]   The choice of word to describe the practice is freighted with political meaning. Those in favor of permitting sex-for-money transactions refer to the exchanges as "sex work." The term which is typically used by those opposed to legalization of this type of exchange is "prostitution." To avoid the bias inherent in selecting a term, I will use both terms and use them interchangeably. *See* JULIE BINDEL, THE PIMPING OF PROSTITUTION: ABOLISHING THE SEX WORK MYTH 72 (2017) (noting the word "prostitution" is becoming replaced by "sex work" and other "euphemisms").

[103]   See TREBILCOCK, *supra* note 49, at 1–22 (providing a valuable summary of the market-based arguments for the "private-ordering paradigm"); *see also* SATZ, *supra* note 49.

They conclude that there is "no logical basis for the current combination of banning compensation for kidney donors while allowing compensation for football players and boxers."[113]

A different argument against legalization of bodily integrity transactions frames the issues in terms of incentives. If we allow the sale of organs or body parts, we may encourage people to sell who might not otherwise have considered engaging in the transaction. For example, college students may be enticed to sell their eggs if the dollar amount is large enough. The same argument is often raised against the legalization of prostitution.[114] If prostitution is legalized, then more women (and the concern is usually with women) may be encouraged to engage in it if they are able to charge large amounts of money. Some arguments are based upon the harmful effects to third parties or to the public generally. For example, one might argue that legalizing prostitution would increase the incidence of sexually transmitted diseases, encourage trafficking and human slavery, and/or increase the incidence of related crimes.[115] These arguments are necessarily speculative or based upon projections since it is difficult to prove a counterfactual or measure a hypothetical situation of legality.

Perhaps the most challenging argument against allowing bodily integrity transactions is that they exploit the poor and promote inequality. Debra Satz argues that "some markets are noxious and need to be blocked or severely constrained if the parties are to be equals in a particular sense, as citizens in a democracy."[116] According to Satz, noxious markets differ from other types of markets because they (1) "produce extremely harmful outcomes"; (2) are "extremely harmful for society"; (3) involve market participants with "very weak or highly asymmetric knowledge and agency"; and/or (4) reflect the "underlying extreme vulnerabilities of one of the transacting parties."[117] A market is "noxious" if it produces "high scores" given these parameters.[118]

Consequently, these transactions essentially make (or have the potential to make) some categories of people (the poor, women, minorities) less valuable than others. Under this view, allowing bodily integrity transactions would legalize the selling of human parts by those subordinated groups for the benefit of dominant groups. Currently, some people may be able to participate in prohibited transactions by paying on the black market and/or traveling to other countries to participate in them. Although medical tourism is difficult to track, existing evidence suggests that trends

---

[113] *Id.*

[114] *See* CATHARINE A. MACKINNON, WOMEN'S LIVES, MEN'S LAWS 151, 155 (2005) (explaining that "prostitution subordinates, exploits and disadvantages women as women in social life, a social inequality that criminal prostitution laws then seal with a criminal sanction" but that "[p]rostitution cannot be decriminalized wholesale on this argument, however").

[115] *See* BINDEL, *supra* note 102, at 72 (providing arguments against legalization of prostitution).

[116] SATZ, *supra* note 49, at 93.

[117] *Id.* at 94–98.

[118] *Id.* at 98.

such as globalization and the Internet are contributing to its growth.[119] The scarcity that results from prohibiting these exchanges may disproportionately affect those who cannot afford to pay to obtain them through other means. Those who can afford to travel outside the country for their transplant or their baby may do so. Those who cannot afford the expense have no choice but to hope for the best before time runs out.

But even for those who are able to afford pursuing alternative channels, the road is not easy. Often, the treatment they receive overseas is risky or unsuccessful. The healthcare standards may be lower than they would be in their home country. International travel itself poses health risks, especially after surgery. Wealth, too, is a relative term. The medical tourist may be wealthier than the donor or surrogate, but the costs are significant even for those who can afford to pay for them. The services typically operate in a murky world without regulation and the quality or competence of the medical personnel and other service providers may not be as advertised. Services may come with significant hidden charges. Medical and legal complications may add to the financial burden.

Focusing solely or primarily on the relative economic power of the parties detracts from the unique character of at least some of these transactions. Many of these are transactions of necessity on both sides. Bodily integrity exchanges raise the specter of unfairness but it is an unfairness of circumstance distinguishable from the terms of the transaction. Exploitation typically means unfair advantage-taking. Unfairness in exchanges typically arises when one party takes advantage of his or her greater bargaining power. That power is often economic but it can also be social or strategic. Bodily integrity transactions, however, involve a different type of unfairness – one involving need on both sides. Consequently, either or both of the exchanging parties may be exploited. In bodily integrity transactions, the consent-seeker includes intermediaries, such as medical providers, clinics, brokers and other third parties. The concern over exploitation is particularly acute with respect to these intermediaries as they – unlike the exchanging parties – are not in a situation of desperation. Desperation makes people vulnerable to exploitation, and there are situations other than financial need which make people desperate. For example, an infertile couple desperate to have children may be willing to "try anything," as Debora Spar explains:

> The clients' demand for the "product" is exceedingly strong. They are willing to try anything – repeated rounds of hormones, multiple surgeries, pregnancy right after cancer – and they are essentially unwilling to give up ... the people who

---

[119] *See* Neil Lunt et al., *Medical Tourism: Treatments, Markets and Health System Implications: A Scoping Review*, OECD (Sept. 20, 2011), www.oecd.org/els/health-systems/48723982.pdf. The report notes key features of the "new 21ˢᵗ Century style of medical tourism" which include "large numbers of people traveling for treatment." *Id.* at 6. The medical treatments include "fertility/reproductive system" services and "organ, cell and tissue transplantation" services. *Id.* at 11. *See also* I. Glenn Cohen, *Transplant Tourism: The Ethics and Regulation of International Markets for Organs*, 41 J. L. MED. & ETHICS 269 (2013) (noting "thriving black markets" in several countries).

receive fertility services don't see themselves as participating in a commercial relationship . . . .

The view from the clinics, by contrast, is more commercial. Although nearly all fertility centers tout their medical expertise and their patient-focused environments, they also reveal a distinctly financial bent. To begin with the obvious, in the United States, at least, fertility is emphatically a for-profit endeavor.[120]

It may also be the case that the desperate situation of each means that *neither* party is exploited, since neither is willing to risk hard bargaining. Rather than denying the potential harms that might result from controversial exchanges, we should try to more specifically address them through regulation if possible. Someone who desperately needs a kidney may not be in a position to bargain for a lower price. Exploitation, like consent, is a conclusion and whether it exists in a given situation depends not solely on the type of transaction, but on the actors involved. For example, the prohibition against sex work stems from a variety of reasons ranging from social and religious conservatives' belief that it is immoral, to the feminist argument that it perpetuates the systemic subordination and oppression of women.[121] Sex workers themselves have very different perspectives and experiences.[122] Some may have been coerced into sex work, some may have turned to it out of economic desperation and still others may view it as a reasonable means of making a living or earning extra income in comparison to available alternatives.[123]

Nevertheless, the objection pertaining to exploitation and subordination of the poor is compelling. It is highly unlikely that wealthy people will be selling their kidneys or other organs. Legalizing bodily integrity transactions would likely exacerbate the unfairness and stratification in a society which values both justice and equality even if it does not always guarantee them. However, prohibiting these exchanges does nothing to alter the social conditions which allow exploitation and subordination to exist. It also does nothing to improve the conditions which have created the situation of desperation. Subordination and exploitation do not typically

---

[120] DEBORA L. SPAR, THE BABY BUSINESS: HOW MONEY, SCIENCE, AND POLITICS DRIVE THE COMMERCE OF CONCEPTION (2006).

[121] *See* BINDEL, *supra* note 102, at xix ("I wish to see an end to prostitution because it is both cause and consequence of women's subjugation at the hands of men and I am, after all, a feminist."); SATZ, *supra* note 49, at 136 ("the most plausible account of prostitution's wrongness turns on its relationship to the pervasive social inequality between men and women."). Satz states that "[i]f prostitution is wrong, it is because of its effects on how men perceive women and on how women perceive themselves." *Id.* at 146.

[122] *See, e.g.*, India Thusi, *Radical Feminist Harms on Sex Workers*, 22 LEWIS & CLARK L. REV. 185 (2018) (arguing that criminalization of sex work and arguments against sex work are often essentialist and harm sex workers of color).

[123] *See generally* BINDEL, *supra* note 102. While Bindel is quite clearly against legalization of prostitution, her book provides a comprehensive survey of the arguments for legalization (which she rejects and rebuts) and provides firsthand accounts of the testimony of those who have worked in the sex trade. *See also* Holly B. Fechner, *Three Stories of Prostitution in the West: Prostitutes Groups, Law and Feminist Truth*, 4 COLUM. J. GENDER & L. 26 (1994) (discussing strategies and objectives of prostitutes' groups).

refer to the *fact* of payment in an exchange; rather, they refer (or should refer) to a failure to pay a fair price and/or the use of a person as a mere means to an end, without regard to that person's human dignity.

The promise of payment, if coercive, is not the only form of coercion. Some women pay for the privilege of having their breasts cut open and filled with silicone sacs to look more attractive to men. Is it fair or accurate to say that they are acting of their own "free will"? Are they less coerced than someone who agrees to receive payment for kidney extraction? Is their human dignity better preserved? From a utilitarian perspective, there is a greater social benefit where someone gets paid to have a kidney removed (a life is saved) than where someone pays to have her breasts altered or her buttocks surgically enhanced.

Furthermore, the absence of payment does not necessarily make a donation *less* coercive. To permit "altruistic" donations and prohibit compensation for the same interaction assumes too much about the surrounding circumstances. Nonpayment does not guarantee an absence of exploitation, coercion or subordination.[124] Family members may feel coerced into giving a kidney or other organ to an ailing relative.[125] The history of "altruistic acts" cautions against taking the meaning of the word at face value. Naomi Duke writes of the danger of historical revisionism which recasts certain acts of violence against African Americans and other subordinated groups as socially beneficial altruistic acts:

> In denying the sanctity and the dignity of bodies of color, the conscription of these bodies as vessels of exploration was publicly, morally, and legally permissible in the name of advancing the nation's interest ... Indeed, as African Americans became the body commons, their oppression became shrouded in altruistic language. Their involuntary servitude and oppression contributed to the "greater good."[126]

Nonpayment, in the context of bodily integrity exchanges, does not mean that *no* money is being paid in the transaction. Michele Goodwin notes that despite the broad language of the federal law prohibiting payment for human organs to be used in human transplantation,[127] "reproductive markets flourish."[128] Jamila Jefferson-

---

[124]   Naomi N. Duke, *Situated Bodies in Medicine and Research*, in THE GLOBAL BODY MARKET: ALTRUISM'S LIMITS 110 (Michele Goodwin ed., 2013) [hereinafter THE GLOBAL BODY MARKET] ("altruism may serve as a 'cover' or proxy for other actions, including manipulation, coercion, and abuse.").

[125]   MICHELE GOODWIN, BLACK MARKETS: THE SUPPLY AND DEMAND OF BODY PARTS 57–58 (2006) (arguing that "exclusive reliance on altruism" creates subsytems of *compelled living donations*, which demands organs from people either unwilling or incompetent to donate and *reproductive altruism*, producing children specifically for organ and tissue harvesting" and that these subsystems "lack voluntary participation, informed consent, and mutual bargaining power, subverting the intention of altruism, with heightened possibilities for coercion, pressure, guilt, and unequal positioning.").

[126]   *Id.* at 109 (citing HARRIET WASHINGTON, MEDICAL APARTHEID: THE DARK HISTORY OF MEDICAL EXPERIMENTATION ON BLACK AMERICANS FROM COLONIAL TIMES TO THE PRESENT 69 (2006)).

[127]   The law is the National Organ Transplant Act, which regulates the process by which organs are procured and allocated and prohibits the transfer of "any human organ for valuable consideration for use in human transplantation." 42 U.S.C. § 274e(a), (b) (2012).

[128]   THE GLOBAL BODY MARKET, *supra* note 124, at xix.

Jones observes that "altruism may be more illusory than real as payments are involved at many levels" of the transplantation system.[129] Under the National Organ Transplant Act (NOTA), "'valuable consideration' does not include the reasonable payments associated with the removal, transportation, implantation, processing, preservation, quality control, and storage of a human organ."[130] As Jefferson-Jones notes, this section provides a kind of loophole:

> This permits hospitals, doctors, organ procurement agencies, and other medical industry providers to receive payment for their services. Donors, on the other hand, are allowed to recoup certain losses, as "valuable consideration" also does not include the "expenses of travel, housing, and lost wages incurred by the donor."[131]

Consequently, allowing paid bodily integrity exchanges might *reduce* exploitation. Under the current system, service providers typically get paid for their work, but the donor is only permitted to recoup losses. Thus, only those who are compassionate and generous enough to put the needs of others before their own suffer the physical risks of the procedure without possibility of economic gain. The system, in other words, rewards selfish or self-preserving behavior and shifts the burden of the organ shortage onto the altruistic, in effect imposing a cost upon them for being humanitarian and self-giving.

Furthermore, pricing puts in stark relief the value that the recipient places upon the exchange. A recipient who has the resources to pay for a procedure to receive a kidney but seeks one "for free" from a relative may be undervaluing the sacrifice which must be made by the relative. One might argue that the recipient values the sacrifice at the market price for kidneys, but such a conclusion ignores that the donor may not have (likely would not have) "sold" the kidney to a stranger for the market price (if there could even be a market price for something as non-fungible as a kidney). It also seems unlikely that allowing some to be paid would diminish the value of the act for those who are willing to donate. It is anomalous to think that, in a society where price is often (and often inaccurately) equated with quality, putting a price on an activity would devalue that activity. With respect to sexual freedom, for example, Debora Spar questions whether it works against women's interest by diminishing the leverage that women had over men.[132] Many girls feel societal

---

[129] Jamila Jefferson-Jones, *Quid Pro Quo Altruism, in* THE GLOBAL BODY MARKET, *supra* note 124, at 91.

[130] 42 U.S.C. § 274e(c)(2) (2012).

[131] Jamila Jefferson-Jones, *Quid Pro Quo Altruism, in* THE GLOBAL BODY MARKET, *supra* note 124, at 92.

[132] DEBORA L. SPAR, WONDER WOMEN: SEX, POWER, AND THE QUEST FOR PERFECTION 56 (2013) [hereinafter SPAR, WONDER WOMEN] ("[t]oday, women no longer see their sexuality as something to be bartered for anything else . . . The question, however, is whether this freedom has come at a cost . . . Yet unless women actually enjoy casual sex as much as men do, and unless they are equally content with no-name, no-commitment relationships, they still, in retrospect, may have struck a deal that works against their own best interests. Because, crude though it may sound, women arguably had more leverage over men when they had the ability and inclination to deny them sex. Presumably, women had greater resources when dating involved a little bit of financial foreplay. So what, then, have young women gained in their pursuit of liberty? And was it worth the price?").

pressure to conform to prevailing and largely male-centric notions of what is sexy, desirable and expected. Technology has exacerbated these social norms and expectations.[133] The prevalence of Internet porn and the ease of shopping for hook-ups on male-created apps like Tinder may pressure women and girls into adaptive sexual behavior and cause them to doubt and dismiss their own intuitions and feelings about what sex and relationships should look and feel like.[134] Conversely, putting a price on sex may create a realization that something which is expected to be free – and thus, devalued – may actually be something which should be appreciated and more highly valued.[135] Deborah Spar writes:

> The question . . . is whether women truly get equal value from a relationship based on "free" sex. Are they equally content to give – and get – sex for nothing, or have they perhaps given men what they want (easy, cheap sex) without getting much in return? In purely economic terms, the answer must simply be no. No, women are not better off giving away something they once bartered. No, women do not gain by losing the power they once had to force men to buy their favors.[136]

A final category of objection is based upon the harmful effects to society or third parties. If legalizing prostitution increases human trafficking, for example, it would outweigh any individual's interest in being able to receive payment for sex. There may be public health concerns, such as the spread of sexually transmissible diseases. Similar arguments about harm to third parties are raised against organ selling. These concerns about harmful societal effects are complex and the problems are often unique to the type of exchange involved. In some cases, regulation might more appropriately address a negative externality than would prohibiting the activity. It is important to note that permitting at least some of these bargains would benefit third parties or provide a societal benefit. Permitting organ sales, for example, might increase the supply of scarce resources and save lives. Legalization might even eliminate or reduce the size of the black market in at least certain types of exchanges.

The desire to eliminate a black market in a particular type of exchange, however, should not justify legalizing practices which are prohibited for public health and safety reasons. For example, the existence of a black market in dangerous, addictive drugs does not mean that they should be legalized, because there is no social benefit to be served by the underlying activity. By contrast, there is a social benefit to be served by permitting paid organ transplants.[137] My objective is to examine the

---

[133] *See generally* PEGGY ORENSTEIN, GIRLS AND SEX: NAVIGATING THE COMPLICATED NEW LANDSCAPE (2016); NANCY JO SALES, AMERICAN GIRLS: SOCIAL MEDIA AND THE SECRET LIVES OF TEENAGERS (2016).

[134] *See* SPAR, WONDER WOMEN, *supra* note 83, at 70–71 (explaining that young women often regret "hook-ups" or non-committal sex because "[r]ather than feeling empowered by their conquests, they feel abandoned by the men they thought might be their boyfriends").

[135] *See id.* at 71–74.

[136] *Id.* at 72.

[137] *See* Philip J. Cook & Kimberly D. Krawiec, *A Primer on Kidney Transplanation: Anatomy of the Shortage*, 77 L. & CONTEMP. PROBS. 1 (2014) (providing data in support of financial inducements for kidney donors).

rationale for prohibiting *payment* for these types of exchanges; it is not to resolve, once and for all, whether all bodily integrity exchanges are socially beneficial. Each type of exchange requires an individualized assessment, public discussion and input from experts who have studied that particular type of exchange.

The payment of money generally does not exacerbate the underlying physical effort or risk involved in the transaction. The procedure and its harms and benefits are (or should be) the same for the transferor and the transferee regardless of whether payment is involved. The perception of the transaction changes because of the meaning society places upon payment and the way payment might adversely affect some members of society or the behavior of the parties.

However, the right to receive compensation for a service should not be equated with the right to engage in the underlying act. The underlying act may be essential to autonomy and constitutive of personhood; however, the receipt of payment for the act is not. For example, an individual's ability to engage in or abstain from sexual activity is integral to her sense of self and tied to both bodily integrity and freedom of expression. Restricting or regulating payment for services does not restrict an individual's freedom to engage in the underlying act. An individual can agree to transfer her kidney without payment, or to engage in sex without payment. These acts enable her to express herself in a fundamental way which the state should limit only in rare instances (i.e. to ensure consent). The right to engage in the underlying activity should be distinguished from the "right" to receive payment for such services, which is more closely associated with the societal value of the free market and the individual right to control personal property.

Yet, it is not altogether appropriate to speak of bodily integrity transactions as exchanges involving personal property. As Margaret Jane Radin writes, to treat the body as "property" presents difficulties:

> The idea of property in one's body presents some interesting paradoxes. In some cases, bodily parts can become fungible commodities, just as other personal property can become fungible with a change in its relationship with the owner: Blood can be withdrawn and used in a transfusion; hair can be cut off and used by a wigmaker; organs can be transplanted. On the other hand, bodily parts may be too "personal" to be property at all.[138]

The fact that a person has control over his or her body is not the same thing as being the "owner" of it, which necessarily implies something external to the self and which can be traded. There is no "title" to the body, and no ability to transfer ownership. Importantly, the Thirteenth Amendment, which prohibits slavery and involuntary servitude, essentially disqualifies the body from being treated as property which may be exploited in every conceivable way.[139]

---

[138] Margaret Jane Radin, *Property and Personhood*, 34 STAN. L. REV. 957, 966 (1982) [hereinafter Radin, *Property*].

[139] U.S. CONST. amend. XIII, § 1 ("Neither slavery nor involuntary servitude, except as a punishment for crime whereof the party shall have been duly convicted, shall exist within the United States, or any place subject to their jurisdiction.").

Although not a perfect way to describe the body itself, property *is* appropriate to discuss the *rights* that an individual has in and over her body. Rights in one's body are similar to other types of intangible property (such as intellectual property rights). I believe that it is essential to retain property concepts, including the concept of ownership, when speaking of the body. Property ownership allows the owner to exclude others from using the property. To treat the body as "unproperty" risks turning the body, especially the female body, into something communal, making it more susceptible to violation. If one does not have ownership rights to one's body, then what right does one have to keep others away from it?

However, owning the rights to one's body does not mean that one can do whatever one wants with it. This has never been the case with any type of property, tangible or intangible. A property owner must still respect the rights of others. The owner of a car cannot drive that car over someone else's lawn. She can, however, prohibit others from driving it. The owner of a patent does not have the right to use the patented invention; the patent grant only allows her to exclude others from using it.[140] Owning one's body justifies the protection of bodily integrity (the exclusion of others from using it) but it does not justify paid bodily integrity transactions (the using of the body).

Rather, the justification for allowing paid bodily integrity transactions is not that the "owner" should be allowed to do whatever she wishes with her "property"; rather, it is that disallowing payment treats these transactions differently from other paid exchanges in a way that is incoherent, and which harms the party wanting to pay for the exchange. If the individual would not be able to participate in the underlying exchange without paying for it, and if that activity pertains to a basic right or freedom, there should be compelling reasons to prohibit payment. A person whose kidney is failing and who would not be able to receive a kidney from a donor deserves an explanation for *why* he cannot pay money to have the kidney of another who is willing to relinquish it. An individual may want to pay for sex because he is unable to find a willing partner. In some cases, the assumption of lack of access may be false. A man may want to pay for sex not because he is unable to find willing partners but because he enjoys the power from the transaction. It may be that social problems will arise after legalization of certain bodily integrity exchanges, which justifies passing laws prohibiting them. The presumption, however, should be in favor of permitting bodily integrity transactions *provided that* it is possible to regulate them to minimize or eliminate any harmful societal effects.[141]

[140]   35 U.S.C. § 154(a)(1) (2012) ("Every patent shall contain a short title of the invention and a grant to the patentee, his heirs or assigns, of the right to exclude others from making, using, offering for sale, or selling the invention throughout the United States or importing the invention into the United States . . . ").

[141]   *See* Michael J. Sandel, What Money Can't Buy: The Moral Limits of Markets 11 (2012). A related question is whether, as Michael Sandel asks, "Do we want a market economy, or a market society?" This book does not attempt to answer that question. Rather, it questions a foundational concept underlying the market – that people consent to market exchanges.

A final category of objection stems from concerns about consent. In exchange for monetary compensation, the individual is engaging in a physically intrusive act which usually involves some level of discomfort or physical vulnerability in exchange for compensation. Empathy, sympathy or disgust may make it difficult to believe that the individual actually consented and wasn't coerced or exploited. It may be difficult to believe that the consent was the result of free will and not the product of desperation. It is the tension between our ideal society and the society we live in that creates a space for exploitation. We may pretend to be fair as a society, but the facts and figures reveal otherwise. As Margaret Jane Radin explains:

> There is always a gap between the ideals we can formulate and the progress we can realize ... Does justice refer to the best general ideals we can formulate? We can call this ideal justice. Or does justice refer to a theoretical working out of what changes would now count as social improvements? We can call this nonideal justice ... To avoid all significant harms to personhood and community may be an ideal of justice, at least of ideal justice. Yet it may also be the case that justice (at least for here and now) instead means only that we should choose the best alternative from among those available to us.[142]

In other words, we may not want to live in a world where someone is willing to have a kidney removed in order to pay for a child's operation, but we do. As Radin explains, our non-ideal world creates a "double-bind"[143] because banning bodily integrity exchanges won't resolve the underlying desperation and the social conditions which cause it.[144]

In our non-ideal world, banning bodily integrity contracts increases the risks for the most vulnerable, and essentially restricts access to certain transactions to the non-law-abiding wealthy. It also ignores that some bodily integrity exchanges reflect actual preferences rather than forced choices. Some of us may find offensive the suggestion that someone would prefer to have sex with a stranger than work double-shifts at Walmart. But the offended sensibilities of some people should not define the choices of others. There are some who would never have sex for money as a matter of principle, but if the underlying act is permissible, then the fact of payment should not render it impermissible without justification (justification based on something other than personal preference or a difference in morality or religious beliefs). Evidence that negative externalities outweigh the benefits of commodification would justify prohibition,[145] as would evidence that the conditions of consent are

---

[142] RADIN, CONTESTED COMMODITIES, *supra* note 49, at 123.

[143] *Id.* at 127.

[144] ("If people are so desperate for money that they are trying to sell things we think cannot be separated from them without significant injury to personhood, we do not cure the desperation by banning sales. Nor do we avoid the injury to personhood.") *Id.* at 125.

[145] *See* Guido Calabresi & A. Douglas Melamed, *Property Rules, Liability Rules, and Inalienability: One View of the Cathedral*, 85 HARV. L. REV. 1089, 1111–14 (1972) (discussing "inalienable entitlements" where "external costs may justify inalienability"); TREBILCOCK, *supra* note 49, at 58–77 (discussing the problem of externalities, particularly pertaining to prostitution and pornography).

unlikely to be sufficiently robust given the risks involved in the activity, the information shared or withheld by the consent-seeker, and the limits of the human mind to calculate the relevant risks.

C. NOVEL/EXPERIMENTAL ACTIVITIES

SpaceX is a company which seeks to make travel to Mars a possibility for ordinary people. The billionaire founder of the company, Elon Musk, will probably not be one of them. He recently remarked that there was a "high" chance of death for the first participants in the program and that they should be "prepared to die."[146] He indicated that he couldn't put himself in that risky position as his children and his company depend upon him.[147]

Mr. Musk wants there to be no mistake that travel to Mars is not for those who plan to live to a ripe old age – or those who have important jobs or dependents. In other words, he wants others to volunteer for a project that is too risky for him to undertake himself. Elon Musk is not the first innovator to risk the lives of others in the name of progress, although he is much more honest and his frankness is refreshing. Other innovators soliciting first volunteers generally were not as forthcoming about the risks involved or even the nature of the project. Many examples come from human experiments in the name of science.

In 1898, a European doctor, Dr. Albert Neisser, had an admirable goal – to find a method of preventing syphilis. His method was far less admirable. He injected serum from syphilis patients into patients without syphilis without their knowledge or consent. Most of the infected patients were prostitutes and when they contracted syphilis, he claimed that it was due to their work, not because he had infected them.[148]

A half-century later and an ocean away, the United States government also conducted an infamous study of syphilis treatment on African American men, known as the Tuskegee Study. The government lied to the subjects about the nature of the study and withheld proper treatment.[149] The shameful history of the Tuskeegee Study led to the creation of the National Commission for the Protection of Human Subjects of Biomedical and Behavioral Research and,

---

[146] Dana Hull, *Musk Seeks Mars Explorers with $200,000, Guts to Risk Death*, BLOOMBERG TECH. (Sept. 27, 2016), www.bloomberg.com/news/articles/2016-09-27/musk-seeks-mars-explorers-with-200-000-gumption-to-risk-death.

[147] *Id.* ("I've got to make sure that if something goes wrong on the flight and I die that there's a good succession plan and the mission of the company continues and it doesn't get taken over by investors who just want to maximize the profitability of the company . . . I would like to see my kids grow up.").

[148] Jochen Vollmann & Rolf Winau, *Informed Consent in Human Experimentation Before the Nuremberg Code*, 313 BRIT. MED. J. 1445, 1445–47 (1996).

[149] *See U.S. Public Health Service Syphilis Study at Tuskegee*, CTRS. DISEASE CONTROL & PREVENTION, U. S. DEP'T OF HEALTH & HUM. SERVS., www.cdc.gov/tuskegee/index.html (last updated Dec. 30, 2013).

eventually, the establishment of the President's Council on Bioethics.[150] But the government's response came too late for the victims. The unwitting participants in the Tuskeegee study suffered from syphilis for the rest of their lives (the study lasted over forty years). Many of them spread the disease to their sexual partners.

During the Nuremberg trials, German doctors and scientists tried to excuse their horrific experiments during the 1930s and 1940s by pointing to the lack of explicit rules governing medical research on humans.[151] Certainly, this was merely a flimsy attempt to explain inexcusably inhumane behavior by medical personnel. A code of ethics strips away this sham of an excuse. Importantly, it provides moral guidance and support during uncertain times or where norms are shifting or unclear. Today, the requirement of informed consent and ethics review committees are part of the operating protocols and procedures for hospitals and research institutions.

Yet, the organizations and agencies which create these protocols and procedures are not infallible and may be subject to their own biases and shortcomings.[152] A code of ethics and ethics review committees are no guarantee that the conditions of consent will be robust enough to constitute valid consent. There are many variations of consent. An informed consent requirement and institutional review are insufficient to prevent harm, abuse and exploitation Many shameful acts were committed in good faith. Today, for example, we consider lobotomies to be a barbaric and misguided practice. But the doctors who performed them in the past generally believed that they were helping their patients.[153] Other practices, such as "conversion therapy" intended to change an individual's sexuality,[154] or operations to alter

[150] *U.S. Public Health Service Syphilis Study at Tuskegee: How Tuskegee Changed Research Practices*, CTRS. DISEASE CONTROL & PREVENTION, U.S. DEP'T OF HEALTH & HUM. SERVS., www.cdc.gov/tuskegee/after.htm (last updated Feb. 22, 2017).

[151] *Id.*

[152] *See, e.g.*, LORI ANDREWS, FUTURE PERFECT: CONFRONTING DECISIONS ABOUT GENETICS 16 (2001) [hereinafter ANDREWS, FUTURE PERFECT] (explaining how some groups that were organized to address uses of genetic technologies were "subject to 'capture' by the governmental or professional organizations that formed them and have not adequately represented the public.").

[153] *See* Barron H. Lerner, *When Lobotomy Was Seen as Advanced*, N.Y. TIMES (Dec. 19, 2011), www.nytimes.com/2011/12/20/health/report-on-eva-peron-recalls-time-when-lobotomy-was-embraced.html (noting that lobotomy as treatment for psychiatric illness "was once seen as a huge advance" and as a way to provide relief from severe and resistant pain).

[154] Stephen Vider & David S. Byers, *A Half-Century of Conflict Over Attempts to "Cure" Gay People*, TIME (Feb. 12, 2015), http://time.com/3705745/history-therapy-hadden/; Rebecca Coffey, *The Colorful Modern History of Gay Conversion Therapy*, PSYCHOL. TODAY (July 25, 2014), www.psychologytoday.com/blog/the-bejeezus-out-me/201407/the-colorful-modern-history-gay-conversion-therapy (stating that "conversion therapy has been damaging and useless from the beginning of its modern history. Indeed, sometimes the injuries afflicted by medical professionals in the name of conversion have been quite literal, reaching far beyond psychic scars that can't be seen."). The American Psychological Association (APA) issued a report that conversion therapy was unlikely to be successful and involved some risk of harm. *Report of the APA Task Force on Appropriate Therapeutic Responses to Sexual Orientation*, APA (2009), www.apa.org/pi/lgbt/resources/sexual-orientation.aspx.

an infant or young child's genitalia or sexual organs,[155] should serve as painful reminders that even well-meaning, medically trained professionals are products of a particular time and place which will be reflected in their research, practices and recommendations.

There is a difference between high-risk activities undertaken by someone with knowledge of those risks, and those which are imposed without the subjects' knowledge. At a minimum, people should not be made to expose themselves to harm without consent for the sake of helping others. But even where the subjects have volunteered to participate and have received information about the nature of the experiment, there are concerns about the validity of consent. Experiments are often complicated and subjects who are unfamiliar with the science or methodology may not fully grasp the information being presented to them.[156] They may understand that there is risk involved, but they may be unable to quantify or assess the risk appropriately.[157]

The payment of money raises concerns about exploiting the poor. Unlike organ transplants, it is legal to pay participants in clinical trials. The Food and Drug Administration (FDA) states that payment to participants is "not considered a benefit, it is a recruitment incentive,"[158] although the distinction seems to be one without a difference. Payment might be used for purposes other than to reimburse research participants for time they take off from work or to cover expenses related to participation. Payment might also legitimize the nature of the research, help overcome mistrust, and increase the diversity of participants involved in the research.[159] The FDA states that incentives should not be "coercive," meaning that they should

155   David Cary, *Pressure Mounts to Curtail Surgery on Intersex Children*, CHI. TRIB. (July 25, 2017), www
       .chicagotribune.com/lifestyles/health/ct-surgery-intersex-children-20170725-story.html (noting that
       the practice of surgeries to alter intersex children's genitalia is "under assault as never before. The
       American Medical Association is considering a proposal discouraging it. Three former U.S. surgeons
       general say it's unjustified."); *A Changing Paradigm: US Medical Provider Discomfort with Intersex
       Care Practices*, HUM. RIGHTS WATCH (Oct. 26 2017), at 2–3, www.hrw.org/report/2017/10/26/changing-
       paradigm/us-medical-provider-discomfort-intersex-care-practices (a report issued by Human Rights
       Watch and InterACT, a group advocating for intersex children, stated that the "evidence is over-
       whelming that these procedures carry risk of catastrophic harm" and "carr[y] the risk of chronic pain,
       nerve damage, and scarring.").
156   LAWRENCE K. ALTMAN, WHO GOES FIRST?: THE STORY OF SELF-EXPERIMENTATION IN MEDICINE 313–14
       (1998) (stating that some doctors believe that "no one can be fully informed about everything
       involved in such a complex thing as an experiment and that probably there is no truly informed
       consent.").
157   DANIEL J. LEVITIN, THE ORGANIZED MIND: THINKING STRAIGHT IN THE AGE OF INFORMATION
       OVERLOAD 219 (2014) (discussing the difficulties people have assessing risks, including problems
       with calculating probability, discerning relevant information, and deferring to authority or experts).
158   *Payment to Research Subjects—Information Sheet, Guidance for Institutional Review Boards and
       Clinical Investigators*, FOOD & DRUG ADMIN., www.fda.gov/RegulatoryInformation/Guidances/
       ucm126429.htm (last updated Jan. 25, 2018).
159   Christine Grady, *Payment of Clinical Research Subjects*, 115 J. CLINICAL INVESTIGATION 1681, 1682
       (2005), www.jci.org/articles/view/25694/pdf ("Some say that financial incentives are also necessary to
       overcome barriers unique to certain subgroups in the population, such as lack of awareness or
       distrust. Consequently, money may not only be important to general recruitment but also helpful in

not "unduly induce subjects to stay in the study when they would otherwise have withdrawn."[160]

The FDA's distinction of "benefit" from "recruitment incentive" is a rhetorical sleight of hand which tries to recast an economic exchange into an altruistic one.[161] There is little empirical evidence indicating whether payment is necessary to recruit clinical participants[162] but it seems unlikely that the wealthy are rushing to participate in medical trials which test cures for ailments they do not have. Even if payment is not the sole motivation for participants, it is often the pivotal one. One participant noted the "high pay" and that "the more invasive the procedures, the more monetary compensation that is provided."[163] That participant also noted that another benefit to participation was that "[i]f it's been a while since your last physical check-up, this is a good way to find out about your health."[164] Bioethicist Carl Elliot commented that clinical trial participants tend to be those who have the time to participate, such as "homeless people, undocumented people, people who are either temporarily or long-term unemployed, people who are out of jail who can't get regular work."[165] In other words, participants are likely to belong to the groups which are most vulnerable to exploitation and most likely to endanger their health for money.

As with bodily integrity transactions, *nonpayment* or underpayment also might be exploitative. For example, participants in certain trials for cancer treatment are often not paid and may even have to cover some of their own costs.[166] It might be that the cost of paying participants in certain trials would be prohibitive, but it may also be that cancer patients (and others suffering from terminal illnesses) are often desperate, and the researcher may not *have* to pay them, given their desperation. In some cases, insurance companies may pick up the costs for the patient, thus creating a disincentive for the researcher to reduce or share the patient's costs.

achieving the goals of racial, ethnic, gender, and social diversity of subjects participating in biomedical research.").

[160] Id.

[161] *See* Cari Romm, *The Life of a Professional Guinea Pig*, ATLANTIC (Sept. 23, 2015), www.theatlantic.com/science/archive/2015/09/life-of-a-professional-guinea-pig/406018/ (discussing a community of clinical trial participants who seek trials that pay more money); Halina Zakowicz, *How to Make Extra Money by Participating in Clinical Trials*, I'VE TRIED THAT (Apr. 9, 2012), https://ivetriedthat.com/2012/04/09/how-to-make-extra-money-by-participating-in-clinical-trials/ (recommending clinical trials as the "answer" if you "don't want the hassle of a minimum wage job" or "need to make a good sum of money quickly because you have bills to pay now.").

[162] Grady, *supra* note 159, at 1482.

[163] *See* Zakowicz, *supra* note 161.

[164] Id.

[165] Romm, *supra* note 161.

[166] *See* NIH: NAT'L CANCER INST., PUB. NO. 16–6249, TAKING PART IN CANCER TREATMENT RESEARCH STUDIES, at 10 (Oct. 2016) (a booklet noting that patients may have to pay "patient care costs and research costs").

Yet, the most problematic aspect of novel procedures is not that they may be exploitative; it is that there are unknown and potentially deadly risks associated with them. The unpredictability of novel procedures and the seriousness of the risks raise concerns about whether the knowledge condition can ever be robust enough to justify consentability.

PART II

Consentability and Contractability

The question of consentability requires answering derivative questions so that, like a Russian nesting doll, all questions must be asked before the answer at its core is revealed. The primary, overarching question, *Should a proposed activity be consentable?*, requires answering two derivative questions: (1) Is it possible to validly consent to the proposed activity? and (2) Are social harms caused by the proposed activity outweighed by its social benefits? If the answer to either of these questions is no, then the proposed activity is *not* consentable. However, answering these two questions is not a simple yes-or-no matter; rather, it requires asking additional questions.

The first derivative question, *Is it possible to validly consent to the proposed activity?*, elicits three additional questions. The first subderivative question is, *What does it mean to consent?* The second subderivative question is, *Does the validity of consent depend on the proposed activity?* In other words, *Should the law require different standards for consent depending upon the nature of the proposed activity?* I will argue that yes, standards for determining consent should (and do) vary depending upon the nature of the proposed activity. The third question (arising from the second subderivative question) is, *What standards should we use to differentiate proposed activities?* In other words, *How do we determine which activities warrant more robust consent conditions and which activities warrant less robust consent conditions?*

The second derivative question, *Are social harms caused by the proposed activity outweighed by its social benefits?*, also leads to two subderivative questions, only one of which may be addressed by a framework. The first subderivative question is, *What are the social consequences of the proposed activity?* This question cannot be answered in the abstract and requires specific inquiry into the societal effects of the proposed activity. Determining whether and to what extent there are negative and positive externalities from a proposed activity requires empirical data relating to that proposed activity, something which is beyond the scope of this book.[167]

---

[167] *See* SANDEL, *supra* note 141, at 8–9 (arguing that a market society promotes inequality and has a corrosive effect on the things exchanged). If, as Michael Sandel argues, certain markets do have a corrosive effect on cherished goods and practices, they should be disallowed; however, this

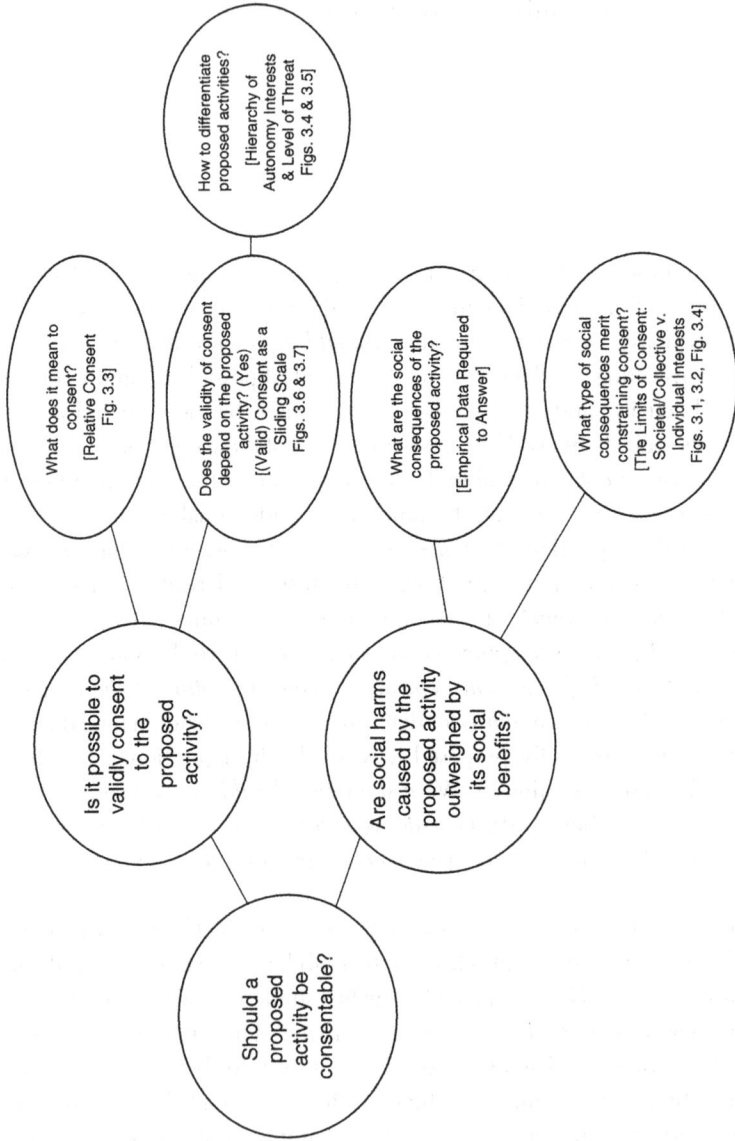

FIGURE II.1 Consentability Framework

A framework can, however, help evaluate the second subderivative question, which is, *What type of social consequences/externalities merit constraining an individual's right to consent to it?*

Figure II.1 provides a broad outline of the consentability framework, the related questions, and a road map of Part II.

Chapter 3 introduces a framework for evaluating consentability. This chapter seeks to answer the questions that sprout from the core question of consentability. Given that the role of consent is promoting autonomy, Chapter 3 begins with a discussion of the meaning of autonomy. It then analyzes the meaning of consent and how consent can diminish or promote autonomy. Chapter 4 discusses how contract law affects consentability. The binding nature of a contract means that it can be a double-edged sword as a tool for promoting autonomy. This chapter examines contract law through the consentability framework and explains how consentability determinations are often based upon contractability. Chapter 4 concludes that, in some cases involving autonomy, social harms would outweigh the benefits of contract enforcement.

---

supposition should be supported by data and other evidence that there is such a corrosive effect and that it is socially harmful.

3

A Consentability Framework

Consentability involves the power of the state. It considers whether – and when – the state should exercise its power to *prevent* an individual from consenting. Because the purpose of consent is to safeguard and promote autonomy, the question of consentability must be addressed within the context of autonomy. I identify five core societal interests or values (see Figure 3.1) which a liberal state seeks to protect: equality or non-discrimination; justice; public safety; democracy and a fair and representative political process; and a free market powered by private, not state, ownership. These societal values roughly correspond to the individual rights granted citizens under the Constitution and other laws (see Figure 3.2).[168] These rights are the right to bodily integrity, freedom of movement, various civil and political rights, and the rights of private property ownership (meaning that a property owner may exercise certain rights regarding the use or disposition of that property). At the core of these interests is autonomy. As Richard Fallon noted, "autonomy holds unique promise to function as the constitutional value of values. A view tracing to Kant maintains that other values possess their worth only because rational autonomous agents find them worth pursuing."[169]

Western societies traditionally place a high value on individual autonomy. Consent is the protector and implementer of autonomy. Yet, what does autonomy mean? Autonomy, like consent, is a multi-faceted concept. Joel Feinberg provided four closely related meanings for the word "autonomy" as it pertains to individuals. The first meaning refers to the capacity to govern oneself or competence.[170] Another meaning refers to the condition of self-government. This condition can mean the actual physical condition or ability to self-govern. For example, a person cannot self-govern if he is enslaved to another, physically overpowered or financially dependent upon another. The condition of self-government also requires freedom from other types of circumstantial and abstract constraints which prevent or limit self-possession or self-identity, such as social and cultural expectations or family pressures.

---

[168] I use the word "citizen" in a broad sense throughout this book to refer to inhabitants of a state.
[169] Richard H. Fallon, Jr., *Two Senses of Autonomy*, 46 STAN. L. REV. 875, 976 (1994).
[170] FEINBERG, HARM TO SELF, *supra* note 52, at 27–51.

SOCIETAL INTERESTS/VALUES

Equality/Non-discrimination	Justice and Due Process	Public Safety	Democracy/Political Process	Free Market/Capitalism

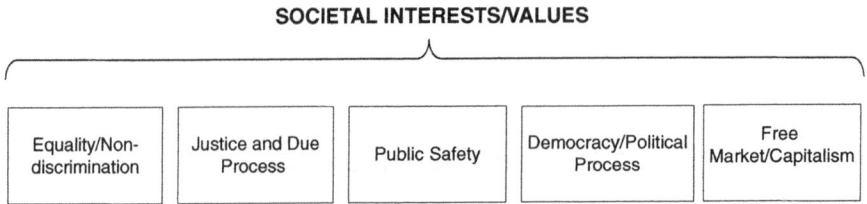

FIGURE 3.1 Societal Interests/Values

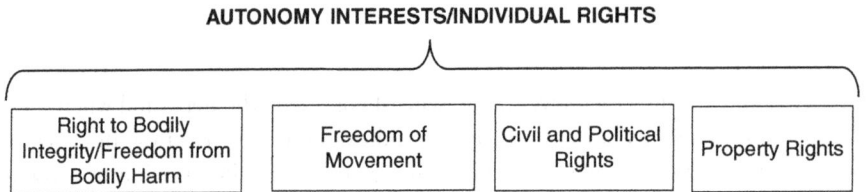

AUTONOMY INTERESTS/INDIVIDUAL RIGHTS

Right to Bodily Integrity/Freedom from Bodily Harm	Freedom of Movement	Civil and Political Rights	Property Rights

FIGURE 3.2 Autonomy Interests/Individual Rights

An autonomous individual (one who satisfies the condition of self-government) is authentic to himself and self-directed, and is not merely doing the bidding of another. Yet another meaning of autonomy refers to an "ideal of character," which derives from the condition of self-government and includes virtues such as self-reliance, personal responsibility, moral authenticity and integrity. Finally, autonomy also refers to the sovereign authority to govern oneself or the "right" to personal sovereignty.[171] Although these conceptions differ, they all presume that autonomy means the power to act and the power not to act, according to one's desires. Autonomy thus means *freedom to* as well as *freedom from*.

But what is the purpose of individual freedom? In his classic essay *On Liberty*, John Stuart Mill wrote that the goal of freedom was utility, but utility in a sense that means more than the most efficient outcomes purportedly assessed according to some objective (majoritarian consistent) norm. It is "utility in the largest sense, grounded on the permanent interests of man as a progressive being."[172] The idea of "man as a progressive being" provides the foundation for liberty:

> It is possible that he might be guided in some good path and kept out of harm's way, without any of these things. But what will be his comparative worth as a human being? It really is of importance, not only what men do, but also what manner of men they are that do it . . . Human nature is not a machine to be built after a model, and set to do exactly the work prescribed for it, but a tree, which requires to grow and

[171] *Id. See also* John Christman, *Constructing the Inner Citadel: Recent Work on the Concept of Autonomy*, 99 ETHICS 109 (1988) (discussing various theories of autonomy).

[172] MILL, *supra* note 51, at 11.

develop itself on all sides, according to the tendency of the inward forces which make it a living thing.[173]

Experience leads to personal development and growth. As Cass Sunstein notes, "mistakes are often productive."[174] People can learn from their past mistakes (and others can learn from them as well). Most of the time, there is no one right decision and "many different kinds of lives can be good."[175]

According to Mill, the government should not compel others to act, or refrain from acting, in ways which are in their own self-interest. The state may not legitimately exercise power over its citizens except to "prevent harm to others":

> The object of this Essay is to assert one very simple principle, as entitled to govern absolutely the dealings of society with the individual in the way of compulsion and control, whether the means used be physical force in the form of legal penalties, or the moral coercion of public opinion. That principle is, that the sole end for which mankind are warranted, individually or collectively in interfering with the liberty of action of any of their number, is self-protection. That the only purpose for which power can be rightfully exercised over any member of a civilized community, against his will, is to prevent harm to others. His own good, either physical or moral, is not a sufficient warrant.[176]

The "Harm Principle" has been invoked by libertarians and free market economists in policy arguments about the role of government regulation in a range of areas.[177]

But the Harm Principle does not address the difficult questions regarding the nature of free will, social and economic inequality, and the limits of human cognition and control. The myriad, complex constraints and the adaptive preferences which impede the conditions of self-government mean that no human being is truly or ideally autonomous all the time. An adult makes decisions for herself, but what if her ability to make decisions is forced by circumstances? What if she suffers cognitive defects (as she most certainly does)? What if she is being manipulated or pressured by someone else? What if her decision is based upon misinformation?

If a woman makes a decision to sell her kidney to buy food for her children, should we treat that decision the same as one made by a wealthy businessman to sell his business for millions of dollars? Can we honestly say that both are the product of "free will" and so the government should not intervene? Is a decision (to sell a kidney), made to avoid a worse consequence (starvation of one's children), still an autonomous act? Agentic power is an ideal that ignores the hard choices which

---

[173] *Id.* at 62.
[174] SUNSTEIN, WHY NUDGE, *supra* note 32, at 94.
[175] *Id.*
[176] MILL, *supra* note 51, at 10.
[177] *See* SUNSTEIN, WHY NUDGE, *supra* note 32, at 3–7 (noting that "the idea of 'consumer sovereignty,' central to modern economics and much political debate, is a close cousin to the Harm Principle … the Harm Principle raises serious doubts about many laws and regulations.").

people must make in a society where the ideal is equality, but the reality is quite different.

Even assuming an ideal world with economic and social equality, human beings are cognitively limited, biased and their decisions may be shaped by social conditions and cultural conditioning. Sunstein writes that the invisible "social background" creates "serious problems for the Harm Principle, because influences on our choices are omnipresent, and we may not even see them."[178] The vast research on human decision-making and its consequences for markets provide important insights which should help us make better decisions, but it cannot guarantee them. In most cases, there is no perfect decision because of the complex, disjunctive and conjunctive nature of many decisions, where outcome depends upon a web of interactions and a chain of events. Should X take a job offer and move to another country or stay and try to get a promotion? Should Y undergo major surgery to remove the tumor, or "wait and see" whether it grows? Should Z marry A or B? A decision is often not the last one, but part of an organic process. It is not always clear that the path not taken would have been the better one, or that the one taken was the worse one. The right decision may not have been the only right decision – just as the wrong decision may not have been the only wrong decision.

Sometimes X knows she made the wrong decision because of the unexpected negative outcome. The tumor that X believed was benign turns out to be a fast-spreading malignant cancer, for example. The outcome did not turn out the way X had hoped, and she regrets her decision profoundly.

But sometimes, the outcome is not what is expected or hoped, yet the decision-maker doesn't think and cannot know that the wrong decision was made. X's job may have ended in a firing, or Z's marriage in divorce, but X is grateful for the lessons learned and Z for the happy memories. The job may have led to a better opportunity and the marriage may have resulted in a close friendship and children. In those cases, the decision-makers are better off as a result of having made the choice, despite the unexpected outcome, and there is no regret.

Sometimes, the outcome is as expected, yet the decision-maker regrets the decision and views it as the "wrong" one. The problem wasn't that X guessed wrong about the outcome, but she guessed wrong about herself. X did not accurately predict how she would react or that her priorities and values would have shifted.

In still other cases, the outcome turned out as expected, and the decision is regretted, not because she was wrong about her future self but because she could not control the behavior of her present self. In these situations, X knew (or would have known if she had stopped to think about it) *at the time* that the decision was made that it was against her (perceived) best interests, but she could not or did not stop herself.

---

[178] *Id.* at 14–15.

Certain factors may hinder the ability of an individual to make choices in her best interest. A preliminary – and perhaps unresolvable – issue is what is meant by "best interest." It may be that best interest is determined by the consenter at a later time from when the decision was made. An adult Y may look back upon decisions she made as a teenager and wonder at the foolishness of her younger self. In some cases, it may mean best interest as determined by the consenter at an earlier time. An adult Y might take measures to guard against her *future* less rational self. The classic example of this is Ulysses having his men tie him to the mast so that he could hear the song of the Sirens without jumping into the ocean to join them. A less dramatic example is people establishing trusts to protect against bad decisions they might make in the future.[179]

Regret is a term which applies to a range of matters, trivial and significant.[180] We may say that we regret having stayed up late to binge-watch our favorite show on Netflix, because we feel sleep-deprived in the morning. That is not the type of regret which is the concern of this book. The regret which is the focus of this book has a permanent negative effect on our happiness and well-being because it limits or damages our *future* autonomy in a significant way.[181] I propose that the state should intervene to minimize or avoid this type of profound regret, which I will refer to as the Regret Principle.

Some may argue that to police a decision out of concern that the decision may be the "wrong" decision for an individual is unduly paternalistic. But it is important to remember that the context in which most consent issues arise is where there is a dispute about its validity. X is claiming that X had a right over Y *because* Y consented; Y, however, is disputing that Y validly consented. The state in some form (the judiciary, an administrative agency) is then called in to resolve the dispute. The accusation of paternalism seems inapt in situations like this where it is the

---

[179] Elizabeth Olson, *The Benefits of a Trust*, N.Y. Times (Mar. 25, 2018), www.nytimes.com/2018/03/22/your-money/trust-wills-inheritance.html.

[180] E. Allan Farnsworth, Changing Your Mind: The Law of Regretted Decisions 20 (Yale Univ. Press, 1998) [hereinafter Farnsworth, Changing Your Mind] (describing regret as "the sensation of distress that you feel on concluding that you have done something contrary to your present self-interest, something that does not accord with your present preferences. But merely making a decision, without taking a second step, is no real cause for regret; it is the second step that causes regret."). Thus, in Farnsworth's view, it is the "second step" of promising to carry out the resolution which may lead to regret, rather than the initial step of resolving to carry out the decision. The definition of regret employed in this book is broader as regret may arise even in situations where there is no "second step" or binding future commitment; regret may arise as a result of actions undertaken without sufficient forethought. The definition of regret then aligns more closely with the definition used by economists such as Barberis, Huang and Thaler, who define regret as "the pain we feel when we realize that we would be better off today if we had taken a different action in the past." Nicholas Barberis, Ming Huang & Richard H. Thaler, *Individual Preferences, Monetary Gambles, and Stock Market Participation: A Case for Narrow Framing*, 96 The American Economic Review 1069, 1084 (2006).

[181] I define autonomy in Chapter 3, section B, as the freedom to move, act or think without assistance or constraint.

consenter who seeks state intervention. Admittedly, the state is not always altruistic or free of self-interested motivations; it is subject to the same social and political influences and biases as the imperfect individuals who comprise its institutions.[182] Nonetheless, because it is usually called upon to intervene when two parties are in a dispute over a matter involving consent, the state is often in the best position to implement rules to avoid or resolve disagreements involving consent.

A society that values autonomy must reconcile the competing interests of its citizens so that the "freedom" of one does not impinge upon the rights of another. It must also recognize that individual freedom depends upon social stability and trust in the rule of law. While a thorough discussion of the role of government is beyond the scope of this book, it should be non-controversial to state that one of the primary roles of the state is to ensure that its citizens peacefully co-exist. Furthermore, the rights of any one individual, no matter how rich or powerful, must not be permitted to trump those of any other. For example, there is a strong societal interest in protecting the bodily integrity and property of individuals. Accordingly, laws criminalize intentional conduct which results in bodily harm to another without regard to the status of the perpetrator or the victim. The rule of law governs and, at least in principle, nobody is above the law.[183] The state must determine what to do when the interests of its citizens conflict, and it must set up rules and systems which minimize the occasion for such conflicts.

Not all state action or regulation is the same. State action which seeks to enhance the conditions of consent promotes, rather than diminishes, agency. Even John Stuart Mill recognized a distinction between coercive actions, such as prohibitions and compulsions, and efforts to enhance decision-making:

> He cannot rightfully be compelled to do or forbear because it will be better for him to do so, because it will make him happier, because, in the opinions of others, to do so would be wise, or even right. These are good reasons for remonstrating with him, or reasoning with him, or persuading him, or entreating him, but not for compelling him or visiting him with any evil, in case he do otherwise.[184]

The label "paternalism" is too often wielded as a cudgel to shut down discussion regarding any form of regulation, but as Mill noted, there is an important distinction between education and compulsion:

> It would be a great misunderstanding of this doctrine, to suppose that it is one of selfish indifference, which pretends that human beings have no business with each other's conduct in life, and that they should not concern themselves about the well-doing or well-being of one another, unless their own interest is involved . . . Human

---

[182] The author thanks Dan Barnhizer for this observation.

[183] *See* Clinton v. Jones, 520 U.S. 681 (1997) (reinforcing that even the President is not immune from being sued); *see also* Zervos v. Trump, No. 150522/17, 2018 N.Y. Misc. LEXIS 900, at *9 (N.Y. Sup. Ct. Mar. 20, 2018) ("No one is above the law.").

[184] MILL, *supra* note 51, at 10.

beings owe to each other help to distinguish the better from the worse, and encouragement to choose the former and avoid the latter. They should be forever stimulating each other to increased exercise of their higher faculties, and increased direction of their feelings and aims towards wise instead of foolish, elevating instead of degrading, objects and contemplations.[185]

Unfortunately, one's fellow human beings may be reluctant to share their unsolicited personal opinions, or meddle in each other's affairs, for fear of harming personal relationships. They may themselves be uninformed or misinformed. Informal networks and peer groups may perpetuate informational inequalities associated with socio-economic and educational disparities. It should not be the case that only those who socialize with medical doctors should be informed of the dangers of smoking, for example. The state, rather than one's fellow citizens, is often in a better position to provide the education which Mill suggests would enhance autonomy.[186]

As Joel Feinberg notes, paternalism is a "pejorative" term, more appropriate as a slur than it is helpful as a description.[187] It is particularly unhelpful and distortive to describe state action which seeks to improve decision-making to prevent later regret. An individual's decisions are not made in a vacuum. Social norms and beliefs reinforce power structures and influence individual behavior. Social pressure and peer influence may force one to act against one's self-interest.[188] Every person and every act, to varying degrees, is the product of its environment. Numerous experiments have demonstrated that individuals may be manipulated, through social pressure or environmental surroundings, to alter their opinions and to act in a way that they did not want and could not have predicted.[189] An act of agency may be a succumbing to cultural, market and social forces rather than an expression of intrinsic desire. It may be possible to know the difference only in retrospect, if at all.

---

[185] *Id.* at 80.

[186] However, this is not to say that the state is untainted by lobbyists or its own political interests. A discussion of how political influences affect governmental disclosures is a subject best left to another day, and another book.

[187] JOEL FEINBERG, HARM TO SELF, *supra* note 52 (discussing the unfortunate negative connotations associated with paternalism). Feinberg notes that the term "paternalism" has unfortunately become a derogatory word which "suggests the view that the state stands to its citizens as a parent (or perhaps a male parent!) stands to his children, and that normal adults might properly be treated as if they were children ... Yet the view that the state has a right to protect persons from their own folly seems to provide the rationale for many criminal statutes that few would wish to repeal ... The pejorative term ... hardly seems fair to those whose views it caricatures. 'Paternalism' is a label that might have been invented by paternalism's enemies." *Id.* at 4.

[188] DellaVigna, *supra* note 29, at 357–59 (summarizing research demonstrating that "excess impact of the beliefs of others" results from the "pressure to conform, or social pressure").

[189] *See id; see also* LEE ROSS & RICHARD E. NJISBETT, THE PERSON AND THE SITUATION: PERSPECTIVES OF SOCIAL PSYCHOLOGY (2011) (discussing various studies which explore how situational determinants affect human behavior); STANLEY MILGRAM, OBEDIENCE TO AUTHORITY: AN EXPERIMENTAL VIEW (1974) (chronicling and explaining Milgram's famous and controversial study of obedience to authority).

Moreover, there are significant limits to human cognition and the power of individuals to understand and control their impulses, desires and behavior. Individuals are limited in their ability to fully understand the implications of their actions, and are subject to emotions which cloud judgment. Economist and Nobel laureate George Akerlof wrote that, unlike the rational, utility-maximizing actor presupposed by classical economic theory, individuals exhibit "behavioral patholo-gies" which prevent them from maximizing their "true" utility:

> The principle of revealed preference cannot therefore be used to assert that the options that are chosen must be preferred to the options that are not chosen. Individuals may be made better off if their options are limited and their choices constrained. Forced pension plans may be superior to voluntary savings schemes; outright prohibitions on alcohol or drugs may be preferable to taxes on their use reflecting their nuisance costs to others; and an important function of management may be to set schedules and deadlines and not simply to establish "appropriate" price-theoretic incentive schemes to motivate employees.[190]

In particular, present bias and projection bias may lead to regretted decisions. Present bias is the human tendency to favor short-term over long-term conse-quences. Projection bias refers to the projection of current preferences onto future periods.[191] Consent may involve a time lag between when it is manifested and when the relevant act is to be performed. This temporal disconnect between the inten-tional manifestation of consent and the performance of the act exacerbates present and projection biases and may lead to suboptimal and regretted decisions.

An individual's preferences might be inconsistent with prevailing social norms but it may not necessarily lead to regret. In other words, the decision made by an individual may be considered eccentric, unhealthy, unwise or otherwise undesirable by most people, but not by the consenting individual. I will refer to this type of situation as one involving *majoritarian inconsistent preferences*. For example, most people would not get a facial tattoo and would consider unwise a decision to get one. Most people might think it is a bad idea to drop out of high school and join a rock band. In each of these examples, a paternalist might determine that the individual's choices must be constrained for his own benefit even if the individual has expressed preferences which are contrary to majoritarian ones.

In another type of situation, flawed decision-making arises where an individual makes a decision which is inconsistent with the individual's own preferences. I will refer to these types of decisions as involving a *self-inconsistent preference*. These preferences may be the same as majoritarian preferences or they may be different. For example, an individual's online shopping habit prevents him from saving for retirement, or a smoker may continue to smoke cigarettes even though she

---

[190]　George A. Akerlof, *Procrastination and Obedience*, 81 Amer. Econ. Rev. (Papers and Proc.) 1, 2 (1991).

[191]　DellaVigna, *supra* note 29, at 342.

desperately wants to stop. Decisions involving self-inconsistent preference are most likely to be regretted, and consequently, these are the decisions where regulation is most warranted.

Often, regret cannot be prevented. Some misfortune occurs due to chance. No government intervention could have changed the course of events. But in other cases, profound regret results from impulsivity, exploitation, excessive optimism, coercion, and lack of information. It is in these situations where government intervention can be most effective. E. Allan Farnsworth divides regretted decisions into two categories. In the first category, the decision to make the promise did not reflect the decision-maker's preferences at the time the decision was made. He refers to cases in this category as those involving "unfairly influenced decisions, uninformed decisions, and ill-considered decisions."[192] In Farnsworth's second category are cases where the promise reflected existing preferences but that promise was later regretted because the decision no longer reflected the individual's preferences. In this category, "[t]ime had to pass for you to have a reason for changing your mind."[193] He includes in this second category "improvident decisions and obsolete decisions."[194] Farnsworth's categories of regretted decisions reflect the concepts of consent construction and consent destruction. The first category seems to capture deficient consent construction; the second category captures those cases where consent is destroyed primarily due to a change brought on by the passage of time, and not because there was a defect in consent construction. Farnsworth's two categories are a useful way to distinguish *ex post* types of regretted decisions (the subject of Farnsworth's book), but like the concepts of consent construction and consent destruction, they do not prove useful as an *ex ante* way to distinguish the types of conditions which lead (or are likely to lead) to regret. Consequently, they do not help resolve the question *how* and *to what extent* may the government intervene to prevent regret? This question highlights a clash between the different conceptions of autonomy. There is a difference between the freedom to make a decision and individual empowerment, which aligns with Feinberg's second definition of autonomy as "self-government." Empowerment requires more than the simple ability to make a choice; it requires being able to make the best decision for oneself according to one's values and interests. An individual may be the best person to decide important matters, but the individual is not necessarily the one with the best information upon which to base those important decisions. If regulation or laws help an individual to avoid making regrettable decisions, autonomy – in its full-bodied sense – is enhanced, not diminished.

Myopia and its consequence, procrastination, are primary reasons for self-inconsistent preferences. George Akerlof notes that procrastination "occurs when present costs are unduly salient in comparison with future costs, leading individuals

---

[192] FARNSWORTH, CHANGING YOUR MIND, *supra* note 180, at 21.
[193] *Id.* at 21.
[194] *Id.*

to postpone tasks until tomorrow without foreseeing that when tomorrow comes, the required action will be delayed yet again."[195] Their immediate desires may over-shadow their future goals, much to their later regret. Procrastinating individuals, according to Akerlof, are both "maximizing and knowledgeable, and yet their decisions are not fully rational."[196] An individual may also misjudge her future preferences, believing her desires to be static rather than dynamic,[197] or as Akerlof writes, "individuals have utilities that do change and, in addition, they fail fully to foresee those changes or even recognize that they have occurred."[198]

There are other factors which affect rational decision-making as well, such as visceral influences[199] like lust, fear and hunger. Janet Metcalfe and Walter Mischel proposed a "hot/cool" system framework to understand the nature of willpower or "the ability to inhibit an impulsive response that undoes one's commitment":[200]

> We propose that there are two types of processing – hot and cool – involving distinct interacting system. The *cool cognitive system* is specialized for complex spatiotemporal and episodic representation and thought. We call it the "know" system. The *hot emotional system* is specialized for quick emotional processing and responding on the basis of unconditional or conditional trigger features. We call it the "go" system.[201]

They noted that "cool control of hot impulses" tended to be impaired under various conditions, most notably stress.

Research conducted by economists and psychologists demonstrate that people generally don't appreciate the effects of visceral influences and may not react optimally to them.[202] George Loewenstein writes:

> When in a hot state, people tend to exaggerate how long the hot state will persist, and, when in a cold state, people tend to underestimate how much future visceral influences will affect their future behavior.[203]

Optimism bias may compound the effects of visceral influences by obscuring rational thinking and making the consenter less likely to consider risks or suboptimal outcomes.[204] Thus, people in love believe they will stay in love, while people who

---

[195] Akerlof, *supra* note 190, at 1.

[196] *Id.* at 5.

[197] *Id.* at 16 (noting that "in making a sequence of small decisions, the decision maker's criteria for decisions gradually changes, with preceding decisions beings the precedent for future decisions.").

[198] *Id.* at 17.

[199] See Shane Frederick, George Loewenstein & Ted O'Donoghue, *Time Discounting and Time Preference: A Critical Review, in* TIME AND DECISION, at 40 (George Loewenstein et. al., eds., 2003) [hereinafter Frederick et. al., *Time Discounting*].

[200] Janet Metcalfe & Walter Mischel, *A Hot/Cool System Analysis of Delay of Gratification: Dynamics of Willpower*, 106 PSYCH. REV. 3 (1999).

[201] *Id.* at 4.

[202] Frederick et al., *Time Discounting, supra* note 199, at 40.

[203] *Id.*

[204] SHAROT, *supra* note 30 (explaining how human beings view the world through optimistic illusions which are critical to our existence).

are not in love may look at decisions made by lovers – such as eloping together – as irrational and something that they would "never" do. Research indicates that often people would prefer not to be in the hot state "even at the moment they are succumbing to its influence."[205] Thus, visceral factors may essentially "drive a wedge between what people do and what makes them happy."[206]

Some moral philosophers, most notably Derek Parfit, argue that there is no one continuous self but a succession of different selves. Under this view, the present self and the future self are discontinuous; accordingly, it is not irrational to make decisions which place more value on the utility of that decision to the present self to the detriment of the future self, or which discount or even entirely ignore the utility to the future self.[207] This book does not adopt the view that our "future selves" are *actually* different people or that our current and future selves are discontinuous (although there may be discontinuous preferences or discontinuous aspects of one's personality). As fascinating as this line of thought may be, it digresses from the primary concern of this book, which is consent. The idea of discontinuous selves fundamentally contradicts the concept of "man as a progressive being" which provides the rationale for autonomy (and autonomy, the justification for consent). An important justification for autonomy is that each individual should be able to determine what is "best" for herself, which assumes that each individual *wants* to make the best decisions for herself and does not view her future self as discontinuous from her current self. Furthermore, society is better off letting people make most decisions for themselves even if they make mistakes because they will presumably learn from their mistakes and become better versions of themselves – not entirely different selves. The assumption is that people are capable of improvement and that they are constantly evolving and learning from their experiences, including their mistakes.

If the present self *were* entirely discontinuous from the future self, then there is no moral authority (and there should be no legal authority) which would permit the present self (X^1) to make decisions for the future self (X^2). If one's discontinuous "future self" is as much a stranger as an actual stranger, then there is no reason to allow one's current self to make decisions for that stranger. Even if most individuals do not act selfishly, most of the time the vast majority of people are unwilling to put another's needs before their own and there is no justification for making X^1 the fiduciary for X^2 *if* they are two completely separate entities (in other words, not X^1 and X^2 but X^1 and Q). Respect for autonomy cannot justify any decision that one makes for one's future if we assume that one's present and future selves are distinct

---

[205] *Id.*

[206] *Id.*

[207] Derek Parfit, *Personal Identity*, 80 PHIL. REV., no. 1, 1971, at 8 ("The alternative, for which I shall argue, is to give up the language of identity. We can suggest that I survive as two different people without implying that I am these people.").

and discontinuous. Accordingly, consent is irrelevant under the extreme view of discontinuous selves because autonomy itself is irrelevant.

The extreme view of discontinuous selves poses another quandary – to which future self should we defer? We may change our values and our perspectives multiple times during the course of our lives.[208] For example, X^1 may undergo surgery. During the recovery process, X^2 (actually Q under the discontinuous selves view) feels so much pain that he regrets what X^1 has done. After the healing process, however, X^3 (or Z under the discontinuous selves view) is grateful for what X^1 has done and has no regrets. As this example indicates, regret often depends upon the outcome of a given decision. For example, if X^1's surgery was complicated and resulted in a disfiguring infection, X^3/Z would regret X^1's decision to have the surgery.

Although this book rejects the extreme view of discontinuous selves, it recognizes the difficulties that human beings face in making decisions which accurately calculate present and future utility.[209] The present self is a fiduciary for the future self, which means that the present self should act in the best interests of the future self. In some cases, the present self carries out those responsibilities; in other situations, it does not.[210] Given the demonstrable limits of human cognition and foresight, there are limits to the efficacy of consent to express individual autonomy. Humans are flawed, and our optimism bias, myopia and other cognitive and emotional limitations cause us to mispredict and misjudge future events, our reaction to them, and even who we are (and want to be). These human limitations should not be used, however, as justification to deprive individuals of decision-making authority. While an individual's choices may not be ideal and individual risk tolerance levels vary, in most cases, permitting an individual to make her own decisions is usually preferable to the alternative of state-dictated mandates.

---

[208] *See* Kaiponanea T. Matsumura, *Binding Future Selves*, 75 LA. L. REV. 71, 99–100 (2014) [hereinafter Matsumura, *Binding Future Selves*] (raising the conceptual question "acknowledging that preferences change, why privilege a person's preferences at the time of a legal dispute?").

[209] *See also* Rebecca Dresser, *Life, Death and Incompetent Patients: Conceptual Infirmities and Hidden Values*, 28 ARIZ. L. REV. 373, 379 (1986) (noting that "a person's interests can change radically over time, so radically that in some cases, it could be said that a different person exists by the time the life and death treatment situation arises.").

[210] A distinction should be made between self-inconsistent preference situations and "bad bet" situations. In the latter situations, there is no conflict of interest, but the outcome from the decision made by X^1 has an adverse effect on X^2. In the self-inconsistent preference situation, there is a conflict between the interests of X^1 and X^2. X^1 disregards X^2 by acting in a way that provides a benefit or gratification for X^1 at the expense of X^2's interests. This is typically not out of spite for X^2 (i.e. self-hatred), but the result of impulse control. By contrast, in the bad bet situation, X^1 wants a positive or beneficial result for X^2 but makes a decision which fails to have the desired result and instead, has negative consequences for X^2. In the conflict of interest scenario, regret is a predictable outcome. X^1 is undertaking an action that it *knows* will lead to X^2's harm and by exercising a self-inconsistent preference, privileging the present over the future. By contrast, in the bad bet situation, regret is not inevitable. On the contrary, X^1 desires the outcome to be positive for X^2. Even if the outcome is not what was expected or desired for X^2, X^2 may not regret having taken the chance. Although both situations may lead to regret, it is more likely in self-inconsistent preference situations.

If, however, the state is to permit most activities, it must also *regulate* potentially harmful activities. This regulation may be through different mechanisms, such as administrative agencies or more local, community-based entities. There are several reasons why regulation is necessary. First, people may assume that the lack of government regulation means that the government has permitted the activity, and by permitting it, has sanctioned it. In other words, they may assume that if an act is legal and consentable, it is because the state has assessed that it is beneficial, safe or, at least, not unduly dangerous. Because a core function of the government is to protect the health and safety of its citizens, people may assume that the state will protect an individual from significant harm, at least where that harm comes from others or where it is not obvious to its victims. Second, people may make decisions without properly considering the consequences. In some cases, these decisions may cause them or others substantial harm which, in turn, may ultimately burden society. Finally, given the unequal allocation of societal resources, some people are in difficult or even desperate situations. Other people may exploit their vulnerabilities unless the state intervenes. Joel Feinberg notes that the Harm Principle covers some types of exploitation:

> When A's exploitative conduct is of a sort that could be expected to adversely affect B's interest and is done without B's voluntary consent, then it can be prohibited and punished by law in virtue of the harm principle. If it is the harm principle that legitimizes the prohibition, then the act is forbidden not because it is exploitative but because it is harmful.[211]

Feinberg adds that the Harm Principle can also justify prohibiting cases of cheating and freeloading.[212] According to Feinberg, however, prohibiting A's exploitative conduct when (1) B has given "full voluntary consent" or (2) B's interests have not been harmed is problematic.[213] But the sliding scale nature of consent means that consent does not necessarily mean *desire*, nor does it necessarily mean that the consented-to act was wealth-maximizing or self-actualizing. As Robin West observed, "It does not follow from the definition of consent that people consent to what they think will make them better off, what will in fact make them better off, what they think will enlarge their freedom, or what in fact will do so."[214] In the

---

[211]   JOEL FEINBERG, HARMLESS WRONGDOING: THE MORAL LIMITS OF THE CRIMINAL LAW 211 (1990) [hereinafter FEINBERG, HARMLESS WRONGDOING].

[212]   *Id.*

[213]   *Id.* at 213 (stating "The principle that warrants the criminal prohibition of unjust gain (exploitation *per se*) even when it causes no unfair loss (harm) can be called the 'exploitation principle' and defined as the doctrine that it is always a good reason in support of a proposed criminal prohibition that it will prevent unjust gain, even when that wrongful gain is not accompanied by unfair loss. The principle is clearly a form of pure legal moralism since its aim is to prevent a kind of non-grievance evil, and it makes no ultimate appeal to the prevention of derivative harms. It is also a kind of strict moralism since the evils it would prevent are instances of immorality (injustice).").

[214]   Robin West, *Authority, Autonomy, and Choice: The Role of Consent in the Moral and Political Visions of Franz Kafka and Richard Posner*, 99 HARV. L. REV. 384, 399–400 (1985).

scenario where A's exploitation harmed B's interest, there may have been a deficiency in the knowledge condition or B might have had motivations other than self-actualization or wealth-maximization. In any event, it might seem doubtful that B's "full voluntary consent" was *truly* knowing and voluntary given what research has shown about the limits of human cognition and the problem of social constraints.

Exploitative conduct has a corrosive effect on society because it stirs emotions and moral outrage, contributing to societal instability. As studies have indicated, people value fairness and punish blatant violations of fairness norms.[215] When someone independently flouts the rules of the game to benefit himself there are two common reactions – others will behave similarly, or they will abide by the rules and feel angry and aggrieved by the "system." Both scenarios breed distrust and from distrust, social erosion follows. Because of the way that people must rely on each other to accomplish their goals, this ultimately diminishes the value of individual autonomy. As Nobel Prize laureate Kenneth Arrow remarked, collective action can "extend the domain of individual rationality . . . Collective action is a means of power, a means by which individuals can more fully realize their individual values."[216] He noted that collective action is necessary for at least two reasons:

> One is simply that the basic resources of the society, its natural resources, its human resources, it technological resources, are limited in supply, and the realization of alternative values or the attempts to find alternative activities for meeting those values imply a competition for these scarce resources. So we need to have a system which will mediate this competition, whether it be a market or an authoritative allocation system . . . We need . . . a social system of some complexity and of some considerable degree of organization in order to regulate the competition for resources to allocate them among the different possible users.
>
> Further, interpersonal organization is needed to secure the gains that can accrue from cooperation . . . We need cooperation to achieve specialization of function.[217]

---

[215]   *See, e.g.,* Daniel Kahneman, Jack L. Knetsch & Richard H. Thaler, *Fairness as a Constraint on Profit Seeking: Entitlements in the Market, in* ADVANCES IN BEHAVIORAL ECONOMICS 263 (Colin F. Camerer et al., eds., 2004) (discussing their study regarding firms' pricing strategies which indicates "a willingness to resist and to punish unfairness and an intrinsic motivation to be fair could . . . contribute to fair behavior in the marketplace."); Ernst Fehr & Klaus M. Schmidt, A *Theory of Fairness, Competition and Cooperation, in* ADVANCES IN BEHAVIORAL ECONOMICS 271 (Colin F. Camerer et al., eds., 2004) (examining conditions where people may be motivated to act by fairness considerations); Ernst Fehr, Georg Kirchsteiger & Arno Riedl, *Does Fairness Prevent Market Clearing?: An Experimental Investigation,* 108 Q.J. ECON. 437 (1993) (reporting results of study showing support for fair wage-effort theory of involuntary unemployment); Christine Jolls, Cass R. Sunstein & Richard Thaler, A *Behavioral Approach to Law and Economics,* 50 STAN. L. REV. 1471, 1492 (1998) (discussing a study that found that people will "behave in accordance with fairness considerations even when it is against their financial self-interest *and no one will know.*" (Emphasis in original.)).

[216]   KENNETH J. ARROW, THE LIMITS OF ORGANIZATION 16 (1974).

[217]   *Id.* at 18–19.

X cannot be expected to be entirely self-sufficient. In order to fulfill certain wants and needs to better X's situation, X will have to seek goods and services from other parties. Consequently, as Kenneth Arrow noted "interpersonal relationships are needed as part of our collective organization, for our mutual improvement."[218] Arrow referred to the invisible institutions" of ethics and morality principles as "agreements" among society's members to supply "mutual benefits."[219] These agreements are "essential to the survival of the society or at least contribute greatly to the efficiency of its working."[220] Arrow noted that essential to these agreements was trust:

> It has been observed ... that among the properties of many societies whose economic development is backward is a lack of mutual trust. Collective undertakings of any kind ... become difficult or impossible not only because A may betray B but because even if A wants to trust B he knows that B is unlikely to trust him. And it is clear that this lack of social consciousness is in fact a distinct economic loss in a very concrete sense, as well of course as a loss in the possible well-running of a political system.[221]

In addition to the potential harm to both A and B described by Arrow, the interaction between A and B may affect third parties unrelated to the transaction. For example, if X knows that A has taken advantage of B, or transgressed rules of fairness in transacting with B, and that A has suffered no resultant legal penalty or social stigma, then X may assume that its future exchange partners will behave like A. As a result, X will likely take extra precautions, increasing transaction costs, and limit exchanges only to those which are absolutely necessary. These self-imposed limitations constrain X's choices and X's ability to pursue its interests. Alternatively, X may also "play dirty" and undermine the rules of fair play if there appear to be no repercussions for doing so.

A society that values individual autonomy must also value the formal and informal societal structures that permit an individual to flourish. The stability of these structures depends upon "social capital." Political scientist Robert Putnam defined social capital as the "features of social life – network, norms, and trust – that enable participants to act together more effectively to pursue shared objectives":[222] Social capital affects economic, emotional and physical well-being. Sociologist Pierre Bourdieu criticized the narrow view of those economists who viewed capital as only the product of self-interested "mercantile exchange":

> It is in fact impossible to account for the structure and functioning of the social world unless one reintroduces capital in all its forms and not solely in the form

[218] Id. at 18.
[219] Id. at 26.
[220] Id.
[221] Id.
[222] Robert D. Putnam, Tuning In, Tuning Out: The Strange Disappearance of Social Capital in America, 28 Ps: POL. SCI. & POL. 664, 665 (1995).

recognized by economic theory. Economic theory has allowed to be foisted upon it a definition of the economy of practices which is the historical invention of capitalism; and by reducing the universe of exchanges to mercantile exchange, which is objectively and subjectively oriented toward the maximization of profit, i.e., (economically) *self-interested*, it has implicitly defined the other forms of exchange as noneconomic, and therefore *disinterested*.[223]

Bourdieu wrote that, contrary to the narrow view of some economists, capital comes in three forms: economic, cultural, and social. Both cultural capital and social capital could be "convertible" in certain conditions into economic capital; economic capital, in turn, was "immediately and directly" convertible into money and could be institutionalized in the form of property rights.[224] By contrast, Nan Lin focuses on the economic function of social capital more emphatically and specifically, stating that "[t]he premise behind the notion of social capital is rather simple and straightforward: *investment in social relations with expected returns in the marketplace.*"[225] David Halpern, on the other hand, defines social capital much more broadly as being composed of a network, a cluster of norms, values and expectancies, and sanctions.[226] Under this conception, social capital has an important effect on all aspects of society, including economic growth, individual health, educational outcomes and effective governance.[227] Despite the differences, all definitions of social capital note that it is integral to social and commercial exchanges. Because social capital is essential for effective cooperation and collective action, it is essential to fulfill the promise of individual autonomy. Trust is constitutive of social capital yet also its product. As Robert Putnam explained, "[t]he theory of social capital presumes that, generally speaking, the more we connect with other people, the more we trust them, and vice-versa."[228]

Trust may be even more important in decentralized governance systems which depend upon common rules and norms. Nobel laureate Elinor Ostrom noted that trust, reciprocity and reputation are the "core relationships" to productive social exchanges.[229] Opportunism, on the other hand, breeds wariness and distrust.

---

[223]   Pierre Bourdieu, *The Forms of Capital, in* Handbook of Theory and Research for the Sociology of Education 241, 242 (J.G. Richardson ed., 1986).

[224]   *Id.* at 243.

[225]   Nan Lin, Social Capital: A Theory of Social Structure and Action 19 (2001) (emphasis in the original).

[226]   David Halpern, Social Capital 10 (2005).

[227]   *See generally id.* at 285 (writing "[S]ocial capital has now been shown to relate to nearly all of the key policy objectives of modern societies and government, and even to the life satisfaction of the population.").

[228]   Putnam, *supra* note 222, at 665.

[229]   Elinor Ostrom, *A Behavioral Approach to the Rational Choice Theory of Collective Action*, 92 Amer. Pol. Sci. Rev. 1, 12 (1998) ("When many individuals use reciprocity, there is an incentive to acquire a *reputation* for keeping promises and performing actions with short-term costs but long-term net benefits. Thus, trustworthy individuals who trust others with a reputation for being trustworthy (and try to avoid those who have a reputation for being untrustworthy) can engage in mutually productive

Ultimately, distrust erodes social capital and impedes collective action and coordination which are necessary to achieving individual goals. Thus, opportunism harms not just the victim of the conduct but all members of society.[230] There is no justification for allowing any one individual to gain by violating societal rules if the cost is that all others are impeded in their efforts to gain. Furthermore, permitting someone to act opportunistically without repercussions (formal or informal) causes people to doubt the reliability of the legal and social institutions – the rules and the rule enforcers – which are charged with sanctioning misconduct.[231] A society without enforceable rules of fair play is a disorderly one where transactions are harder to complete because the potential parties distrust each other and cannot rely upon institutional mechanisms of enforcement to compensate for that distrust.

I propose a complement to the Harm Principle, which I will refer to as the "Opportunism Corollary," which holds that the state should prevent individuals from benefitting through actions which knowingly harm or exploit others. Exploitation and opportunistic conduct hinder a functioning society and thus, limit the value of individual autonomy for all members of society. Consequently, to protect the collective autonomy interest, the state must disfavor or underweight the opportunistic actor's interests in order to prevent the actor from gaining through his misdeed and to establish a precedent which deters future wrongdoing.

The purpose of the Opportunism Corollary is to preserve trust in relationships and in the institutions which police misconduct. The smooth functioning of society requires that its members trust each other to a certain extent; at a minimum, people should not fear that others will cause them harm and suffer no repercussions for their misconduct. If A tries to get B to act in a way that benefits A but that A knows is harmful or detrimental to B, A is acting opportunistically *regardless* of whether B manifested consent.[232] On the other hand, if B acts in a way that B knew would make A think B had consented and that would cause A to act in reliance upon B's manifestation of consent in a way that benefits B, B has acted opportunistically. The Opportunism Corollary recognizes the mutuality of human interactions involving consent and thus applies to the conduct of both parties in a consent scenario. The Regret Principle seeks to improve the conditions of consent and discourages people from engaging in acts which they will profoundly regret because these acts

---

social exchanges ... so long as they can limit their interactions primarily to those with a reputation for keeping promises.").

[230] *See generally* HALPERN, *supra* note 226 (providing a comprehensive account of how social capital contributes to individual life-satisfaction and well-being as well as economic growth).

[231] As David Halpern noted, sanctions, along with network and norms, are one of the three major components of social capital. *Id.* at 10.

[232] FEINBERG, HARMLESS WRONGDOING, *supra* note 211, at 214 (noting that exploitative conduct can also include conduct which neither harms the victim nor benefits the wrongdoer, but "when both wrongful harm *and* wrongful gain (exploitation) are missing, I can see no case at all for criminalization."). I agree with Feinberg's view and note that the Opportunism Corollary only applies where the wrongdoer believed that conduct would harm the victim.

will have diminished their (future) autonomy. Both the Regret Principle and the Opportunism Corollary are essential to evaluating consent and consentability.

Opportunism is a concept that is distinct from consent although it is intertwined with it. Opportunistic conduct may affect the consenter in such a way that the manifestation of consent does not constitute valid consent. For example, A may withhold information from B which makes B's consent invalid. In some cases, however, one may take advantage of another *with* her valid consent.[233] For example, A and B may have the same information, but B's judgment regarding the harm posed by that information may differ from A's judgment. Opportunism concerns the wrongdoer's state of mind, not the victim's. The victim's state of mind is relevant only insofar as it affects the wrongdoer's motivation or knowledge. If A believes that B truly wishes to participate in a particular activity, it may affect A's belief that the activity is harmful or beneficial to B. If A, however, believes that B is consenting for reasons other than self-interest (for example, in order to please A, or because B is acting rashly in a "hot" state), then A's act of seeking consent may be viewed as opportunistic. The Opportunism Corollary recognizes that members of society have some responsibility toward each other and that, as a general matter, people should not try to benefit themselves by persuading others to act in a way that harms their self-interest. This does not mean that members of society are fiduciaries for each other. They do not have to maximize the interest of their neighbors or act in a way that is detrimental to themselves. It also does not mean that they must put the interests of others before their own. But they should not enrich themselves by getting others to act in a way that will cause these others harm. Different situations require different standards of behavior so that the greater the potential harm to the consenter from the proposed activity, the better the behavior expected of the consent-seeker. X may approach Y and try to persuade Y to sell Y's car. X should not, however, approach Y and try to persuade Y to sell Y's kidney on the black market. Interestingly, the current "altruistic" model of organ transplantation allows and even encourages opportunism by permitting those in need of an organ to solicit and pressure others for one without even having to pay for it.

Harm is caused by acting without the consent of another, but it may also be caused by acting in a way that knowingly harms another's interests even when that person desires the harmful activity. B may have self-inconsistent or adaptive preferences that do not maximize her well-being and which threaten her autonomy. If A is aware of the harmful nature of B's desires or preferences, the fact that B agreed to the harmful act does not excuse the wrongfulness of A's conduct. For example, B may consent to A giving B heroin, but that does not mean A's conduct is not harmful. Under the Opportunism Corollary, A should not be able to benefit from conduct which A knows harms B regardless of whether B manifested consent. Thus, A may

[233] *Id.* at 176 (noting that "[a] little-noticed feature of exploitation is that it *can* occur in morally unsavory forms without harming the exploitee's interests and, in some cases, despite the exploitee's voluntary consent to the exploitative behavior.").

not sell heroin to B even if B desires it. The Opportunism Corollary protects B but it also protects other members of society. If A is able to benefit from doing something which A knows is harmful to another, A is more likely to continue engaging in that behavior and to harm others who have not consented. The definition of opportunism is to take advantage so it is to be expected that opportunism left unchecked tends to breed more opportunism.

The Opportunism Corollary discourages or prevents benefitting from wrongdoing regardless of whether there was a manifestation of consent to the wrongful act because opportunism harms the collective by propagating distrust, creating social instability and impeding social and commercial exchanges. The Opportunism Corollary is normative and prescriptive, but it is also descriptive in that it captures what the law seeks to accomplish with amorphous concepts such as "bad faith," and "reasonableness." In contract law, for example, the courts tend to assess the relative blameworthiness of the parties.[234] The "reasonable" interpretation of terms often turns on whether one party knew what the other party meant.[235] Certain contract defenses, such as unilateral mistake, unconscionability and intoxication, weigh the relative blameworthiness of the parties.[236] Whether a party knew (or should have known) that its behavior was harmful requires consideration of expected norms of behavior, given the context and the proposed activity. For example, commercial dealings require conformance with norms of good faith and fair dealing, attorneys and physicians have special duties and must act in conformance with professional standards, and agents must act in accordance with fiduciary standards in dealings with their principals.

A. RELATIVE CONSENT

As previously noted, there are three consent conditions: a manifestation of consent, knowledge and voluntariness. Motive, while not an independent condition, is an essential component of each of the three consent conditions. Motive considers the consenting party's purpose as it pertains to each consent condition. For example, someone who signs a document that he believes is an insurance form has not manifested consent if it turns out that the document was actually a contract for the sale of his house. Similarly, if he signed the document because he was threatened with a beating if he refused, his motive (to escape physical harm) reveals a lack of the voluntariness condition. Motive also relates to the dynamic nature of consent and is especially relevant when there is a lag between the time consent is granted and

---

[234] *See* discussion, Chapter 4.
[235] *See, e.g.*, Embry v. Hargadine, McKittrick Dry Goods Co., 105 S.W. 777 (Mo. Ct. App. 1907) (finding that a reasonable person should have known how plaintiff would have interpreted language); RESTATEMENT (SECOND) OF CONTRACTS § 201 (AM. LAW INST. 1981); *see also* Kim, *Relative Consent, supra* note 6, at 178–88.
[236] *See* discussion, Chapter 4; *see also* Kim, *Relative Consent, supra* note 6.

the time the act requiring consent is to occur. In other words, does consent *still* exist at the time performance is due? Consent may be subject to certain assumptions or conditions. If the reason that the party consented no longer applies, due to intervening circumstances, consent no longer exists. Thus, motive is tied to the continuation of consent over time.

Voluntariness requires that the consenting party act with *volition*, meaning that the act was not reflexive. It requires asking whether the consenting party *wanted* to engage in the act or activity. In assessing voluntariness, the actions of the consent-seeker must be considered. For example, if the consent-seeker threatened or pressured the consenter, the level of volition is lower than it would be without the pressure. If the consenter was motivated by fear of the threat, rather than a desire to enter into the transaction, there is a failure of the condition of voluntariness. Knowledge requires that the consenter understood the material facts involved in making his or her decision. Again, the actions of the consent-seeker would be relevant. If that party withheld certain information or provided false or misleading information, the level of knowledge is considered diminished.

I propose a "relative consent" approach which examines each of the conditions of consent and renders more explicit and transparent the process by which consent

Act/Manifestation of Consent

- •Intentional?/Motive
- •Physical (Reflexive? Compelled?)
- •Cognitive (understand nature of the act)
- •Other Party Knowledge/Behavior
  - •Reasonable to assume manifests consent?

Knowledge

- •Information
- •Other Party Knowledge/Behavior
  - •Withholding information?
- •Understanding
- •Motive/Purpose
- •Cognitive capabilities
- •Other Party Behavior
  - •Deceptive? Unfair?

Voluntariness

- •Volitional
- •Desire/Motive
- •Other Party Knowledge/Behavior
  - •Physical force? Coercion? Manipulation?

FIGURE 3.3 Consent Construction/Assessing the Conditions of Consent

should be assessed. The concept of relative consent recognizes the importance of context and the relationship between the parties. Consent or "valid consent" is merely a conclusion that the relevant action, which would be impermissible without consent, is justified because it does not harm the consenter's autonomy; on the contrary, it enacts it. But in order for consent to justify the action, certain conditions must have been satisfied.

Discussions of consent and free will must recognize the complexity of human behavior and the reality of human irrationality. A relative consent approach recognizes that tension exists not only between and among individuals, but within individuals who usually have conflicting desires and interests. A recognition of the complex and dynamic nature of consent better promotes the value of autonomy. Too often, artificial notions of autonomy are used to justify governmental laissez-faire which is at best uncaring and at worst, harmful and perpetuates inequality. By distilling what it means to exercise free will, and discarding false assumptions about human behavior and motivations, the government is in a better position to preserve, protect and promote autonomy.

The very word – autonomy – conjures up images of rugged individualism and self-sufficiency. But this definition of autonomy is blinkered and incomplete. To value the autonomy of any one individual necessarily means valuing the autonomy of all individuals. But an autonomy-enhancing act of one individual might restrict or threaten the autonomy of other individuals. As important as the autonomy interest of the consenting party is, it is not always the paramount interest and rarely the only interest implicated in an act involving consent.

Evaluation of each consent condition is relative because it requires consideration of the mindset and behavior of both the consenting party and the party seeking consent (Figure 3.3). The motive of the consenting party and the behavior of the consent-seeker affect the degree to which each of the conditions must be found (i.e. their requisite robustness level). Bad faith or opportunism on the part of the consent-seeker is an important factor in assessing consent, consistent with the Opportunism Corollary. Negative behavior on the part of the consent-seeker means that the consent conditions must be more robust in order for consent to be found. For example, in a commercial transaction, if the party seeking consent is acting in good faith, the requisite robustness levels for the consent conditions are minimal. If the party seeking consent acts in bad faith by hiding information which he knows is material to the other party, however, the existence of the consent conditions must be stronger. A contracting party who takes advantage of the other party's ignorance may find the contract can be avoided in some situations.[237] Egregious behavior by the consent-seeking party, such as unlawful threats or lies, may invalidate the other party's consent and the contract. Thus, whether a party has "freely" or

---

[237] *See* discussion, Chapter 2.

"validly" consented depends upon whether the consent-seeker manipulated, exploited or coerced the ostensibly consenting party.

B. A HIERARCHY OF AUTONOMY INTERESTS

Consentability requires understanding both the meaning of consent and its underlying purpose as a mechanism for autonomy. Autonomy and consent are context-dependent. An act of agency does not exist in a vacuum. The nature of consent itself is not fixed, but complex and dynamic. Personal values and opinions may shift over time, the result of changes both internal and external. Given the unpredictability and irrationality of human behavior, acts which limit future capacity may promote one's present autonomy but risk limiting one's future autonomy. It is impossible to know in advance which future limitations an individual might regret. Put another way, a decision by X^1 might enhance X^1's autonomy, but greatly diminish X^2's autonomy. For example, X^1 could make an uncoerced decision to cut off his legs which would fulfill his present self's desires and lead to greater self-actualization of his present self, but it is an act which results in hindering his future mobility and so would pose a high-level threat to autonomy. X^1 may not care about the loss of his mobility; in fact, that may be what he sought in making the decision. The decision to limit his autonomy then could be viewed as an exercise of autonomy itself; *however*, because X^1's decision impacts X^2's autonomy in such a fundamental and important way, the threat level to his autonomy interest is very high.

Although there are different definitions of "autonomy,"[238] I use the term in the context of the hierarchy of autonomy interests in its most literal sense to mean *freedom to move, act or think without assistance or constraint.* Thus, a proposed activity would pose a threat to the consenter's autonomy if it would limit the consenter's capacity to act and think independently and without assistance. Under this definition, a decision which provides more opportunities and options for the consenter enhances autonomy, while one that reduces them diminishes autonomy. This definition for the purpose of determining the threat level to autonomy differs from other definitions which focus on self-actualization.[239]

The hierarchy as shown in Figure 3.4 is a spectrum; each interest is a band or range which depends upon different factors or variables associated with the threat. Figure 3.5 outlines the relevant factors to consider in determining the threat to the autonomy interest. The top row indicates the type of threat; the column beneath each type of threat indicates the factors or variables which should be considered to determine the severity of the type of threat. In my proposed hierarchy, both the type of threat and the degree to which it is affected by an act (determined by the "Factors to Consider") affect the consentability of that act. The threat level to the autonomy

---

[238]   *See* discussion, Chapter 3 (intro).
[239]   *Id.*

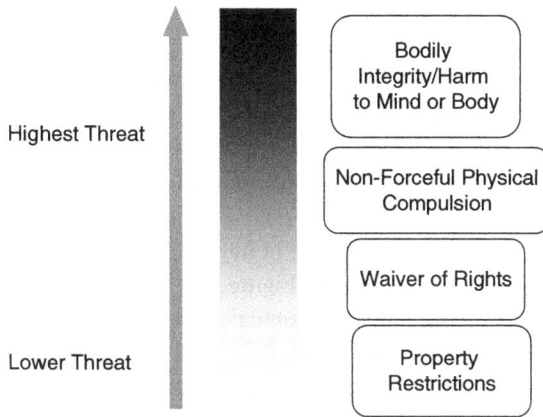

FIGURE 3.4 Hierarchy of Autonomy Interests

| | TYPE OF THREAT | | |
HIGHEST LEVEL			LOWEST LEVEL
BODILY INTEGRITY/ HARM TO MIND AND/OR BODY	**NON-FORCEFUL PHYSICAL COMPULSION**	**WAIVER OF RIGHTS**	**PROPERTY RESTRICTIONS**
Duration	Duration of compulsory service or exposure	Duration of waiver	Duration of restriction
Impact/severity of threat (Permanence/irreversibility, diminishment v. enhancement)	Condition/nature of threat	Type of Right/Importance	Type of restriction
Pain	Degree of physical exertion or offensiveness	Likelihood of exercising right	Type of property/importance
Availability of alternatives to bodily harm	Alternatives (Working conditions and degree of difficulty to avoid)	Availability of alternatives to waiver	Alternative of compensation for restriction

(Left margin: **Factors to Consider**)

FIGURE 3.5 Relevant Factors in Assessing Threat Level to Autonomy

interest depends upon both the nature of the threat and the interest being threatened. Thus, one has a greater interest in preserving one's body from intrusion which is excruciatingly painful and permanent, than one that is merely unpleasant and temporary. This distinction on the basis of pain and intrusiveness is one that is already recognized in the law, even if not always explicitly.[240]

[240] For example, the 9th Circuit distinguished bone marrow donations using the aspiration method from those using the apheresis method, finding that donations using the former could not be compensated under the National Organ Transplant Act, but the latter could. *See* Flynn v. Holder,

The hierarchy of threats to the autonomy interests illustrates the importance of each type of interest to individual liberty in a literal sense. The hierarchy of autonomy interests is not a hierarchy of values, nor is it based upon what activities are most essential for a properly functioning society or for a self-actualized self; rather it is a hierarchy of which interests *if violated* would most diminish the future self's options by constraining the future self's freedom to act and think independently.

The correlation of threat level to type of interest (Figure 3.4) is not direct, precise or fixed, but depends on the factors (Figure 3.5) which should be considered in determining the significance of the threat to the autonomy interest. The first factor is the duration of the threat. The second factor concerns the nature of the threat and its effects. The more severe the threat, the greater the threat to autonomy. Intrusive acts which are likely to result in irreversible or permanent diminishment of the mind or body of the consenting party constitute the most significant threat to autonomy. Acts which are likely to result in changes which ultimately enhance movement or capability (such as corrective or rehabilitative surgeries) or which improve mental health or emotional well-being (therapeutic medical procedures), on the other hand, pose a lesser threat to autonomy. The third factor is pain (or a variant of pain, such as discomfort). An act which is painful or uncomfortable (or creates a situation which results in pain or discomfort) poses a greater threat to autonomy than one that is not, because pain/discomfort is a state from which one would prefer to be free. Pain/discomfort is subjective, however, and this criterion considers how unpleasant the activity will be to the consenter. Some people may enjoy an activity which others would consider painful, and the threat to the autonomy interest would be much lower for those who do not find the activity painful than for those who do. The final factor is whether there are alternatives to the proposed, autonomy-threatening activity. This factor is of most relevance where mandatory laws are concerned. If alternatives exist, then the proposed activity poses less of a threat to autonomy because the consenter has the power to opt out. For example, a law which requires mandatory vaccinations for school-aged children is less of a threat to autonomy if it permits home-schooled children to opt out of the vaccinations. Similarly, a law which requires motorists to submit to chemical testing for alcohol or drugs is less of a threat to autonomy if one may opt for a breath test instead of a blood test, because a breathalyzer is less intrusive and painful than a blood draw.

684 F.3d 852, 860–65 (9th Cir. 2012). Apheresis, unlike the aspiration method, does not invade the bone for marrow and is less painful for the donor. *Id.* at 856–57. The Court described aspiration as "a painful, unpleasant procedure for the donor" which "requires hospitalization and general or local anesthesia and involves commensurate risks." *Id.* at 856. Apheresis, on the other hand, beings with "five days of injections" to accelerate blood stem cell production and then "with no need for sedatives or anesthesia, a needle is inserted into the donor's vein ... Complications for the donor are exceedingly rare ... the new process makes bone marrow donations much like ordinary blood donations." *Id.* at 857.

The autonomy interests themselves are part of the assessment of threat level to autonomy, with the most serious threat to autonomy involving threats to bodily integrity which are painful and permanent. Physical harm assumes physical constraint. By contrast, physical constraint unaccompanied by violence or physical harm is a lesser, but still high, threat to individual autonomy. This second type of threat to autonomy – non-forceful, physical compulsion – involves a different type of "force." For example, someone who is contractually obligated to perform services is not being physically forced to perform; nevertheless, that individual's physical freedom is restricted. An employee may be required to work in unpleasant circumstances because she signed a contract that requires her to do so. Although not as severe as physical constraints, non-forceful compulsion limits an individual's freedom to move or change his or her circumstances or requires an individual to hear views or see acts which that individual finds deeply offensive or upsetting.

The third type of autonomy interest pertains to various civil and political rights. These rights enable members of society to engage in the political process and participate in civic life. These rights include constitutional rights, such as the right to speak freely, and statutorily created rights, such as the copyright granted to non-employee authors of creative works. Autonomy includes the power to exercise or waive these rights. Acts which inhibit or restrict these rights pose a threat to the autonomy interest; the threat level depends upon the type of restriction. A temporary restriction on the right to speak freely or one that is limited to certain places or times poses less of a threat than a ban on speech.

The fourth type of autonomy interest involves the power to allocate or reallocate property rights. This right is associated with property ownership. A primary benefit of property ownership is the ability to use, share, transfer, sell or trade it. Restrictions on these rights limit the owner's autonomy to varying degrees, depending on the nature of the restriction. For example, temporarily closing access to a street leading to someone's home in order to conduct government business (such as repairing the street or capturing a criminal) poses a minimal threat to autonomy. On the other hand, government taking of private property for public purposes poses a much greater threat to autonomy. This does not mean that the government is prohibited from taking private property, but the justification for doing so must be stronger than the justification for closing the street for a day

Some may disagree with this ordering or the list of autonomy interests. Some may also disagree about which interest they value more. Some, for example, might value the freedom to speak more highly than bodily integrity.[241] But the exercise of the

---

[241] Such a view, however, would likely be in the minority. As one judge noted, "our society acknowledges a profound ethical imperative to respect the human body as the physical and temporal expression of the unique human persona." Moore v. Regents of Univ. of Cal., 51 Cal. 3d 120, 128 (1990) (Mosk, J., dissenting).

right to speak is not possible if one is dead (the highest-level threat to individual autonomy). One may value the right to vote more highly than the right to be free from false imprisonment, but one may not vote if one is physically restrained and unable to obtain a ballot. The hierarchy of threats to the autonomy interests is based upon the potential harm to an individual's ability to act autonomously, not upon the value that any individual places on a particular interest or right. Accordingly, violations of bodily integrity are generally greater threats to autonomy than violations of personal property rights. However, the type of threat does not necessarily reflect the actual threat that an act might pose to a person's autonomy in any given case. The threat level will depend upon both the type of autonomy interest and relevant associated factors which indicate the degree of harm. For example, an individual who is accidentally pushed in a crowded room has had her bodily integrity violated, but has been caused little physical or emotional harm, suffers minimal pain and is left with no lasting injuries. Consequently, the threat to autonomy is lower than a restriction on an individual's ability to sell her house, which prevents her from moving to accept a job in another location. The threat level is a sliding scale which depends upon context, not simply categorization. All threats to a particular autonomy interest are not equivalent, but depend upon consideration of the relevant factors. Both a punch to the jaw and a shot to the chest violate an individual's bodily integrity; the latter threatens individual autonomy much more, as it is more painful, physically harmful, and will result in permanent damage. Bodily intrusions which are permanent, painful and harmful represent the most extreme threat to bodily integrity. Offenses to bodily integrity which are fleeting and not physically harmful or painful, such as third degree assault or offensive touching, constitute threats to autonomy, but they are not as severe as those which maim, cause permanent damage or destroy. Similarly, waivers of certain rights are a greater threat to autonomy than are waivers of other rights.

The ability to think and act autonomously is intimately and crucially connected to bodily integrity. My definition of bodily integrity includes the brain/mind. While some may distinguish between the mind and the body, this book does not for a pragmatic reason: the brain is part of the body and controls its movements.[242] The mind cannot exist without the brain. Damage to the brain affects the ability to think, which is the most fundamental aspect of the autonomy interest. The ability to think – to deliberate, reflect, plan and imagine – differentiates human beings from other living creatures. Accordingly, under my proposed approach, a prison term would be less of a threat to autonomy (although still a high-level threat) than

---

[242]   *See* JONATHAN WESTPHAL, THE MIND-BODY PROBLEM (2016) (providing a helpful overview of the mind-body problem). Westphal writes that "[m]ind-body dualism was a popular view until roughly the 1960s, though it is less and less so these days, at least with professional philosophers. They have for the most part thrown in their lot with those scientists who have adopted a materialistic or naturalistic worldview – nature is all there is." *Id.* at 25.

a forcible lobotomy which removes the frontal cortex of the brain. Depression may be more debilitating than physical impairments (and it can also cause them).

The ability to "think," however, is not the same thing as the ability to *express* one's thoughts. Although an important civil right for a free society, the freedom of expression may be restricted under certain circumstances. By contrast, the ability to think private thoughts is the most fundamental and essential aspect of being human. Without the ability to think, no other act is considered an autonomous one. Accordingly, attempts to prevent an individual from thinking (e.g. frontal lobe lobotomies, brainwashing, hypnosis or brain transplants) pose the highest level of threat to autonomy. While a mind transplant and other types of mind control are still in the realm of science fiction, developments in science and technology indicate that we are not too far from a world where minds and bodies can be engineered in astonishing and formerly unthinkable ways. Already, scientists have successfully tested a brain implant which noticeably improved word recall by sending electrical pulses to the brain.[243] The implant is designed to help those with severe memory loss from dementia, injury or stroke.[244] The entrepreneur Elon Musk announced a new venture which would develop implantable brain chips, with the ultimate goal of a "whole brain interface."[245] Advancements in medicine and technology suggest a future where the very DNA of humans may be manipulated and engineered – as well as hacked and remotely controlled. Implants may be used to improve memory, but in the future they also might be used to create false memories. In fact, scientists reportedly created a false memory in a mouse with the use of lasers.[246] It is in these types of "novel" situations that a consentability framework may prove most useful as they distinguish between those implants which enhance autonomy and those which make people more vulnerable to losing it.

My proposed approach to consentability is both normative and descriptive, as it is consistent with existing law and captures the balancing of interests which courts currently conduct. For example, the U.S. Supreme Court has long considered the nature of bodily intrusion when assessing the constitutionality of government

---

[243] Benedict Carey, *Brain Implant Enhanced Memory, Raising Hope for Treatments, Scientists Say*, N.Y. TIMES (Feb. 7, 2018), www.nytimes.com/2018/02/06/health/brain-implant-memory.html.

[244] *See* Jon Cohen, *Memory Implants: A Maverick Neuroscientist Believes He Has Deciphered the Code By Which the Brain Forms Long-Term Memories*, MIT TECH. REV. (2016), www.technologyreview .com/s/513681/memory-implants/ (noting that the idea of a memory implant was considered "audacious" and "far outside the mainstream of neuroscience" just a few years ago).

[245] Samantha Masunaga, *A Quick Guide to Elon Musk's New Brain-Implant Company, Neuralink*, L.A. TIMES (April 21, 2017), www.latimes.com/business/technology/la-fi-tn-elon-musk-neuralink-20170421-htmlstory.html.

[246] David Noonan, *Meet the Two Scientists Who Implanted a False Memory Into a Mouse*, SMITHSONIAN MAG. (Nov. 2014), www.smithsonianmag.com/innovation/meet-two-scientists-who-implanted-false-memory-mouse-180953045/?page=2; James Gorman, *Scientists Trace Memories of Things That Never Happened*, N.Y. TIMES (July 25, 2013), www.nytimes.com/2013/07/26/science/false-memory-planted-in-a-mouse-brain-study-shows.html.

actions. In Birchfield v. North Dakota, for example, the Court distinguished the level of bodily intrusion involved in breathalyzer tests from blood tests:

> First, the physical intrusion is almost negligible. Breath tests "do not require piercing the skin" and entail a "minimum of inconvenience." [Citation omitted] . . . there is nothing painful or strange . . . Finally, participation in a breath test is not an experience that is likely to cause any great enhancement in the embarrassment that is inherent in any arrest . . .
>
> Blood tests are a different matter. They "require piercing the skin" and extract a part of the subject's body. [Citation omitted] . . . It is significantly more intrusive than blowing into a tube . . . In addition, a blood test, unlike a breath test, places in the hands of law enforcement authorities a sample that can be preserved and from which it is possible to extract information beyond a simple BAC reading. Even if the law enforcement agency is precluded from testing the blood for any purpose other than to measure BAC, the potential remains and may result in anxiety for the person tested . . .
>
> Because breath tests are significantly less intrusive than blood tests and in most cases amply serve law enforcement interest, we conclude that a breath test, but not a blood test, may be administered as a search incident to a lawful arrest for drunk driving. As in all cases involving reasonable searches incident to arrest, a warrant is not needed in this situation.[247]

For the commission of crimes, the state generally limits an individual's freedom to an extent that is equivalent to the harm that the individual has caused. This is both an application of and an extension of the Harm Principle. Society finds violations of bodily integrity and physical coercion so reprehensible that the offender is punished by the state in an equivalent manner. The greater the violation of bodily integrity, the greater the risk to the offender's own bodily integrity. Offenses such as assault in the third degree or offensive touching are typically misdemeanors. The offender usually serves little or no jail time and/or pays a fine. The injury to the victim's bodily integrity and society's interest in deterring crime is weighed against the offender's own autonomy interest in bodily integrity and/or property. The more intrusive invasions of bodily integrity and physical coercion are felonies, and result in incarceration for substantial periods of time. Crimes posing the highest-level threat to autonomy, such as torture, involve both mind control and bodily intrusion. Accordingly, punishment for their commission is harsh, and may even include life imprisonment. In jurisdictions which still permit it, the death penalty is typically used only where the offender has committed murder (a complete deprivation of autonomy). As these examples indicate, the graver the threat to autonomy posed by the act, the more severe the punishment for its commission.

In only one situation does an autonomy-threatening act actually *promote* autonomy, and that is when a person consents to it. The conditions necessary for valid consent – intentional manifestation of consent, knowledge, voluntariness – are

[247]   Birchfield v. North Dakota, 136 S. Ct. 2160, 2176–78 (2016).

necessary to ensure autonomy even in one-party actions. Consentability depends on whether the autonomy-enhancing effect of being able to make the decision out-weighs the autonomy-diminishing effect of having made the decision. Perfect consent conditions, however, are elusive. Accordingly, as section C explains, the adequacy of the conditions should depend upon the nature of the act to which consent is sought.

C. (VALID) CONSENT AS A SLIDING SCALE

Consent transforms the nature of the act from one that is autonomy-threatening or autonomy-diminishing to one that is autonomy-enhancing. This, however, is subject to one very important condition – that the consent is valid, meaning that the necessary conditions of consent are sufficiently robust. To assess their robustness requires under-standing the values served by a requirement of consent. Consent allows an individual to exercise autonomy and it protects her from actions which diminish her autonomy.

Consent is complex and dynamic – less a threshold to be crossed than a sliding scale which can be (and should be) adjusted depending upon the context. Given the elasticity and the context-dependent nature of consent conditions, how can one determine that they have been met to a sufficient degree to justify actions that, absent consent, are autonomy-threatening?

The framework proposed in this book recognizes the variable and dynamic nature of consent by assessing the robustness of the conditions of consent (Figure 3.3) in light of the potential threat the proposed activity presents to the autonomy of the consenter (Figures 3.4 and 3.5). I propose that the robustness level of the consent conditions must correlate to the threat level to the autonomy interest so that the greater the threat to the autonomy interest, the more robust the consent conditions must be in order to find valid consent.[248] If the threat to the autonomy interest outweighs the robustness of the consent conditions, there is no valid consent (Figure 3.6). Similarly, if the conditions of consent outweigh the threat to autonomy, there is valid consent (Figure 3.7).

Assessments of consent conditions are "relative," meaning that they are on a sliding scale which considers the conduct of both parties and the nature of the transaction. Opportunistic conduct on the part of the consent-seeker discounts the consent-seeker's interest and reduces the robustness or strength of the consent conditions (which, in turn, makes it more difficult to find valid consent). If, for example, the consent-seeker knew that the consenter was ignorant of certain informa-tion, the consenter's knowledge condition would be considered more deficient than if the consenter's ignorance were not known to the consent-seeker. Transactions

---

[248]   My approach to a sliding scale conception of consent shares similarities with Joel Feinberg's variable concept of voluntariness; it differs, however, in that it considers all the conditions of consent, not just voluntariness. It also differs in that the two-part framework considers both the conditions of consent and the potential harm posed by the act to which consent is being given in order to determine consent validity.

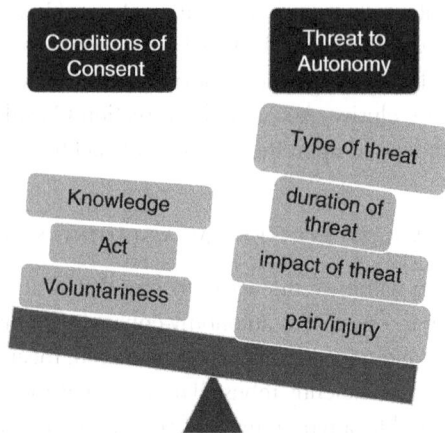

FIGURE 3.6 Figure Showing No Valid Consent

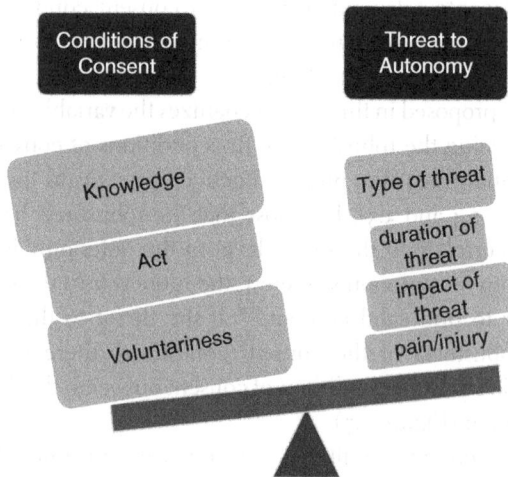

FIGURE 3.7 Figure Showing Valid Consent

which pose a greater threat to the autonomy interest require more robust consent conditions. For example, consent to sell a kidney requires that the consenter demonstrate more robust consent conditions – a stronger manifestation of consent, more volition, more information and knowledge – than if the consenter were agreeing to a less risky transaction, such as buying a toaster from an online website.

The requisite robustness level can be compared to standards of proof. If the proposed act would cause physical harm and suffering, and could result in permanent disfigurement, the conditions of consent must be established with absolute certainty, the equivalent of the judicial standard "beyond a reasonable doubt." Consent to major surgery, for example, requires information about the nature of the procedure, including relevant risks and side effects, and a waiting period. Valid transfers of property require consent, but the conditions of consent are subject to the lesser standard of "reasonable certainty." Thus, parties to a contract generally are not required to fully disclose all relevant information, although there are exceptions, such as where the parties are fiduciaries or where the information results in a basic assumption error.

The sliding scale approach to consent is already reflected in the law's differing consent standards. Contract law, for example, does not require *actual* (subjective) knowledge. Instead, contract law substitutes *capacity* and *access to information* or *notice* for knowledge. The requirement of capacity serves two purposes.[249] The first is to simplify assessment of whether the party had sufficient understanding to consent. Minors generally lack the capacity to consent. Incapacity may be temporary, such as in the case of intoxication or a psychological episode which temporarily impairs function or understanding. In some respects, the presumption of incapacity is overbroad. For example, some minors may be able to understand the consequences of their consent more keenly than some adults. Yet, they are deemed incapable of consent. The second purpose of capacity is to safeguard against coercion and to simplify assessment of whether consent was voluntary. Children, adults with certain mental illnesses and those under the influence of drugs or alcohol, are deemed to be particularly vulnerable to pressure and less able to guard against it. They may also be more prone to impulsive behavior and less able to control themselves.

The knowledge condition in the context of medical procedures will have different requirements than consent to a commercial transaction because of the higher-level threat to the autonomy interest. Consequently, there must be *informed* consent to medical procedure rather than the less robust condition required for contract formation.[250] The voluntariness condition is suspect if the decision *not* to consent would put the individual in a situation that poses a high-level threat to autonomy. While discussing the constitutionality of implied consent laws, the Supreme Court stated:

> Petitioners do not question the constitutionality of those laws, and nothing we say here should be read to cast doubt on them. It is another matter, however, for a State not only to insist upon an intrusive blood test, but also to impose criminal penalties on the refusal to submit to such a test. There must be a limit to the consequences to which motorists may be deemed to have consented by virtue of a decision to drive

---

[249] *See* RESTATEMENT (SECOND) OF CONTRACTS § 12 (AM. LAW INST. 1981) (stating that a "natural person" has "full legal capacity" to enter into contracts "unless he is (a) under guardianship, or (b) an infant, or (c) mentally ill or defective, or (d) intoxicated").

[250] *See* THE LIMITS OF CONSENT: A SOCIO-ETHICAL APPROACH TO HUMAN SUBJECT RESEARCH IN MEDICINE (Oonagh Corrigan et al. eds., 2009) (providing a valuable overview of the complex issues relating to informed consent).

on public roads . . . we conclude that motorists cannot be deemed to have consented to submit to a blood test on pain of committing a criminal offense.[251]

Generally, the role of the state in regulating, limiting or prohibiting the acts to which an individual may consent should be (a) to prevent people from making decisions that will ultimately harm their autonomy interests in a way that they will profoundly regret; (b) to do so by strengthening the conditions of consent; (c) to prevent people from limiting or harming the autonomy of others; and (d) to do so by implementing rules, processes or policies to safeguard against opportunism. The state should restrict or prohibit those activities which pose a high-level threat to an individual's autonomy and it should permit those activities which pose a low-level threat to autonomy. The greater the threat to the autonomy interest, the more robust the requisite consent condition must be and consequently, the greater the state's role in regulating the consenting process. For highest-level threat acts, the requisite robustness levels for valid consent may be difficult to obtain. Given the difficulty of ensuring valid consent in highest-level threat situations, the state would be justified in implementing a mandatory law or prohibition as long as the law or prohibition is not more restrictive (i.e. does not pose more of a threat to autonomy) than the harm that it seeks to prevent.

State intervention is also justified to prevent the exercise of an individual's agency in order to protect another individual's greater autonomy interest or to mediate where there are conflicting autonomy interests. This approach privileges *collective autonomy*[252] over individual autonomy where autonomy interests are equivalent. In doing so, the following presuppositions apply:

First, the autonomy interests of individuals are often in tension with each other. In the event of conflict, the level of threat to each individual's autonomy interest and (where relevant) to the collective autonomy interest, must be considered. Opportunistic conduct by the consent-seeker diminishes the consent-seeker's autonomy interest and increases the robustness level (i.e. the burden of proof) required for valid consent.

Second, autonomy interests are not absolute, fixed or uniform. There are various factors (permanence, duration, enhancement or diminishment, physical, mental and emotional pain) which affect the degree to which the autonomy interest might be threatened (see Figures 3.4 and 3.5). The greater the number and degree of applicable factors in a given situation, the greater the threat to the autonomy interest. The evolving threat to autonomy should be considered as it relates to the consenter, the consent-seeker, and to society.

Third, for consent to be an effective gatekeeper of autonomy, the requisite conditions for its validity must be established. The robustness level required to

---

[251]   *Birchfield, supra* note 247, at 2185.
[252]   Collective autonomy is defined as the interest that all members of society have in a particular right. The concept is discussed *infra* at Chapter 3 section D.

establish consent conditions varies depending upon the threat level to the autonomy interest. This means that consent conditions must be established to a standard equivalent to a burden of proof standard[253] such as "beyond a reasonable doubt," "by clear and convincing evidence" or "by a preponderance of the evidence." A "beyond a reasonable doubt" or "by clear and convincing evidence" burden of proof standard applies where the act poses the highest- or high-level threat to autonomy. A lesser burden of proof, such as "by a preponderance of the evidence" standard, applies where the act poses a moderate- or low-level threat to autonomy. The greater the potential harm to the autonomy interest (taking into consideration the relevant factors), the more certainty (i.e. the higher the burden of proof) required to establish the necessary consent conditions. This approach is one that states have already adopted in regard to burdens of proof which correspond to the interests at stake.[254] Where only the loss of money is at stake, the burden of proof is lower (i.e. by a preponderance of the evidence) than where constitutional due process rights or public policy considerations are implicated.[255] For example, the "clear and convincing" standard rather than the lower "by a preponderance of the evidence" standard is generally applied in actions to terminate parental rights[256] and in actions to recover punitive damages for fraud or misconduct.[257] The state plays an essential role in ensuring that consent conditions have been met to the standard commensurate with the threat level. In some cases, the threat level to autonomy is so high that the requisite robustness level is unlikely to be met. Accordingly, those activities should be prohibited because they pose too great a threat to autonomy.

The **final** presupposition pertains to adequate solutions or remedies and is particularly relevant to breaches of contract. Where autonomy interests conflict, there must be some effort to balance or adjust the conflicting interests to achieve a fair result. The threat level to the autonomy interest in light of the relevant contextual factors should determine the remedy.

---

[253] *See, e.g.*, CAL. EVID. CODE § 115 (2014) ("'Burden of proof' means the obligation of a party to establish by evidence a requisite degree of belief concerning a fact in the mind of the trier of fact or the court. The burden of proof may require a party to raise a reasonable doubt concerning the existence or nonexistence of a fact or that he establish the existence or nonexistence of a fact by a preponderance of the evidence, by clear and convincing proof, or by proof beyond a reasonable doubt.").

[254] *See* In re Marriage of Peters, 52 Cal. App. 4th 1487, 1490 (1997) (stating that "facts are subject to a higher burden of proof only where particularly important individual interests or rights are at stake.").

[255] *See, e.g.*, Baxter Healthcare Corp. v. Denton, 120 Cal. App. 4th 333, 365 (2004) (noting that the burden of proof "serves to allocate the risk of error between the parties, and varies in proportion to the gravity of the consequences of an erroneous resolution … Generally, a higher burden of proof applies only where particularly important individual interests or rights, which are more substantial than the loss of money, are at stake.") (Citations omitted).

[256] *See* In re Michael G., 63 Cal. App. 4th 700, 709 (1998).

[257] *See* CAL. CIV. CODE § 3294(a) (Deering, LEXIS through 2018 Reg. Sess.) (stating that "where it is proven by clear and convincing evidence that the defendant has been guilty of oppression, fraud, or malice, the plaintiff, in addition to the actual damages, may recover damages for the sake of example and by way of punishing the defendant.").

D. THE LIMITS OF CONSENT

There are different reasons why an act might be deemed inconsentable. Sometimes, an act is deemed inconsentable because it violates moral or religious beliefs or simply disgusts most people on a visceral level.[258] But morality is an unreliable and undesirable justification for government interference because it is an evolving and dynamic concept which often reflects majoritarian norms, prejudices and biases.[259] Morality-based laws are often difficult to reconcile in a pluralistic society that values diversity and religious freedom. In particular, morality-based laws which are intended to promote a particular religious view threaten our society's core belief in autonomy as they would impose values or beliefs upon those who may not adhere to them and who may even oppose them. The objective of a consentability framework is to provide a systematic way to analyze rules and norms which, in turn, promote the objectives of freedom, fairness and respect for diversity. Morality and culture are fluid concepts. In the not-too-distant past, same-sex relations were considered immoral, slavery unremarkable, and interracial marriage shocking. Social norms are constantly in flux, and rules based upon majoritarian views may perpetuate the subordination of minority populations. The power of the mob – amplified through the social media echo chamber – makes the already dubious wisdom of the crowd seem even less wise. The framework – the "rules" – of consentability should be flexible enough to recognize and accommodate cultural shifts while being firm enough to provide some predictability.

There is value in encouraging diversity of viewpoints because doing so encourages individual flourishing. John Stuart Mill warned against "wearing down into uniformity all that is individual" in oneself as it is only by "cultivating and calling forth . . . that human beings become a noble and beautiful object of contemplation" which leads to the human race itself "infinitely better worth belonging to."[260] History is replete with mavericks and renegades who challenged and eventually changed conventional wisdom. It is also filled with tragic tales of forced sexuality conversions, lobotomies, and violence inflicted upon those who dared to cross religious, racial, gender or other socially constructed barriers. An act of agency may be an act of rebellion, a challenge to the existing cultural and social structure. Informal (social) forces and formal (legal) forces may suppress these challenges to the status quo simply to preserve existing power structures.

But even the inclination to react against majoritarian norms is itself shaped by those norms. There is no counterculture without a mainstream culture; there is no rebellion without something to rebel against. Impulsiveness, unrestrained passion

---

[258]   Martha C. Nussbaum, Hiding From Humanity: Disgust, Shame, And The Law, at 2 (2004) (noting that disgust serves "sometimes as the primary or even sole reason for making some acts illegal.").

[259]   *See id.* at 14 (arguing that disgust "should never be the primary basis for rendering an act criminal, and should not play either an aggravating or a mitigating role in the criminal law where it currently does so.")

[260]   Mill, *supra* note 51, at 66.

and rebelliousness are compelling characteristics of movie heroes and literary protagonists. In real life, however, these same characteristics might be evidence of immaturity, mental instability, ignorance or abuse. Similarly, the desire to differentiate oneself in a dramatic and even shocking way may result in self-actualization – but it may also result in profound regret. Given the limits of human cognition and the existence of opportunistic, manipulative and deceitful bad actors, the state should seek to ensure that the conditions under which consent to certain activities is given promote, rather than diminish or degrade, autonomy. It is unrealistic to believe that decision-making certainty is always attainable and that regret and exploitation can be eliminated entirely; nevertheless, the state should strive to get its citizens as close to certainty in decision-making and as far away from profound regret and exploitation as practicable. Individual freedom and respect for autonomy is promoted by ensuring that people understand the risks associated with their actions; however, efficiency concerns and practical constraints dictate that governmental efforts should be commensurate with the potential harm flowing from these acts. Some acts are inconsentable because there is a strong suspicion that consent would be too flimsy or that a person or class of persons is being exploited. The suspicion also arises in novel situations where there is limited information. New technologies have unpredictable outcomes. Parts loosen, gadgets break, the human body reacts in unexpected ways. The level of risk involved with activities created by new technologies is impossible to assess. Novel situations also make it difficult to make predictions regarding one's future emotional state because there are no predecessors who can pass along experienced wisdom. An individual's reaction to a new experience may differ from what was anticipated.

The state also plays a role in enforcing and enhancing individual autonomy as a *value*. Consent's magical powers are naturally limited. They only extend where the consenter has authority to grant permission. The power of consent is personal and (except in situations involving legal guardians) does not give one the power to affect the person or personal belongings of another. The Harm Principle requires the state to act to prevent someone from exercising free will when doing so would cause harm to others but to refrain from intervening when the only harm would be to self. The Opportunism Corollary extends the Harm Principle to require the state to prevent or discourage its citizens from profiting by taking knowing, harmful advantage of others.

My proposed consentability framework is not based upon promoting and protecting the autonomy interest of *any one individual* but upon promoting the interests which members of society *collectively* have in their autonomy. Rather than simply viewing autonomy as an individual right affecting a particular individual, the concept of "collective autonomy" reflects the importance of autonomy as a societal value. A society that values autonomy and liberty must not favor *any one individual's* autonomy and liberty over any other individual's autonomy and liberty unless there is a principled and neutral basis for doing so. Furthermore, *if the individual autonomy interest and the collective autonomy interest are on the same level on the hierarchy of autonomy interests* (Figure 3.4), *in the event of a conflict, the collective autonomy interest prevails over the individual autonomy interest.*

The concept of collective autonomy recognizes that a consent act has the potential to affect three parties: (1) the consenter; (2) the consent-seeker; and (3) collective members of society. If A enters into a contract to purchase goods from B, the contract directly affects both A and B but it may also affect others indirectly. B may have agreed to purchase goods from C with the proceeds from the sale with A. If A breaches her contract with B, it may affect the willingness of C in the future to enter into the same type of contract with D. C and D may then undertake time-consuming precautions to avoid the same result as the contract between A and B. The precedent established by A and B's contract affects other members of society. A collective autonomy approach recognizes the communitarian nature of society and the interrelationship of individuals. The concept of collective autonomy also explains public health and safety laws, such as laws against texting and driving which protect drivers from their own bad driving, but also protect the lives (i.e. the bodily integrity) of others from bad drivers.

Mandatory laws aimed at preventing self-harm tend to address two types of situations. The first situation is when the self-harming act also harms others. In this type of circumstance, state intervention is justified if the threat to the individual's autonomy from such intervention is lower than the threat to the group if the act were allowed. In other words, a mandatory law is justified when the individual autonomy interest is outweighed by the collective autonomy interest. For example, California passed a law that required all children enrolled in public or private schools or day cares to be vaccinated against a variety of contagious diseases, regardless of the religious or personal beliefs of their parents.[261] The hierarchy of autonomy interests would put the collective autonomy interest in avoiding a contagious disease (i.e. bodily integrity right) above an individual's interest in adhering to religious beliefs (i.e. civil and political rights). The mandatory vaccination requirement is an example of non-forcible physical compulsion. The individual must choose between getting his child vaccinated in contravention of his religious beliefs or having his child home-schooled. There is an alternative to compliance (home schooling) which poses less of a threat to autonomy than the bodily intrusion posed by vaccination, and the right to religious freedom can be exercised in exchange for the right to a non-home schooled education (with both being at the same level on the hierarchy of autonomy interests).[262] Importantly, the California law provides an exemption for medical reasons. If there are medical

---

[261] S.B. 277, 2015 Leg., Reg. Sess. (Cal. 2015), www.leginfo.ca.gov/pub/15– 16/bill/sen/sb_0251–0300/ sb_277_bill_20150630_chaptered.pdf.

[262] *Cf.* Erwin Chemerinsky & Michele Goodwin, *Compulsory Vaccination Laws are Constitutional,* 110 Nw. U. L. Rev. 589, 594 (arguing that the California law "does not go far enough" and that "[a]ll

reasons for a child not to be immunized, requiring that a child be immunized or forgo public schooling does not actually offer a choice. The child is essentially forced to forgo public schooling. The government-mandated option should pose the same or a lesser threat to the autonomy interest than the consequence for the failure to comply. Coercive actions, however, may be justified in emergency situations to protect the collective autonomy interest even at the risk of harming any one individual's autonomy interest if that collective autonomy interest is greater than or on the same level as the individual's autonomy interest on the hierarchy of autonomy interests.

The second situation is where state intervention poses less of a threat to autonomy than the act itself poses. For example, mandatory seat belt laws are minimally restrictive compared to the harm which would likely result from failing to wear one and getting into an accident. Deficient consent conditions dilute the autonomous nature of an act. Most people who object to wearing seat belts do not object to wearing them *in the event of an accident*. They object because they do not believe they will get into a serious accident. Their cognitive biases may prevent them from calculating the risks appropriately. They may underestimate the probability of getting into a serious accident or believe that because they have not been in a serious accident before that it won't happen to them. They may prioritize the immediate inconvenience of wearing a seat belt over the injuries that their future self might suffer. They may not have accurate information or realistic expectations regarding what would happen to them in the event of an accident – they may, for example, believe that they will be "thrown clear" of the accident or that they could more easily escape without a seat belt.[263] State intervention is justified because the government intervention poses only a low-level threat to autonomy (temporarily and minimally restricting one's movements while in a car or risk paying a fine), while the harm poses the highest-level threat to autonomy (death or serious bodily injury).

Generally, state intervention should take the form of regulation which is intended to police the consenting process to ensure the adequacy of the consent conditions. In some cases, however, the situation warrants presuming that the individual's knowledge condition is deficient. For example, it is unlikely that many would actually "consent" to the consequences of not wearing a seat belt in a car accident; rather, the decision not to wear a seatbelt is attributable to the inability to adequately assess the risks and understand the consequences of such a decision.

Finally, the right to bodily integrity pertains only to one's body; it does not extend to what that body has produced. Nobody owns the fruits of her body's production

children should be vaccinated, to protect them and to protect others from the spread of communicable diseases.").

[263] *See, e.g.*, *Myths and Facts About Seat Belts*, MICH. STATE POLICE, www.michigan.gov/msp/0,4643, 7–123-72297_64773_22760–13689–,00.html (last visited June 6, 2018) (addressing several common myths about wearing seat belts, including that the driver would be "thrown clear in a crash" which, as the website explains, "is almost impossible").

because nobody may "own" another human being. A pregnant woman should have the power to decide whether to continue or terminate her pregnancy. Once she gives birth, however, her right to autonomy does *not* extend to the infant. Whatever rights she has or does not have over the infant results from her status by law (as a parent) or by contract (as a surrogate). After birth, the infant is a human being, and no longer *part* of the woman's body. A person's parental rights are determined by legal status; autonomy interests, therefore, are relevant to the extent that there might be a contract which reallocates the rights determined by law. Once the woman ceases to be the source of life, she no longer has a claim predicated on bodily integrity. Of course, she may have rights as a *parent* but that is not the same as an autonomy interest in the infant that is born. Consent and contract play important roles in these situations. The law determines the rights and responsibilities of birth parents; this book argues that the parties should be permitted to allocate those rights and responsibilities through contract, but consent is a prerequisite to that contract.

While the consenter in the above scenario is a woman, it is foreseeable that in the future, the consenter may be a man; the embryo or fetus may also contain the genetic material from more than two parents.[264] It is also foreseeable that the tissue may develop entirely outside of a human womb.[265] Artificial reproductive technologies, such as in vitro fertilization or surrogacy, have raised difficult questions regarding control and responsibility. In the future, these questions may extend to include life created through other means, including cloning, bioengineering and artificial intelligence. In these situations, it is not within the power of any individual to "consent" to what may or may not happen to another human being. The woman who has contributed the egg and the man who has contributed the sperm – or any person who has contributed any genetic material – is not the "owner" of that (or any) living person. The question of autonomy and consent in this case arises at the moment that the genetic material is contributed, not after it has developed into an independent living human being. One may not own another human being in a free society. Consent is a tool of individual autonomy which may only be used by the consenter; it has no claim on the autonomy of another. As technology advances and scientific progress creates novel situations, it is imperative to remember the critical role of consent – and its limits.

---

[264] *See* Michael Reilly, *A Three-Parent Child Was Conceived in Mexico, Because the U.S. Won't Allow It*, MIT Tech. Rev. (Sept. 28, 2016), www.technologyreview.com/s/602499/a-three-parent-child-was-conceived-in-mexico-because-the-us-wont-allow-it/ (reporting that in Mexico, a child was born from genetic material from two mothers and fertilized with the father's sperm); Gina Kolata, *Birth of Baby with Three Parents' DNA Marks Success for Banned Technique*, N.Y. Times (Sept. 27, 2016), www.nytimes .com/2016/09/28/health/birth-of-3-parent-baby-a-success-for-controversial-procedure.html.

[265] *See* Olga Khazan, *Babies Floating in Fluid-Filled Bags*, Atlantic (April 25, 2017), www.theatlantic .com/health/archive/2017/04/preemies-floating-in-fluid-filled-bags/524181/ (reporting a study where premature lambs were gestated for four weeks in an artificial womb); Jessica Hamzelou, *Artificial Womb Helps Premature Lamb Fetuses Grow for 4 Weeks*, New Scientist (April 25, 2017), www .newscientist.com/article/2128851-artificial-womb-helps-premature-lamb-fetuses-grow-for-4-weeks/.

4

Consent and Contracts

John Stuart Mill explained that an individual should not be permitted to bind himself to slavery because doing so would undermine the principle of freedom:

> The ground for thus limiting his power of voluntarily disposing of his own lot in life, is apparent, and is very clearly seen in this extreme case. The reason for not interfering unless for the sake of others, with a person's voluntary acts, is consideration for his liberty. His voluntary choice is evidence that what he so chooses is desirable, or at the least endurable, to him, and his good is on the whole best provided for by allowing him to take his own means of pursuing it. But by selling himself for a slave, he abdicates his liberty; he foregoes any future use of it, beyond that single act. He therefore defeats, in his own case, the very purpose which is the justification of allowing him to dispose of himself. He is no longer free; but is thenceforth in a position which has no longer the presumption in its favor, that would be afforded by his voluntarily remaining in it. The principle of freedom cannot require that he should be free not to be free. It is not freedom, to be allowed to alienate his freedom. [266]

Joel Feinberg, however, observed that if the reason to prohibit slavery contracts (as opposed to slavery, which would be without consent) is to preserve personal freedom, then we have embarked on a slippery slope which would also ban euthanasia and all manner of unhealthy activities, such as eating fried foods or smoking cigarettes.[267] Feinberg discussed an alternative argument, which is that it is extremely unlikely that "the agreement to become another's slave can satisfy the requisite high standards of voluntariness":[268]

> Since the renunciation of rights is both total and irrevocable in this kind of transaction, the standards of voluntariness employed must be higher than for any other kind of agreement (except perhaps suicide pacts and voluntary euthanasia

---

[266] MILL, supra note 51, at 110.
[267] FEINBERG, HARM TO SELF, supra note 52, at 77.
[268] Id. at 79.

requests). The risks are so great that the possibility of mistake must be reduced to a minimum. It is by no means impossible for a given slavery agreement to be voluntary, but the grounds for suspicion are so powerful that the testing would have to be thorough, time-consuming, and expensive.[269]

This argument captures the weighting of factors in assessing consent construction. Because the threat to autonomy is so high (the highest, other than death), the consent conditions may be extremely difficult to establish. Difficult, but not impossible.

I think a better explanation for the prohibition on slavery contracts is that the concept of "contract" itself makes little allowance for consent destruction. A person might consent to being a slave and then later change her mind. Under a consentability framework, one should be permitted to change one's mind if the autonomy interest that one has at stake is greater than the autonomy interest at stake for the other party. Thus, one should *always* be permitted to remove oneself from the condition of slavery, given that one's autonomy interest in physical and legal freedom will always outweigh the other party's economic interest in owning a slave. It is thus more accurate to say that while one may consent to the condition of being a slave, one may not *remain* a slave if one no longer consents. "Contract," however, means that one is obliged to perform even if later one changes one's mind and so no longer consents at the time of performance. Thus, slavery must be made incontractable.

It is not necessary to refer to such an extreme example as slavery to make the point that the relative autonomy interests determine the power of the parties to enforce a contract. Contracts for almost any kind of personal service or employment may not be specifically enforced. An individual may not have the right to breach such a contract, but she does have the power to do so. This means that an employer may not force an employee to continue working, although the employee might have to pay monetary damages for breach of an employment contract. The employee's personal freedom outweighs the employer's economic interest in having that employee perform; this does not, however, mean that the employee has no obligation whatsoever.

An individual may consent to do something but change her mind prior to the time of performance. In most cases, she will have the right to do so. Someone consenting to marry has the right to break off the engagement. Someone consenting to sex may withdraw consent at any time, even during the activity. Someone may consent to meet someone for dinner but then cancel or leave the table before the main course has arrived. The consent-seeker may be disappointed, but typically has no right to force performance. The exception is when the parties have entered into a contract.

Because a contract expresses a present intent to bind oneself to do something in the future, there always lurks the potential for a party to change her mind. But the very purpose of a contract is to ensure performance even when a party at a later time no longer wishes to perform. Where the consenting party changes her mind, in essence she is *no longer consenting* to perform. But if a contract binds her, in most cases, she is obligated to perform despite her later non-consent. She must perform (or pay damages for non-performance) despite consent destruction because her *earlier* self consented. In this situation, there are two primary reasons for privileging the autonomy interest of the earlier self over the autonomy interest of the later self. The first is that the later self's interest in avoiding the contract must be balanced against the consent-seeker's interest in enforcing it. The consent-seeker may have restricted his freedom somehow (by, for example, not purchasing another piece of property) in reliance upon performance. The second reason for contract enforcement is that there is a societal interest in protecting the concept of private property ownership and the free market, which can only function by ensuring the security of transactions. Commerce and a credit economy depend upon contracts as reliable planning tools. Where the interests of the party are equivalent (e.g. where both parties are exchanging property), the societal interest in protecting the security of transactions (which in turn, promotes the collective autonomy interest in controlling one's property) tips the balance in favor of enforcement.

All contracts require consent, but not all consentable acts are – or should be – contractable. There is a saying that hard cases make bad law, meaning that a decision rendered to address a particular set of facts in an unusual case may create a precedent that is ill-suited for the majority of cases raising the same issue. In the same way, it might be said that hard choices make bad contracts. Contract law recognizes that consent is measured by degrees, but assumes the best unless shown evidence of the worse. In other words, a manifestation of consent – a signature on a page, a click of an "I accept" icon, a nod of the head – presumes assent unless one of the parties presents convincing evidence that the manifestation was not of *consent* at all but was the product of coercion, mistake, fraud or a similar invalidating cause. The manifestation results in the presumption, but the law also requires consideration. The requirement is a low bar in most arm's-length transactions. Where the requirement of consideration becomes more complicated is where personal relationships are involved. Guilt, sorrow and a desire for affection prompt one to make ill-considered promises – and provide the plotline for first-year contracts cases. In Schnell v. Nell,[270] for example, a woman leaves her three friends some money in her will; the only problem is that it is the year 1861, so she owns no property in her name and has no money to give. Her grief-stricken husband writes out a note that he will make good on his wife's bequest. Later, presumably when the fog of grief has lifted, he changes his mind. The court finds there was no consideration for the note.

Relationships between friends and family members are murky and promises between them are often exchanged without deliberation. Furthermore, it would

---

[270] Schnell v. Nell, 17 Ind. 29 (1861).

unnecessarily constrain personal relationships to expect people to act the same way with friends and family as they do with strangers or business associates. It serves no societal purpose and burdens the judiciary to treat promises between friends and family the same as promises between business acquaintances. The exception, of course, is where the parties clearly intended a promise to be binding.

The requirement of consideration serves to promote deliberation and intentionality.[271] In some cases, however, a party may be able to escape a contract despite a manifestation of consent and consideration, on the grounds of unconscionability or public policy. Unconscionability has always been an amorphous and controversial doctrine. Courts seem to be frightened of its indefinability and its lack of precision, but it is exactly those qualities that make the doctrine suitable for situations where the existence of consideration does not necessarily mean the existence of consent. The doctrine of unconscionability seeks to capture the sliding scale nature of consent. A contract entered into under a high degree of procedural unconscionability does not require the contract terms to be as egregious as where there is low procedural unconscionability. Procedural unconscionability, or "bargaining naughtiness," suggests a deficiency of the knowledge condition, in that one party may not have been aware of the relevant terms.[272] Substantive unconscionability, or terms that "shock the conscience,"[273] suggests a deficiency of the voluntariness condition. The other party may not have coerced the victim, but the victim seems to have entered into the transaction due to a lack of alternatives. The other party may not be responsible for the victim's dire or unfortunate situation, but was certainly aware of it. It is this fact – deliberately taking advantage of someone else's misfortune – that makes the transaction "unconscionable."

Consent has an inversely proportional relationship with exploitation. Exploitation can be separated into two different categories. The first is where the party benefitting from the transaction manipulates the victim in some way. Contract law recognizes this type of exploitation in the doctrines of fraud, duress, nondisclosure, unilateral mistake and undue influence.[274] The party benefitting from the transaction is a wrongdoer (to a greater or lesser degree), and thus, blameworthy for diminishing or eliminating one of the necessary conditions of consent. The wrongful act might be obvious, such as a threat (in the case of duress), or it may be less blatant, such as misleading another party in some way (in the case of nondisclosure or some cases

---

[271] Lon L. Fuller, *Consideration and Form*, 41 COLUM. L. REV. 799 (1941) (discussing the purposes of consideration, including to encourage deliberation). See id. at 799 (noting that "it is said the enforcement is denied gratuitous promises because such promises are often made impulsively and without proper deliberation.").

[272] Arthur Allen Leff, *Unconscionability and the Code – The Emperor's New Clause*, 115 U. PA. L. REV. 485, 487 (1967) ("I shall often refer to bargaining naughtiness as 'procedural unconscionability,' and to evils in the resulting contract as 'substantive unconscionability.'").

[273] Harrington v. Atlantic Sounding Co., 602 F.3d 113, 126 n. 7 (2d Cir. 2010) (noting that New Jersey law requires that an unconscionable contract "shocks the conscience.").

[274] See generally KIM, RELATIVE CONSENT, supra note 6.

involving unilateral mistake). Accordingly, a contract which results from this type of opportunism is void or voidable, depending upon the relative blameworthiness of the parties.

The second type of exploitation results from factors external to the contracting parties. The preexisting imbalance between the parties – the fact that one is richer, more powerful, or more knowledgeable than the other – creates the conditions which make exploitation possible. However, the stronger party is not responsible for those conditions, unlike in the first type of exploitative situation. What makes the situation exploitative is that the stronger party is aware of the bargaining imbalance and seeks terms that take advantage of the other party's weaker position. Contract law generally treats this type of exploitation differently from the first type. The wrongful act of the stronger party (the taking advantage of the party in dire straits) is apparent in the terms of the transaction itself. By contrast, the wrongful act of the party in the first type of exploitation is distinct from the transaction; the terms of the transaction themselves might not be objectively unfair. The exploitation in the first type of situation derives from the conduct of the consent-seeker (the benefitted party), not from the terms of the transaction. By contrast, in the second type of situation, the exploitation results from the terms of the transaction itself. Given the non-egregious (or not-as-egregious) conduct of the consent-seeker, the substantive terms of the transaction in the latter type of situation must be severe. Contract law recognizes the interplay of these two types of exploitation in the doctrine of unconscionability.[275] Courts have been reluctant to use the doctrine as a defense in the absence of terms that "shock the conscience," although bad behavior (or less socially acceptable behavior) on the part of the stronger party will decrease the degree to which the terms must be found shocking. The sliding-scale nature of unconscionability thus seeks to balance the blameworthiness of the stronger party with the harmfulness of the terms. In some jurisdictions, an absence of any procedural unconscionability may still result in a finding of unconscionability, if the terms are harmful or egregious enough.[276] On the other hand, contracts made under circumstances of extreme procedural unconscionability but without unfair terms are more likely to be challenged using the defenses of fraud, duress, unilateral mistake or non-disclosure.[277]

---

[275] *Id.*, see also RESTATEMENT (SECOND) OF CONTRACTS § 153 (AM. LAW INST. 1981) (recognizing the second type of exploitation in the doctrine of unilateral mistake in jurisdictions that follow the Restatement).

[276] See, e.g., Maxwell v. Fidelity Financial Servs., 907 P.2d 51, 59 (Ariz. 1995) (concluding that under Arizona law, "a claim of unconscionability can be established with a showing of substantive unconscionability alone, especially in cases involving either price-cost disparity or limitation of remedies.").

[277] *Id.* (noting that "[i]f only procedural irregularities are present, it may be more appropriate to analyze the claims under the doctrine of fraud, misrepresentation, duress and mistake, although such irregularities can make a case of procedural unconscionability.").

A. THE CONSENT CONDITIONS IN CONTRACT DOCTRINE

Melvin Eisenberg argued that modern contract law has become more substantive, subjective, individualized and dynamic, and less formalistic, objective, binary and static.[278] The balancing of interests contained in modern contract doctrine takes into account the complexity of human relationships, the limits of human cognition, and the unpredictability of the future.[279] Contract law balances these interests through the vehicle of consent. Consent is an essential prerequisite of a contract but whether someone has consented to a contract is often the subject of dispute. Contractual consent differs from consent in other contexts. For example, the consent required to enter into a contract is not the same as the consent required for a medical procedure. Although rarely articulated by courts, consent differs even within the contractual context. Consent to a mass consumer form contract differs from consent to a merger and acquisition contract between two multinational corporations. The nature of the consent varies depending upon the relationship of the parties and the type of transaction. When courts refer to the presence (or absence) of contractual consent, they are rendering a judgment based upon the circumstances of the transaction. These circumstances include the words and deeds which manifest consent, but are not limited to them. If a party signs an agreement under duress, a court will find that she did not consent, regardless of the act of signing her name on the signature line. On the other hand, a court may find that a person has consented to an agreement by engaging in certain activity, such as proceeding on a website, clicking on an online box, or opening a package, even if that person never read or noticed the associated terms.[280] The courts may find consent if the party acted in a way that the *court* determined should indicate consent, even if the party herself was unaware of the meaning conveyed by her actions. A contract is law between private parties, allowing them to transfer their rights, create obligations for themselves and bind each other. A contract binds only the parties but gives the state the power of enforcement. In this way, the state plays an essential role in the redistribution of private property. But why should the state intervene in purely private matters?

There are several justifications for state interference in contractual matters.[281] One of the most often cited justifications is that a contract promotes the autonomy of

---

[278] Melvin Aron Eisenberg, *The Emergence of Dynamic Contract Law*, 88 CAL. L. REV. 1743, 1745 (2000).

[279] See id. at 1765 (stating that "[p]romissory transactions seldom occur in an instant of time. They have a past, a present, and a future" and the demarcation between and among them may not be clear).

[280] See ProCD v. Zeidenberg, 86 F.3d 1447 (7th Cir. 1996); see also NANCY S. KIM, WRAP CONTRACTS: FOUNDATIONS AND RAMIFICATIONS 35–44 (2013) [hereinafter KIM, WRAP CONTRACTS] (providing an overview of the case law discussing various forms of non-negotiated contracts); Nancy S. Kim, *Online Contracting*, 72 BUS. LAW. 243 (Winter 2016–2017); Nancy S. Kim, *Wrap Contracting and the Online Environment: Causes and Cures*, in RESEARCH HANDBOOK ON ELECTRONIC COMMERCE (John A. Rothchild ed., 2015).

[281] See STEPHEN A. SMITH, CONTRACT THEORY (Oxford Univ. Press, 2004) (discussing a variety of contract law theories).

individuals by allowing them to decide how to allocate their property rights.[282] Thus, a contract permits an individual to rent out a room in her home or sell her car. Another common justification is that while a contract may directly affect only the two contracting parties, it may indirectly affect other parties. A contract where X agrees to sell Y her farm might have led Y to sell his farm to Z, and Z to buy horses from A. Even if there is no secondary transaction which results from the contract, the enforceability of the contract – whether it is respected and upheld – may affect whether future parties enter into contracts. State enforcement provides reliability and security of transactions, which is necessary to the stability of a credit-based economy.[283] A credit-based economy allows more utility from property ownership and a more sophisticated and expansive marketplace.[284] For example, credit permits a farmer to use a tractor now and pay for it after the harvest. Without credit, the tractor would sit idle, there would be fewer crops, and the farmer would have less money after the harvest to buy goods and services from others. Without the backing of the state, the future performance of an individual would depend upon his word – or the brute strength of the one to whom performance was owed. Without contracts, commercial exchanges would be local, limited to barter exchanges, and enforced by the threat of vigilante justice.

At a minimum, a contract requires consent.[285] As Brian Bix writes, "[C]onsent, in terms of voluntary choice, is – or at least appears to be or purports to be – at the essence of contract law."[286] The law typically views contracts made without consent as not being contracts at all. A promise made under duress, for example, is void or voidable.[287] Although the promisor made a promise, the lack of consent makes

---

[282] See Owen M. Fiss, *The Autonomy of Law*, 26 YALE J. INT'L L. 517, 518–519 ("Contract law is ... indispensable to assure parties who are bargaining with each other that their promises will be enforced. Neither contracts nor property law, nor any other body of law ... that might be needed for market functioning, are self-enforcing.").

[283] See Morris Cohen, *The Basis of Contract*, 46 HARV. L. REV. 553, 576 (1933) (stating that the law will enforce contracts "in the interest of the general security of business transactions.").

[284] See KIM, WRAP CONTRACTS, supra note 280, at 17–34 (providing a general discussion of how contract shapes and is shaped by a credit economy and marketplace changes).

[285] AAA Constr. of Missoula, L.L.C. v. Choice Land Corp., 264 P.3d 709, 713 (Mont. 2011) ("Identifiable parties capable of contracting, consent, a lawful object, and sufficient consideration comprise the essential elements of any contract."); Marseilles Homeowners Condo. Ass'n. v. Broadmoor, L.L.C., 111 So.3d 1099, 1111 (La. Ct. App. 2013) ("Consent is an absolute necessity to the formation of a contract ... Importantly, consent envisions agreement on all elements of a given sale or contract"); Se. Grading, Inc. v. City of Atlanta, 324 S.E.2d 776, 779 (Ga. Ct. App. 1984) ("An offer and an acceptance are essential prerequisites to the creation of every contract. Thus, the law requires that the parties consent to the formation of a contract." (citations omitted)).

[286] See Brian H. Bix, *Contracts*, in THE ETHICS OF CONSENT: THEORY AND PRACTICE 251 (Franklin G. Miller & Alan Wertheimer eds., 2010).

[287] United States ex rel. Trane Co. v. Bond, 586 A.2d 734, 738 (Md. 1991) (summarizing several cases and noting that they "as well as the Restatement (Second) of Contracts §§ 174, 175 (Am. Law Inst.1981), distinguish between duress by physical compulsion, which may render a contract void, and duress by threat, which renders a contract voidable by the victim except where the other party to the contract in good faith, and without reason to know of the duress, either gives value or relies materially on the contract.").

breaking that promise permissible, even socially desirable. Scholars debate whether, how, and to what extent the morality of promise-keeping justifies contract law,[288] but without consent, it is immoral to enforce a promise against a party because it would deprive the promisor of agency and reward the promisee for bad behavior. Thus, the moral prerequisite for allowing the courts to adjudicate contractual disputes is that the parties have consented. Their consent subjects the parties to state interference into their private affair.

Contract formation requires offer, acceptance, mutual assent, and consideration. Each of these doctrines essentially determines whether a requisite condition of consent has been met in a given case. A failure of a consent condition means that the contract has not been properly formed. Consent in the context of contractual assent does not require a high level of knowledge. A party to a contract does not need to understand the meaning of all – or even most – of its terms. Furthermore, contract law does not require actual assent. It requires only a *manifestation* of assent. A manifestation of assent does not mean that a party has actually assented.[289] It means only that a reasonable person would have understood the manifestation to indicate that the party assented. An objective standard is necessary to respond to the problems of deception and of faulty memories. Thus, it balances the interests of the promisor and the promisee who, in good faith, believed there was assent and a contract.

While consent is a moral prerequisite to a contract, the mere fact of having consented to a contract does not justify its enforcement.[290] Certain types of promises are too oppressive to keep and their oppressiveness makes breaking them an act of maturity or responsibility. In certain circumstances, it would be immoral not to break a promise. For example, if Jane promises to meet Frank for dinner at 6:00 p.m. but Jane's mother suffers a heart attack at 5:00 p.m., it would be immoral for Jane to refuse to take her mother to the hospital in order not to break her promise to Frank. A philosophy which requires promise-keeping in all situations quickly proves rigid and unworkable. If it is to justify contract law, the morality of promises must be based upon something other than the mere fact of having made the promise.

If consent provides the moral foundation for promises, what is the justification for enforcing a contract where the promisor has subsequently changed her mind?[291]

---

[288]   See, e.g., CHARLES FRIED, CONTRACT AS PROMISE: A THEORY OF CONTRACTUAL OBLIGATIONS (1981); Seana Valentine Shiffrin, *The Divergence of Contract and Promise*, 120 HARV. L. REV. 708, 709 (2007); Steven Shavell, *Is Breach of Contract Immoral?*, 56 EMORY L.J. 439 (2006).

[289]   RESTATEMENT (SECOND) OF CONTRACTS § 19(3) (AM. LAW INST. 1981) (stating that a party's conduct "may manifest assent even though he does not in fact assent.").

[290]   See Chunlin Leonhard, *The Unbearable Lightness of Consent in Contract Law*, 63 CASE W. RES. L. REV. 57, 60 (2012) (noting that "consent is an amorphous, difficult-to-define concept that is made increasingly more difficult by the marketplace manipulations of human decision-making biases.").

[291]   See Robin Kar, *The Art of Promise and Power of Contract*, JOTWELL (June 13, 2016), http://juris.jotwell .com/the-art-of-promise-and-power-of-contract/ (reviewing Dori Kimel, *Personal Autonomy and Change of Mind in Promise and in Contract*, in PHILOSOPHICAL FOUNDATIONS OF CONTRACT LAW 96 (Klass, Letsas & Saprai eds., 2015)).

A contract implicates the autonomy of both parties and requires mutual consent. Contract law can best be understood as a free society's interest in protecting the rights of all of its individual members to determine how to use, distribute, allocate and reallocate their property interests.[292] Given the increased value and utility from contracting, state intervention is an important part of private property ownership. Consequently, the subsequent change in desire of one of the parties does not release that party from its obligation unless the other party also changes its mind. The act of consent both protects and promulgates the property rights of both parties. The right of one party to change its mind does not prevail over the other party's desire to retain the contract. But the party who wishes to enforce the contract also does not necessarily prevail over the desire of the party to escape the contract. Enforcement depends upon the relative behavior of both parties. Thus, the morality of contract law is reflected in the way it considers blameworthiness within assessments of consent.

1. How Contract Law Addresses Consent Construction and Destruction

The three conditions necessary in order for consent to be properly constructed (an intentional act or manifestation indicating consent, knowledge and voluntariness) are captured and expressed in contract law doctrines. At the most basic level, all contracts require a manifestation, some act or statement which indicates consent to the contract. The manifested act can be a statement, a signature, a click on an "accept" icon, or a nod of the head. The act (whether word or deed) is the "manifestation of consent," and triggers a presumption of consent. Where the manifestation of consent is a promissory statement, it may raise problems relating to the interpretation of words. Where the manifestation of consent is an action, such as a signature on a written agreement or a click on an "agree" icon, it may raise problems relating to the identity of the actor or whether the actor understood the meaning of the act. The presumption of consent which arises from an action, such as signing a document or clicking on an "accept" icon, is entwined with the "duty to read."[293] Rather than being an affirmative obligation, the duty to read is a presumption that someone who has signed a document (or clicked to accept online terms) has read the terms that the document contains.[294]

---

[292] See Randy E. Barnett, *A Consent Theory of Contract*, 86 COLUM. L. REV. 269, 297 (1986) (stating that "contract law concerns enforceable obligations arising from the valid transfer of entitlements that are already vested in someone, and this difference is what makes consent a moral prerequisite to contractual obligation.").

[293] See E. ALLAN FARNSWORTH, CONTRACTS, § 4.26 (4th ed. 2004) (noting that one who manifests assent "may not later complain about not having read or understood it."). The duty to read is a presumption that one who has manifested assent to a contract has read the terms.

[294] See Charles L. Knapp, *Is There a "Duty to Read"?*, in REVISITING THE CONTRACTS SCHOLARSHIP OF STEWART MACAULAY: ON THE EMPIRICAL AND THE LYRICAL 315, 320 (Jean Braucher, John Kidwell & William C. Whitford eds., 2013) (stating that "in practice, the presumption created by signing an

The law typically views consent as the moment when the manifestation of consent occurred. The presumption of consent may be overcome by evidence that shows that the other consent conditions – voluntariness and knowledge – are deficient. Where the manifested act itself was involuntary or conducted in ignorance, there is no contract – the agreement is void. Often, however, the manifested act was voluntary but undertaken without full knowledge, with a heavy heart or under pressure. The difficulty is in determining *how much* of each condition is required in order to reach the conclusion that there was consent or no consent. The assessment of the consent conditions is on a sliding scale where the requisite robustness of each condition depends upon the relative blameworthiness of the parties in light of their relationship, third party effects, and societal impact.

Given the important role of consent in determining the validity and enforceability of contracts, to limit the meaning of "consent" to the subjective state of one party would be foolish – and would threaten the role of contracts in facilitating commercial transactions. The consent-seeker cannot ascertain with certainty the internal state of the consenting party. This is a fundamental and unavoidable weakness of consent. Furthermore, the human mind is error-prone, and neuroscience and social science research in the past fifty years has revealed how much.[295] Some people may lie if it suits their best interests to do so, such as if a contract no longer proves as profitable as expected, but others lie without intending to do so, simply because they are human. Daniel Levitin observes that "[p]erhaps the biggest problem with human memory is that we don't always know when we're recalling things inaccurately . . . This faulty confidence is widespread and difficult to extinguish."[296] Not only is our recollection of events incomplete and inaccurate, false memories are common and suggestible. Levitin explains that "the act of recalling a memory thrusts it into a labile state whereby new distortions can be introduced; then, when the memory is put back or restored, the incorrect information is grafted to it as though it were there all along."[297] Accordingly, the standard of reasonableness serves an important purpose because it enables the decision-maker (the judge, the jury, the arbitrator) to make a determination about the internal state of another individual that would otherwise be susceptible to distortion. The distortion may be intentional (the individual is lying) or unintentional (the individual's recollection is faulty). The perception of the consent-seeker is integral to an analysis of consent. The intentional "manifestation of consent" is a communicative act, the meaning of which depends both on how the act is communicated and how it is perceived. A party should not be permitted to behave in a way that leads another party to predictably suffer loss; on the other hand, a party should not unreasonably respond to

agreement is not regarded as truly conclusive, nor is the duty absolute" and noting several doctrines which may be a defense against its application).

[295] See discussion, Chapter 2.
[296] LEVITIN, supra note 157, at 50.
[297] *Id.* at 56.

the words or conduct of another and incur a loss. Each party then is responsible for how her act is perceived by the other party. Imposing an objective standard upon the manifestation of consent condition protects both parties by requiring them to behave in a manner that conforms to social norms.

A contract involves a promise.[298] A promise by definition always implicates the future, and contracts relate to only future performance on the part of the parties. (In the case of unilateral contracts, the future performance pertains only to one party, the offeror.) Consent, on the other hand, can involve future or past action. In some cases, consent grants permission; this permission pertains to future action and protects the party seeking consent from legal prosecution for doing what would otherwise be unlawful without such consent. In other cases, consent (such as ratification) is approval of action already taken which protects the consent-seeker from liability. A contract involves both a promise and consent; the term "assent" captures both concepts.[299] Motive becomes especially relevant when it comes to contracts because contracts involve two different time periods: contract formation and contract performance. As circumstances evolve, consent which exists at the time of formation may no longer exist at the time of performance.

A person's reason for agreeing to a contract may be undermined by subsequent events. Despite a "manifestation of consent," the consenter may seek to avoid contract enforcement by using one of several contract claims or defenses. The basis for avoidance may be either that the party never consented (consent was never constructed and so there was no contract formation) or that, due to additional information or changed circumstances, the party no longer wishes to perform (consent was destroyed). Consent destruction, like consent construction, has a sliding scale. Intent impacts the knowledge condition, which is essential to consent (and assent).[300] Importantly, courts should consider the intent of both parties, not just the intent of the party seeking to escape the contract. Consent (or the absence thereof) at the time of performance is an important consideration, but it is not determinative in light of consent at the time of contract formation. Contract defenses have different effects and may render a contract void, voidable or unenforceable.

---

[298] See RESTATEMENT (SECOND) OF CONTRACTS § 1 (AM. LAW INST. 1981) ("A contract is a promise or a set of promises for the breach of which the law gives a remedy, or the performance of which the law in some way recognizes as a duty.").

[299] See KIM, RELATIVE CONSENT, supra note 6, at 178 (stating that although courts may use the terms assent and consent interchangeably, assent "includes the concept of consent (i.e. permission) but also involves the promissory element involving future participatory activity or performance."). But see Randy E. Barnett, Contract is Not Promise; Contract is Consent, 45 SUFFOLK U. L. REV. 647 (2012).

[300] See RESTATEMENT (SECOND) OF CONTRACTS § 24 (AM. LAW INST. 1981) ("An offer is the manifestation of willingness to enter into a bargain, so made as to justify another person in understanding that his assent to that bargain is invited and will conclude it.").

2. Void, Voidable and Illegal Contracts

The distinction between "void" and "voidable" has confused many law students, attorneys and more than a few legislators.[301] One court noted that there are "innumerable cases in which the word 'void' when used in statutes, ordinances, and in a variety of other contexts has been interpreted to mean 'voidable.'"[302] A void contract is a misnomer and not a contract at all (although I will continue to use the term for lack of a suitable alternative). It cannot bind anyone.[303] A voidable contract may be rescinded by the affected party; however, that party may also ratify the contract.[304] A voidable contract typically has legal consequences *until* the power of avoidance is exercised. Only if a party avoids it is the contract void. On the other hand, if the party ratifies it, the power of avoidance is terminated.[305] A void contract may not be ratified and there is no legal remedy for its breach.

The consequences of a contract being void or voidable may be significant to third parties. For example, a void contract cannot be enforced even by an innocent third party, such as a good faith purchaser or assignee. It also affects the burden of proof, as a party seeking to enforce a contract has the burden of establishing its existence, but a party seeking to avoid a contract must bear the burden of proving grounds for avoidance.[306]

The term "unenforceable" only adds to the confusion.[307] The term encompasses a wide variety of contracts. Void contracts are unenforceable but they are not actually contracts at all.[308] Voidable contracts are those which may not be enforced

---

[301]   See Yannuzzi v. Commonwealth, 390 A.2d 311, 332 (Pa. Commw. Ct. 1978) (noting that the word "void" is "not always used with technical precision."); see also Larkin v. Saffarans, 15 F. 147, 152 (W.D. Tenn. 1883) (noting that "what is only voidable is often called void.").

[302]   Yannuzzi, 390 A.2d at 332.

[303]   RESTATEMENT (SECOND) OF CONTRACTS § 7 cmt. a (AM. LAW INST. 1981) (noting that a void contract is "not a contract at all; it is the 'promise' or 'agreement' that is void of legal effect. If the term 'contract' were defined to refer to the acts of the parties without regard to their legal effect, a contract could without inconsistency be referred to as 'void.'"); Guthman v. Moss, 150 Cal. App. 3d 501, 507 (1984) ("A void contract is no contract at all; it binds no one and is a mere nullity.").

[304]   RESTATEMENT (SECOND) OF CONTRACTS § 7 (AM. LAW INST. 1981) ("A voidable contract is one where one or more parties have the power, by a manifestation of election to do so, to avoid the legal relations created by the contract, or by ratification of the contract to extinguish the power of avoidance."); see also Norfolk S. Corp. v. Smith, 414 S.E.2d 485 (1992) (noting that a voidable contract may be ratified); Tsvetana Yvanova v. New Century Mortg. Corp., 62 Cal. 4th 919, 930 (2016) ("Despite its defects, a voidable transaction, unlike a void one, is subject to ratification by the parties.").

[305]   Fumai v. Levy, No. Civ.A. 95-1674, 1998 WL 42297, at *3 (E.D. Pa. Jan. 16, 1998).

[306]   See JOSEPH M. PERILLO, CONTRACTS § 9.22, at 324 (7th ed. 2014).

[307]   Fumai, 1998 WL 42297, at *3 (noting that there is "more than a little confusion" surrounding the terms "void contract," "voidable contract," and "unenforceable contract" and that the "term 'unenforceable contract' is perhaps the source of the most confusion."); Jesse A. Schaefer, *Beyond a Definition: Understanding the Nature of Void and Voidable Contracts*, 33 CAMPBELL L. REV. 193, 193 (2010) (noting that the meanings of "void," "voidable" and "unenforceable" are "persistently and maddeningly slippery.").

[308]   See ARTHUR LINTON CORBIN, CORBIN ON CONTRACTS § 7, at 11 (1952) ("In the term 'void contract,' there is self-contradiction. This is because the term 'contract' is always defined so as to include some element of enforceability.").

if a party exercises her power of avoidance. The Restatement states that voidable contracts "might be defined as one type of unenforceable contract."[309] Yet there are other contracts for which judicial remedies are unavailable but which are neither void nor voidable.[310] These contracts have some effect upon the legal relations of the parties and may be enforceable by non-judicial methods. These "unenforceable" contracts include those subject to the Statute of Frauds or Statute of Limitations.[311] The Restatement (Second) Contracts defines an "unenforceable contract" as "one for the breach of which neither the remedy of damages nor the remedy of specific performance is available, but which is recognized in some other way as creating a duty of performance, though there has been no ratification."[312] Unlike with voidable contracts, these unenforceable contracts create legal consequences other than through ratification.[313] But, as Corbin noted, "there are important differences in the legal relations that are created by the various agreements that are called unenforceable contracts."[314]

To compound the confusion, variations of the same defense may have different effects. Fraud, for example, can render a contract either void or voidable, depending upon the type of fraud. Duress, too, can render a contract either void or voidable depending upon the type of duress visited upon the victim. The broad category of illegal contracts may be unenforceable and/or void or voidable.[315]

Most of the defenses seek to determine whether the conditions of consent have been established to such an extent as to justify enforcement. An analysis of the conditions of consent considers more than the subjective perspective of the consenting party. While consent is typically discussed by courts and commentators as something analogous to the will or desire of the consenting party, it is applied by courts as something that requires a careful balancing of interests and an assessment of both parties' conduct. For example, one of the considerations relevant to determining whether a contract is void or voidable is the policy against forfeitures. The standard remedy for a party seeking to avoid a contract is rescission. A party seeking to rescind a contract must make restitution. A voidable contract then allows a party to return to status quo. A void contract, on the other hand, means there is no contract. A void contract has the potential to harm innocent third parties. Where an agreement is void, courts may grant an equitable remedy even if a legal one is lacking. Restitution may be granted in situations where there is no contract and so

---

[309] RESTATEMENT (SECOND) OF CONTRACTS § 8 cmt. a (AM. LAW INST. 1981)
[310] CORBIN, supra note 308, § 8, at 12–13.
[311] Id.
[312] RESTATEMENT (SECOND) OF CONTRACTS § 8 (AM. LAW INST. 1981).
[313] Id. at cmt. a.
[314] CORBIN, supra note 308, § 8, at 13.
[315] See PERILLO, supra note 307, § 22.1, at 773 ("As a general rule, an illegal bargain is unenforceable and, often, void."); Corbin, supra note 308, § 7, at 12 ("Most bargains that are described as 'illegal' are not wholly void of legal effect; but an agreement by two parties for the doing of acts that both know to be a felony would have no legal operation and be 'void,' although the acts themselves, when performed, would have very important effects indeed.").

nothing to rescind. Even when a statute classifies a contract as void, courts may still grant restitution of benefits conferred if necessary to avoid a forfeiture.[316] Where the party negatively affected by the forfeiture is also the wrongdoer, the courts will consider the relative culpability of the parties and may grant restitution without recognizing a contract. In such cases, they assess whether the harm to the underlying law (which makes the contract illegal) outweighs the harm of forfeiture.

The effect of a claim or defense upon a contract – whether it renders the contract void, voidable or unenforceable – relates to the conditions of consent. An intentional manifestation of consent – one that is made voluntarily and with knowledge that the act communicates consent – creates a presumption that the other conditions have been met. This presumption may be rebutted but requires a balancing of competing interests.

One important factor is the behavior of the party seeking to enforce the contract. A void "contract" essentially means that there was no effective manifestation of consent. Consideration is often evidence of the manifestation of consent. Without consideration, a contract is void. Duress which voids a contract requires physical force (or, in some jurisdictions, threat of imminent physical injury) which shows that the manifestation of consent was not intentional. Accordingly, there is no contract – nor was there ever. A voidable contract means that although there was a manifestation of consent, there was a defect in consent construction. An unenforceable contract that is neither void nor voidable falls outside of consent meaning that the reason for unenforceability has nothing to do with whether there was consent. Rather, some policy – the need for record-keeping, for example – provides the rationale for rendering the contract unenforceable.

While illegal contracts are commonly said to be void, that statement is not entirely correct.[317] The category of "illegal contracts" often leads to confusion because it is imprecise and too broad, capturing contracts which have different legal effects.[318] It includes agreements which are void, voidable or unenforceable as against public policy.[319] The Restatement Second avoids using the term "illegal bargain" and refers

---

[316] See Veridyne Corp. v. United States, 83 Fed. Cl. 575, 586 (2008) ("Forfeiture is an inappropriate remedy for common-law fraud except when a conflict of interest is perpetuated . . . or where an agent of a contractor obtains a contract through a conflict of interest. The case law, properly read, does not support defendant's argument that the appropriate remedy for any contract that is void ab initio is forfeiture of monies already paid or the denial of recovery in quantum meruit or quantum valebat.").

[317] See SAMUEL WILLISTON, A TREATISE ON THE LAW OF CONTRACTS § 12.4 (Richard A. Long ed., 4th ed. 1995) ("It is commonly said that illegal bargains are void. This statement, however, is not entirely correct.").

[318] See Chunlin Leonhard, *Illegal Agreements and the Lesser Evil Principle*, 64 CATH. U. L. REV. 833, 834–35 (2015) (discussing illegal agreements and advocating for explicit adoption of the lesser evil principle to resolve disputes involving illegal agreements).

[319] See CORBIN, supra note 308, § 8, at 12–13 (discussing unenforceable contracts). Contracts which are unenforceable, but which are neither void nor voidable, involve neither the adequacy of a consent condition nor wrongdoing on the part of the party seeking enforcement. Rather, this category of contract is unenforceable either because of external circumstances or requirements outside the

to bargains which are unenforceable on grounds of public policy.[320] The source of the illegality spans a wide spectrum, from felonies to improper licenses. The traditional rule is that an illegal contract is not enforceable[321] and that a court will leave the parties to an illegal contract where it finds them.[322] The reality is more complicated.[323] In assessing the enforceability of an illegal contract, the courts generally consider three important factors: the culpability of the parties, the policy underlying the relevant law, and the risk of forfeiture. If the parties are not in pari delicto, meaning that they are not equally culpable, courts are more inclined to enforce the contract, provided that doing so does not undermine the reason for the law or harm public welfare.[324] The greater the risk of forfeiture and the better the moral standing of the party seeking enforcement, the more likely a court is to find the contract enforceable.[325] Conversely, a party in pari delicto is likely to get little sympathy from the courts even when there is the risk of forfeiture.[326]

Courts consider the effect of designating an illegal contract as void or voidable on innocent third parties.[327] While a statute may designate a particular type of bargain as "void," courts may disregard that designation if policy considerations suggest that the agreement should actually be voidable.[328] On the other hand, they may refuse to enforce a contract which is valid on its face if the party seeking enforcement has engaged in illegal conduct.[329] If the act itself is illegal, the party has no power to

control of either party. Those circumstances may simply be the passage of time which runs afoul of the Statute of Limitations. Another type of external circumstance is a formal requirement, such as the requirement of a writing, which is intended to safeguard consent construction. These unenforceable contracts may still have legal consequences. Because the basis for non-enforceability is not based upon a lack of consent or wrongdoing, these types of unenforceable contracts may be rehabilitated in circumstances where there is no harm to the underlying policy.

[320] RESTATEMENT (SECOND) OF CONTRACTS § 178 (AM. LAW INST. 1981).
[321] Id.
[322] See, e.g., Trees v. Kersey, 56 P.3d 765, 771 (Idaho 2002) ("When a court invokes the illegality doctrine, it denies enforcement of the contract, leaving the parties where it finds them.").
[323] Id. ("Courts on occasion . . . apply an exception to the illegality doctrine where both parties concur in the illegal act, but the parties are not equally at fault by reason of the fact that one party commits fraud, or there is duress, oppression, or undue influence over the other. In such a situation the courts have allowed the less guilty party to recover.") (citations omitted).
[324] Geis v. Colina Del Rio, L.P., 362 S.W.3d 100, 107 (Tex. App. 2011) ("The defense of in pari delicto requires Texas Courts, as a general rule, to decline to enforce illegal contracts when the contracting parties are equally blameworthy.").
[325] U.S. Nursing Corp. v. Saint Joseph Med. Ctr., 39 F.3d 790 (7th Cir. 1994) (noting public policy reasons for determining whether a contract is unenforceable).
[326] Id. at 794.
[327] See Bankers Trust Co. v. Litton Sys., Inc., 599 F.2d 488, 493-94 (2d Cir. 1979) (finding that although defense could be raised against a party engaged in bribery, it could not be raised against a holder in due course). The Second Circuit noted that there was an important distinction between the lease contracts for the photocopiers, which were "not themselves illegal," and the contract to bribe a person in connection with those lease contracts, which was illegal. Id. at 491.
[328] See Williston, supra note 317, at 38–41 ("Statutes may and sometime do make bargains absolutely void, but even though a statute states in its terms that a particular bargain is 'void,' this has often been held to mean 'voidable.'").
[329] Id.

consent to it. If the underlying act is a crime, the reason for its illegality is that it harms third parties, and causing this harm is not within the parties' power. For example, an agreement to steal property and split the profits is not something to which the parties may consent. Although they may reallocate their property rights, they lack the authority to decide what happens to property which is not theirs. If, however, the underlying act is permissible, then the courts assess the conditions of consent, including the relative blameworthiness of the parties, in determining the effect of the illegality.

Contracts involving inconsentable acts are generally deemed void as against public policy. These are acts to which no party may consent; accordingly, no contract may be formed to perform them. But, as the next section explains, inconsentability may often be due to the limitations of contract law, rather than because the acts are irredeemably socially harmful.

B. CONTRACTABILITY AND THE PROBLEM OF TIME

A contract gives parties power they would not otherwise have over each other. Consent legitimizes the contract and contract legitimizes the power of the state over the parties. Consentability defers to the power of an individual and contractability – the power of individuals to consent to a contract – defers to the power of the state. Both consentability and contractability involve the problem of regret. Even if the conditions of consent are met, one may later regret the act. Because human beings are fallible, they will inevitably make bad choices. The government's role is not to eliminate that possibility but to reduce its incidence and magnitude. People should be allowed to make mistakes even at the risk of later regret; it is the price of being human and the gift of living in a free society. It is also the risk undertaken by parties when they enter into a contract.

There is a significant difference, however, between consentability and contractability. The problem of consentability (provided that consent conditions are met) involves a present desire to engage in an act which one may later regret. Regret is speculative; its magnitude and occurrence are uncertain. If the act of consent occurs at approximately the same time as the act to which one is consenting, there is no conflict between the present self and the past self. The future self's interests are affected but the desires of that future self are unknown.

The problem of contractability is altogether different because it involves regret after the moment of formation but before the time for performance. Contract disputes arise when the potential conflict between the desires of the present (now past) self and those of the future (now present) self becomes actualized. Regret is no longer speculative but realized. As Farnsworth notes, "Feeling like a different person may bring relief in one's own mind, but it will not bring relief from one's promises."[330]

---

[330] Farnsworth, supra note 180, at 26.

Anthony Kronman refers to a "different selves" rationale to explain paternalistic restrictions on the ability to contract away too much of one's personal liberty (such as contracts of self-enslavement or antenuptial agreements which waive the right of divorce).[331] He explains that the nature of these types of agreements results in regret and not mere disappointment:

> There is an important difference between regret and disappointment. Disappointment, does not by itself undermine a person's confidence in the rationality of his own choices; regret can and often does.

But the primary difficulty with bodily integrity *contracts* is not that a person suffers regret (which may occur with any type of contract); rather, Kronman suggests, it is with the remedy available for their breach:

> Normally, when a person makes a contract he later comes to regret, he is free to abandon the agreement and simply compensate the other party for his loss … A reminder of this sort may intensify the promisor's regret and make it more difficult for him to forget what now seems like an irrational decision, but this cannot be avoided entirely … If, however, the promisor is required to perform as he had originally agreed – if he is barred from substituting damages for the specific performance of his obligations – his feelings of regret are likely to be intensified … When the promisor's own values have changed dramatically, the compulsory performance of a contract requiring his personal cooperation with the other party may pose a special threat to his integrity or self-respect.[332]

A party to a contract who later changes her mind faces legal consequences. These consequences are typically in the form of monetary damages. In some cases, however, they may take the form of specific performance or an injunction. A contract is a tool of autonomy; it does not, however, substitute for it. In the world of commercial exchanges, contracts are enforceable because the societal interest in ensuring the security of transactions generally outweighs an individual's interest in being able to change her mind regarding the disposition of her property. Undermining the security of transactions essentially destabilizes everyone's contract and thus, *everyone's* interest in being able to control her own property. The collective interest of the members of society in being able to reallocate property rights outweighs the right of any one individual to do the same. The collective interest in the security of transactions tilts the balance toward contract enforcement where there is a conflict between the past self and present self over the disposition of personal property.

But contract law recognizes its limitations when the transaction involves personal services because of the specter of involuntary servitude. As Kaiponanea Matsumura notes, when the contract involves "certain matters of great personal significance,"[333] courts have refused to enforce them on the grounds that they violate public policy.

[331] Anthony Townsend Kronman, *Paternalism and the Law of Contracts*, 92 YALE L.J. 763, 774–85 (1983).

[332] *Id.* at 783–84.

[333] Matsumura, *Binding Future Selves*, supra note 208, at 73.

Even ordinary employment "contracts" are typically terminable at will, provided the parties act in good faith. Even where employment is for a stated duration, courts will not force the parties to continue working together. Instead, courts will order the payment of damages rather than specific performance. The Thirteenth Amendment of the U.S. Constitution reflects the primacy of bodily integrity over the property rights of others by specifically prohibiting involuntary servitude. Private law created by the parties cannot override this constitutional prohibition.

Contract law is best suited for traditional commercial transactions[334] and often lacks the language or the rules to address the unique issues raised by bodily integrity transactions. Bodily integrity contracts do not lack consideration, yet they are not arm's length transactions involving fungible goods. A "sale" of a kidney is not like the sale of a car. Existing contract law defenses prove inadequate to address concerns about forced services. For example, the doctrine of changed circumstances discharges the performance of a party to a contract where an event occurs whose "nonoccurrence" was a "basic assumption" upon which the contract was made, where the event makes performance impracticable or where the party's purpose in entering into the contract is "substantially frustrated" unless the contract or the circumstances indicate otherwise.[335] The doctrine of changed circumstances requires that the party seeking discharge is not at fault for the changed circumstances. With bodily integrity contracts, the change will often be internal to the party seeking discharge, rather than an external event, and the changed circumstances doctrines would not be applicable. The doctrine of unconscionability also proves inadequate for bodily integrity exchanges. These situations do not involve a greedy corporation or businessperson. Instead, the parties are generally both desperate, even if one of them has much more money than the other. While it is not uncommon to characterize the "buyer" in such transactions as exploitative, that characterization is often misleading and unfair. A person who needs a kidney transplant is in no position to bargain for the best deal. A woman or couple seeking an egg donor is also not likely to treat the donor as merely another service provider who can be dismissed at will. On the other hand, the "provider" is someone who is submitting to bodily intrusion in return for money. It is this economic disparity between the buyer and the provider which makes it tempting to categorize the relationship as exploitative. But the relationship is not inherently exploitation (nor is the contract unconscionable) if each party truly needs what the other party has to offer and the terms of the transaction are fair by objective measures. The relationship between the parties in such exchanges resists simplistic labels, as it is often neither exploitative nor entirely voluntary (on either side).

While consent is essential to the exercise of free will and to our conception of autonomy, certain acts fall outside the realm of individual freedoms. While parties

---

[334]   See generally Nathan B. Oman, *The Dignity of Commerce: Markets and the Moral Foundations of Contract Law* (2017).

[335]   RESTATEMENT (SECOND) OF CONTRACTS §§ 261, 265 (AM. LAW INST. 1981).

may craft their own law with a contract the subject matter of the contract must be one that is consentable. It cannot, in other words, have an unlawful objective or one that is against public policy. There are some acts to which courts or lawmakers have determined that parties may not consent and, consequently, some contracts which may not be formed. The parties may intend to enter into a contract, they may mutually agree to the terms, they may do so gladly and willingly – but they will not be able to harness the power of the state to enforce the terms.

Making certain acts consentable is problematic because of the difficulties of enforcing a contract involving those acts. A party may seek to avoid or invalidate a contract on several grounds and courts will do so depending upon the circumstances. Contract law contemplates and addresses exploitation and other consent construction deficiencies. A party who was manipulated or coerced by the other party can avoid the contract. A party who was deceived or misinformed may also escape performance. But contract law does not adequately address situations involving a party's change of heart. Changed circumstances doctrines address only situations caused by supervening events outside the control of the party seeking to be excused. Contract law does not excuse performance where a party experiences an internal change. On the contrary, one of the primary uses of contracts is to ensure that parties perform their obligations even if they no longer want to do so.

Contracts involve consent at two distinct time periods – formation and performance. Given the period of time between formation and performance, the potential for regret is ever-present. As previously noted, human beings tend to be myopic. Their immediate wants loom large and their future needs are obscured. A decision made at an earlier time may prove undesirable or unwise at the time for performance. Cognitive limits and other constraints at the time of the manifestation of consent may mean that, after more careful deliberation, someone may later withdraw consent. In non-contractual settings, such withdrawal typically suffices for future activities; however, in contractual settings, such withdrawal typically does not suffice, a fact which is not surprising since the very purpose of a contract is to ensure future performance.

Yet, contracts are not enforced in every circumstance. A contract means that a private obligation is enforceable by the state. But without consent, the rationale for contract disappears unless there is another societal justification for the commitment of state resources needed for enforcement. In cases involving commercial contracts, that societal justification is ensuring the security of transactions in a credit economy. Accordingly, courts have tended to enforce commercial contracts where the party has at one time consented, even if the party no longer wishes to perform and so *no longer* consents. The passage of time increases the likelihood that there will be a change in circumstances. The more time that passes, the greater the probability of events occurring which may cause an individual to regret an obligation incurred at an earlier time.

The potential for a change of heart due to both internal and external circumstances seems especially likely with bodily integrity transactions. Consenting individuals may be more susceptible to shifting emotions and personal dynamics because these transactions involve matters of an intimate nature. Many bodily integrity transactions don't fit into the two predominant types of contracts – negotiated, arms-length agreements or adhesive form contracts involving relatively minor, mass consumer transactions. It is a failure of contract law that it does not have a language – or rules – to express these non-commercial or not-primarily-commercial transactions. A woman agreeing to serve as a surrogate for another couple may fall in love with someone who wants her to terminate the surrogacy contract. The couple seeking the surrogate's services may fall out of love. The surrogate may move far away to take up a job opportunity, or she may develop an illness. The couple may conceive. Life marches on and bodily integrity transactions, more than commercial ones, are likely to get tangled up in its footsteps.

Contract law has ways to address situations involving exploitation and coercion. The defenses of undue influence, duress and unconscionability address these types of consent deficiencies. Contract law also has ways to address situations involving a basic assumption error or where circumstances arise which are contrary to a factual assumption made by the parties. But contract law has no way to deal with the regretted situation where the changed condition is an internal one. Given the mercurial nature of human emotions and the intimate nature of the expected performance, bodily integrity contracts are generally deemed to be "against public policy" because contract law provides no other alternatives where a party seeks avoidance of a commitment due to a change of heart rather than "changed circumstances."

Another problem with contractability relates to the commodities problem. Contracts are tools for businesses. Margaret Jane Radin describes contract as a "linchpin of the commodified conceptual scheme."[336] Contract law is built on cases dealing primarily with commercial contracts. The purpose of contract law, unlike tort law or criminal law, is to facilitate marketplace transactions. Bodily integrity transactions, however, are not marketplace transactions. The services involved in these transactions are fundamentally more intimate and intrusive than services in other types of transactions. Getting the language right is about more than semantics; it is important in order to accurately describe the interaction, its implications and its consequences. Radin writes:

> Why should discourse matter? .... Why should it matter if someone conceptualizes the entire human universe as one giant bundle of scarce goods subject to free alienation by contract, especially if reasoning in market rhetoric can reach the same result that some other kind of normative reasoning reaches on other grounds? Three answers suggest themselves: it matters because the rhetoric might lead less-than-

[336] RADIN, CONTESTED COMMODITIES, supra note 49.

perfect practitioners to wrong answers in sensitive cases; it matters because the rhetoric itself is insulting or injures personhood regardless of the result; or it matters because there is no such thing as two radically different normative discourses reaching the "same" result.[337]

The language of commodification frames the issues of bodily integrity interactions in terms of sales of goods. As a descriptive matter, it is simply wrong and fails to capture their character. It is misleading to refer to a kidney "sale." Under the Uniform Commercial Code (UCC), sale means the "passing of title from the seller to the buyer for a price."[338] There is no title transferred in bodily integrity transactions. The UCC defines "goods" as "things ... which are movable at the time of identification to the contract" but a kidney is not a "good" or a thing and does not exist independently of the consenting party. The payment of money is not payment for the "thing," but payment to engage in a complex process involving the transfer of the "thing."

The language of commerce offends and misleads. Radin notes that "the way we conceive of things matters to who we are. To conceive of something personal as fungible assumes that the person and the attribute, right, or thing are separate."[339] To conceive of human body parts as fungible goods may ultimately lead to a loosening of regulations which is truly repugnant, or the opposite, the reactionary restoration of prohibitory laws to redress the affront to humanity.

These types of exchanges are not as clean and neat as the term "sale" would imply. A person receiving the kidney is not a "buyer" of a kidney, and the person from whom the kidney is being removed is not the "seller." These transactions are examples of what Margaret Jane Radin refers to as "incomplete commodification," which cannot accurately be described as a "sale of things" because there is "an irreducibly nonmarket or nonmonetized aspect of human interaction going on between seller and recipient, even though a sale is taking place at the same time."[340] Thus, Radin rejects the "clean compartmentalization"[341] of commodification and noncommodification:

> As an alternative to compartmentalization, I think we should recognize a continuum reflecting degrees of commodification that will be appropriate in a given context. An incomplete commodification – a partial market-inalienability – can sometimes reflect the conflicted state of affairs in the way we understand an interaction. And an incomplete commodification can sometimes substitute for a complete noncommodification that might accord with our ideals but cause too much harm in our nonideal world.[342]

---

[337] *Id.* at 84.
[338] U.C.C. § 2-106 (Am. Law Inst. & Unif. Law Comm'n 2002).
[339] See RADIN, CONTESTED COMMODITIES, supra note 49, at 93.
[340] *Id.* at 107.
[341] *Id.* at 106.
[342] *Id.* at 104.

This book tries to avoid use of the term "commodification" and the language of markets altogether because they fail to adequately capture the complexities of bodily integrity exchanges.[343] One cannot simply purchase a kidney the way that one may purchase an item at the grocery store. A kidney transplant is not an off-the-shelf product; nor is it a specially manufactured good. It is more akin to the provision of services than the sale of a good, but even referring to it using the language of services is inappropriate and misleading. The kidney provider is not providing services and would not be liable if the transplant went awry, for example. Rather, an exchange involving the transfer of a body part from one human being to another in order to save the recipient's life is *sui generis*. A kidney transplant is a process that involves multiple relationships, medical and psychological testing and invasive and painful bodily procedures. Bodily integrity exchanges vary in terms of their complexity. In a surrogacy arrangement, for example, the parties may agree to a relationship that is more than a one-shot transaction. They may agree that the surrogate will remain part of the family or that she will participate in certain milestone events.[344]

The rhetoric of commodification and contracts is downright gruesome in the context of remedies in the event of breach. The difficulty posed by enforcement of bodily integrity contracts is compounded by the language of commodification. If a kidney is a "good" and a kidney transfer a "sale," then a breach of a contract involving the transfer might be treated the same way as breaches of other sales contracts. But how to assess damages? The UCC provides a buyer with several possible remedies in the event of a breach by a seller.[345] The buyer can "cover" by buying substitute goods and recover from the seller the difference between the cost of cover and the contract price, along with incidental or consequential damages.[346] The idea of forcing the seller in this situation to pay for cover damages is offensive, even cruel. Given that money may have been the motivating factor, it is unlikely that the seller would have the resources to pay the judgment. The difference is likely to be high. If the buyer does not cover, the buyer can still recover the difference between the contract price and the market price.[347] But what is the market price of a kidney? In both scenarios, the buyer may recover incidental and consequential damages. In the context of bodily integrity exchanges, it would be costly to go through the process of finding another "seller." The medical team would have to

---

343 Certainly, there are scholars and commentators who disagree. See, e.g., DEBORA L. SPAR, THE BABY BUSINESS: HOW MONEY, SCIENCE, AND POLITICS DRIVE THE COMMERCE OF CONCEPTION xv (2006) (arguing that "despite popular protests to the contrary, and despite the heartfelt sentiments of parents and providers, there is a flourishing market for both children and their component parts. Eggs are being sold; sperm is being sold; wombs and genes and orphans are being sold; and many individuals are profiting handsomely in the process.").

344 See, e.g., MARTHA M. ERTMAN, LOVE'S PROMISES: HOW FORMAL AND INFORMAL CONTRACTS SHAPE ALL KINDS OF FAMILIES (2015) (arguing that contracts and "deals" help people shape and sustain their families).

345 U.C.C. § 2-711 (Am. Law Inst. & Unif. Law Comm'n 2002).

346 *Id.* § 2-712.

347 *Id.* § 2-713.

be reserved for another date. The delay might have negative health ramifications for the buyer. Accordingly, the amounts might be large enough to drive the seller into bankruptcy or worse – performance despite consent destruction.

The UCC provides another remedy which might help the buyer in this situation – it is the right of replevin.[348] The buyer may seek specific performance if the goods are "unique" if after "reasonable effort" he is unable to effect cover or the circumstances indicate that such efforts would be "unavailing."[349] This situation is likely to arise with some frequency in breaches of contracts for the sale of commodified body parts. But specific performance would be a gruesome and inhumane remedy, a solution only in a nightmarish, dystopian society and one which would justify banning all bodily integrity contracts.

Given the nature of bodily integrity contracts and the existing remedies for breaches of contract, the seller *should* be allowed to escape the contract if the seller has a change of heart. Unlike commercial contracts, a seller's motivation for seeking avoidance of this type of contract is not to avoid a financial loss. Given the high-level threat to autonomy, there should be no doubt about the willingness of the consenting party to undergo the procedure. Consent should be robust, not just at the time of contract formation, but at the time of performance. Someone who gets cold feet prior to an operation during which his kidney will be surgically removed should not be forced to proceed simply because he entered into a contract. The situation is unlike one where someone changes his mind regarding a decision to enter into a contract to sell chairs, for example. A kidney is not a fungible item, and despite the temptation to use the language of markets, there can never be a market for kidneys that functions the same way as markets for goods (at least not until kidneys are manufactured in a laboratory).

Bodily integrity exchanges raise complicated issues when it comes to remedies for breach.[350] While these types of contracts should be enforceable against the party breaching an obligation to pay, they should not be enforced against the party breaching an obligation to undergo the bodily intrusion. Specific performance should never be granted where the act involves a high-level threat to the autonomy interest. Even an award of damages against someone changing her mind about undergoing an exchange involving bodily intrusion would be unconscionable, since the impetus for entering into the contract was likely economic need. Furthermore, damages would be difficult to assess. The standard measure of recovery for breach of contract is expectation. In the context of bodily integrity exchanges, expectation damages would be difficult to calculate with reasonable certainty.

---

[348] *Id.* § 2-716.
[349] *Id.*
[350] See Matsumura, *Binding Future Selves, supra* note 208, at 91 (stating that "courts' discomfort with available remedies" is a prime concern in determining the enforceability of intimate agreements).

One might argue that, gruesome as it may be, the pricing of body parts and intimate acts has long been a part of our justice system.[351] Plaintiffs have been allowed to recover in tort for loss of limbs, pain and suffering, and loss of consortium. But this argument fails to recognize a fundamental distinction between actions based in tort and those based in contract. A plaintiff in a tort action is suing because the other party has transgressed a social norm (of reasonable behavior) which caused the plaintiff's injury. The basis for the monetary compensation is determined by the jury or the court; not determined by the plaintiff based upon what he has "bargained." The freedom to contract has its limits, and certain provisions exceed the power of the parties. The assessment of damages is one of them. The burden would be too great on courts to assess the value of a kidney, an hour of sexual relations or a baby.

The argument against contract enforcement does not apply to an award of damages against the party breaching an obligation to pay, because the agreed-to performance was monetary, and so readily calculable. Consequently, in order to permit the contractability of bodily integrity exchanges or other high-risk activities, the law must recognize a paradigm shift in contract enforcement. Given the asymmetric nature of what each party is bargaining away, there must be an asymmetry in the available remedy. A party agreeing to an intrusive act such as organ removal is consenting to an act involving a high-level threat to that party's autonomy. The party agreeing to pay for the other party's performance, however, is bargaining to pay money as that party would in a standard commercial transaction.

The model of traditional contracts breaks down when applied to bodily integrity exchanges where the autonomy interests involve something greater than control over property. Contract law as currently conceived adopts a categorical approach that an agreement is either a contract and enforceable, or a non-contract and unenforceable. If an agreement is a contract, the injured party can seek either specific performance or expectation damages. Yet, in the context of bodily integrity exchanges, the traditional approach to remedies is unpalatable as a way to address breaches of contracts.

On the other hand, a prohibition against all bodily integrity contracts is overbroad and unnecessarily restricts individual freedom. If an act is consentable then the parties should be able to make promises and enter contracts which bind them; however, certain accommodations should be made in light of the complex nature of bodily integrity transactions. This does not mean that a contract involving bodily integrity services may *never* be enforced. But mutuality of remedy should not apply. Breach of the contract by the party promising to pay should be subject to expectation

---

[351] Monetary values are routinely placed upon lives and body parts in a variety of contexts, ranging from personal injury lawsuits to insurance claims to human rights violations, but doing so has moral implications. See William Aceves, *Valuing Life: A Human Rights Perspective on the Calculus of Regulation*, 36 L. & INEQ. 1 (2018); Eric A. Posner & Cass R. Sunstein, *Moral Commitments in Cost-Benefit Analysis*, 103 VA. L. REV. 1809 (2017).

damages. If, however, the breaching party is the one expected to perform, expectation damages should not be available. The appropriate remedy for breach of a bodily integrity contract should depend upon the threat level to autonomy posed by enforcement. Expectation damages are readily calculable where the breaching party is the one who promised to pay money. Forcing the breaching buyer to pay what he promised is non-controversial and resembles a standard commercial transaction *because the injured party's expectation interest was mere money.* By contrast, where the breaching party is the one who has agreed to provide services, the damages question is more complicated so that restitution – and not damages – would be the appropriate remedy. The asymmetric or "mismatch" nature of the consideration in these types of transactions leads to a need for mismatch remedies. The range and scope of consentable activities necessitates a paradigm shift in the law governing contracts which, paradoxically, requires very little change to the doctrines themselves. The issue of mismatch remedies is further discussed in Chapter 6.

The dually desperate nature of some exchanges also makes it difficult to treat them like ordinary commercial exchanges. The usual contract remedies and standards, such as reliance and expectation, are inappropriate in a situation involving bodily integrity. For example, a person relying upon a kidney from someone who then changes his mind may have missed an opportunity to receive a kidney from someone else. On the other hand, someone who agreed to the kidney removal should not be forced to submit to the operation simply because he entered an agreement to do so. But, one might argue, shouldn't the provider be made to keep her word, especially if the other party is relying upon it? If transactions are consentable, shouldn't they also be contractable? The answer is a very qualified yes. The transaction may be contractable *provided that* the remedy does not treat these transactions like ordinary commercial transactions.

Contract law does not explicitly distinguish between commercial and non-commercial contracts, but various doctrines safeguard against the consent deficiencies that tend to distinguish non-commercial contracting scenarios. The requirement of consideration guards against contracts entered into too casually or unintentionally. Undue influence and duress guard against the kind of pressure more often wielded by intimates than those bargaining at arm's length. Unconscionability guards against exploitation by employers and monopolistic businesses. Traditional contract doctrine was forged over centuries, yet its principles and rules are remarkably consistent with modern research in the fields of neuroscience and psychology. A blanket rule that bars minors from being legally responsible for their contracts might have seemed overbroad, but modern research on the human brain indicates it was quite wise.[352] The doctrine of consideration counters the natural human tendency to act impulsively, especially when it comes to emotional situations. Promises to make a gift are not enforceable but a completed gift is not recoverable, reflecting both a recognition of the

---

[352] See discussion infra Chapter 5, section E.

endowment effect as well as the need for the security of transactions. Unconscionability and equitable doctrines, such as restitution, recognize the human desire for justice and fairness. In these ways and others, today's research confirms the general wisdom of traditional contract law; it also suggests a need to further refine its applications if contract law's reach is extended beyond the commercial realm. Contract doctrines should accommodate the differences between bodily integrity and commercial contracts. Given the intimate nature of a bodily integrity exchange, the covenant of good faith and fair dealing in the context of a bodily integrity contract should mean the parties must treat each other with mutual respect and in a manner which preserves their human dignity. For example, degrading comments by the consent-seeker about the consenter's body would violate the covenant of good faith and fair dealing.[353]

Although a contract can protect against exploitation, it may also be used to promote it. The concern about economic exploitation is a serious one, particularly in countries where basic human needs are not guaranteed. Controversial exchanges, such as the sale of human organs, cannot be viewed as voluntary where economic necessity threatens survival. The poor suffer many hardships, but governmental and societal structures affect the type of hardship and the level of desperation. Consent is a privilege in that it exists only in societies where basic human needs are being met. The concept of consent does not exist where an individual and her family are starving, or where basic liberties are threatened. "Consent" cannot justify legalizing sex work or the sale of body parts in a country without rule of law or which fails to provide basic human needs, because consent depends upon having alternatives. People without options cannot consent; they submit. There may be utilitarian or welfarist rationales for allowing certain bodily integrity exchanges in these circumstances, but the justification for legalization cannot be based upon autonomy arguments. Where an individual must choose between two actions which both pose a high-level threat to the autonomy interest, the choice should not be viewed as voluntary. There is no real choice if the status quo (the other "option") threatens survival.

---

[353] See Gene Maddaus, *"Flipping Out" Surrogate Mom Sues Bravo Over Filmed Birth*, VARIETY (June 12, 2018), https://variety.com/2018/biz/news/flipping-out-bravo-trent-1202844060/ (discussing lawsuit by surrogate mother against reality television show for filming birth where one of the parents made "disgusting" comments about her vagina which were broadcast on the show).

PART III

The Regret Principle and the Opportunism Corollary: Application

In a free society, the government should respect individual autonomy and restrict very little between two consenting adults. It should, however, ensure that both adults are actually consenting. This book has questioned the traditional conception of consent and referenced the important body of research conducted by social scientists such as Daniel Kahneman and Amos Tversky which challenged a core assumption underlying the free market, that individuals process information appropriately and make rational choices which maximize utility.[354] Research in social psychology and behavioral economics shed light on human cognitive processing and the myriad ways in which it can fail to serve the best interests of the decision-maker. It also revealed that human beings are highly susceptible to social influence, context and pressure.[355] Thus, the foundation upon which much of the thinking about autonomy was based is cracked and crumbling. Individuals do not make decisions in a vacuum; often, they are unable to clearly assess a situation due to blind spots, false assumptions, social influences and other human limitations.

Given the insights garnered from this social science research and the contextual, responsive, and evolving nature of consent, this book has proposed a reconceptualization of consent which requires assessing a variety of factors to determine the robustness of certain conditions which comprise consent. These factors consider the impact of the most common cognitive biases and shortcomings on the consenter. However, my proposed model of relative consent does not require perfect consent conditions; it merely adjusts the requisite robustness of the consent condition depending on what is at stake. Perfect consent is rare, perhaps even unattainable, and hard choices abound in real life. Consent is not a stationary line

---

[354] See discussion, Chapter 1; see also DellaVigna, supra note 29, at 315 (categorizing three ways in which individuals deviated from the standard model of the rational decision-maker: nonstandard preferences, nonstandard beliefs and nonstandard decision-making, and surveyed empirical evidence on these three classes of deviations. Nonstandard preferences included time preferences, risk preferences and social preferences. Nonstandard beliefs included overconfidence and projection bias. Nonstandard decision-making included framing and limited attention, persuasion and social pressure and emotions).

[355] Id.

to be crossed or an all-or-nothing binary proposition; rather, this book argues that valid consent is a sliding scale which depends upon the threat that the consented act poses to autonomy. Perfect consent conditions are not required because perfection is impossible where human beings are involved; yet the greater the potential for harm, the closer to perfection (i.e. the more robust) the consent condition should be.

A relative theory of consent is a reconceptualization of consent that shifts the focus away from the *manifestation* of consent to the conditions of consent. If consent is to mean an expression of individual autonomy, then the criteria used in reaching that conclusion must reflect realistic assumptions about human intent and behaviors, not idealized ones. When the stakes are high and pose a grave threat to autonomy, the conditions of consent must be at their most robust. If they are not, then the rhetoric of consent should not be used to provide either the legal or moral justification for the consent-seeker's actions.

Consent is one of the two determinants of consentability. The other determinant is the social harm of the act relative to its social benefit. This factor might pose the threat of the slippery slope, as it risks becoming a catchall for objections based upon prejudices and personal beliefs. But it need not be if what we understand to be "social harm" is simply "harm to the autonomy interest of others." The "harm to others," captured in the Harm Principle, should not be limited to physical harm. It should also include opportunism, which is already captured in our law in various guises in flexible and contextual standards such as bad faith, reasonableness, intentional wrongdoing, fairness, etc.[356] The Opportunism Corollary underlies the concepts of exploitation, injustice and unfairness. It enforces the rules of fair play which distinguish a civilized and orderly society from a gang of barbarians. Although society should be concerned about sliding down the slippery slope to restricting freedom, it should be equally concerned about tumbling down the other side of that slope and ending up in a place where the brutes and the bullies always win. Fair rules are required to prevent unfair fights. Setting the rules of conduct is not the same thing as dictating what conduct is permissible, and the rhetoric of consent should not be used to justify opportunism.

Technology will continue to push the boundaries of what society thinks is acceptable. In some cases, the changes will be gradual, occurring first on the fringes of society and undetected by the public. The early adopters or practitioners might be cultural rebels or scientists, and their actions will go undetected by mainstream society. In other cases, technology will announce changes much more loudly or visibly. The early adopters will be mainstream members of society or the technology will be part of a corporation's vision. The practice might involve the human body, such as cloning or genetic engineering, or it may affect social relations in a fundamental way, perhaps involving technology such as augmented reality or

---

[356] *See* Oren Bar-Gill & Omri Ben-Shahar, *An Information Theory of Willful Breach*, 107 MICH. L. REV. 1479, 1481 (2009) (noting two views of willful breach: "one that deems fault to be irrelevant and another that attaches harsher consequences to different types of willful, blameworthy breach").

artificial intelligence. Sometimes, the changes will go undetected because they are not visible or obvious to most people. As Lori Andrews observed in the context of genetics policy, "When technologies are introduced incrementally and policies are adopted in small units to deal with a few isolated issues, there is less opportunity to stimulate a social debate about whether we are moving in a direction in which we wish to go."[357] Companies, skilled in the art of marketing and sales, may try to manipulate the public and intimidate lawmakers into accepting products and services which degrade, rather than enhance, social relations. Legislators will be indifferent or reluctant to act until there is some sort of social outcry or the impact on society is too great to ignore.[358] The law will arrive too late, after social norms have already been established and when it is much more difficult to reverse society's course.

The consistency of a framework helps resist the distortions of self-interested marketers and lobbyists, who too often use the rhetoric of consent and consumer choice to justify their opportunistic conduct. For example, a company that creates a product that records a person's conversations and collects images and sends them to third-party marketers should not be able to justify those actions by claiming that its customers consented by clicking "agree" to the company's terms and conditions. The threat to autonomy posed by such products requires much more robust consent conditions. By contrast, a simple click may be sufficient to constitute consent to the business's description of services or scope of license, as these terms do not diminish or affect the consenter's autonomy in any significant way.

Valid consent depends upon the robustness of the conditions of consent in relation to the potential threat that the activity poses to personal autonomy. "But if someone consents, why should anyone care?" is a plaint too often raised in response to an act of perceived paternalism. As the hard cases demonstrate, the question is inapt because it presupposes that there was, in fact, consent. The consentability framework looks beyond the *manifestation* – the spoken word Yes, the click of an "agree" icon, the passive acquiescence – to determine whether the activity promotes or diminishes autonomy and whether the consent conditions are sufficiently robust in light of the nature of the activity. Chapter 5 addresses the first guiding principle of the consentability framework, the Regret Principle, and suggests some ways to improve the conditions of consent. Chapter 6 addresses the second guiding principle of the consentability framework, the Opportunism Corollary, and suggests ways to reduce opportunism. Because the particulars of each proposal depend upon the specific activity involved, the proposals are broad. These proposals are not intended to be exhaustive or definite. They are merely starting points in discussions of how to enhance consent, prevent regrettable decisions and reduce opportunism. These proposals might be implemented by a central governing authority or by more local

---

[357] ANDREWS, FUTURE PERFECT, *supra* note 152, at 17.
[358] For example, this is happening in the area of personal data and online privacy.

governing authorities which may be more responsive to community needs.[359] All of them should prompt an individual to think about the impact of, and the influences affecting, an important, personal decision. Chapter 7 revisits the hard cases and explains how the proposals in Chapters 5 and 6 might affect consentability.

---

[359]   Elinor Ostrom, writing about the advantages of decentralized governing systems, explained: "[w]hen only a single governing authority makes decisions about rules for an entire region, policymakers have to experiment simultaneously with *all* of the common-pool resources within a jurisdiction with each policy change. And, once a change has been made and implemented, further changes will not be made rapidly." Elinor Ostrom, *Polycentricity, Complexity and the Common*, 9 Good Soc'y 37, 37 (1999).

5

Improving the Conditions of Consent

Research in the past sixty years has revealed that human beings are prone to heuristics and biases, have difficulty assessing very complex information, make impulsive or ill-considered choices under time constraints, and are manipulable and subject to social pressures. These human fallibilities impair decision-making and may lead to regretted actions which impair future autonomy.[360] But it is not just human cognitive limitations which make certain acts inconsentable; it is also the nature of information itself. Information is limited yet boundless, in the sense that additional or different information can be later acquired which may change existing knowledge. A person might have all available information at the time a decision is made, but new information or changed circumstances may alter the effect of the original information.

Imperfect and dynamic information is only part of what constrains optimal decision-making. The other part is voluntariness. Even if we had perfect information, with the ability to process it like a computer, our social and economic circumstances would create limitations. The robustness of the voluntariness condition depends upon the availability of alternatives. The choice between a rock and a hard place is not much of a choice at all.

Consentability of a risky activity is advisable only where it is likely that the conditions of consent will be properly constructed in light of the gravity of the consequences resulting from the risky activity. Regrettable decisions are the byproduct of constraints on human cognition and the limits imposed by socio-economic conditions. As imperfect humans in an imperfect and unfair world, we can expect some degree of regret over our past decisions. But sometimes the level of regret is so profound that the decision should never have been made.

A. A MORE DEFINITE MANIFESTATION OF CONSENT

One way to strengthen consent is to require more deliberate, unambiguous and intentional manifestations of consent. The requisite manifestation(s) should depend upon the consented-to act. For example, a click on an "accept" icon may be all that

[360] *See* discussion *supra*, Chapter 3.

is required for certain acts, but not for others. Users might be asked to consent to a social network's terms of service which prohibit harassing other users by clicking "accept." On the other hand, a single click should not suffice to transfer the copyright to users' content from the users to the website. Similarly, while a signature at the end of a contract should be sufficient to manifest consent to a transaction involving the purchase and sale of commercial goods, it should not suffice to manifest consent to a bodily integrity contract where the consenter agrees to transfer his kidney. The law already requires stronger manifestations of consent for certain activities. Certain provisions in agreements, such as waivers of rights, for example, often need to be separately signed or drafted in a particular way.[361]

Consent to participate in an activity where the participant lacks knowledge about what the activity entails *cannot* be valid consent to that activity. Because the knowledge condition is absent or deficient, consent to the unknown can only mean consent to proceed, not consent to the non-specifically disclosed consequences. Where the consented-to activity is progressive and novel, or involves bodily integrity, the consenting party should confirm consent as the activity progresses. This confirmation might be in the form of multiple staged manifestations of consent, depending upon the nature of the consented-to activity.

Some laws already reflect the idea of progressive and specific consent, most notably in the area of sexual activity. For example, the idea of progressive consent underlies California's affirmative consent law, which has been misrepresented (and unfairly ridiculed) by popular media. In fact, the law captures the essence of consent by stating that "affirmative consent" means "affirmative, conscious and voluntary agreement to engage in sexual activity [which] must be ongoing throughout a sexual activity and can be revoked at any time."[362] The California law also captures the concept of relative consent and blameworthiness, stating that "[i]t is the responsibility of each person involved in the sexual activity to ensure that he or she has the affirmative consent of the other or others to engage in the sexual activity."[363] The affirmative consent law recognizes that consent to one type of physical contact (such as kissing) does not mean consent to any other type of physical contact (sexual intercourse). The more intrusive the activity, the greater the threat to bodily integrity, and the more definite should be the manifestation of consent. Consent should not be presumed to the progression of an activity. On the other hand, consent which has been granted to an activity which is ongoing is presumed to continue for the

---

[361] See, e.g., CAL. CIV. CODE § 1542 (Deering, LEXIS through 2018 Reg. Sess.) ("general release does not extend to claims which the creditor does not know or suspect to exist in his or her favor at the time of executing the release, which if known by him or her must have materially affected his or her settlement with the debtor."); see also U.C.C. § 2–209(2) (AM. LAW INST. & UNIF. LAW COMM'N 2002) ("A signed agreement which excluded modification or rescission except by a signed writing cannot be otherwise modified or rescinded, but except as between merchants such a requirement on a form supplied by the merchant must be separately signed by the other party.").

[362] Id.

[363] Id.

duration of that activity *unless* the consenter communicates (verbally or non-verbally) that consent is being withdrawn. Although it is the responsibility of the consenter to indicate that the consenter wishes to cease an ongoing activity, the consent-seeker has the responsibility to ensure that there is continued consent. This means that the consent-seeker should be attentive and receptive to signs that consent is being withdrawn; it also means that the consent-seeker should verify that the consenter is able to communicate a desire to withdraw consent (and is not fearful of doing so).

The need for staged manifestations of consent for progressive activities and the need for shared responsibility for continued consent to ongoing activities (i.e. the consenter's responsibility to communicate consent withdrawal and the consent-seeker's responsibility to ensure continued consent) are highlighted by "rough sex" defenses by men who have harmed or killed women during allegedly consensual sexual activity.[364] According to the man, the death or injury was accidental, even though the act that led to it was intentional. Regardless of whether the woman initially consented to sadomasochistic activity, he should have ensured that she *continued* to consent (and had the ability to do so) as the activity progressed, rather than assuming that her initial consent meant continued consent to escalating harm. The burden on the consent-seeker in this situation is slight and impedes freedom very little, and the potential harm to the consenter's autonomy is so great, that there should be no excuse for failure to obtain additional manifestations of consent and to ensure continued consent.

B. STRENGTHENING THE KNOWLEDGE CONDITION

A relative consent approach requires evaluating capacity and information in light of the *motive* of the consenting party and the actions of the *other party*. The other party may provide misinformation or may conceal information. In some cases, the other party may have an affirmative obligation to provide the consenting party with information. The extent of the other party's responsibility for the information depends upon the type of activity to which the party is consenting. The greater the threat to the consenting party's autonomy,[365] the higher the standard for the consent-seeker's conduct. Acts that affect the bodily integrity of the consenting party and which are painful and irreversible require the party seeking consent to affirmatively provide all material information. Acts that involve property transfers, on the other hand, typically require only that the consent-seeker be honest and refrain from concealing information.

The knowledge condition requires that the consenting party have access to accurate, adequate and relevant information. The information provided must be

---

[364] *See* George E. Buzash, Comment, *The "Rough Sex" Defense*, 80 J. CRIM. L. & CRIMINOLOGY 557 (1989) (providing an overview of the legal issues associated with "rough sex" as a defense in criminal prosecutions).

[365] A hierarchy of autonomy interests is provided in Chapter 3 section B.

evidence-based and relevant to the risks associated with the activity; it should not be motivated by the consent-seeker's own personal or political views. In some cases, too much information may lead to unnecessary mental anguish, without helping the consenter make a better decision. Too much information is counterproductive because complexity inhibits understanding. In the context of informed consent to medical procedures, some courts have recognized that excessive disclosure of remote risks may frighten a patient and negatively affect her ability to make sound decisions.[366] The human capacity for processing multiple items or cumulative risks is limited. Too much information may result in overload and an inability to process the information.[367] It may also obscure material information and lead to worse outcomes.

Access to information is not enough to satisfy the knowledge condition. The consenting party must have access to the information in a form and at a time which helps that party *understand* material and relevant information and the consequences of consent. The presentation of the information must take into account the realities of how humans make decisions in given contexts, instead of presupposing a rational actor making decisions under ideal circumstances (unlimited time, sufficient resources, technical or specialized knowledge of the subject matter, detached emotional state).

This section is not intended to provide a comprehensive set of disclosure strategies, nor is it suggested that sophisticated and costly strategies to enhance the knowledge condition must be adopted in every situation where consent is sought. Disclosure alone is inadequate and often ineffective.[368] However, the fact that disclosure can often be ineffective does not mean that consent-seekers should be absolved of responsibility for disclosure; doing so would only reward them for their half-hearted, lackluster efforts. Successful businesses know how to reach consumers – they employ battalions of marketers, spend vast amounts of money, hire focus groups and advertise the appeal of their products and services through various methods, such as limited time offers and special promotions. Companies whose businesses pose a high risk to the autonomy interest of their customers – doctors performing cosmetic surgeries, brothels, hospitals involved in organ transfers, companies engaged in space travel, and intermediaries in bodily integrity transactions – should be expected to expend reasonable efforts to communicate relevant information to prospective consenters. While the extent of disclosure efforts will depend

---

[366] *See, e.g.*, Cobbs v. Grant, 8 Cal. 3d 229, 246 (1972) (noting that disclosure of risks may "seriously upset" the patient, and affecting the ability to weight the risks of undergoing treatment); Moore v. Regents of Univ. of California, 51 Cal. 3d 120, 131 (1990) (acknowledging that disclosure "may corrupt the patient's own judgment by distracting him from the requirements of his health.").

[367] Naresh K. Malhotra, *Information Load and Consumer Decision Making*, 8 J. CONSUMER RES. 419, 427 (1982) (finding "dysfunctional effects of information overload" when consumers were provided with ten or more alternatives, or information on fifteen or more attributes).

[368] *See generally* OMRI BEN SHAHAR & CARL E. SCHNEIDER, MORE THAN YOU WANTED TO KNOW: THE FAILURE OF MANDATED DISCLOSURE (2014).

upon the resources available to the business, even the smallest companies can create a questionnaire which tests the consenter's understanding of the activity for which consent is sought. Reviewing the results of the questionnaire would also reinforce important but overlooked aspects of the procedure.

Given the limits of human cognition and human susceptibility to manipulation and distraction, valid consent requires more than merely making relevant information available. Information must be presented in a way that enhances knowledge, thus it must be both understandable and salient. Too often, disclosure has been interpreted as coverage of information, a way to protect against legal liability rather than as an *effective means of communication*. Technical disclosure is rarely effective without a corresponding consideration of the audience and the method of disclosure. How the information is disclosed is just as important as what is disclosed. Most people will not read pages of fine print; this is especially true if doing so is unlikely to expand their choices or alter the outcome (i.e. if they lack bargaining power).

The requirement of disclosure should not be deemed satisfied simply because information was provided; information must be presented in a way that is understandable to the layperson. Furthermore, too much information may reduce comprehension, so efforts should be made to convey only information relevant and material to the consenter.[369] In one study, Stanford undergraduate students were given a long and a short consent form, adapted from a standard consent form for an MRI scan.[370] The short consent form had the detail and redundancy of the long form deleted. The researcher found that subjects who received the short form answered more of the specific questions regarding the MRI procedure than those who had received the long consent form.[371] Of greater concern, however, was that *all* the fifty-three subjects (those who received the long form and those who received the short form) failed to understand important information contained in the forms. In fact, the subjects answered only 60 percent of the specific questions correctly, leading the researcher to conclude that "subjects in this experiment did not give a valid consent," despite signing the consent form.[372]

The format and style in which the information is presented should also be considered. Important information and information which is relevant to the particular individual making the decision should be presented first. Information should be presented in a way that is easy for the recipient of the information to process. People are more likely to read short text in large font which is visually textured or

[369] *See* Lisa A. Robinson, W. Kip Viscusi & Richard Zeckhauser, *Consumer Warning Labels Aren't Working*, Harv. Bus. Rev. (Nov. 30, 2016), https://hbr.org/2016/11/consumer-warning-labels-arent-working (noting that the current "cluttered system of warnings" fails to distinguish between major and minor risks, and thus fails to empower people to make informed decisions).

[370] Traci Mann, *Informed Consent for Psychological Research: Do Subjects Comprehend Consent Forms and Understand Their Legal Rights?* 5 Psychol. Sci. 140 (1994).

[371] *Id.* at 141.

[372] *Id.* at 142.

interesting, than multiple pages of fine print.[373] Processability is a critical factor in comprehension and refers to both the physical (stylistic) presentation of the information as well as the substantive presentation. Disclosure requirements should incorporate research on how best to convey information.[374] Extensive research demonstrates that the same information presented in different formats affects consumer understanding in different ways.[375] Studies testing nutrition label formats show that the type of information and the way it is presented on the label affects subjects' comprehension and preference.[376] Warning icons have been proven effective at deterring consumers from buying junk food, while information regarding daily intake recommendations of sugar, salt and fat have not, presumably because the message is presented in a more complex manner.[377] Format changes to information on residential energy use were shown to produce more efficient consumer choices.[378]

Consumers respond differently to verbal or textual advertising stimuli than they do to visual advertising stimuli.[379] As Baruch Fischhoff and Julie Downs state:

[373]   Thomas D. Barton, Gerlinde Berger-Walliser & Helena Haapio, *Visualization: Seeing Contracts for What They Are, And What They Could Become*, 19 J. L. Bus. & Ethics 47 (2013) (explaining how visual strategies may better raise awareness of contract terms and improve commercial relationships); Nathaniel S. Good, Jens Grossklags, Deirdre K. Mulligan, & Joseph A. Konstan, *Noticing Notice: A Large-Scale Experiment on the Timing of Software License Agreements*, Sch. Info.: U. Cal. Berkeley (2007), http://people.ischool.berkeley.edu/~jensg/research/paper/Grossklagso7-CHI-noticing_notice.pdf (demonstrating that short notices were effective at informing users about spyware); Matthew Kay & Matthew Terry, *Textured Agreements: Re-envisioning Electronic Consent* (July 2010), www.mjskay.com/papers/soups_2010_textured.pdf (last visited Mar. 24, 2018) (a paper presented to the Symposium on Usable Privacy and Security (SOUPS) showing how the use of text bubbles and visual images captures user interest and attention).

[374]   *See* James R. Bettman, John W. Payne & Richard Staelin, *Cognitive Considerations in Designing Effective Labels for Presenting Risk Information*, 5 J. Pub. Pol'y & Marketing 1, 2 (1986) (noting that while "bounded rationality does not necessarily reduce the need for information provision programs, it does increase the need to be careful in designing programs to inform people about risks.").

[375]   *See id.* at 14 (noting that "particular formats and methods for organizing information can greatly influence the ease with which various types of processing can be carried out.").

[376]   Alan S. Levy, Sara B. Fein & Raymond E. Schucker, *Performance Characteristics of Seven Nutrition Label Formats*, 15 J. Pub. Pol'y & Marketing 1, 10 (1996) (noting that format features such as "summary indicators of nutrient levels" and "use of a common metric for quantitative information" had the "greatest impact"); Scot Burton, Abhijit Biswas & Richard Netemeyer, *Effects of Alternative Nutrition Label Formats and Nutrition Reference Information on Consumer Perceptions, Comprehension and Product Evaluations*, 13 J. Pub. Pol'y & Marketing 36, 44 (1994) ("Label format and inclusion of reference value information appear to have effects on consumer perceptions and evaluations.").

[377]   Azam Ahmed, Matt Richtel & Andrew Jacobs, *U.S. Objects to Warnings on Junk Food*, N.Y. Times (March 21, 2018), www.nytimes.com/2018/03/20/world/americas/nafta-food-labels-obesity.html.

[378]   *See* Wesley A. Magat, John W. Payne & Peter F. Brucato, Jr., *How Important is Information Format? An Experimental Study of Home Energy Audit Programs*, 6 J. Pol'y Analysis & Mgmt. 20 (1986).

[379]   Elizabeth C. Hirschman, *The Effect of Verbal and Pictorial Advertising Stimuli on Aesthetic, Utilitarian, and Familiarity Perceptions*, 15 J. Advert. 27, 33 (1986) (noting that the use of text "should act to create a perception of heightened rationality and factualness" and visual depictions were more likely to "provide the consumer with a perception of greater familiarity with the product than if s/he were confronted with the same information in a printed format.").

The value of information is situation dependent. An important fact in one context can be entirely irrelevant in another. Consider, for example, the information needs of an individual when betting in a March Madness pool and when contemplating elective surgery, or when considering the surgery with and without coverage by health insurance. As a result of such differing information needs, interventions must consider the particulars of specific decisions. The design of such interventions should benefit from the knowledge of both specialists in the domain and specialists in decision-making.[380]

The purpose of disclosure is to provide information that is relevant to the disclosees to "help them achieve whatever goals they themselves happen to have."[381] In contract law, this objective is framed as fulfilling the intent of the parties. The level of engagement required to ascertain intent depends upon the nature of the transaction and the threat level to autonomy. Too much information may impede, rather than enhance, the knowledge condition. For example, in an arm's-length commercial transaction, there is no affirmative duty to disclose but the parties should not conceal information. In transactions involving a higher level of threat to the autonomy interest, more affirmative and effective disclosure is required. A physician seeking consent to surgery, for example, should inform the patient of potential risks and benefits of the procedure. She should also provide information about alternative treatments. The physician should not merely provide answers to questions; she should seek to find out the patient's motive in undergoing the procedure by asking the patient questions. What does the patient expect as a result of undergoing the procedure? What is the likelihood of these anticipated outcomes – and what are the risks that might diminish the value of the patient's expected outcomes?

The recipient of information should be able to understand risks in their appropriate context but this is not likely when the information requires specialized knowledge.[382] Complex information should be simplified with images or a combination of text and images which convey a message clearly. The objective is to ensure that the consenting party deliberates before undertaking an action which might have harmful long-term effects on autonomy. Consent to actions involving high-level threats to autonomy, such as participation in the first trip to Mars or involvement in an experimental drug trial with a risk of substantial bodily injury,

---

[380]   Baruch Fischhoff & Julie Downs, *Accentuate the Relevant*, 8 PSYCHOL. SCI. 154 (1997).

[381]   *Id.* at 157.

[382]   *See* Kenneth Boyd, *The Impossibility of Informed Consent*, 41 J. MED. ETHICS 44 (2015) (discussing the complex issues, and shortcomings, associated with informed consent); *see also* Marc Ginsberg, *Informed Consent: No Longer Just What the Doctor Ordered? The Contributions of Medical Associations and Courts to a More Patient Friendly Doctrine*, 15 MICH. ST. U. J. MED. & L. 17 (2010); Nadia N. Sawicki, *Modernizing Informed Consent: Expanding the Boundaries of Materiality*, 2016 U. ILL. L. REV., no. 3, 821 (2016). Some commentators question whether informed consent to medical procedures is even possible, especially where the patient is not medically trained. *See generally* Boyd, *supra* (summarizing various debates surrounding informed consent, including whether it was possible for most patients).

requires a robust knowledge condition which, in turn, requires evidence of effective disclosure. Companies and institutions seeking participants for activities involving a high threat to autonomy should have proof that the participants understood the relevant information, not simply that the information was disclosed. Given the vast research on how humans process information and assess risk,[383] it should be insufficient for a company or institution seeking consent to acts which may result in serious bodily injury to merely provide information; they should have the burden of proving that the information was also *understood* by the participant. In situations involving non-therapeutic procedures, it might help to counter emotionalism with emotionalism. Imagery which evokes a visceral response may enhance the salience of risks which might be overshadowed by optimism bias or the visceral desires or emotionalism of an activity. For example, images of what may go wrong on a Mars expedition might counter the heroic images of returning astronauts held by the consenter. Photos of cosmetically enhanced patients could show both the best- and worst-case scenarios. However, where the individual's choice is constrained (such as in medically necessary procedures), showing negative images might only exacerbate faulty and irrational decision-making and should be avoided.

Disclosure alone may not result in different or better decisions. One study measured the effectiveness of salient credit card disclosures and found that it had little to no change on consumer behavior and the reduction of consumer debt.[384] As Omri Ben-Shahar notes, the problem is often not that there is insufficient disclosure, it is a lack of available options:

> More fundamentally, the failure of the smart disclosure reminds us that the problem for most indebted consumers is not information. People know intuitively when they borrow too much, even if they cannot quantify this intuition. The problem for low-income borrowers is, well, ... poverty. They borrow to pay towards urgent needs ... mandated disclosure – including the most methodologically sound version – is not a panacea.[385]

Where consumers have few alternatives, even information which is salient and prominently disclosed will have little effect on behavior.

But the failure of some types of disclosure to affect certain behavior in some cases where individuals lack options does not mean that disclosure is ineffective in all situations or that it is futile to try to improve disclosure mechanisms. Where the consenter has viable alternatives, disclosure may prevent people from making bad

---

[383] See LEVITIN, *supra* note 157, at 219–67 (noting the obstacles to accurately assessing risk).

[384] See Enrique Seira, Alan Elizondo & Eduardo Laguna-Müggenburg, *Are Information Disclosures Effective? Evidence from the Credit Card Market*, 9 AM. ECON. J.: ECON. POL'Y 227 (2017).

[385] Omri Ben-Shahar, *More Failed Nudges: Evidence of Ineffective "Behaviorally Informed" Disclosures*, JOTWELL (Aug. 10, 2017), https://contracts.jotwell.com/more-failed-nudges-evidence-of-ineffective-behaviorally-informed-disclosures/ (reviewing Enrique Seira, Alan Elizondo & Eduardo Laguna-Müggenburg, *Are Information Disclosures Effective? Evidence from the Credit Card Market*, 9 AM. ECON. J. ECON. POL'Y 277 (2017)).

choices due to the lack of information. For example, consumers may be less likely to take out a credit card with a high interest rate if they are able to take out a credit card with a lower interest rate. It may also prevent some consumers from being seduced by the attractive features of the card (e.g. rewards program) while ignoring the unattractive features of the card (high interest rates and annual membership fee). It may turn out that textual disclosures are generally ineffective because the mathematical calculations are too complex for the average consumer but that certain images or other visual disclosures are effective. Warning icons, such as stoplight signals, hazard signs or symbols, may be more effective at conveying a message than fine print.[386]

Disclosures may be more effective at changing behaviors of only some groups of people. One type of disclosure may reach one group but leave another one unaffected, depending upon the style, the method of delivery or the language. The fact that some disclosures may not change negative behavior for all groups of people does not mean that all disclosures are ineffective for all groups of people. But even assuming, for the sake of argument, that salient disclosure fails to change behavior (an assumption belied by the available literature), this does not mean that disclosure has failed or is irrelevant. The purpose of disclosure is *not simply or solely to change behavior; the purpose of disclosure is to inform.*[387] Salient disclosures enhance knowledge. Knowledge is an essential component of consent. That salient disclosures may fail to alter behavior (at least in some situations) does not make them irrelevant to establishing consent. Consequently, where consent is required, effective disclosure is a necessity.

C. THE VOLUNTARINESS CONDITION AND EXTERNAL FACTORS

Salient disclosures may create a robust knowledge condition but are not enough to establish valid consent. Consent also requires the condition of voluntariness. The conditions of knowledge and voluntariness are often interrelated but they are not the same. If, for example, a patient is not informed of available alternatives to treatment, disclosure is ineffective (the knowledge condition is deficient), and consent is defective. If there are no available alternatives, the condition of voluntariness is deficient. In a situation where someone has the option only to "take it or leave it," the provision of more information may do little to alter behavior if there are no available options. While the consent-seeker may not be physically forcing the individual to *take it*, the option of *leave it* may not be a realistic one.

---

[386] *See* Kim, Wrap Contracts, *supra* note 280 ("Given that websites are visually oriented, a drafter should use images to encourage visitors to read legal terms" such as warning and danger icons); *see also* Ian Ayres & Alan Schwartz, *The No-Reading Problem in Consumer Contract Law*, 66 Stan. L. Rev. 545, 553 (2014) (arguing that consumer protection law should focus on disclosing unexpected, unfavorable terms in a "warning box" with a standardized border).

[387] Disclosure may also help keep opportunism in check, as discussed in Chapter 6.

The lack of reasonable alternatives indicates a diminished condition of voluntariness. In situations which require that the condition of voluntariness be robust (i.e. where the threat to the autonomy interest is high), a lack of reasonable alternatives may mean consent has not been properly constructed. The condition of voluntariness may be difficult to ascertain, given the susceptibility of humans to pressure from others. On one end of the spectrum is physical force. An individual who is physically forced to manifest consent is not consenting voluntarily, nor is a person who experiences an automated or reflexive bodily response, such as a sneeze. An individual who is threatened with physical violence is also not consenting voluntarily. In addition to physical force, bodily reflexes and threats of physical force, there is a range of circumstances which diminish or degrade the condition of voluntariness.

For example, a Wisconsin-based technology company, Three Square Market, offered to have microchips implanted in its employees which would permit them to open office doors and pay for food with a swipe of a hand.[388] The employees were not required to accept the offer, but more than forty-one out of eighty-five of them did.[389] The company had its employees implanted at a "chip party" held at company headquarters.[390] Although the company did not force its employees to get microchipped, simply making the offer could exert pressure on its employees. The culture of the technology company might be such that a non-participating employee would be perceived as a technophobe, and not a good "fit." The vocal enthusiasm of the chief executive (who stated that he, his wife and two sons were all going to be microchipped)[391] could have influenced employees wishing to please and impress their boss with their willingness to support his initiative. The employee/employer relationship, the technology-oriented company culture, and the enthusiasm of peers and supervisors create the type of social pressure which might have made it difficult for an employee to refuse. A vice-president at the company expressed her initial apprehension, stating, "I planned for the worst and it wasn't bad at all."[392] Her statement doesn't demonstrate eagerness so much as relief at not having a worse outcome.

The condition of voluntariness implicates the consenting party's agency. Consent is an expression of autonomy only if the consenting party is expressing his or her own will. Many factors might influence a person into acting against her true desires,

---

[388]   Maggie Astor, *Microchip Implants for Employees? One Company Says Yes*, N.Y. Times (July 25, 2017), www.nytimes.com/2017/07/25/technology/microchips-wisconsin-company-employees.html.

[389]   Jeff Baenen, *Wisconsin Company Holds "Chip Party" to Microchip Workers*, Chi. Trib. (Aug. 2, 2017), www.chicagotribune.com/bluesky/technology/ct-wisconsin-company-microchips-workers-20170801-story.html.

[390]   *Id.; see also* A.J. Dellinger, *Majority of Three Square Market Employees "Excited" to Insert Biochip in Hand*, Int'l Bus. Times (July 26, 2017), www.ibtimes.com/majority-three-square-market-employees-excited-insert-biochip-hand-2570669.

[391]   *See* Astor, *supra* note 388.

[392]   *See* Baenen, *supra* note 389.

including social pressure.[393] The relational nature of consent in most situations means that the behavior of the other party is often the most relevant influential factor. I propose there are three principles which should be considered in assessing the voluntariness conditions.

The first principle is that the voluntariness condition varies depending upon the behavior of the consent-seeker. The consenter may lack agency even when the other party is not using physical force. Someone being manipulated or emotionally coerced by another to manifest consent is not acting voluntarily. Contract law recognizes the way that choice affects voluntariness in the definition of duress, which is defined by the Restatement as "an improper threat" which leaves a person with "no reasonable alternative."[394] The "no reasonable alternative" means that the voluntariness condition is weak, but whether it is so weak that it is deficient depends upon whether the consent-seeker's behavior warranted disregarding his interests. Generally, if the consent-seeker was responsible for the consenter's tough situation (i.e. the consent-seeker made an improper threat), the voluntariness condition will be considered deficient.

The second principle is that the consent-seeker has a duty of reasonable care.[395] This is a general societal rule, part of our social contract, and an integral part of tort law. In the context of voluntariness, it means that the consent-seeker should not take unfair advantage or manipulate the consenter in a way that would cause the consenter harm. It differs from the first rule in that it applies even where the consent-seeker is not responsible for the tough situation of the consenting party. While this rule is based in tort law, the general concept is also captured in contract doctrines, such as the doctrine of unconscionability and unilateral mistake, where the consent-seeker has taken advantage of a vulnerability or weakness of the consenting party but was not responsible for creating that vulnerability or weakness.[396]

The third principle is that, if the motive for the "consent" is to escape a harm which poses a high-level threat to autonomy to oneself or to a third party, then the

---

[393] *See generally* JONAH BERGER, INVISIBLE INFLUENCE: THE HIDDEN FORCES THAT SHAPE BEHAVIOR (2016) (discussing research, including Muzafer Sherif and Solomon Asch's studies, which shows how social pressure affects judgment and behavior); *see also* LEE ROSS & RICHARD E. NJISBETT, THE PERSON AND THE SITUATION: PERSPECTIVES OF SOCIAL PSYCHOLOGY (2011) (discussing various studies which explore how situational determinants affect human behavior).

[394] RESTATEMENT (SECOND) OF CONTRACTS § 175 (AM. LAW INST. 1981).

[395] RESTATEMENT (THIRD) OF TORTS: LIABILITY FOR PHYSICAL AND EMOTIONAL HARM § 3 (AM. LAW INST. 2010) ("A person acts negligently if the person does not exercise reasonable care under all the circumstances. Primary factors to consider in ascertaining whether the person's conduct lacks reasonable care are the foreseeable likelihood that the person's conduct will result in harm, the foreseeable severity of any harm that may ensue, and the burden of precautions to eliminate or reduce the risk of harm."); *see also* RESTATEMENT (THIRD) OF TORTS: LIABILITY FOR PHYSICAL AND EMOTIONAL HARM § 7(a) (AM. LAW INST. 2010) ("An actor ordinarily has a duty to exercise reasonable care when the actor's conduct creates a risk of physical harm.").

[396] *See* Kim, *Relative Consent, supra* note 6, at 205–10.

voluntariness condition is deficient. In this case, consent has not been properly constructed; it is defective.

Defective consent is the purgatory between valid consent and no-consent. In the world of defective consent, consent's magic is neither entirely morally transformative nor completely ineffectual. The practical effect of defective consent is that the consent-seeker is not absolved of liability simply because the other party has manifested consent. Rather, the actions of the consent-seeker should be viewed under the second principle (did the consent-seeker act reasonably and with due care under the circumstances?). (Defective consent is discussed further in Chapter 6 section E.)

If the only viable alternative to the act poses a high risk to the autonomy interest, providing salient disclosure may inform but it fails to establish voluntariness. Consequently, there are some situations where consent cannot be established because the voluntariness condition is insufficiently robust. Necessary services provided on a "take it or leave it" basis, health conditions which require medical intervention,[397] medical emergencies and similar situations are ones where an individual is forced to manifest consent or else suffer high-level harm to autonomy. Accordingly, the voluntariness condition is lacking and so the individual cannot be said to have validly consented. This does not mean that the act or service should not or must not be provided; it does, however, mean that consent is defective, and the act or service should not be subject to private ordering. Without valid consent, there should be no enforceable contract. Consequently, contract cannot be the way the terms of the interaction are established. The state (through a regulatory agency or a professional organization licensed by the state) must establish standards for the procedure. A patient who must undergo a medically advised surgery may technically grant "informed consent," but it is defective consent, which is neither valid consent nor non-consent. Defective consent may save the physician from being sued for battery, but it does not provide the basis for contract, nor does it safeguard against claims of negligence. The terms of the procedure should not be subject to bargaining; rather, they should be subject to professional codes and state regulations and laws governing medical procedures. Accordingly, the patient should not be made to sign an "agreement" containing terms which, for example, limit the liability of the surgeon for malpractice or require the patient to agree to mandatory arbitration in the event of a dispute. If state legislators determine that it is good policy to limit the liability of surgeons, they should pass legislation providing such protection. But it should not be permitted under the guise that the patient "consented" by signing a contract (and relevant legislation should not make "consent" the basis for a waiver of liability).

---

[397] Most medical procedures which are technically "elective" are therapeutic and not fully voluntary. For example, it is the very rare individual who *desires* surgery to remove a tumor or to have an abortion. The decision is a forced choice. The medical context is different from other situations for this reason.

Absent physical force or unlawful threats, classical economics (which continues to influence many areas of the law, including contract law) assumes that decision-makers act in their self-interest, meaning that in assessing utility, the decision-maker considers only its own payoff.[398] Yet, experiments in psychology and neuroscience reveal this assumption to be false.[399] Motive is relevant to assessing the condition of voluntariness. An individual being manipulated to carry out another party's actions has diminished agency. The level of agency required to constitute consent depends upon the nature of the consented-to act. Interactions which involve only low or moderate-level threats to autonomy, such as most commercial exchanges, may require only that there was no threat of physical violence or other unlawful behavior. The greater the threat to autonomy, the higher the standard required to show agency – and the greater the scrutiny of the other party's influence. For example, the CEO of a company should not force employees into a situation where they must either have a microchip implanted underneath their skin or be excluded from a company-wide function (i.e. a "chip party"). The situation is tainted with coercion because an employee may fear she is risking her economic livelihood if she declines to participate. At the very least, the event should not be hosted onsite by the company and the participants should not be publicly announced or celebrated, as that might make non-participants fearful of being identified and ostracized.

D. DISCOURAGE IMPULSIVITY AND ENCOURAGE DELIBERATION

One way to improve consent would be to establish a consenting environment which encourages deliberation and discourages impulsivity. This subsection focuses on two procedural measures: cooling periods and counseling sessions.

Where there is no concern that inaction will exacerbate, harm or otherwise irreversibly alter an existing condition, procedural requirements should be put into place which slow down the process of obtaining consent to high-level threat procedures. As George Loewenstein observed, "much behavior is non-volitional or only partly volitional – even in situations characterized by substantial deliberation."[400] In many situations, more information may encourage deliberation, but the allure of the activity may make resistance futile. Someone in a "hot" state requires a change in emotional and physical surroundings.[401] The duration of the cooling period should depend upon the gravity of the act and should vary depending

---

[398] Stefana DellaVigna, *supra* note 29, at 336.
[399] *See* discussion Chapter 1, section A.1.
[400] George Loewenstein, *Out of Control: Visceral Influences on Behavior*, 65 ORG. BEHAV. & HUM. DECISION PROCESSES 272, 289 (1996).
[401] *See* Dan Ariely & George Loewenstein, *The Heat of the Moment: The Effect of Sexual Arousal on Sexual Decision Making*, 19 J. BEHAV. DECISION MAKING 87, 97 (2006) (suggesting that "efforts to promote safe, ethical sex should concentrate on preparing people to deal with the 'heat of the moment'" or avoid the situation altogether).

on the risk to autonomy. It should commence after the details of the exchange have been finalized or, if there is a contract, after its execution by the consent-seeker.

A waiting period enables the consenting party to reflect upon the consequences of the act and the particular aspects of the exchange which may have been negotiated and finalized. During the waiting period, the consent-seeker should not contact the consenter, although the consenter may contact the consent-seeker with questions. The consenter should seek a change of physical environment and remove herself from the presence of those (i.e. the consent-seeker(s)) who are affected by her decision and who may be influencing it in overt or subtle ways. As social psychologists have explained, an individual's situation may affect her behavior in ways that may be antithetical or inconsistent with her personality or self-image.[402] The stress associated with the physical environment, the presence of others, and her own mental, emotional and physical state may all impede decision-making. The individual must be given a chance to withdraw from the activity without penalty at any time during the waiting period.

A waiting period is not advisable, however, where a rapidly changing condition is at issue, because inaction may pose a greater threat to the autonomy interest than action. A waiting period in this case poses its own risks, or increases the risks involved in the procedure and is, therefore, inappropriate and inadvisable. For example, an operation to remove a growing, malignant tumor poses a high-level threat to autonomy, but the decision to postpone its removal may pose a greater threat. Similarly, waiting periods are not advisable for medical emergencies, as they would result in greater harm.

Waiting periods are a politically charged issue as they relate to abortions, but the very purpose of a framework is to avoid forcing or prohibiting actions based upon religious and moral beliefs. It is worth noting that the definition of autonomy which I have adopted refers to freedom in a literal sense, and refers specifically to the freedom of the consenter's future self to move, act or think without assistance or constraint.[403] By this definition, pregnancy, childbirth and parenting all diminish autonomy in substantial ways because they restrict a woman's freedom to act freely and without constraints. Abortions, particularly when performed in the first trimester, are generally a very safe procedure and pose only a low- or moderate-level threat to the autonomy interest. Waiting periods should only be required with respect to procedures posing a high-level threat to autonomy. Moreover, pregnancy is a rapidly changing condition where the risks to the woman's health increase as time passes. An abortion performed by a medical professional is much safer than pregnancy and delivery, and poses

---

[402]   Ross & Nisbett, *supra* note 46, at 4 (discussing how situational variables make "quite a bit of difference" and occasionally "[make] nearly all the difference, and information about traits and individual differences . . . proves all but trivial").

[403]   *See* discussion Chapter 3 section B.

a lower risk to the autonomy interest.[404] A waiting period for abortions would exacerbate the risk involved in the procedure. Abortions at later stages pose a greater threat to the autonomy interest, so that postponing the procedure only increases the health risks. Accordingly, waiting periods for abortions are inadvisable as increase the threat level to autonomy.

In addition to a cooling period, procedural requirements should include an information session with a physician and, where the situation involves a high-level risk to autonomy and is not prompted by a medical emergency, a counseling session with a mental health professional. Counseling should guide the patient into making the best decision given the available information and the relevant circumstances. Information should be evidence-based, factually accurate, and disclose available alternatives; the availability of possible alternatives should not be withheld because of the information provider's religious, political, or other personal beliefs.[405]

The information sessions should address and remedy, to the extent possible, the typical cognitive limitations and heuristic biases which lead individuals to make less than optimal personal decisions. Research reveals that the availability heuristic may cause one to underestimate or ignore the risks involved with familiar procedures. For example, a woman who knows someone who had an uncomplicated breast implant procedure with favorable results might assume the procedure will be just as uncomplicated and favorable for her.[406] Optimism bias and complexity may cause her to miscalculate the costs involved in the procedure or the maintenance costs of future procedures. A report on cosmetic interventions commissioned by the U.K. Department of Health notes that many of the study participants did not consider the "long term cost implications" of their breast implants, including their need to be replaced every ten years:

> This may not be that surprising, as even a patient in her 20's who had clearly been fully informed regarding 10-year replacement, was postponing thinking about the costs involved two years later, and not thinking beyond the next replacement. Indeed, none of the patients with breast implants included in this study had plans for meeting the costs of replacement. However, if this is thought through, and young women do realize that they may therefore be facing, and having to find the funds for, five or six replacement operations, it may be a deterrent from considering breast enlargement at a young age.[407]

---

[404] E. G. Raymond & D. A. Grimes, *The Comparative Safety of Legal Induced Abortion and Childbirth in the United States*, 119 Obstet. Gynecol. 215 (2012) (finding that the pregnancy-associated mortality rate was 8.8 deaths per 100,000 live births and the mortality rate related to induced abortion was 0.6 deaths per 100,000 abortions).

[405] *But see* Nat'l Inst. of Family & Life Advocates v. Becerra, 138 S.Ct. 2361 (2018) (ruling that petitioners were likely to succeed on their claim that a California law which requires anti-abortion clinics to provide specific information about family planning, including abortion, violated the First Amendment).

[406] U.K. Dept. of Health Report, *supra* note 75, at 43 (noting that "personal experience, knowing someone who has had a particular procedure carried out successfully, can be an overriding influence and outweigh any other considerations in evaluating the risks involved.").

[407] *Id.*

Counseling should inform the consenter of the risks and "worst case" scenarios to counter the consenter's optimism and imaginability biases and to help the consenter better prepare for potential problems arising from the activity or procedure. Gary Klein refers to this strategy as a "premortem":

> A premortem is the hypothetical opposite of a postmortem. A postmortem in a medical setting allows health professionals and the family to learn what caused a patient's death. Everyone benefits except, of course, the patient. A premortem in a business setting comes at the beginning of a project rather than the end, so that the project can be improved rather than autopsied. Unlike a typical critiquing session, in which project team members are asked what might go wrong, the premortem operates on the assumption that the "patient" has died, and so asks what did go wrong. The team members' task is to generate plausible reasons for the project's failure.
>
> A typical premortem begins after the team has been briefed on the plan. The leader starts the exercise by informing everyone that the project has failed spectacularly. Over the next few minutes those in the room independently write down every reason they can think of for the failure – especially the kinds of things they ordinarily wouldn't mention as potential problems, for fear of being impolitic ... Next the leader asks each team member, starting with the project manager, to read one reason from his or her list; everyone states a different reason until all have been recorded. After the session is over, the project manager reviews the list, looking for ways to strengthen the plan.[408]

Counselors should engage in a variation of the "premortem" strategy that has the consenter consider how the procedure or activity could fail or go wrong and how the consenter would handle negative outcomes. Such an approach may help debias the consenter and improve decision-making. It may also help the consenter better understand the nature of the risk that he is about to undertake. The premortem approach has its limits, however. Unlike the business participants engaged in a typical premortem exercise, the consenter in many of the "hard case" scenarios will have little control over *how* to perform the activity. Accordingly, a premortem strategy can only help the consenter determine whether to engage in the activity at all, not how to prevent potential problems in the performance of the activity. Thus, a premortem may be more helpful in situations where the status quo poses no risk; it will be less helpful, and potentially harmful, where the consenter's choice is more constrained (i.e. where the activity involves a medically advised or medically necessary procedure).

A primary objective of counseling is to counter any misinformation obtained from advertising or popular culture. Even the status of an act as legal or consentable may mislead. People may assume that if a product or procedure hasn't been banned either the government has determined that it is safe or the government is regulating

---

[408]   Gary Klein, *Performing a Project Premortem*, HARV. BUS. REV. (Sept. 2007), https://hbr.org/2007/09/performing-a-project-premortem.

it so that it will be safe.[409] This assumption may be entirely false. The setting or other cues may be deceptive. Someone may erroneously assume that the individual wearing the white lab coat wielding the hypodermic needle to administer the toxin which paralyzes her facial muscles is a medically trained professional. The familiarity of a procedure may cause someone to be misinformed or inadequately informed, affecting her risk assessment. The U.K. Dept. of Health Report noted that study participants perceived cosmetic procedures as riskier when they were properly informed about what they entailed:

> When informed about these procedures, they were felt to be more risky than had been anticipated – the idea of putting acid on to the face with a chemical peel, how "Botox" acts by paralyzing muscles, the fact that dermal fillers can be permanent – all of these increased perceptions of how risky these procedures are.[410]

Finally, formalities should be instituted to reinforce the seriousness of the undertaking. The consenting party might be asked to manifest consent by signing a written consent document on more than one occasion. If there is a risk of death or incapacity, the individual should be made to fill out a health directive or living will, designating a guardian, next of kin and the course of treatment in the event of incapacity.

E. AGE AND MATURITY

Age and maturity are important factors to consider in determining consentability. Adolescence and young adulthood is a particularly fraught time for a variety of reasons, including rapid physical and social changes, growing independence, and the increasing responsibilities of adulthood. To add to this particularly dynamic time, the brains of those in their teens and twenties are still developing and the prefrontal cortex, which is responsible for executive function, is not fully developed until an individual is about twenty-five years of age.[411]

The law generally recognizes the vulnerabilities of the young. Minors who commit acts which would be criminal or tortious if committed by an adult are

---

[409] For example, many consumers believe that the government regulates vitamin supplements for safety and efficacy. *See* Joanna Sax, *Dietary Supplements Are Not All Safe and Not All Food: How the Low Cost of Dietary Supplements Preys on the Consumer*, 41 AM. J. L. & MED. 374, 377 (2015) ("Consumers are not necessarily aware that dietary supplements . . . are not tested for safety and efficacy prior to market entry.").

[410] *Id.* at 40.

[411] *See* Sara B. Johnson, Robert W. Blum & Jay N. Giedd, *Adolescent Maturity and the Brain: The Promise and Pitfalls of Neuroscience Research in Adolescent Health Policy*, 45 J. ADOLESCENT HEALTH 216, 216 (2009) [hereinafter Johnson et al.] (noting that a "growing body of longitudinal neuroimaging research has demonstrated that adolescence is a period of continued brain growth and change . . . The frontal lobes, homes to key components of the neural circuitry underlying 'executive functions' such as planning, working memory, and impulse control, are among the last areas of the brain to mature; they may not be fully developed until halfway through the third decade of life.").

typically not charged or, if they are, suffer lesser punishment or penalties. The Supreme Court recognized the relevance of neuroscience studies on the developing brain in Roper v. Simmons,[412] when it ruled that "the Eighth and Fourteenth Amendments forbid imposition of the death penalty on offenders who were under the age of 18 when their crimes were committed."[413] In that case, the defendant, Christopher Simmons, was convicted and sentenced to death for murdering a woman during the course of a robbery committed when he was seventeen years old. His attorneys argued that his youth made him less culpable for his crime and therefore he should not be subject to the death penalty. The Supreme Court agreed, based in part upon neuroscience evidence provided by the defense, and briefs submitted by, among others, the American Psychological Association.

There are crimes (most notably, statutory rape) which involve acts committed with or against minors which would not be considered crimes if committed with or against adults. For example, sex with a minor is a crime even if the minor consents. While the law provides protection for children, there is a sharp dividing line at the age of eighteen. Those aged eighteen and older are deemed to have the same degree of maturity and are accorded as much legal responsibility and culpability as someone much older. Yet, given what scientists have learned about the way the brain develops (and that it doesn't fully develop until the early twenties), that line seems arbitrary.[414] Some research suggests that while there is no real difference in the cognitive capacities of young adults and older adults, there is a marked difference with respect to psychosocial maturity (measured by impulsivity, risk perception, resistance to peer pressure and thrill-seeking).[415] For this reason, some car rental companies employ a minimum age requirement, which is typically twenty-five.[416] Some laws recognize that simply turning eighteen does not magically confer the emotional and economic stability of adulthood. For example, in most of the United States, adults under the age of twenty-one are prohibited from purchasing or

---

[412]   Roper v. Simmons, 543 U.S. 551 (2005) (O'Connor, J., dissenting).

[413]   *Id.* at 578.

[414]   *See also* Johnson et al., *supra* note 410, at 217 (observing that "there is little empirical evidence to support age 18, the current legal age of majority, as an accurate marker of adult capacities.").

[415]   *See id.* at 220 ("Among the many behavior changes that have been noted for teens, the three that are most robustly seen across cultures are: (1) increased novelty seeking; (2) increased risk-taking; and (3) a social affiliation shift toward peer-based interactions."); *see also* Dustin Albert & Laurence Steinberg, *Age Differences in Strategic Planning as Indexed by the Tower of London*, 82 CHILD DEV. 1501, 1515 (2011) (the authors report that "strategic planning and problem solving undergo continued refinement well into late adolescence and, in some respects, early adulthood."). *See also* Laurence Steinberg et al., *Age Differences in Future Orientation and Delay Discounting*, 80 CHILD DEV. 28 (2009) (finding younger adolescents demonstrate a weaker orientation to the future than older adolescents).

[416]   *See* BUDGET, www.budget.com/budgetWeb/html/en/common/agePopUp.html (last visited June 12, 2008); *see also* Lisa Fritscher, *Age Requirement to Rent a Car*, USA TODAY, http://traveltips.usatoday.com/age-requirement-rent-car-62294.html (last updated Mar. 13, 2018) (renters under twenty-five are subject to additional rules and surcharges, including restrictions on the type of vehicle available for rent).

consuming alcohol. The Patient Protection and Affordable Care Act requires insurers to permit those under twenty-six years of age to remain on their families' health insurance plan.[417] Most laws, however, do not distinguish between an eighteen-year-old and a twenty-eight-year-old or, for that matter, a fifty-eight-year-old.

Current rules and standards regarding the age of consent should be reconsidered in light of research that shows that neurological development is typically not complete until people reach their mid-twenties. This does not mean someone *else* should be able to make decisions on their behalf, or that those between eighteen and twenty-five years of age should not be able to make decisions regarding their bodily integrity; it does, however, mean that safeguards should be in place to protect the young from opportunistic behavior by those seeking to prey upon their vulnerabilities. For example, limits should be placed upon the ability of businesses to target this particular demographic group. In cases involving a high-level threat to autonomy, the legal age of consent should be raised from eighteen to twenty-five years old, when the brain is more likely to be fully developed. These safeguards are further discussed in Chapter 7.

Those under eighteen years of age are in a different position, legally, regarding their ability to consent. Generally, the law prohibits minors (those under eighteen) from making most legal decisions. Yet, it allows minors to undertake or undergo some high-level threat actions with parental consent. The substitution of a parent's consent for that of the minor's is often necessary and justifiable; however, it may be problematic in cases where the consent pertains to the physical well-being of the child and there is a possible conflict of interest between the parent and the child. In such cases, additional safeguards are imperative. Michele Goodwin addresses the troubling issue of children who become organ donors to their siblings, and notes that the "pressure to donate is so strong that it may veer into the coercive. Importantly, there is no negotiation process for the child who surrenders her bone marrow or organ."[418]

---

[417] 42 U.S.C. § 300gg-14(a) (2012) ("A group health plan and a health insurance issuer offering group or individual health insurance coverage that provides dependent coverage of children shall continue to make such coverage available for an adult child until the child turns 26 years of age."); *see also Dependent Health Coverage and Age for Healthcare Benefits*, NAT'L CONF. ST. LEGISLATURES (Nov. 1, 2016), www.ncsl.org/research/health/dependent-health-coverage-state-implementation.aspx (noting that prior to the federal law, "at least 31 states required carriers to extend coverage to young adults").

[418] Michele Goodwin, *Compelled Body Part Donations, in* THE GLOBAL BODY MARKET, *supra* note 124, at 73. Goodwin proposes the following balancing test: "First, it must be clearly understood that compelled living donations from children and incompetent persons are the least desired forms of procurement ... Alternatives must be considered for desperate parents and siblings beyond the reach of the most vulnerable members of their families ... Second, minors younger than thirteen years old should be prohibited from participating in living donation procedures ... Third, a *guardian ad litem* should always be appointed in child donor cases. Fourth, psychological screenings for the children involved as well as the adults in their lives should be required to assess how well the parties understand the risks, benefits, and long-term consequences of their actions. Fifth, an independent physician must be appointed for the prospective donor to prevent conflicts of interest. Finally,

In most cases, parents will have the best interests of their child in mind and there is no or little reason for concern. However, where there is a potential conflict of interest, such as a disagreement based upon religious beliefs or where a parent makes a decision with the potential to harm one child in order to save another, there must be safeguards. At a minimum, the child and the parent(s) should be made to undergo a screening and/or interview process to ensure mental and emotional fitness. In cases involving a high-level threat activity, the state should be permitted to prevent the action if the status quo poses no harm to the child. For example, the state should not be permitted to override the decision of a parent about whether the child should undergo a particularly risky medical treatment for a potentially fatal disease. The state, however, should, be permitted to prohibit a particularly risky or painful treatment or procedure which would provide little or no benefit to the child. While the judgment of the state should not substitute for that of the parent, the state should be permitted to intervene and halt any action on behalf of the child if the child expresses such a desire, the parent is deemed unfit to make the decision, or the proposed action poses a substantial risk of harm to the child's autonomy with no countervailing potential benefit to the child's autonomy.

In situations involving a dynamic condition, allowing the minor to consent may pose a lesser degree of harm than disallowing consent to the activity. If, for example, a blood transfusion would save a minor's life, the parents should not be permitted to refuse the transfusion against the wishes of the minor. Consenting to a blood transfusion poses less of a threat to autonomy than *not* allowing the minor to consent. The profound consequences to the minor's autonomy from refusing a transfusion outweigh the parents' autonomy interest in imposing their religious beliefs upon their child.

Furthermore, in some cases, there is a countervailing threat to the autonomy interest which is greater than the potential harm from undergoing the action. Pregnancy and the decision whether to get an abortion provides an example. In an ideal world, a minor should voluntarily seek parental consent prior to getting any medical procedure and her parents would be supportive and understanding; however, the reality for many teenaged girls is that revealing an unplanned pregnancy would have traumatic and profound negative consequences. Moreover, if teenagers are deemed too immature to decide whether to have an abortion, they are certainly too immature to have a baby and bear the responsibilities of raising a child or to make the emotionally difficult decision to give one up for adoption. Assessing consentability requires considering the procedure itself – and not the moral or religious beliefs associated with it, as those may differ depending upon the individual. Abortion is widely perceived as a safe procedure. The alternative of pregnancy and childbirth poses a greater threat to the autonomy interest because there is

a statement should be issued to the court from the donor explaining why she desires to participate as an organ or tissue donor." *Id.* at 85–86.

a greater risk of physical harm and the procedure is more intrusive. Furthermore, being a parent itself constrains the future self's freedom. A non-decision or inaction in this situation will have a permanent and irreversible outcome involving great physical pain, which will also impede future autonomy. Given the profound consequences of delay and the harm to the autonomy interest, a minor should be permitted to make the decision whether to have an abortion without seeking parental consent. On the other hand, the minor may decide to remain pregnant, and her parents should not have the authority to compel her to undergo an abortion.

By contrast, a teenaged girl seeking breast augmentation surgery is not facing a dynamic condition. The procedure poses a high-level threat to her autonomy interest as the surgery itself is risky and has long-term health consequences which are not widely known. In the absence of a countervailing high-level threat to her autonomy (such as detriment to her mental health if she is unable to have the surgery performed), she should wait until she is twenty-five, an age when her brain as well as her body is more likely to be fully developed.

6

Reducing Opportunism

Each of the conditions of consent depends to a certain degree upon the behavior of the other party. The relational nature of consent means that the actions of the parties influence each other. The voluntariness condition, for example, may be more or less robust depending upon whether and to what extent the consent-seeker acted to persuade the consenting party. Similarly, the knowledge condition may be affected by information provided by the consent-seeker. Even the manifestation of consent may be influenced by the consent-seeker. For example, a company might design its website to make it more likely that visitors will "manifest consent" by clicking reflexively to "accept" its terms of service.[419] Default settings which assume consent, such as opt-out rather than opt-in terms, indicate a less robust manifestation of consent condition.

But, there is another rationale for reducing opportunistic conduct which is independent of its influence on the consenter. Opportunism has a destabilizing effect on society, and if unchecked, may lead to social conditions which may demonstrate the wisdom of the Hobbesian vision of man. The justification for state intervention then is not solely that the opportunistic conduct undermined the conditions of consent (although it may have), but that opportunism diminishes social cohesion and impedes cooperation by making people more distrustful.

The likelihood of opportunism increases where the act for which consent is sought is one which the *consent-seeker* would refuse to undertake. Someone who tries to get another to do an act which he himself wouldn't do because it is too dangerous, painful or degrading could be taking advantage of another and acting opportunistically *regardless* of whether the other person consented. On the other hand, the consent-seeker could be acting in good faith, and acts are not necessarily opportunistic simply because the consent-seeker is herself unwilling to participate. The consenter may be in a better position to undertake the risky activity, or the consent-seeker may need to handle other aspects of the activity. For example, the

[419] *See* KIM, WRAP CONTRACTS, *supra* note 280, at 53–69 (discussing the ways companies use the form of digital contracts to facilitate consumer actions that constitute manifestations of consent despite lack of knowledge).

National Aeronautics and Space Administration (NASA) selects astronauts to perform dangerous tasks because their skills, physical attributes and training make them
best-suited to perform them successfully. It may, however, be helpful to scrutinize
more closely those situations where the consent-seeker *was* qualified to undertake
the activity, but instead sought another to do it for her.

A. DUTY OF CANDOR

The law generally discourages or prohibits someone from using her position of trust
for personal gain. An agent, for example, must disclose conflicts of interest to
a principal. Even parties to a commercial transaction must, after entering into
a contract, be forthcoming with relevant information as part of their contractual
duty of good faith.[420] Contract law recognizes a difference in the disclosure obligations of parties before and after they have entered into a contract. Judge Richard
Posner, writing for the Seventh Circuit, explained:

> Before the contract is signed, the parties confront each other with a natural wari-
> ness. Neither expects the other to be particularly forthcoming, and therefore there is
> no deception when one is not. Afterwards the situation is different. The parties are
> now in a cooperative relationship the costs of which will be considerably reduced by
> a measure of trust. So each lowers his guard a bit, and now silence is more apt to be
> deceptive.[421]

While parties to a commercial contract have a duty of good faith, they do not have
a duty of candor.[422] The duty of contractual good faith is, as Posner described it,
"halfway between a fiduciary duty (the duty of *utmost* good faith) and the duty
merely to refrain from active fraud."[423]

However, parties in transactions involving a high-level threat to autonomy should
be viewed differently from those in a commercial transaction. Even if they are not
fiduciaries in the strictest sense, the relationship is not one at arm's length, given the
nature of the transaction.[424] Rather, trust and a duty of candor should be prerequisites to transactions which pose a risk of serious bodily injury to one or both of the
parties. Unlike the parties to a commercial contract, parties to a bodily integrity
exchange should act in good faith even prior to committing themselves to

---

[420] Mkt. St. Assoc. v. Frey, 941 F.2d 588, 594 (7th Cir. 1991) (noting that taking "deliberate advantage of
an oversight by your contract partner concerning his rights under the contract" is "sharp dealing" and
without social value).
[421] *Id.*
[422] *Id.* ("The duty of honesty, of good faith, even expansively conceived, is not a duty of candor.").
[423] *Id.* at 595.
[424] The California Supreme Court made this very observation in discussing the "fiduciary duty" of
physicians to their patients, noting, "In some respects, the term 'fiduciary' is too broad. In this context
the term 'fiduciary' signifies only that a physician must disclose all facts material to the patient's
decision. A physician is not the patient's financial adviser." Moore v. Regents of Univ. of California,
793 P.2d 479, 485 n.10 (Cal. 1990).

contractual terms. The nature of the transaction is fundamentally different from a commercial transaction because the stakes are much higher and involve more than just property or money. Accordingly, the parties should be forthcoming about relevant information and should not take advantage of the consenting party's "incapacity, ignorance, inexperience, or even naivete."[425] The "parties" may include more than the two people physically affected. In a kidney exchange, for example, the consent-seeker would be the recipient of the kidney (the payer), as well as the various intermediaries, such as the medical personnel, broker or clinic. The consent-seeker (the payer and the intermediaries) in transactions posing a high-level threat to autonomy (e.g. surrogacy, organ transactions) should be viewed as having fiduciary-like duties to the consenting party, similar to those that medical professionals have to their patients. In Moore v. the Regents of the University of California, the California Supreme Court stated, "a physician has a fiduciary duty to disclose all information material to the patient's decision."[426] This includes disclosure of "personal interests unrelated to the patient's health, whether research or economic, that may affect the physician's professional judgment" and is not limited to information about medical risks.[427]

As part of a discussion of alternatives, medical professionals must disclose whether they will reap a financial reward for recommending one procedure over another[428] or for referring the patient to a particular physician or organization.[429] It is this author's opinion that they should also disclose whether they hold religious or personal beliefs that might influence their recommendations. Patients generally expect their medical professionals to have their best interests in mind and do not consider that they may have other, potentially conflicting, motivations. People who are considering whether to submit to a physically taxing and potentially dangerous undertaking – such as undergoing pregnancy and delivery, or having surgery to have a kidney removed – may assume the consent-seeker is acting in good faith and is providing relevant and material information. For example, a surrogate concerned about the safety of continuing with her pregnancy would want to know whether her physician's personal objection to abortion affects his professional opinion. Certainly, it should not; unfortunately, it may. Notions of fairness and reciprocity mandate that each party have a duty of candor to the other where one of them is consenting to an activity which implicates a high-level threat to autonomy.

---

[425] *Mkt. St. Assoc.*, 941 F.2d at 593.
[426] *Moore*, 793 P.2d at 483.
[427] *Id.*
[428] *Id.* ("Indeed, the law already recognizes that a reasonable patient would want to know whether a physician has an economic interest that might affect the physician's professional judgment.").
[429] *Id.* at 130 ("[a] physician may not charge a patient on behalf of, or refer a patient to, any organization in which the physician has a 'significant beneficial interest, unless [the physician] first discloses in writing to the patient that there is such an interest and advises the patient that the patient may choose any organization for the purposes of obtaining the services ordered or requested by [the physician].'" (citing BUS. & PROF. CODE § 654.2(a) (Deering, LEXIS through 2018 Reg. Sess.)).

The requirement of disclosure in conflict of interest situations serves three purposes. It forces disclosers to double-check their own motivations and recommendations. It also allows the disclosees to assess the situation and make their own determination about the relevance of any potential conflict of interest. Finally, it shifts the burden of making the inquiry regarding conflicts. Patients may hesitate to ask a physician (or other consent-seeker) about conflicts of interest because they fear angering or upsetting the very person who will be in control of their safety when they are at their most vulnerable.[430] The act of inquiry itself may create an unnecessarily stressful situation for both parties as it introduces an element of suspicion and mistrust into the relationship. A requirement which makes disclosing potential conflicts of interest part of the standard procedure of informed consent thus has the potential to minimize the stress of inquiry on both parties, deter the discloser from engaging in self-dealing, and reduce the incidence of inappropriate or unnecessary procedures.

Disclosure of conflicts of interest may be inadequate to eliminate problems, including those of bias and dishonesty.[431] In some cases, an outright ban on conflicts of interest may be appropriate.[432] For example, a doctor prescribing a particular brand of drug should not receive payment or gifts from the pharmaceutical company manufacturing the drug. An outright ban, rather than mandatory disclosure, in this situation makes practical sense. It is awkward for a patient to have to question her doctor about potential conflicts of interest. A patient may be wary of appearing to doubt the trust that patients should have in their medical providers. She may be afraid that her doctor may dislike her if she asks questions and provide her with a lower quality of care. As a result, she may decide not to risk asking such questions at all.

In other cases, however, banning the conflict of interest may be impractical due to the nature of the transaction. For example, a scientist seeking volunteers for an experimental study has an inherent conflict in that the scientist benefits from having enough participants to perform the study. In this situation, disclosure and a duty of candor provide a more practical way to address the problem of conflicts of interest provided that the disclosure is effectively communicated in a manner which enhances the consenter's knowledge.[433]

---

[430] For that reason, a federal law, known as the Federal Anti-Kickback Statute, prohibits accepting payments for influencing referrals of business to federal health care programs. 42 U.S.C. §1320a-7b (2012).

[431] LORI ANDREWS & DOROTHY NELKIN, BODY BAZAAR: THE MARKET FOR HUMAN TISSUE IN THE BIOTECHNOLOGY AGE 57 (2001) (noting that "when academic researchers and institutions go commercial" there is a concern about the quality of medical care and that "outside corporations with economic interests" which fund research at universities may "sometimes try to suppress publication of findings that are not in their favor.").

[432] *See supra* note 430; *see also* Joanna Sax, *Financial Conflicts of Interest in Science*, 21 ANN. HEALTH L. 291, 308 (2012) (discussing the problem of conflicts of interest in academic research and noting that "[t]he current policy of disclosure does not appear to work well.").

[433] The problem of effective disclosures, and suggestions for improving them, are discussed in Chapter 6 section B and Chapter 7 section B.

Although physicians, lawyers, scientists, and other professionals are constrained by their profession's code of ethics and standards of care, they are also human and subject to human fallibilities. Research has shown that gifts influence behavior, yet people may believe that they are immune from corruption. Neuroscientist Tali Sharot refers to this as an "introspection illusion," which is "the strong sense people have that they can directly access the processes underlying their mental states. Most mental processes, however, are largely unavailable for conscious interpretation. The catch is that people are unaware of their unawareness."[434] Despite what they may consciously believe, even the most well-intentioned people can have their opinions, judgments and actions swayed with enticements. Unsurprisingly, governments, institutions and businesses have strict rules against accepting gifts. Reputable researchers also disclose the source of their funding.

The crime of bribery recognizes the power of gifts to influence behavior. It is not even necessary for the bribe to succeed in influencing the conduct; the mere act of giving the gift is recognized as corrosive. Given the potential of money to influence behavior, and the human tendency for self-deception and rationalization, a consent-seeker should disclose *any direct or indirect payment or financial benefit that he or she expects as a consequence of the proposed activity.*

Mandatory disclosure by the consent-seeker of benefits and conflicts of interest enables the consenter to assess for herself whether they affected the consent-seeker's actions or tainted the information that was provided by the consent-seeker. A failure to disclose a benefit or conflict of interest would mean the consent was defective. The consent-seeker would be subject to a lawsuit under existing tort and contract law, and subject to damages and/or restitution, including disgorgement of financial benefit.[435]

B. NO SOLICITATIONS: LIMITING THE INFLUENCE OF SOLICITORS, ADVERTISEMENTS AND MARKETERS

There is a greater likelihood of opportunism where the consent-seeker solicits or instigates the consenting party to engage in the act than where the consenter initiates contact. One way that consent-seekers are able to solicit large groups of potential consenters is through advertising. Generally, marketing efforts seek to persuade or entice people into taking a particular action, such as using a product or service, by promoting its benefits. Advertisers and marketers are skilled at persuading consumers to purchase goods or services and in creating a desire or need with the use of words and images. In a free market society, there are minimal restrictions on their ability to do so. The primary limitation is that advertisements must not be false,

---

[434] SHAROT, *supra* note 30, at 18.
[435] RESTATEMENT (THIRD) OF RESTITUTION AND UNJUST ENRICHMENT § 3 (AM. LAW INST. 2011) ("A person is not permitted to profit by his own wrong.").

deceptive or misleading.[436] The laissez-faire governmental approach to advertisements does not apply where there is great potential harm to consumers. For example, the Federal Drug Administration (FDA) regulates the marketing of prescription drugs.[437] Advertisements for alcoholic beverages are subject to disclosure requirements, including disclosure of alcoholic content.[438] Tobacco companies may not advertise their products on broadcast television.[439] Similarly, the government should regulate advertisements for activities which pose a high-level threat to autonomy. At the very least, advertisements for high-level threat activities should contain a disclosure regarding the source of funding for the advertisement.

In ordinary contexts, advertising may be palatable or socially beneficial. However, when marketers tout activities which pose a high-level threat to autonomy (i.e. high degree of bodily intrusion, permanent consequences, physical and emotional pain and suffering), they prey upon the vulnerable. An example of advertising which should be regulated is that aimed at potential egg donors, a practice which seems particularly prevalent at elite universities.[440] A college student, young and cash-strapped (a reasonable assumption, given her youth and the high cost of college tuition), may not yet be ready to appreciate the long-term impact of agreeing to be an egg donor.

The level of regulation should depend upon the level of threat to autonomy. There should be no advertisement permitted for highest-level threat activities (such as advertisements by manufacturers of drugs to be used in assisted suicide). Activities which constitute high-level threats to autonomy, such as kidney or egg sales, should have restrictions regarding where they may be advertised (e.g. not on college campuses) and what they may say. Targeted advertisements and advertisements on social media sites should not be permitted for any high-level threat activities. Unlike advertisements in public places, these types of advertisements force content upon the recipient. Repeated exposure to the advertisements, in turn, essentially brain-

---

[436] See, e.g., CAL. BUS. & PROF. CODE § 17500 (Deering, LEXIS through 2018 Reg. Sess.) (making unlawful advertisements which are "untrue or misleading, and which is known, or which by the exercise of reasonable care should be known, to be untrue or misleading"); 15 U.S.C. § 45(a) (2012) (under federal law, section 45 of the Federal Trade Commission Act (FTC) prohibits "unfair or deceptive acts or practices in or affecting commerce.").

[437] See *Background on Drug Advertising*, FOOD & DRUG ADMIN., www.fda.gov/Drugs/ResourcesForYou/ Consumers/PrescriptionDrugAdvertising/ucm071964.htm#authority(last (updated June 19, 2015) (noting its authority based on a number of federal laws to oversee the "approval and marketing of prescription drugs" including prescription drug advertising).

[438] 27 U.S.C. § 205(f) (2012).

[439] Public Health Cigarette Smoking Act of 1969, 15 U.S.C. 1331–38; see also Sapna Maheshwari, *Why Tobacco Companies Are Paying to Tell You Smoking Kills*, N.Y. TIMES (Nov. 24, 2017), www.nytimes .com/2017/11/24/business/media/tobacco-companies-ads.html.

[440] See Gina Kolata, *$50,000 Offered to Tall, Smart Egg Donor*, N.Y. TIMES (Mar. 3, 1999), www.nytimes .com/1999/03/03/us/50000-offered-to-tall-smart-egg-donor.html; Editorial Board, *Egg Donor Wanted, "B" Students Need Not Apply*, STAN. DAILY (May 30, 2012), www.stanforddaily.com/2012/ 05/30/egg-donor-wanted-b-students-need-not-apply/.

washes the recipients and normalizes the advertised activity.[441] Using a consentability framework, the interest that a company has in being able to advertise its services through direct marketing approaches (such as targeted ads, discount services, or through social media postings) is outweighed by the potential harm which the audience suffers as a result of being exposed to the advertisement.

Advertisements with regard to high-level threat activities should both market the benefits and disclose the risks at the same time and in the same manner. The greater the risk to the autonomy interest, the more conspicuous the disclosure component of the advertisement should be relative to the marketing component. For example, advertisements seeking egg donors generally promote the large financial benefits and the emotional rewards of being a donor; they do not mention the potential grave risks to the donor's health or the emotional aspects of undergoing the donor process. Advertisements for cosmetic procedures only show the glowing successful results, not the painful recovery process or the unsuccessful outcomes.

The disclosure component should not be measured in terms of quantity of information; it should be determined by the effectiveness of communication. Disclosures often overwhelm the reader with complex information presented in a way that makes it difficult for the reader to synthesize and understand. Most disclosure requirements focus only on the textual requirements, such as the type of information that should be conveyed, or the conspicuousness of the font size or style. They do not typically require companies to provide evidence that their disclosures have been effective at communicating the information. Not surprisingly, companies typically make only those efforts necessary to meet the technical requirements to comply with regulations. Advertisers know how to communicate effectively, but are unwilling to use that knowledge to convey the risks and disadvantages of their products and services in an effective manner. A relatively straightforward way to improve the effectiveness of advertisements would be to require that disclosures be presented in the same manner as the marketing information.

Some argue that to require companies to disclose certain information or to disclose it in certain ways violates their First Amendment free speech rights.[442] For example, in the United States, graphic packaging efforts have been successfully challenged as unconstitutional by tobacco companies.[443] However, tobacco companies were also ordered to

---

[441]   Normalization may result even from one prior exposure. Daniel Kahneman writes, "A single incident may make a recurrence less surprising." He describes his surprise at meeting a colleague by chance while vacationing with his wife on a small island resort. Two weeks later, he happens to be seated next to this colleague at a theatre in another country (not their home town). He states that the previous surprise encounter lessened – rather than increased – his surprise at meeting his colleague on the second encounter. The colleague was now "the psychologist who shows up when we travel abroad." KAHNEMAN, *supra* note 19, at 72.

[442]   *See* ADAM WINKLER, WE THE CORPORATIONS: HOW AMERICAN CORPORATIONS WON THEIR CIVIL RIGHTS (2018) (chronicling how corporations gained civil rights, including First Amendment expression rights).

[443]   *See* R. J. Reynolds Tobacco Co. v. Food & Drug Admin., 696 F.3d 1205 (D.C. Cir. 2012) (affirming that graphic warning requirements violated the First Amendment); *see also* Maheshwari, *supra* note

issue "corrective statements" about their products as part of a lawsuit settlement where they were charged with deceiving the public about the dangers of their product. The settlement required them to air television commercials and print advertisements educating the public about the hazards of cigarette smoking and disclosing the tobacco companies' shameful and deceptive business practices.[444] Tobacco companies, however, fought successfully to dilute the force of the original corrective statements.[445] As their strenuous efforts demonstrate, tobacco companies understand that moral outrage is often a more effective way to convey a message than factual disclosures.[446]

Advertisements play a large role in establishing and shaping both social norms and individual expectations. The average human being is ill-equipped to fend off the marketing messages propagated by corporations with multi-million-dollar budgets. The government should help individuals make the best decisions for themselves, rather than leave them at the mercy of sophisticated and seasoned advertisers who aim to seduce them into committing acts of enormous consequence to their autonomy. People may expect that certain types of advertising are already subject to some type of regulation. For example, a U.K. study on cosmetic interventions noted that there was a "widespread assumption" that advertising of these types of procedures was monitored or had been checked for accuracy, even though there was no such monitoring.[447]

In order to be effective, regulations should govern both the content of the advertisements (e.g. the potential risks, who is paying for the advertisement) as well as the manner, form and mode in which it is presented. Given the way the human brain processes information, information that is presented visually may be more relevant and useful to the average consumer. One study tested the reactions of U.S. smokers and non-smokers aged 18–24 years to Canadian cigarette warning labels, which include both text and graphic images, and U.S. cigarette warning labels, which are text-only.[448] The study participants reported that the Canadian

---

439. *But cf.* Cigar Ass'n of Am. v. Food & Drug Admin., No. 1:16-cv-01460, 2018 WL 2223653, at * 20–*21 (D.D.C. May 15, 2018) (finding that health warning on cigar packages which made up 30 percent of the cigar package was constitutional because cigar manufacturers retained sufficient space (70 percent) to communicate their own messaging).

444 *See* Maheshwari, *supra* note 439.

445 *Id.* (noting that "Proposed versions of the ads in 2011 appeared tougher ... Tobacco companies argued that the initially proposed statements were 'forced public confessions' designed to 'shame and humiliate them.'").

446 *See* Chuck Stanley, *Tobacco Companies Settle Long-Running Health Warning Dispute*, Law360 (Apr. 25, 2018), www.law360.com/consumerprotection/articles/1037281/tobacco-cos-settle-long-running-health-warning-dispute?nl_pk=0f3b3b3b-80ff-46e8-a41c-efb7f15de8b9&utm_source=new sletter&utm_medium=email&utm_campaign=consumerprotection (reporting that the tobacco companies and the federal government reached a settlement on how the language should be presented on cigarette packaging). As of this writing, the details of the packaging (such as font size and background colors) had not been announced.

447 U.K. Dept. of Health Report, *supra* note 75, at 23.

448 Michelle O'Hegarty et al., *Young Adults' Perceptions of Cigarette Warning Labels in the United States and Canada*, Ctrs. Disease Control & Prevention, U.S. Dep't of Health & Hum. Servs. (Apr. 2007), www.cdc.gov/pcd/issues/2007/apr/06_0024.htm.

warning labels were more visible and informative than the U.S. text-only warning labels. Smokers reported that they did not pay attention to the U.S. labels but that they did remember the Canadian graphic labels. The following comments made by the young adult study participants are instructive and worth quoting in their entirety:[449]

> **Sample Comments from Young Adult Study Participants on Canada Graphic Warning Labels**
>
> It puts a visual picture in your head to go along with words that you've been hearing. So here's something like you can see, not just the words behind it. It's something you can see, so it's going to affect you maybe a little bit more . . .
>
> American cigarettes – I've read the warning labels, and they all say the same thing. But Canada – that makes me think a little bit more because they're so blunt about it. They really say – smoking is going to kill you. That's on the label.

The study's findings are not surprising, given what is known about the way humans process information. Reading text takes more effort than viewing visual images, especially given the context in which the labels are viewed. Visual depictions make information more salient to individuals. Young adults, accustomed to images on their phone and computer screens, may be more attuned and receptive to information conveyed with text and images than they are to text alone. Furthermore, given myopia and time-inconsistent preferences, people may be inclined to discount the risks of an activity which causes insidious harm. Because the allure of smoking is visceral, the risks may be too attenuated and remote to be appropriately weighed.

To reduce cognitive overload from too much information, consent-seekers should present material information in a way that is relevant and accessible to the target audience. The greater the threat to the autonomy interest, the more effort that the consent-seeker should make to personalize the information for the target audience. Again, research on cigarette warning labels is particularly illuminating in understanding effective disclosure. One study indicated that the prevention of wrinkles may be a more powerful motivator to stop smoking than prevention of emphysema or other health-related illnesses caused by smoking.[450] Teenagers and young adults, in particular, may be more likely to pay attention to the short-term consequences of smoking (bad breath, smelly clothing) than the health consequences, which may be

---

[449] Id.
[450] See Marie-France Demierre et al., *Public Knowledge, Awareness, and Perceptions of the Association Between Skin Aging and Smoking*, 41 J. AM. ACAD. DERMATOLOGY 27–30 (1999) (finding that smokers, especially younger ones, believed that information about the aging effects of smoking would be relevant to smokers in deciding to quit).

more difficult for them to imagine. Visual images, too, may help convey information more effectively. Studies have found that a combination of textual warnings with strong, graphic images is more helpful in increasing smokers' intentions to quit smoking than only text or only graphic images.[451] One study indicated that it was not the information conveyed in the warnings which was effective, but the fear that the images evoked.[452] The more graphic and negative images evoked fear which enhanced smokers' intentions to quit smoking.[453] That study also found that graphic images with text were effective in prompting smokers to at least try to quit smoking.[454] Smokers who received graphic pictorial warnings with text were significantly more likely to have made an attempt to quit smoking during the trial period than those who received text-only warnings.[455] While nearly all smokers now know the health dangers of smoking, these dangers may not be at the forefront of their mind when they are craving a cigarette. Graphic labeling addresses the myopia and impulsivity associated with the decision (or more accurately, the habituated response) to smoke. It makes the harmful effects of smoking salient, forcing the smoker to confront what he may, in the moment, be ignoring. Nicotine is addictive and the craving which smokers suffer requires a countervailing emotional force, such as fear. Pictorial warnings, such as those implemented in Canada, elicit fear and other strong affective responses. Packaging requirements which conjure negative associations have also proven quite effective at deterring smokers and would-be smokers. Australia, for example, mandated that all cigarettes be sold in opaque, greenish-brown boxes. Referred to as the world's ugliest color, "opaque couché" has

---

[451] Noel Brewer et al., *Effect of Pictorial Cigarette Pack Warnings on Changes in Smoking Behavior: A Randomized Clinical Trial*, JAMA INTERNAL MED. (June 6, 2016), https://jamanetwork.com/jour nals/jamainternalmedicine/fullarticle/2526671; see also Jeremy Kees et al., *Tests of Graphic Visuals and Cigarette Package Warning Combinations: Implications for the Framework Convention on Tobacco Control*, 25 J. PUB. POL'Y & MARKETING 212, 218 (2006) ("significant effects of the inclusion of the visual warning" and "the combination of message and visual used . . . resulted in stronger personal intentions to quit than both the message statement alone and no warning information at all.").

[452] Brewer et. al., *supra* note 454 (finding that pictorial cigarette pack warnings illustrating a health harm increased quit attempts from 34 percent to 40 percent).

[453] *Id.*

[454] *Id.*

[455] *Id.* The four pictorial warnings contained text as originally proposed by the Family Smoking Prevention and Tobacco Control Act of 2009 (codified at 21 U.S.C. sec. 387a-1 (2012).) *Id.* The text-only warnings were the Surgeon General warnings that have been used in the United States since 1985. *Id.* Participants brought an eight-day supply of cigarettes to visits at which they completed computer surveys. While they completed the surveys, the warnings were placed on their cigarette packs. At weekly follow-up visits, participants were asked whether they had quit smoking for one day or longer during the week. At the week 4 follow up, they were also asked whether they had stopped smoking for one day or longer since the start of the study. *Id.* Forty percent of smokers who received the pictorial with text warnings reported a quit attempt lasting a day or longer, compared to 35 percent who received only the text warnings. *Id.* Furthermore, 5.7 percent of smokers exposed to pictorial warnings had stopped smoking for at least seven days by the end of the trial, compared to 3.8 percent of those who had received text-only warnings. *Id.*

been described as looking like "death, filth, lung tar or baby excrement."[456] Cigarette boxes were also covered with pictures of rotted teeth, tongues with tumors and worrisomely tiny newborns along with warnings about the hazards of smoking.[457] The warning text was in type larger than the cigarette brand names.[458] Recent data indicates that Australia's anti-smoking efforts have been quite successful.[459]

Research in the area of nutritional labeling provides additional insight into effective disclosure. Studies have indicated that traffic light labels are effective in helping consumers understand nutritional information; this is especially true with consumers who lacked numeracy skills, were generally unfamiliar with the relationship of calories to obesity and obesity to health, or lacked self-control. But while studies have shown that traffic light labels were more effective than numeric calorie information, context matters. One field study indicated that presenting numeric caloric information reduced the caloric value of lunch orders.[460] In that study, researchers Eric M. Van Epps, Julie S. Downs and George Loewenstein created an online lunch ordering system for employees of a large health care company. They created a control condition of participants who ordered without any calorie labels. There were three experimental conditions, with calories presented in numbers only, traffic lights only, and numbers and traffic lights. They found a "significant reduction in calories ordered among those exposed to labels."[461] Interestingly, they found there was no reduction on the *number* of items purchased,[462] which seems to indicate that diners were making choices based upon caloric information rather than price.[463] The researchers noted that while previous research in the full-service

---

[456] Donald G. McNeil, Jr., *How to Get Smokers to Quit? Enlist World's Ugliest Color*, N.Y. TIMES (June 21, 2016), www.nytimes.com/2016/06/21/health/cigarette-packaging-ugliest-color.html.

[457] See Australia Competition and Consumer (Tobacco) Information Standard 2011, www.legislation .gov.au/Details/F2011L02766 (last visited Mar. 31, 2018).

[458] *Id.*

[459] See *Evaluation of Tobacco Plain Packaging in Australia*, Dep't of Health, Austral. Gov't, www.health .gov.au/internet/main/publishing.nsf/Content/tobacco-plain-packaging-evaluation (last updated 23 Oct. 2017) (referring to post-implementation review of Tobacco Plain Packaging, which concluded that "tobacco plain packaging measure has begun to achieve its public health objectives of reducing smoking and exposure to tobacco smoke in Australia and it is expected to continue to do so into the future"); for report, see Post Implementation Review of Tobacco Plain Packaging, Austral. Gov't (Feb. 26, 2016), http://ris.pmc.gov.au/2016/02/26/tobacco-plain-packaging (concluding that evidence shows that requirements of the Tobacco Plain Packaging Act are succeeding in reducing prevalence of smoking and is likely to have greater positive impact, as intended).

[460] Eric M. Van Epps et al., *Calorie Label Formats: Using Numeric and Traffic Light Calorie Labels to Reduce Lunch Calories*, 35 J. PUB. POL'Y & MARKETING 26–36 (2016).

[461] *Id.* at 31.

[462] *Id.*

[463] *Id.* at 32. The researchers concluded: "Traffic light labels appear to be just as effective on their own as they are in combination with exact calorie numbers, which implies that detailed numeric information may not contribute much to one's decision-making process when ordering, beyond providing a simple signal regarding which menu options are relatively healthier than others." *Id.* at 32–33. Furthermore, the researchers noted that their finding of the effectiveness of numeric labeling was

restaurant setting "painted a pessimistic picture of the efficacy of numeric calorie labeling," their study showed that "both numeric and traffic light calorie labels had promising effects when ordering food online."[464] This study indicates that the context in which information is presented affects its salience. A diner sitting in a crowded restaurant has his attention focused on competing stimuli – his dining companion, the waiter, the menu, the people around him. The diner ordering from an office cubicle has his attention on the computer screen and can better focus on the presented information. Accordingly, certain types of disclosures may be more effective in some environments than in others.

Information should be tailored for the targeted audience. For example, immediate social consequences may be more salient than health consequences to younger (and healthier) smokers, who may be more concerned with their current social standing than their future health condition.[465] Younger smokers are likely not as concerned as older smokers with the possibility that smoking may lead to male impotence. Even graphic warnings have only limited effect on persuading smokers from quitting who have become chemically addicted. They may, however, have a much stronger impact on dissuading *potential* smokers.

The best method of disclosing risks would be to require that they be contained within the advertisement itself and presented in the same format (same font, color and style). If, however, they are not, the mode of communicating disclosures should be one which reaches the intended audience. For example, disclosures intended to reach young adults should focus on social media and online sites, rather than newspaper print ads. Generally, however, the mode of communication for disclosures should be the same as that used to advertise the product or service.

Finally, the government should engage in public awareness campaigns to educate the public of the broader social issues related to consentable but risky acts. (The funds might come from taxes or license fees associated with the activity.) Rather than focusing solely on dispassionate factual disclosures, state-sponsored ads can raise the types of moral and ethical questions addressed in this book. For example, an ad might depict a perfectly healthy woman using her hard-earned money to undergo risky plastic surgery and then show her wealthy plastic surgeon

inconsistent with other studies which found that numeric information alone had little effect on consumer decision-making. "This inconsistency with our results may result from differences between the environments in which the choices were made. Although consumers in a full-service restaurant might require traffic light (or other prescriptive) labels to guide them to choose more healthful items, the current study shows that consumers can use both numeric-only and graphic-only labels to choose lower-calorie meals when placing orders online." *Id.* at 33.

[464] *Id.*

[465] *See* Kees et al., *supra* note 454, at 223 (noting that research shows that "the use of graphic warnings may depend in part on the consequences conveyed by the warning ... Some research suggests that warnings emphasizing social consequences can be more effective because they are more salient among younger populations") (citing Karen H. Smith & Mary Ann Stutts, *Effects of Short Term Cosmetic Versus Long-Term Health Fear Appeals in Anti-Smoking Advertisements on the Smoking Behaviour of Adolescents*, 3 J. CONSUMER BEHAVIOR no. 2, 2003, at 157–77).

investing that money into the stock market and driving a Tesla. The resistance of the tobacco industry to ads which may trigger moral outrage indicates that appeals to moral outrage may be especially effective at attracting audience attention and increasing an issue's salience. For example, as part of a settlement, tobacco companies had to issue corrective statements in ads. One proposed ad stated,

> We told Congress under oath that we believed nicotine is not addictive. We told you that smoking is not an addiction and all it takes to quit is willpower. Here's the truth: Smoking is addictive. And it's not easy to quit. We manipulated cigarettes to make them more addictive.[466]

Not surprisingly, the tobacco companies resisted, claiming that the ads shamed them. Shaming, of course, is what would have made these ads effective.

The argument made by corporations against government regulation of advertising on First Amendment grounds is puzzling.[467] Commercial speech is – and should be – subject to greater regulation than political speech.[468] Advertising which promotes a product or service implicates the company's economic or property interest and differs from corporate statements on political or social issues, which implicate an expressive interest (even though they may also have the effect of promoting a corporation's brand). Furthermore, the government may outright forbid or regulate the sale of dangerous substances, as it does with certain drugs and chemicals, and prohibit or regulate harmful activities, as it does with drunk driving. If the First Amendment is deemed to prohibit the regulation of advertising for high-level threat to autonomy activities, then these activities should be prohibited altogether because the risk of defective consent and the likelihood of regret would be too high to be socially acceptable. The issue of advertising and free speech then becomes irrelevant as the First Amendment does not apply to illegal activities.[469]

Admittedly, even governmental regulation of advertisements and solicitations may be an imperfect solution to the problem of opportunism. Oversight may be lax, constrained by a lack of resources and subject to political influence. While governmental regulation is necessary to restrain opportunism, it may be ineffective

---

[466]   Maheshwari, *supra* note 438.

[467]   *See* Zauderer v. Disciplinary Counsel of Supreme Court of Ohio, 471 U.S. 626, 650–52 (1985) (distinguishing disclosure requirements from prohibitions on speech and holding that advertisers' rights are adequately protected if disclosure requirements are reasonably related to the state's interest in preventing consumer deception); *Cigar Assn. of Am.*, 2018 WL 2223653, at 27–44 (applying the *Zauderer* standard to find factual disclosure requirements on cigar packaging constitutional).

[468]   *See* Posados de Puerto Rico Assocs. v. Tourism Co. of Puerto Rico, 478 U.S. 328, 340 (1986) (noting that commercial speech receives a "limited form of First Amendment protection so long as it concerns a lawful activity and is not misleading or fraudulent.").

[469]   *See* Cent. Hudson Gas & Elec. Corp. v. Pub. Serv. Comm'n of New York, 447 U.S. 557, 566 (1980) (establishing a four-part test to resolve First Amendment challenges involving commercial speech, including that activity must be lawful); *see also Posados de Puerto Rico Assocs.*, 478 U.S. at 340–41; Greater New Orleans Broad. Ass'n v. United States, 527 U.S. 173, 183 (1999) (stating that First Amendment protects only commercial speech which concerns a lawful activity).

at doing so. If governmental regulation of advertisements for an activity which poses a high-level threat to autonomy proves to be a failure, the underlying activity should not be consentable.[470]

C. REGULATING PROVIDERS AND PROCEDURES

Governmental regulation of acts which implicate a high-level threat to autonomy is an important and necessary part of determining their consentability. Because the state has the power to impose regulations to protect public health and safety, the public may believe it always does so. Some people may believe that if an act is lawful, then it must have passed state scrutiny and is at least reasonably safe. Consentability confers upon an act a legitimacy that it may not deserve. For example, participants in a British study regarding cosmetic interventions believed that non-surgical interventions, such as dermal fillers and Botox, were regulated. There was "genuine shock" that surgical cosmetic procedures could be performed by non-specialists, and a consensus that this should not be permitted.[471] The public should not be misled about something that could have serious consequences for public health and safety. State medical boards often don't restrict doctors from performing procedures which are outside of their specialty area.[472] Plastic surgeon Dr. Anthony Youn writes that the lack of regulation in the area of cosmetic surgery has "allowed an increasing number of doctors of all types – including gynecologists, general surgeons and even emergency medicine physicians – to perform tummy tucks, liposuction, facelifts and breast enhancement."[473]

If consent is to provide the justification for permitting even those acts which pose a high risk of harm, the conditions for consent must be robust. Consent to an act which is based upon a mistaken assumption that it has been preliminarily screened for public safety means the knowledge condition is deficient – and so consent is defective. The risks of certain acts may be self-evident, but other risks may not be. Disclosure of risks alone is insufficient to overcome public misperception that providers of services have undergone some sort of training or passed a licensure requirement. Because some states require even those who simply braid hair to obtain a cosmetology license (which often requires nearly two years of schooling),[474] consumers may assume that someone conducting risky and invasive procedures

---

[470] See Garrett Hardin, *The Tragedy of the Commons*, 162 SCI. 1243, 1246 (1968) (noting that prohibition is "easy to legislate," although temperance is not).

[471] U.K. DEPT. OF HEALTH REPORT, *supra* note 75, at 48.

[472] See Anthony Youn, *Plastic Surgery: "Wild West" of Medicine*, CNN (July 25, 2012), www.cnn.com /2012/07/25/health/youn-wild-west-medicine/index.html.

[473] *Id.*

[474] Jacob Goldstein, *So You Think You Can be a Hair Braider?*, N.Y. TIMES (June 12, 2012), www.nytimes .com/2012/06/17/magazine/so-you-think-you-can-be-a-hair-braider.html?_r=1&ref=magazine&page wanted=all; Hair Braiding Requirements, AM. ASS'N COSMETOLOGY SCH., http://beautyschools.org /hair-braiding-requirements/ (last visited June 13, 2018).

will have undergone training and be subject to regulation which is much more rigorous.[475] In reality, the requirements vary from state to state. New York state, for example, has only minimal and vaguely defined requirements for body art providers, although it is currently in the process of implementing new regulations.[476] The primary regulations governing body piercing studios in the state of New York appear to be a prohibition on piercing minors without written parental or guardian consent[477] and a requirement that only single-use needles be used.[478] A report issued by the American Academy of Pediatrics stated that although most states had a law in place regulating tattooing (especially of minors), even with these regulations "72% of states do not effectively regulate sanitation, training and licensing, and infection control."[479] The same is true of state laws governing piercing.[480]

Service providers may provide input on how to regulate a given practice, but attempts to self-regulate should be viewed with skepticism. Self-regulation where for-profit businesses are involved is as effective as leaving foxes to guard the henhouse. As a rule, the more intrusive and potentially harmful the activity is, the more carefully the state should regulate how it is conducted.

D. REMEDIES AND ENFORCEMENT

The issue of remedies is unavoidable in discussing consentability and contractability. Given the gatekeeper function of consent, the consequences of a finding of no-consent may be grave. A doctor, for example, who performs a procedure erroneously believing that the patient has consented would be liable for battery. The question of remedies is particularly important as it relates to contractability. A contract means that the promise is legally enforceable. The standard remedy for breach of contract is

---

[475] *Frequently Asked Questions – Cosmetic Treatments*, Med. Bd. California, www.mbc.ca.gov /Licensees/Cosmetic_Treatments_FAQ.aspx (last visited June 13, 2018) (some states do regulate procedures such as Botox. In California, only physicians, registered nurses, or physician assistants under physician supervision may inject Botox).

[476] *Body Art – Tattooing and Body Piercing*, N.Y. St. Dep't Health, www.health.ny.gov/community/ body_art/ (last visited Mar. 30, 2018) (New York's Public Health Law article 4A requires that body piercing studios obtain a permit, but does not indicate any licensing or educational requirements); N.Y. C.L.S. Pub. Health § 461(3) (LEXIS through 2018 Ch. 1–47, 50–58) ("The department shall issue a permit if the body piercing specialist and body piercing studio or tattooist and tattoo studio are in compliance with this article, penal law and the state sanitary code are not otherwise disqualified under this article.").

[477] *Id.* at § 460-a.

[478] *Id.* at § 467.

[479] Cora C. Breuner, David A. Levine & The Committee on Adolescence, Clinical Report: Adolescent and Young Adult Tattooing, Piercing, and Scarification 11 (2017), http://pediatrics .aappublications.org/content/pediatrics/early/2017/09/14/peds.2017–1962.full.pdf (published online in PEDIATRICS, the official journal of the American Academy of Pediatrics).

[480] *See Tattooing and Body Piercing*, Nat'l Conf. St. Legislatures (Aug. 1, 2017), www.ncsl.org /research/health/tattooing-and-body-piercing.aspx (collecting state tattoo and body piercing regulations and noting that, as of January 2009, over twenty-nine states restrict or prohibit adolescents from getting tattoos or body piercings).

damages. Damages for breach of a bodily integrity contract would be inadequate and difficult to calculate. In a contract for the transfer of a kidney, would damages be measured by the market value of a kidney? The value of X's life? How would something as non-fungible as either a kidney or a life be calculated?

Even if it were possible to calculate with reasonable certainty, expectation damages in transactions involving a high-level threat to autonomy would be awkward and cumbersome at best, and coercive at worst, given the asymmetry of what the parties are exchanging. Currently, if a participant in a clinical drug trial has second thoughts and wishes to end her involvement in the study, federal law requires that she be permitted to do so without penalty.[481] The result should be the same in any situation which involves bodily integrity.

In typical commercial transactions, the consideration offered by each party may vary in value, but does not differ in kind – it is property (money, personal or real property) or a right or encumbrance affecting property. Accordingly, when one party changes her mind, judicial enforcement is sound because the same *type* of interest is at stake for both parties. In "mismatch" transactions, the nature (distinct from the value) of the transaction is different. One party is offering a body part or an act which involves a risk of bodily injury, while the other party is offering only money. This transaction might be money exchanged for a body part as part of a transplant, but it might also be payment for participating in an ultimate fighting match or an experimental drug trial. The transaction is a mismatch because the parties are not undertaking the same *type* of risk.

A contract requires mutuality of obligation, but it does not require mutuality of consideration; however, the disparate nature of consideration in a mismatch transaction affects the nature of the obligation in a way that is more than simply a matter of degree or value. A court order forcing someone to physically perform and risk bodily injury is more coercive than ordering someone to pay money or sell property. Not surprisingly, courts often find contracts involving a mismatch transaction to be against public policy. For example, certain types of maternal surrogacy contracts are deemed to be void as against public policy.[482] Given the offensiveness of enforcing the contract, courts may simply refuse to recognize it as a contract at all.

In mismatch transactions, courts should recognize the contract but not specifically enforce it. Generally, the equitable remedy of specific performance will not be ordered if doing so would violate public policy.[483] Accordingly, specific

---

[481] 45 C.F.R. § 46.116(b)(8) (LEXIS through June 13, 2018 issue of the Fed. Reg.) (requiring that investigators inform participants in research that they may "discontinue participation at any time without penalty or loss of benefits to which the subject is otherwise entitled.").

[482] *See generally* Matsumura, *supra* note 2; Zalesne, *supra* note 2.

[483] RESTATEMENT (SECOND) OF CONTRACTS § 365 (AM. LAW INST. 1981) ("Specific performance or an injunction will not be granted if the act or forbearance that would be compelled or the use of compulsion is contrary to public policy.").

performance is rarely ordered in cases involving breach of an employment contract.[484] Specific performance is typically granted when damages would be inadequate; nevertheless, even when the parties expressly agreed to it in their contract and damages are inadequate, courts will refuse to order specific performance for breach of an employment contract.[485] The policy against specific performance in employment cases recognizes the relational nature of employment and the need for cooperation and trust in working relationships. It also seeks to minimize the administrative burden on the judiciary.[486]

If specific performance of employment contracts raises the disquieting specter of involuntary servitude, specific performance of bodily integrity contracts would be even more disturbing and would likely violate the Thirteenth Amendment.[487] Assume, for example, that X enters into an agreement where X will pay Y $40,000 if Y agrees to have a kidney removed so that it can be transplanted into X's body. On the day of the operation, Y changes Y's mind. Y should have the power to withdraw consent even though the language of contracts and promise-keeping suggests otherwise.[488]

The hierarchy of autonomy interests provides a way to think about bargains that reflects society's core values. Y's autonomy interest in Y's bodily integrity outweighs X's autonomy interest in X's property. Although X's body is affected by the contract, it is not the consideration for the contract. The consideration supplied by X is the $40,000; that is the only thing that X is giving up in order to get what Y is offering. Y, on the other hand, is offering to give up his kidney in order to get that $40,000.

An underlying reason for judicial squeamishness with mismatch transactions may be that there is no palatable remedy for breach of a contract when the breaching party is the one who is offering up his or her bodily integrity. Yet, the need to limit the remedies for breach of contract in transactions involving a high risk to autonomy does not mean that the contract should be void or the transaction incontractable.

---

[484] Zannis v. Lake Shore Radiologists, Ltd., 392 N.E.2d 126, 128 (Ill. App. Ct. 1979) ("It is well settled that, with reference to such contracts, when specific performance is sought, a court should not compel an employee to work for his employer, nor compel an employer to retain an employee in his service."); RESTATEMENT (SECOND) OF CONTRACTS § 367(1) (AM. LAW INST. 1981) ("A promise to render personal service will not be specifically enforced.").

[485] *Id.* ("As stated, there are strong policy reasons for the rule against compelling an employer to retain an employee against his wishes. Furthermore, these reasons indicate the rule is designed not only for the benefit of the parties to a personal services contract, but also for the sake of both efficient judicial administration and society in general. Consequently, the mere fact that the parties to a personal services contract may have agreed therein to specific performance as a remedy cannot alter the necessity for imposing the general rule against compelling an employer to retain an employee.").

[486] *Zannis*, 392 N.E.2d at 129.

[487] One might argue that such servitude is not "involuntary" if the individual had agreed to it contractually. But it is involuntary in the sense that the consenter no longer wishes to perform; in other words, consent was destroyed. *See* discussion, Chapter 4 section B.

[488] *See also* Ariel Porat & Stephen Sugarman, *Limited Inalienability Rules*, 107 GEO. L.J. (forthcoming 2018) (proposing a "limited inalienability rule" that allows the holder of an entitlement to transfer it but still possess an inalienable right to revoke the transfer at a later stage, with no penalty).

Instead, I propose that contracts involving mismatch transactions be treated analogously to unilateral contracts. A unilateral contract is one where an offer is made which can only be accepted by performance.[489] Acceptance and contract performance occur simultaneously. If the offeree discontinues performance, the offeror cannot compel completion or sue for damages because the contract was never formed. By contrast, the commencement of performance by the offeree creates an "option contract" which restricts the offeror's power to revoke the offer.[490] Therefore, if the offeree completes performance, the offeror must also perform, or be liable for breach. An offer for a unilateral contract may thus bind the offeror without binding the offeree.

However, the comparison of bodily integrity contracts to unilateral contracts is imperfect. Both parties must intend to form a bodily integrity contract, as these exchanges involve progressive and mutually dependent performances. Accordingly, either party or both parties may have commenced performance at the time of breach. In the above scenario for example, X may have made payments to Y prior to Y's breach. Y should have the absolute right to refuse to perform up until the time of the operation, but X should be able to recover damages. Rather than expectation damages, restitution would be the more appropriate remedy for breach by Y. Restitution would require Y to return to X any benefit conferred from the transaction.[491] To make restitution instead of expectation damages the standard remedy for breach of a bodily integrity contract does not mean that a contract was not formed or that contracts involving mismatch transactions are void.

Specific performance should not be available where performance involves bodily integrity; however, an injunction *would* be appropriate where the order does not require the breaching party to risk bodily integrity. For example, if Y breaches the contract with X because Y has found another party, Z, willing to pay more for the kidney, X may seek an injunction to prevent Y from undergoing the operation even if X cannot compel Y to perform. The injunction essentially stops Y from making a bad faith, opportunistic breach, but it does not pose a threat to Y's bodily integrity. It only limits Y's freedom to contract – in other words, it does not offend any fundamental societal value and does not pose a high-level threat to Y's autonomy. It also does not prevent Y from seeking medical care or any other medical procedure. It *does* deter Y from breaching the agreement with X in order to make more money. Permitting an

---

[489] RESTATEMENT (SECOND) OF CONTRACTS § 45 cmt. a (AM. LAW INST. 1981) (stating that "where the offer does not invite a promissory acceptance" is has "often been referred to as an 'offer for a unilateral contract.'").

[490] *Id.* at § 45(1) ("Where an offer invites an offeree to accept by rendering a performance and does not invite a promissory acceptance, an option contract is created when the offeree tenders or beings the invited performance or tenders a beginning of it.").

[491] Craig Purshouse & Kate Bracegirdle, *The Problem of Unenforceable Surrogacy Contracts: Can Unjust Enrichment Provide a Solution?*, MED. L. REV. (Feb. 7, 2018), at 3, https://academic.oup .com/medlaw/advance-article/doi/10.1093/medlaw/fwy001/4841967?searchresult=1 (proposing that an unjust enrichment theory would be more fair to the intended parents than the status quo, but without subordinating the best interests of the child).

injunction in this scenario treats the interests of the parties similarly *when they are similar.* In the original scenario, Y has a good faith concern about the operation and wishes to avoid harm to his body. Although X's motive for entering into the contract involves his bodily integrity, X is not using his body as consideration (it is not being offered as part of the transaction, the way that Y's body is). X's consideration is mere money and his interest is only economic. Thus, Y's interest in preserving his bodily integrity outweighs X's economic interest. Furthermore, the societal interest in prohibiting involuntary servitude outweighs the societal interest in promoting the security of transactions. By contrast, in the scenario where Y wishes to breach in order to receive more money from a third party, an injunction prohibiting him from doing so recognizes that Y's interest is no longer in preserving bodily integrity; rather, it is an economic interest, similar to X's. If bodily integrity exchanges are to be recognized as *contracts* then they must be enforceable in some way, even if the nature of their enforcement is limited and recognizes the mismatch nature of the transaction.

There is a related policy reason for permitting the issuance of an injunction where Y breaches to make more money – by committing an "efficient breach," Y is both acting opportunistically (triggering the Opportunism Corollary) and treating his body like a commodity. Y should not be permitted to treat his body like a commodity simply because it is *his* body, for the reasons discussed earlier in this book.[492]

Under my suggested approach, X may not seek specific performance or expectation damages for breach by Y because a bodily integrity contract is different in kind from other types of contracts. But that does not mean that the contract is void. Y, for example, would be able to fully enforce the contract if X refused to pay. Furthermore, an injunction should be available for the consent-seeker in situations involving opportunistic breaches like Y's described above. In ordinary commercial transactions, an injunction is available where the plaintiff can show that there is no adequate remedy at law, such as where damages would be hard to measure.[493] Given the inadequacy of damages in cases involving bodily integrity contracts, an injunction should be available to prevent opportunistic breaches where the breaching party's motive is simply to make more money.

Given the nature of bodily integrity contracts, mental distress damages may also be available. Mental distress damages are generally not recoverable in breach of contract cases; however, there are exceptions where mental distress was a reasonably

---

[492] *See* Chapter 2 section B.

[493] Register.com, Inc. v. Verio, Inc. 356 F.3d 393, 404 (2d Cir. 2004) (stating that "irreparable harm may be found where damages are difficult to establish and measure"); O'Neill v. Poitras, 551 N.Y.S.2d 92, 93 (N.Y. App. Div. 1990) ("Injunctive relief is not appropriate in actions involving breach of contract where a plaintiff has an adequate remedy at law."); *see also* RESTATEMENT (SECOND) OF CONTRACTS §360 (AM. LAW INST. 1981) ("In determining whether the remedy in damages would be adequate, the following circumstances are significant: (a) the difficulty of proving damages with reasonable certainty, (b) the difficulty of procuring a suitable substitute performance by means of money awarded as damages, and (c) the likelihood that an award of damages could not be collected.").

foreseeable consequence of the breach.[494] Mental distress damages would be foreseeable where the consenter breaches a bodily integrity contract in bad faith and the consent-seeker has relied upon performance. It may be especially useful where the breach is a partial breach (and so does not excuse contract performance). For example, a surrogate who drinks during pregnancy in violation of a "no-drinking" clause may be liable for mental distress damages (which should be in an amount less than expectation damages for these situations), even if the breach would not excuse performance of the contract by the couple that hired her. Mental distress damages may also be available to the consenter in the event of a breach by the consent-seeker. Given the intimate nature of transactions involving the body, it is foreseeable that some breaches would degrade the consenter and cause mental distress even if the contract price were paid. As previously noted, the covenant of good faith and fair dealing as applied to bodily integrity contracts should mean that the parties treat each other with mutual respect and in a way that preserves each other's human dignity.[495] For example, a surrogate who is subjected to degrading comments about her reproductive organs as she is delivering a couple's baby has suffered a harm that is unique to a bodily integrity contract. Mental distress is a foreseeable consequence of this type of breach.

As previously mentioned, restitution should be available to the consent-seeker (X) in the event of even a good faith total breach by the consenter (Y) in a bodily integrity contract. Restitution seeks to undo the transaction and return to each party any benefit it has conferred on the other party by way of part-performance or reliance.[496] Any prepayments made by X, for example, would have to be repaid by Y if Y decided to breach by not undergoing the exchange. To require Y to return money that was paid in anticipation of Y's performance does not raise the same troubling issues as requiring Y to pay expectation damages; on the contrary, to allow Y to retain money that X paid in anticipation of Y's performance would be unfair to X and encourage opportunism by those in Y's position. Restitution would also be available to the *consenter* where the consenter had already performed but where there was defective consent. Disgorgement of profits might be an especially effective remedy where the consent-seeker was an intermediary in a bodily integrity contract or a business or entrepreneur in a novel/experimental activity scenario. Some of the hard cases discussed in Chapter 2 raise other complex problems regarding breach and remedy,

---

[494] *See* RESTATEMENT (SECOND) OF CONTRACTS § 353 (AM. LAW INST. 1981) ("Recovery for emotional disturbance will be excluded unless the breach also caused bodily harm or the contract or the breach is of such a kind that serious emotional disturbance was a particularly likely result."); *see also* Huskey v. Nat'l Broad. Co., 632 F. Supp. 1282, 1293 (N.D. Ill. 1986) (finding that knowing invasion of privacy could reasonably be expected to cause emotional disturbance and constituted breach of contract to abide by regulations prohibiting nonconsensual photography of inmates); Ross v. Forest Lawn Mem'l Park, 153 Cal. App. 3d 988, 996 (1984) (finding that claim for emotional distress damages was compensable as a result of breach of promise to provide private funeral and burial services).

[495] *See* discussion *supra* Chapter 4 section B.

[496] RESTATEMENT (SECOND) OF CONTRACTS § 344 (AM. LAW INST. 2011).

and resolution of these problems should reflect the hierarchy of threats to the autonomy interest. The hard cases are discussed further in Chapter 7.

In addition to reinforcing the prohibition against involuntary servitude, allowing wide latitude to individuals to withdraw from activities which affect their bodily integrity will likely have positive effects on the consenting process. The consent-seeker may be more forthcoming with information at the outset, to reduce the likelihood that the consenter will withdraw upon later learning of additional information. It also encourages consent-seekers to act more responsibly. For example, a researcher might more carefully design the experiment and gather preliminary data to minimize the likelihood of participants withdrawing. Allowing withdrawals without repercussions may also provide an incentive to consent-seekers to be more thorough in their screening of participants to make sure that they are emotionally, physically and mentally prepared to complete performance.

The judicial system is a costly and time-consuming mechanism to redress grievances, and measures should be taken to avoid litigation by reducing occasions for conflict. For example, in bodily integrity transactions, the total sum of money due the consenter should be placed in escrow upon contract execution to reduce the number of disputes regarding the timing and amount of payments. Regulatory agencies should also craft standard terms to prevent hard bargaining and exploitation in bodily integrity transactions. These standard terms might, for example, prohibit waivers for negligence and require payments on a set schedule. With the use of smart contracts and other blockchain technology, the problem of costly enforcement mechanisms could be eliminated or greatly reduced. Given the realities of litigation and the potential abuses of bodily integrity contracts (such as renegotiating payment terms after the parties have begun performance), if the technology becomes more widely available, the use of automated enforcement mechanisms may be particularly useful.

E. PRESUMPTION OF DEFECTIVE CONSENT

The prevailing notion of consent is that it is a subjective state of mind communicated through an outward manifestation which is evaluated under an objective standard. Consequently, a manifestation of consent is often used as a substitute for *actual* consent if a "reasonable person" would have understood it as such. In practice, this means that it is the *manifestation* that justifies the subsequent actions, and places the terms of an interaction into the realm of contract and mutual agreement.[497] A finding of consent has a psychological effect in that it changes the way the consenter is perceived, by herself and society. As Lee Ross and Richard Nisbett note, "Social processes unfold quite differently when people believe they have freely chosen their behavior, as a direct expression of their goals and attitudes,

---

[497] See discussion *supra* Chapter 4 section A.

than when they believe the behavior was coerced or was under the control of extrinsic reinforcing agents."[498] The focus on the consenter's actions, the "manifestation of consent," thus often results in shifting blame onto the consenter for ensuing events while too prematurely and too comprehensively absolving the *consent-seeker* from responsibility. On the other hand, to ignore the effect that the manifestation of consent has on the consent-seeker would absolve consenters from taking responsibility for *their* actions, and treat unfairly those consent-seekers who act in good faith on a consenter's expressions. Consent is mutual and relational. The current absolutist conception of legal consent is ill-suited for flesh-and-blood human beings and does not reflect the complexities, dynamism and nuances of human interactions.

I propose recognizing a special, flexible category of *defective consent* which recognizes that a consenter may manifest consent because the consent-seeker has manipulated the context in some way. Defective consent recognizes that the consenter, too, may act irresponsibly and opportunistically. There are degrees of wrongfulness, and consent is a shared responsibility; neither party is immune from opportunistic behavior. The general concept of defective consent is already captured in the law, although in implied or abstruse ways. Contract law recognizes the defenses of duress, undue influence, mistake, and unconscionability which allow the consenter to avoid a contract despite a manifestation of consent. Criminal and tort law also recognize the concept of defective consent in "mitigating circumstances" which may reduce the severity of the crime charged or the extent of the defendant's liability.

Generally, the law distinguishes between acts where there was no consent and acts where there was defective consent. For example, in the context of medical malpractice, a physician who has failed to obtain consent (i.e. no-consent) has committed battery, while one who has failed to obtain informed consent (i.e. defective consent) is liable under a duty of care or negligence standard.[499] The nature of the patient's consent determines whether the physician is liable for battery or negligence (or in some situations, like emergencies, nothing at all). In Cobbs v. Grant,[500] the Supreme Court of California distinguished between consent to the *type* of treatment, and consent to treatment without adequate disclosure:

> Where a doctor obtains consent of the patient to perform one type of treatment and subsequently performs a substantially different treatment for which consent was not obtained, there is a clear case of battery . . . However, when an undisclosed potential

---

[498] Lee Ross & Richard E. Nisbett, The Person and the Situations: Perspectives of Social Psychology 16 (1991).

[499] *See* Daum v. SpineCare Med. Grp., Inc., 52 Cal. App. 4th 1285, 1313 (1997) (noting that the "battery theory should be reserved for those circumstances when a doctor performs an operation to which the patient has not consented ... However, when the patient consents to certain treatment and the doctor performs that treatment but an undisclosed inherent complication with a low probability occurs, no intentional deviation from the consent given appears; rather, the doctor in obtaining consent may have failed to meet his due care duty to disclose pertinent information.").

[500] Cobbs v. Grant, 8 Cal. 3d 229, 237 (1972).

complication results, the occurrence of which was not an integral part of the treatment procedure but merely a known risk, the courts are divided on the issue of whether this should be deemed to be a battery or negligence ... Dean Prosser surveyed the decisions in this area and concluded, "The earliest cases treated this as a matter of vitiating the consent, so that there was liability for battery ... [T]he prevailing view now is that the action ... is in reality one for negligence in failing to conform to the proper standard .... "[501]

The California Supreme Court concluded that although it was a "close question ... the trend appears to be towards categorizing failure to obtain informed consent as negligence."[502] It also implied that if the "undisclosed potential complication" *were* an "integral part of the treatment procedure," rather than merely a "known risk," then the performance of the procedure would be without consent and the doctor would be liable for battery.[503]

Defective consent results where the consenter has manifested consent, but at least one of the other conditions of consent is deficient in light of the threat to the autonomy interest. I propose that in some situations, one or more conditions of consent is likely to be deficient, and consent should be *presumed* to be defective regardless of whether the consenter has manifested consent. One example is where a patient consents to a medical procedure which poses a high-level threat to the autonomy interest. In that situation, the patient likely does not have a robust enough knowledge condition given the threat to autonomy and the specialized nature of the information regarding medical procedures. Accordingly, medical procedures involving a high-level threat to the autonomy interest must not be subject to private ordering and (1) must be performed in accordance with professional standards; and (2) the terms between the parties, including the economic terms, must be fair and reasonable. Conflicts of interest must be disclosed; a failure to do so should be the equivalent of failing to disclose a material risk of the procedure, and treated like a failure to obtain informed consent.

Another situation in which consent should be presumed defective is where someone under twenty-five years of age has undergone a high-level threat to autonomy activity. The consent-seeker could overcome the presumption with evidence that (1) the activity was initiated by the consenter; (2) the terms of the activity or exchange were substantively fair and equitable; and (3) the activity or exchange was performed in accordance with professional standards. Contract law already presumes minors lack capacity to enter into contracts. This presumption should also be extended *ex post* in high-level risk activities (i.e. where a bodily integrity contract has already been performed) to those aged under twenty-five years. For example, a twenty-year-old (X) who sold her eggs to an intermediary (Y) could argue that her consent was defective. Y could then try to rebut the presumption by showing that X approached

[501]   *Id.* at 239 (citing PROSSER ON TORTS at 165–66 (4th ed. 1971) (footnotes omitted)).
[502]   *Id.*
[503]   *Id.*

Y, that the economic terms were fair and equitable, and that the care she received was performed by a qualified professional and in accordance with that profession's standard of care. A failure to meet this burden would subject Y to a claim by X for unjust enrichment or disgorgement of profits. Depending upon the circumstances, Y could also be liable under tort or criminal law. A consent-seeker who acts unreasonably but in good faith deserves a more lenient punishment and his interests deserve more consideration than one who acted in bad faith and with total disregard for another's autonomy.[504] My approach is similar in this respect to that proposed by Alasdair Maclean who, writing about informed consent in the medical context, stated that a "healthcare professional acting with a wholly selfish motive and no intention to benefit the patient should be subject to a greater sanction than the healthcare professional whose intention and motive are consistent with his or her basic obligation of beneficence even if they act in a way that is unjustifiably paternalistic."[505]

If there is defective consent, there must be some independent basis – independent of the manifestation of consent – which justifies the consent-seeker's action that results in the harm or injury. Default rules will usually determine whether that independent basis exists. These default rules are the laws and norms that govern society and human behavior. In cases involving actions by members of a profession, such as doctors or lawyers, the standards of that profession's governing body will fill the gap left by defective consent.[506] In cases where there is no governing body or professional code of conduct, reference should be made to social and business norms to determine conformity with standards of reasonableness, good faith and fair dealing. In the absence of an independent justification for the action, the consent-seeker would be liable for injury directly caused by the action.

The acknowledgment of defective consent provides several significant contributions to the current way of thinking about consent. First, it recognizes that consent is not an all-or-nothing proposition where either one party or the other wins or loses. It recognizes that people have a responsibility to each other for the harmful consequences of their actions. In addition, in some situations, it shifts the burden of consent onto the party who is in the better position to ensure the conditions of

---

[504] But, as Peter Alces has suggested, people may not be as fully in physical control of their actions, and so not as morally culpable, as "folk psychology" might suggest. *See* PETER ALCES, THE MORAL CONFLICT OF LAW AND NEUROSCIENCE, at 7 (2018) (referring to folk psychology as "what we *imagine*" to be going on in the minds of others, which differs from cognitive neuroscience, which "seeks to identify the physical cause of the actor's behavior, the underlying neural aberration").

[505] ALASDAIR MACLEAN, AUTONOMY, INFORMED CONSENT AND MEDICAL LAW: A RELATIONAL CHALLENGE 231–38 (2009) (proposing a "relational model of consent" in the doctor–patient context and a "new category of civil claim" that allows for a range of remedies depending on the precise nature of the breach).

[506] *See* Kurt M. Hartman & Bryan A. Liang, *Exceptions to Informed Consent in Emergency Medicine*, HOSP. PHYSICIAN (Mar. 1999), at 53–59, www.turner-white.com/pdf/hp_mar99_emergmed.pdf (noting that a doctor who performs an emergency procedure to save a patient's life would not be liable for battery or negligence if it was performed in accordance with professional standards).

consent given the context. Finally, expressly recognizing the concept of defective consent permits the crafting of remedies which better reflect blameworthiness.[507]

F. DISCLOSURE, DEFECTIVE CONSENT AND LIABILITY

A proper assessment of the knowledge condition of consent requires understanding how disclosure affects consent. The following questions illuminate the relationship between disclosure and consent and provide guidance on how to address situations where defective consent results from a failure of the consent-seeker to provide adequate disclosure.

1. Was information properly disclosed in light of the threat level to autonomy? Did the consenting party have knowledge of the potential risks?

   The disclosure requirement is not a mere technical requirement. The consent-seeker cannot defend herself simply by showing that information was presented to the consenter. The information must be presented in a way that was understandable in light of the objectives of the consenter. The volume of information sufficient to meet this standard will depend upon the threat level to the autonomy interest (i.e. the nature of the transaction) and its relevance to the consenter.

2. If the information was not properly disclosed, then there may be either defective consent or no-consent, depending on the nature of the omitted information.

   The failure to disclose *all* information does not necessarily mean there was no-consent; however, the party has consented only to what was explicitly disclosed. A failure to disclose material risks associated with the procedure means there was defective consent to the procedure. On the other hand, a failure to disclose the type of treatment means there was no-consent. For example, a patient consenting to one type of surgical procedure has not given consent for the physician to perform another type.[508]

3. If there is defective consent, then the consent-seeker is not immunized from liability, although the punishment for defective consent should differ from that for no-consent.

   Defective consent does not mean the same thing as no-consent. Defective consent means that consent does not provide the justification for the act and does not immunize the consent-seeker from liability. The consent-seeker must then try to justify her actions by reference to laws or professional or social norms. For example,

---

[507] Orit Gan has suggested, if "consent is recognized as a continuous process, different degrees of consent may result in different measures of damages." *See* Gan, *supra* note 14, at 634.

[508] *See* Cain v. Howorth, 877 So. 2d 566, 581–82 (Ala. 2003) (finding that patient's consent to perform a total hip arthroplasty did not constitute consent to a bipolar hip arthroplasty; there was no consent for the latter procedure); *see also* Cobbs v. Grant, 8 Cal. 3d 229, 239 (1972) (noting that where "a doctor obtains consent to perform one type of treatment and subsequently performs a substantially different treatment for which consent was not obtained, there is a clear case of battery.").

if a physician fails to get informed consent (i.e. there is only defective consent), she would be liable for injuries which materialized but whose risks were not adequately disclosed.[509] If the patient had not suffered injury, the physician would not have any liability. By contrast, where the patient has refused treatment altogether, there is no-consent (not defective consent) and, with the exception of emergencies (where consent is generally not required),[510] the physician would be liable for battery even if the procedure had been performed reasonably because the touching itself constitutes the injury.[511] As previously noted, if the nature of the undisclosed information is so material and relevant that its omission means the patient has not consented, then the physician has committed battery. For example, a patient who has consented to one type of procedure has not consented if the doctor performs another one.[512]

---

[509] *See* White v. Beeks, 469 S.W.3d 517, 525 (Tenn. 2015) (where there was no informed consent "a physician would be liable to a patient for injuries resulting from the procedure, 'regardless of whether such injuries resulted from negligence or otherwise'" (citing Ray v. Scheibert, 484 S.W.2d 63, 71 (Tenn. Ct. App. 1972)).

[510] *Cobbs*, 8 Cal. 3d at 243.

[511] *See, e.g.*, Doctors Hosp. of Augusta, L.L.C. v. Alicea, 774 S.E. 2d 114, 126 (Ga. Ct. App. 2015) (noting that a "competent adult patient has the right to refuse medical and surgical treatment" and that medical touching without "basic consent" to treatment constitutes the intentional tort of battery); Lawson v. Bloodsworth, 722 S.E.2d 358, 359 (Ga. Ct. App. 2012) ("A cause of action for battery will lie for any unlawful touching, that is, a touching of the plaintiff's person, even if minimal, which is offensive.").

[512] Erickson v. Garber, 2003 Mass. App. Div. 125 (S.D. 2003) (oral surgeon obtained patient's obtained consent to install dental implants but did not consent to the extraction of her remaining teeth).

7

Revisiting the Hard Cases – Some Final Thoughts

A. SELF-DIRECTED ACTIVITIES

Although the discussion of self-directed acts in Chapter 2 focused on two ends of a range – suicide and body modifications – the consentability framework applies to all self-directed acts, including bad habits such as smoking and eating junk food. Under the framework, smoking would be much more heavily regulated, banned in all public places, and eventually available only via prescription (i.e. for those already addicted, for whom quitting suddenly might be mentally or physically harmful). Banning cigarette smoking may sound like an audacious proposal and an unbearable limitation of individual freedom, but resistance to such a change might be explained by the endowment effect[513] – because smoking is already legal, banning it feels like a punishment. But there is no such thing as a right to smoke, and smoking does not further any of the autonomy or state interests. On the contrary, the evidence indicates overwhelmingly that smoking is highly addictive, detrimental to health, and disproportionately affects already vulnerable groups, such as children.[514] There

---

[513] The "endowment effect" is generally understood as an "exaggerated preference" for goods that one already has and as "distaste for losing" what one already has. *See* Colin F. Camerer & George Loewenstein, *Behavioral Economics: Past, Present and Future, in* ADVANCES IN BEHAVIORAL ECONOMICS, at 3, 15 (Colin F. Camerer, et al., eds., 2004); *see also* Hardin, *supra* note 470, at 1248 ("Every new enclosure of the commons involves the infringement of somebody's personal liberty. Infringements made in the distant past are accepted because no contemporary complains of a loss. It is the newly proposed infringements that we vigorously oppose; cries of 'rights' and 'freedoms' fill the air. Burt what does 'freedom' mean? When men mutually agreed to pass laws against robbing, mankind became more free, not less so."). The same could be said of passing laws that prohibit businesses from selling addictive and physically harmful products.

[514] *See* CTRS. FOR DISEASE CONTROL & PREVENTION, U.S. DEP'T OF HEALTH & HUM. SERVS., A REPORT OF THE SURGEON GENERAL: HOW TOBACCO SMOKE CAUSES DISEASE ... WHAT IT MEANS TO YOU (2010), www.cdc.gov/tobacco/data_statistics/sgr/2010/consumer_booklet/pdfs/consumer.pdf; *see also* Smoking & Tobacco Use: Health Effects, CTRS. FOR DISEASE CONTROL & PREVENTION, U. S. DEP'T OF HEALTH & HUM. SERVS., www.cdc.gov/tobacco/basic_information/health_effects/index.htm (last updated Feb. 9, 2017) (stating that cigarette smoking can harm "nearly every organ in the body" and "causes one of every five deaths in the United States each year); *Health Effects of Cigarette Smoking*, CTRS. FOR DISEASE

are harmful effects to the collective autonomy interest from smoking which detrimentally affect the bodily integrity of those who inhale secondhand smoke. Furthermore, the tobacco industry deceived the public for decades into believing its products were safe, even when it knew they were not.[515] Under the consentability framework, highly addictive products which pose harmful societal effects and provide no (or very little) countervailing benefits should not be permitted. Addiction poses special problems for consent as it negatively impacts both the voluntariness and knowledge conditions. While first-time smokers may be making a voluntary decision, they may later become addicted, which makes their subsequent smoking a compulsion rather than a choice. First-time or beginner smokers may underestimate or discount the likelihood that they will become addicted, or the health harms that might result from an addiction. Given the high-level threat to the autonomy interest, the conditions of voluntariness and knowledge are unlikely to be sufficiently robust. Furthermore, under the Opportunism Corollary, the bad behavior of the cigarette industry warrants discounting its economic interest (which is also a lesser interest under the consentability framework than consumers' bodily integrity interest). The opportunistic conduct of cigarette companies (actively marketing to get people to engage in an activity that the companies *knew* was harmful and concealing that information) created a thriving market for cigarettes which users, once hooked, found hard to quit. The potential for profound regret on the part of future smokers is too high and the "opportunism cost" (the failure to prevent and deter future similar wrongdoing) too great to allow a handful of tobacco companies to profit from their past misdeeds and their harmful products.

By contrast, snack foods with little nutritional value, often referred to as "junk food," should be regulated but not banned. There are a wide variety of snack foods, some with more nutritional value than others. They are not addictive in the same way as cigarettes, nor do they cause as much harm to health.[516] Some of the harm, such as weight gain or high blood pressure, may be reversed. There are also some benefits of fast food. They might be high in calories and sodium, but they are cheap and filling. Unlike cigarettes, which are addictive and provide no health benefit, snack foods are not addictive for most people and have *some* nutritional benefit. If,

CONTROL & PREVENTION, U.S. DEP'T OF HEALTH & HUM. SERVS., www.cdc.gov/tobacco/data_statistics/ fact_sheets/health_effects/effects_cig_smoking/index.htm (last updated May 15, 2017) (providing information about the health problems associated with smoking, including that it causes about 90 percent of all lung cancer deaths and 90 percent of all deaths from chronic obstructive pulmonary disease).

[515] *See* United States v. Philip Morris USA, Inc., 449 F. Supp. 2d 1 (D.D.C. 2006).

[516] DIAGNOSTIC AND STATISTICAL MANUAL OF MENTAL DISORDERS (5th ed. 2013). Currently, the American Psychiatric Association does not acknowledge food addiction, except for binge eating disorders. Some research has indicated, however, that there are areas where food addiction and DSM-5 eating disorders may overlap. *See* Marco Aurélio Camargo da Rosa, *Overlap between Food Addiction and DSM-5 Eating Disorders in a Treatment Seeking Sample*, NAT'L INST. OF DRUG ABUSE (2015), www .drugabuse.gov/international/abstracts/overlap-between-food-addiction-dsm-5-eating-disorders-in-treatment-seeking-sample; Tori DeAngelis, *Fighting Food Addiction*, AM. PSYCHOL. ASS'N (Nov. 2011), www.apa.org/gradpsych/2011/11/food-addiction.aspx.

however, there is research that finds that *certain* snack foods, or ingredients in them, are addictive or unsafe even in small quantities, those substances, like other addictive or dangerous substances, should be prohibited or heavily regulated. For example, there has been no proven safe level of consumption for partially hydrogenated oils, which prompted the FDA to ban them.[517]

Although a ban on all snack foods would be an overbroad and premature measure, there should be more regulation of advertisements and more required effective disclosures of snack foods, so that consumers understand what they are buying and how it might affect them.[518] Snack food marketers should not target children or create advertisements especially designed to appeal to them, a measure that researchers and public health experts have advocated for years without success.[519] In Chile, the government has already banned certain advertising methods aimed at children, such as the inclusion of toys with snack food purchases, and the use of cartoon characters to promote products.[520] Corporations might argue that marketing and advertising regulations restrict their free speech, but under the consentability framework, free speech restrictions are justified by the collective autonomy interest that consumers have in their bodily integrity. In other words, the threat to the corporations' autonomy interest (in property and civil rights) is outweighed by the collective autonomy interest (in bodily integrity).[521]

There is always potential for opportunism whenever a person (whether an individual or a multinational corporation) profits by selling to another a product that has the potential to impede health. A consentability framework provides a way to assess how the state should address these situations. The potential for regret is not as great when eating a bag of Doritos for the first time as it is with smoking a cigarette for the first time – and in neither case is the potential for regret as high as it is with injecting heroin for the first time. The consumption of low-nutritional-value snack

---

[517] Sabrina Tavernise, *FDA Sets 2018 Deadline to Rid Foods of Trans Fats*, N.Y. TIMES (June 16, 2015), www.nytimes.com/2015/06/17/health/fda-gives-food-industry-three-years-eliminate-trans-fats.html.

[518] The author recognizes that the success of any state regulation depends on the will and politics of the leaders in power. The Trump administration, for example, has shown little inclination to expand the disclosure requirements of snack food manufacturers. On the contrary, the administration has objected to greater disclosure requirements and, as of this writing, is seeking to limit the ability of its NAFTA partners, Mexico and Canada, to implement such warnings. *See* Azam Ahmed, *supra* note 377.

[519] Eliza Barclay, *Scientists Are Building a Case for How Food Ads Make Us Overeat*, NPR (Jan. 29, 2016), www.npr.org/sections/thesalt/2016/01/29/462838153/food-ads-make-us-eat-more-and-should-be-regulated ("[researchers] believe more strategies and policy options to reduce children's exposure to food advertising are needed – not just in the U.S., but everywhere."); Sujit Sharma, *Are Fast Food Ads Killing Us?*, CNN (Apr. 27, 2017), www.cnn.com/2017/04/27/opinions/overeating-the-new-tobacco-opinion-sharma/index.html ("[O]ur culture has unwittingly accepted a marketing scheme which promotes a lifestyle that is literally killing us.").

[520] Andrew Jacobs, *In Sweeping War on Obesity, Chile Slays Tony the Tiger*, N.Y. TIMES (Feb. 7, 2018), www.nytimes.com/2018/02/07/health/obesity-chile-sugar-regulations.html.

[521] It is the author's belief that corporations do not have an autonomy interest at all, given they are not natural persons, but that is an argument that must be made another day and in a different book.

foods does not harm third parties the way secondhand smoke from cigarette smoking does. All addictive products should be regulated, but it is the nature of the addiction and the degree of potential harm that should determine the extent of the regulation. Because users do not have the power to consent to harm to others, the use of certain products which directly harm third parties (such as smoking tobacco or marijuana cigarettes in public places) should not be consentable at all.

1. Suicide

The Regret Principle requires that the state prohibit most suicides. Studies have indicated that suicide attempts are often impulsive[522] or occur during periods of high stress, such as after the death of a loved one.[523] Individuals who have attempted suicide are often depressed or mentally ill, and many have either been drinking or are under the influence of drugs at the time of the suicide attempt.[524] The permanence of the act, the mental anguish and the physical pain that accompanies most attempts mean that suicide poses the highest level of threat to autonomy. Given the individual's agitated or altered emotional and mental state and the novelty or uncertainty of the act, the consent conditions are likely defective. People who attempted suicide often report that they are grateful that they have failed[525] or regretful that they made the attempt.[526] Given the threat level to autonomy and the fragile emotional and mental state of those contemplating suicide in most cases, it would be difficult to establish any of the conditions of consent – much less all of them – with the requisite robustness level.

However, an individual suffering from an extremely painful and incurable disease or illness has had time to deliberate on her situation and to consider available alternatives. She has had the opportunity to discuss with doctors and other experts

---

[522] See Charles Nemeroff, *Ask an Expert: Suicide*, KPBS, www.pbs.org/wgbh/takeonestep/depression/ask-suicide_1.html (last visited June 8, 2018) ("impulsivity is something to really worry about … because it's associated with suicidality.").

[523] See A SANE AUSTL. & UNIV. OF NEW ENG., LESSONS FOR LIFE: THE EXPERIENCES OF PEOPLE WHO ATTEMPT SUICIDE: A QUALITATIVE RESEARCH REPORT 23–24 (2015), www.sane.org/images/PDFs/lessons-for-life.pdf [hereinafter "SANE STUDY"] (stating that a number of "adverse life events" can lead to attempted suicide).

[524] *Id.* at 21–22 ("Twenty-seven of the participants (89 percent) reported having been diagnosed with at least one mental illness. This finding is consistent with research that indicates up to 90 percent of people who die by suicide have a mental health problem" (citing J. T. Cavanugh et al., *Psychological Autopsy Studies of Suicide: A Systematic Review*, 33 PSYCHOL. MED. 395–405 (2003))).

[525] Tad Friend, *Jumpers: The Fatal Grandeur of the Golden Gate Bridge*, NEW YORKER (Oct. 13, 2003), www.newyorker.com/magazine/2003/10/13/jumpers (noting that those who jump off the Golden Gate Bridge and survive "often regret their decision in midair, if not before." One survivor recalled that after jumping, "I instantly realized that everything in my life that I'd thought was unfixable was totally fixable – except for having just jumped." Another survivor recalled, "My first thought was What the hell did I just do? I don't want to die.").

[526] SANE STUDY, *supra* note 523, at 25 (describing a range of emotions after suicide attempt, including anger, confusion, shame, regret and relief and happiness about having survived).

her predicament. Furthermore, the pain and the medical treatments required to sustain her may be intrusive and diminish her autonomy. An individual may prefer to discontinue painful treatments which prolong life but diminish its quality. Refusing life-support and other life-saving measures is generally accepted as lawful.[527] Many hospitals use Physician Orders for Life-Sustaining Treatment (POLST) forms, which is an approach to end-of-life planning.[528] These forms are viewed as "tools" for "patients with serious illness or frailty . . . for whom a health care professional would not be surprised if they died within one year."[529] By providing an alternative to the current standard of care, which involves taking all possible measures to save a patient, the POLST forms give the patient more control over the type of treatment to be received.[530] To force life-saving measures upon someone constitutes a high level of bodily intrusion and diminishes individual autonomy but may be justified where the patient is unconscious, depressed or otherwise unable to give consent. However, treatment imposed contrary to the patient's expressed wishes, which leaves the patient in a helpless condition – unable to care for himself and completely dependent upon medical equipment and personnel to keep him alive – poses the highest level of threat to autonomy. Not only is the individual unable to exercise and/or communicate his will after such intervention, he is now at the mercy of others. For some, death would be the more preferable alternative.

Assisted suicide differs from refusing life-support or life-prolonging measures in that it does not merely refuse an intrusive but life-sustaining measure, it involves an affirmative (bodily intrusive) act which has fatal (permanent, irreversible) consequences. Many opponents of assisted suicide or "right-to-die" legislation argue that it is immoral to terminate a life. Sometimes the reason is based upon religious principles.[531] But in a free society, the state should not impose morality based upon religion; rather, it should seek to ensure that its citizens make the best decisions

---

[527] See Paula Span, *The Patients Were Saved. That's Why the Families Are Suing*, N.Y. TIMES (April 10, 2017), www.nytimes.com/2017/04/10/health/wrongful-life-lawsuit-dnr.html (noting that some patients and their families have sued hospitals because health care personnel have disregarded advance directives and resuscitated patients against express instructions).

[528] See *About the National POLST Paradigm*, NAT'L POLST PARADIGM TASK FORCE, NAT'L POLST, www.polst.org/about-the-national-polst-paradigm (last visited June 16, 2018) ("The National POLST Paradigm is an approach to end-of-life planning that emphasizes patients' wishes about the medical treatment they receive . . . The decisions from these conversations may be documented as actionable medical orders on a POLST Paradigm Form.").

[529] *Id.*

[530] See *Patient FAQs: Does a POLST Form Limit the Type of Treatment I Can Get? What if I develop a simple infection?*, NAT'L POLST PARADIGM TASK FORCE, NAT'L POLST, http://polst.org/faq/ (last visited June 10, 2018) ("POLST Form medical orders give you more control over receiving treatments you want to receive and avoiding treatments you do not want to receive in the event you are unable to speak for yourself during a medical emergency.").

[531] Many faith-based organizations oppose assisted suicide. Organizations which are part of the coalition opposing assisted suicide in California, for example, include California Catholic Conference, Alliance of Catholic Health Care, Clergy Community Coalition and Catholics for the Common Good. See *Organizations that Oppose Assisted Suicide*, CALIFORNIANS AGAINST ASSISTED SUICIDE,

taking into consideration human cognitive limitations and the realities of decision-making. These realities include the pressures an individual may feel if family members are worried about the financial cost of medical care or the emotional toll of caregiving. Even without overt pressure from others, a patient may be concerned that she is a burden and decide to terminate her life. The patient may feel depressed as a result of medical treatment. Californians Against Assisted Suicide, a coalition of organizations opposing physician-assisted suicide, raised several concerns about California's assisted suicide legislation, including that it did not require a psychiatrist evaluation, did not require notification of a family member, and did not require trained medical personnel to be present at the time the fatal dose was taken.[532] The patient should be informed that the actual experience may not be as simple or painless as she may be envisioning. Rather than dying a peaceful death, she may have an adverse reaction which causes prolonged suffering. The patient should be required to consider and perhaps leave explicit directives about what to do in the event that the prescription does not work as planned. The concerns raised about the validity of consent in these situations should be taken very seriously. It is imperative not to slide down the slippery slope which right-to-die legislation might create. Strict parameters should be placed around such legislation, perhaps the most important being to minimize any discrepancy between one's present and future desires. As Rebecca Dresser notes:

> When competent people make judgments on the conditions under which they desire to live and die, their judgments reflect their existing capacities and the activities that make their present lives worth living. Decisions about the future health care that will advance their interests are inextricably intertwined with their current conceptions of the good. But people experiencing various life events, including set-backs in their physical and mental functioning, may revise their goals, values, and definitions of personal well-being. As a consequence, their notions of a life worth living can be modified as well. As long as individuals remain competent, they can incorporate their transformed ideas into the decisions they make. But incompetent patients lose this opportunity. If their interests diverge from those served by their previously articulated preferences, decisions based on the earlier preferences could deviate from what would maximize their current interests as incompetent patients.[533]

A healthy individual today may think she would want to die in the event she had Alzheimer's, but there is no way to be absolutely certain of her future desires. A patient with Alzheimer's or dementia may enjoy her new life even if she no longer

http://noassistedsuicideca.org/about/organizations-that-oppose-assisted-suicide-legalization (last visited Apr. 2, 2018).

[532] *Why We Oppose SB 128: California's Assisted Suicide Bill*, CALIFORNIANS AGAINST ASSISTED SUICIDE (May 6, 2015), http://noassistedsuicideca.org/images/CAASCoalitionLettertoCASenatev2.pdf (letter from various organizations to members of California State Senate).

[533] Dresser, *supra* note 209, at 379.

remembers her old one. Thus, any prediction about how one may feel in a future state should be greatly discounted, perhaps even ignored, if the present self expresses desires contrary to those previously expressed.

In certain limited cases, however, control over the manner of death may be the only way for an individual to preserve her autonomy. It may be more cruel to leave an individual to suffer in unspeakable pain (or to be numbed and unintelligible from pain medication) than to end that suffering. But given the potential discrepancy that might exist between one's present and future preferences and the threat level to autonomy, assisted suicide should only be available in situations where the patient is undergoing extreme physical suffering and predicted to die in the near term (three to six months) or where the individual is suffering from dementia or Alzheimer's and rapidly losing control of her body. Diseases that deprive an individual of her mind pose as great a threat to autonomy as those which deprive her of bodily functions. An individual should have the right to make life-or-death decisions while she is still mentally competent; however, those decisions must be subject to the later self's ability to override or defer them. There are degrees of consciousness and mental capability, and an individual who is diagnosed with dementia or Alzheimer's may retain mental faculties for a long period of time. An individual suffering from dementia may no longer be able to recall certain information and may not even recognize a loved one, but she may still enjoy activities and wish to continue living. In such a case, it is only when she is no longer aware and cannot control what she is doing that her past self's directive should take effect.

Safeguards should be implemented to ensure valid consent. There should be a waiting period and a formal written request process to winnow out impulsive requests. California's right to die legislation, for example, applies only to adults who have a "terminal disease," which means an "incurable and irreversible disease" which will, "within reasonable medical judgement, result in death within six months."[534] The legislation contains other safeguards to ensure the robustness of consent conditions. It requires patients to submit two oral requests fifteen days apart and one written request in the presence of two witnesses.[535] It also requires the physician to determine that the individual has "capacity to make medical decisions, is acting voluntarily, and has made an informed decision," and makes it a felony to "knowingly coerce or exert undue influence" to request a life-ending drug.[536] The law also clearly distinguishes and does not authorize physicians to engage in "active euthanasia" or directly terminate the patient's life, such as with a lethal injection.[537] It does not, however, require that the patient be undergoing progressive,

---

[534]   CAL. HEALTH & SAFETY CODE § 443.1(q) (West 2018).
[535]   *Id.* at §§ 443.2, 443.3.
[536]   *Id.* at § 443.17.
[537]   *Id.* at § 443.18 ("Nothing in this part may be construed to authorize a physician or any other person to end an individual's life by lethal injection, mercy killing, or active euthanasia.").

rapid and significant mental and physical deterioration or severe physical pain as a result of the disease – but under a consentability framework, it should.[538]

2. Body Modification

An individual's desire for a particular type of body modification should be no more or less consentable depending upon whether it is conventional or unconventional, whether it conforms to societal expectations and stereotypes or rejects them. What should determine consentability is whether the requisite conditions of consent are capable of being met, given the potential harm to autonomy. What matters, in other words, is the safety of the procedure, its potential risks, its purpose and effects, and whether there is adequate information available for the individual to make a decision she won't regret. The threat level to autonomy may change over time. If the procedure or technique improves, it would lower the risk to autonomy; on the other hand, if it is later determined that the activity is more harmful than previously realized, the threat level would increase. Procedures which are painful, irreversible and hinder the future autonomy of the individual – sterilizations, amputations, forms of genital mutilation which foreclose sexual satisfaction – require the highest levels of scrutiny and must meet the most robust conditions of consent. In many cases, valid consent is unlikely to be found and the procedure should not be performed. But consent conditions which are unachievable now may become achievable at a later time with technological advancements. For example, a doctor today may refuse to perform a voluntary amputation because it would leave the patient's mobility permanently limited and diminish her autonomy. But should a doctor refuse such a procedure if the purpose is to replace the healthy human limb with a much better functioning prosthetic? What if the surgery could be made safe and painless, with little risk of error or failure? What if it could somehow be made reversible?

The underlying motive for the modification affects the analysis of consent. Individuals engage in body modification for different reasons. These reasons should be considered in assessing consent. A person seeking a body modification as a way to enhance her appearance or increase her body's functionality may have unrealistic expectations. She may believe it will propel her to stardom or social success. These unrealistic expectations may be the result of misinformation or naïve optimism. The desire to undergo the modification may be the result of external pressure from friends, partners, employers or generalized societal pressure to conform. Acts which result in a greater threat to the autonomy interest should require more robust conditions and more safeguards to ensure consent.

[538] The California law was overturned by a state court at the time this book was being printed. The state of California is expected to appeal the ruling. Soumya Karlamangla, *Riverside Judge Overturns California's Doctor-Assisted Suicide Law*, L.A. TIMES (May 15, 2018), www.latimes.com/local/lanow/la-me-ln-end-of-life-option-act-20180515-story.html.

While the law should not discriminate based on the aesthetic appeal of a given body modification, there are very good reasons to prohibit or restrict and regulate body modifications in general, whether they render one more conventionally attractive or more unconventional and even, by society's standards, freakish. The risk associated with a particular type of modification should determine the level of restriction and regulation. The risks from the modification may be minor and curable, such as a rash or skin irritation – or they might be severe, even life-threatening, such as damaged nerves, a severed artery and reduced mobility. The modification itself may be temporary or permanent; its impact may be profound or superficial. The extent of the risk (i.e. the threat level to autonomy) should determine the extent of regulations. The state should regulate the skill level and qualifications of the person performing the modification, the conditions and setting under which the modification is to be performed, and whether there should be a waiting period. Generally, all procedures which result in permanent body modifications and pose a risk of serious bodily injury (i.e. those which pose a high-level threat to autonomy) should be performed only by medically trained personnel. Acts, such as some piercings and tattoos, which pose a lesser level of threat to autonomy should require a license and training.

The novelty of certain body modifications and the dearth of scientific studies or reliable and fact-based information about them may make it difficult for an individual to fully grasp their consequences. One man had a sensor implanted into his arm that measured his body heat and pulse and transmitted that information to his cell phone. Afterward, he reported having panic attacks about the device, which was the size of a pack of cards, felt heavy and bulged noticeably underneath his skin. He eventually had it removed.[539] Even if participants understand the experimental nature of a modification, they may underestimate the risks.[540] They may also fail to accurately predict the desirability of the modification to their future selves. It may prevent them from getting a particular type of job or cause unexpected problems.[541] One body modification artist said that he sees several people every month who want to remove or upgrade implants for various reasons, "For example, horns, really visible implants, if people got them done when they were young and then it's affecting their life, they can't find a job or something like that."[542] A woman reported that magnets that she had embedded into her fingers were interfering with her ability to play the guitar.[543] Another had a hand magnet removed because it caused her computer to go to sleep when she was using it.[544] In addition, technology changes and improves so that an upgrade may be desirable. Whatever the reason, removal of

---

[539] Rose Eveleth, *The Half Life of Body Hacking*, MOTHERBOARD (June 25, 2015), http://motherboard.vice.com/read/the-half-life-of-body-hacking.
[540] *Id.*
[541] *Id.*
[542] *Id.*
[543] *Id.*
[544] *Id.*

an implant may be desired, and the subject may have failed to consider how difficult, painful and expensive it may be to have it removed. Furthermore, extreme body modifications are often performed in non-sterile environments and/or by non-medical professionals.[545]

But it is not only novel biohacks and other unconventional modifications which impede the knowledge condition. Conventional modifications pose challenges for a different reason – their familiarity and popularity may cause someone to underestimate the pain and risk involved.[546] Because tattoos are prevalent, especially among those between 18 and 35 (47 percent in this age group reported having one or more tattoos),[547] people may assume there are no or only very minor health risks associated with the practice. Dr. Greg Hall, a primary care physician, started a popular website to educate the public about permanent body art because information was difficult to find. Most people may understand that there is a risk of infection associated with getting a tattoo but may not be aware of the seriousness of the risk. They may also not have considered that tattoo inks can react negatively with magnetic resonance imaging scans, may affect their immune system, and can contain carcinogenic chemicals.[548]

Liposuction is a familiar procedure to most women; however, women seeking to have it done may be unfamiliar with some of its consequences, especially if those consequences are not readily apparent. For example, they may not realize that the fat that is suctioned out will return and that when it does, it may distribute unevenly to areas of their body which have more fat cells, such as the upper abdomen, triceps and shoulders.[549] They may have failed to consider that an alteration of one feature changes the balance of the face or the proportion of the body.[550] They may also discount the probability of accidents or unexpected reactions which may force them to undergo subsequent corrective operations or live with the resulting deformities.[551]

---

[545] *See* Anthony Youn, *Body Modification – or Mutilation?*, CNN (Nov. 7, 2013), https://edition.cnn .com/2013/11/07/health/youn-body-modification/ (stating that extreme body modifications are "almost never performed by actual physicians. These treatments are more often associated with tattoo parlors than medical offices.").

[546] *See* U.K. DEPT. OF HEALTH REPORT, *supra* note 75, at 29 ("Moreover, the increasing availability and presence of cosmetic interventions resulted in the procedures being seen as less risky.").

[547] Larry Shannon-Missal, *Tattoo Takeover: Three in Ten Americans Have Tattoos, and Most Don't Stop at Just One*, HARRIS POLL (Feb. 10, 2016), https://theharrispoll.com/tattoos-can-take-any-number-of-forms-from-animals-to-quotes-to-cryptic-symbols-and-appear-in-all-sorts-of-spots-on-our-bodies-some-visible-in-everyday-life-others-not-so-much-but-one-thi/.

[548] Greg Hall, *Tattoos Affect Your Health: Long-Term Side Effects Ink Has on Your Immune System and Disease Risk*, MED. DAILY (Nov. 15, 2016), www.medicaldaily.com/tattoos-affect-your-health-long-term-side-effects-ink-has-your-immune-system-404404.

[549] Gina Kolata, *With Liposuction, the Belly Finds What the Thighs Lose*, N.Y. TIMES (Apr. 30, 2011), www.nytimes.com/2011/05/01/weekinreview/01kolata.html?_r=1&ref=health.

[550] Jenna Goudreau, *The Hidden Dangers of Cosmetic Surgery*, FORBES (June 16, 2011), www.forbes.com /sites/jennagoudreau/2011/06/16/hidden-dangers-of-cosmetic-surgery/#122afa7d8805.

[551] *Id.* (discussing the disastrous financial and emotional consequences of botched operations).

Unreasonable expectations may impede the knowledge condition. One report found that teenagers and young women were particularly susceptible to media images of "perfection" which shaped their expectations.[552] Some viewed cosmetic interventions as a way to achieve somewhat unrealistic goals, such as wanting to have a breast enlargement in order to "try and become a model."[553]

While some people who elect cosmetic surgery are deciding to do so to make themselves feel better, I suspect many of them feel intense societal pressure to look a certain way. They may fear losing their jobs or romantic partners if they age naturally. Social pressures may create a less than ideal voluntariness condition. While a person might not be threatened or forced by a specific individual into having a body modification performed (although this, too, may happen), societal expectations and the desire to conform to them may compel someone to undergo a procedure. Social pressures may not eliminate the voluntariness condition but – given the high-level threat to the autonomy interest of many types of body modifications – they do necessitate safeguards, such as counseling and a psychiatric evaluation. A person desperate to gain approval from her peers by having a cosmetic procedure may not have considered that having the procedure may not result in social acceptance.[554] The U.K. Dept. of Health study on cosmetic interventions reported:

> There was ... recognition among participants that there are prospective patients who are vulnerable and that this can be for a wide range of reasons, such as having unrealistic expectations, hoping the procedure will be the answer to more fundamental problems, having mental health/psychological problems, being impressionable or gullible, or very young, and those "addicted" to cosmetic change. It was felt to be vital that there is safeguarding in place that enables the vulnerable to be identified at an early stage and counselled/assessed accordingly, and that there should be definite requirements or guidelines that ensure this e.g. via thresholds for the number of procedures undertaken, an age limit below which counseling and assessment is mandatory.[555]

By contrast, those seeking unconventional body modifications which subvert traditional notions of beauty will typically exhibit greater robustness of the voluntariness condition.[556] Individuals seeking such procedures have generally made their

---

[552] U.K. Dept. of Health Report, *supra* note 75, at 35.
[553] *Id.*
[554] Goudreau, *supra* note 550 (describing how one woman who experienced peer disapproval after breast augmentation surgery had her implants removed).
[555] U.K. Dept. of Health Report, *supra* note 75, at 64.
[556] Morgen L. Thomas, *Sick/Beautiful/Freak: Nonmainstream Body Modification and the Social Construction of Deviance*, Sage Open 1, 7 (2012), http://journals.sagepub.com/doi/pdf/10.1177/2158244012467787 (stating that those who engaged in unconventional body modifications show a "unique kind of agency" and "the negative comments and reactions of others do little to stop a Mod from modifying"); Thomas defines a "Mod" as practitioners of "nonmainstream body modifications." *Id.* at 1.

decision to do so independently and without social pressure.[557] On the contrary, they often act with the express disapproval or discouragement of friends and family precisely because they are transgressing social norms.[558] They are thus acting with greater volition (i.e. a more robust voluntariness condition) than someone undergoing cosmetic surgery who aspires to conform to majoritarian standards of beauty. However, the extreme, nonconformist nature of some modifications may raise concerns about underlying mental or emotional issues.[559]

People going through a major life change (such as adolescents and young adults, people suffering from the loss of a parent or spouse, or those in the aftermath of a divorce or other emotional trauma) may be especially vulnerable to body modifications that they later regret. Children and teenagers, may be particularly susceptible to advertisements and media messages. A U.K. National Health Service report found that the media through various channels directed at children normalized cosmetic procedures, which may prime them to get the procedures in the future.[560] According to the American Society of Plastic Surgeons, 64,470 cosmetic surgical procedures and 161,700 cosmetic minimally invasive procedures were performed on teenagers aged thirteen to nineteen in 2015.[561] That same year, 7,840 teenagers aged eighteen to nineteen years old received breast implants.[562] Non-therapeutic cosmetic procedures upon children and adolescents is particularly troubling because

---

[557] *Id.* at 11 (noting that "Mods" realize that "their unconventional body practices directly challenge society's expectations of beauty and health norms, gender expression and roles, corporeal presentation, and symbolic inscription simply by moving *away* from Western appearance ideals (beauty) and *toward* its perceived opposite (monstrosity)").

[558] *Id.* at 7 ("nowhere is the disapproval Mods experience more egregious than in the family milieu.").

[559] *See, e.g.,* Youn, *supra* note 545 (asking whether body modification might be a sign of "underlying psychiatric issues"). *But see* Thomas, *supra* note 556, at 5 (critically observing that "because Western society continues to create and perpetuate arbitrary dualisms in every aspect of human behavior, there is only one other category available" to those who engage in unconventional body modifications, which is "that of the unwell, the sick, physically and psychologically"). Thomas further notes that the "language used in psychological literature implies, not so covertly, that individuals who intentionally cut themselves, burn themselves, or otherwise inflict pain on themselves, for whatever reason, suffer from some inherent mental defect or have experienced some type of emotional trauma in their lives that drives them to harm themselves." *Id.*

[560] *Regulation of Cosmetic Interventions: Research Among Teenage Girls,* CREATIVE RESEARCH (Mar. 11, 2013), at 5, https://assets.publishing.service.gov.uk/government/uploads/system/uploads/attachment_data/file/192030/Report_on_research_among_teenage_girls.pdf ("It is possible that children are being exposed to cosmetic interventions at an early age due to the wide availability of, and their exposure to, TV programmes and magazines that include interventions as part of their core material ... While the media create awareness of the interventions, set down the standards of perfection that many people strive to meet and promote 'role models' for procedures in the form of celebrities, many girls see their influence as benign and largely a source of entertainment. However, others recognize that the expectations they communicate put unrealistic pressure on young people and feed the greatest pressure of all for teenagers, the judgment of their peers.").

[561] *Briefing Paper: Plastic Surgery for Teenagers,* AM. SOC'Y PLASTIC SURGEONS, www.plasticsurgery.org/news/briefing-papers/briefing-paper-plastic-surgery-for-teenagers (last visited Apr. 6, 2018).

[562] *Id.*

their bodies are still developing, and the long-term effects are unknown. Diana Zuckerman, president of the National Center for Health Research,[563] writes:

> Cultural phenomena such as surgical makeovers on numerous television programs ... make it increasingly difficult to agree on what constitutes a 'normal' appearance and when the desire to improve one's appearance is questionable or even crosses the line to psychopathology.[564]

Zuckerman notes that there are "no epidemiological studies or clinical trials on the safety and long-term risks" of cosmetic procedures on developing teens, and that physical changes that girls undergo as teenagers and young adults should prompt a reassessment of whether procedures like breast augmentation and liposuction should be permitted.[565] Given that those under 25 are still developing and are particularly susceptible to cognitive limits, such as short-term thinking, the presumption should be against allowing them to receive elective (non-therapeutic) cosmetic surgeries which pose a high-level threat to autonomy, such as breast augmentations and liposuction. As Zuckerman notes, however, certain types of cosmetic surgeries have a beneficial, therapeutic effect:

> There is no question that reconstructive surgeries can benefit children and youth. Surgical procedures to correct cleft lips and palates, for example, are not controversial. Plastic surgery to correct unattractive facial features that can attract ridicule from other children, such as prominent noses and ears, are generally accepted in the United States.[566]

As previously mentioned, it is difficult for the government to categorically distinguish non-therapeutic from therapeutic procedures.[567] The burden would thus be on the prospective young adult patient to obtain a neutral doctor's opinion that the high-level threat procedure is therapeutic and not simply cosmetic. Given the limited nature of this requirement (the burden disappears when the individual reaches twenty-five years of age), it does not impose the same administrative burden or the same restriction on individual freedom as it would if it were applied to all adult members of society.

While all surgical procedures are risky and pose a threat to autonomy, the threat to autonomy increases with the complexity of the surgery. During any type of surgery, the patient is abdicating power over some part of her body, but for surgeries that require general anesthesia, the patient loses consciousness and control over her

---

[563] *See* www.center4research.org/ (formerly the National Research Center for Women & Families).

[564] Diana Zuckerman, *Teenagers and Cosmetic Surgery*, 7 ETHICS J. AM. MED. ASS'N, no.3, Mar. 2005, at 1, http://journalofethics.ama-assn.org/2005/03/oped1-0503.html.

[565] *Id.* ("In addition to development that may occur in the late teens, growth charts indicate that the average girl gains weight between 18 and 21, and that is likely to change her desire or need for breast augmentation as well as liposuction.")

[566] *Id.*

[567] *See* discussion *supra* Chapter 2 section A.

mind and her body. Some surgeries pose a greater risk of injury than others, and the degree of required consent condition robustness should depend upon the threat level to the autonomy interest. Even non-surgical procedures such as piercings, Botox and collagen injections pose some risk to individuals, including the risk of necrosis, infection and disfigurement, which is heightened if the procedures are administered by non-medical personnel. The consenter may discount these risks because of the familiarity of the procedures and the prevalence of advertisements which depict only a positive outcome. One doctor, for example, stated that because people erroneously think certain non-surgical cosmetic procedures are "completely safe," they "don't know how to deal with the complications of procedures and that's why I think they need to regulate this industry properly."[568] In addition, a person who seeks to modify her body in any way – conventional or unconventional – may be disappointed by the result. She may have misjudged the effect of her new appearance on strangers. While any type of body modification carries the risk of an unintended or undesired outcome, the reaction of others to the procedure is a particularly uncontrollable and unpredictable variable.[569] Younger adults may not consider the impact that tattoos may have on their job prospects. Dr. Anthony Youn, a plastic surgeon, writes that plastic surgeons and dermatologist are seeing "more and more people who want their tattoos removed, often because they worry that the tattoos could cause problems with employment."[570]

Given the risk associated with even non-surgical procedures, all body modifications should be performed only by licensed and trained professionals. The extent of required training should depend upon the risk associated with the procedure. Because surgical procedures pose a high-level threat to autonomy, they should only be conducted by medical professionals certified in the type of surgery they will be performing. Breast augmentation surgeries, for example, should not be performed by dermatologists.

Few medical professionals are willing to perform unconventional body modifications.[571] Certainly, doctors are justified in refusing to expose their patients to unnecessary risks – but in doing so, they may be inadvertently exposing them to greater risk, as those seeking unconventional modifications are forced to seek the services of those with no professional training who often work in non-sterile and poorly equipped environments. The refusal of the medical profession to recognize and respond to the needs of the body modification community is hypocritical, given its willingness to recognize and train its

---

[568] U.K. Dept. of Health Report, *supra* note 75, at 80.

[569] *Id.* at 32 (finding that some people desired cosmetic procedures because they were sensitive to how others judged their appearance).

[570] Anthony Youn, *Suffering from "Tattoo Regret,"* CNN (Apr. 8, 2013), www.cnn.com/2013/04/08/health/youn-tattoo-regret/index.html.

[571] *See* Youn, *Body Modification, supra* note 545 (in discussing the risks of extreme body modification and the likelihood they would not be performed by doctors, Dr. Anthony Youn stated, "In fact, I've never heard of a single plastic surgeon who's admitted to performing extreme body modification.").

members to perform purely cosmetic, non-therapeutic surgeries. Furthermore, as discussed above, those seeking unconventional modifications typically demonstrate a greater robustness of the voluntariness condition. Rather than succumbing to societal pressure to conform, they typically have to confront societal obstacles and live with social rejection because of their unconventional modifications. They must search harder to find someone willing to perform the procedure. An individual seeking a procedure as an end in itself exhibits a higher degree of the voluntariness condition than does an individual seeking a procedure as a means to achieve another objective, such as social approval.

Under my approach, a doctor performing *any* type of body modification which poses a high-level threat to autonomy – including traditional cosmetic surgery – would be susceptible to a claim of defective consent. In order to rebut this claim, the doctor would need to show that a reasonable doctor would have determined the procedure was medically advisable and that it was performed in a reasonable manner according to the standards of the relevant medical specialty. This approach deters unnecessary body modifications but does not ban them. The patient presumably would only bring a claim if he was unhappy with the result and suffered an injury. The doctor would then have to prove that the procedure was medically advisable and performed in accordance with professional standards. If the doctor performed in accordance with professional standards but the procedure was not medically advisable, then there might be no injury to the patient and no damages. This approach may have the socially desirable effect of deterring opportunistic providers from persuading patients into unnecessary procedures for economic gain.

Cognitive limitations and heuristic biases necessitate state intervention when the potential harm to individuals is grave or permanent. Psychiatric evaluations, counseling (both before the procedure and during the recovery period) and a waiting period should be required for anyone seeking modifications which pose a high-level threat to autonomy (generally those involving surgery, such as breast implants). The purpose of mandatory counseling is to educate or inform by providing the consenter with accurate, evidence-based information about what to expect as a result of the procedure.

The state has an important interest in protecting the health and safety of its subjects. A person consenting to a tattoo is not *also* consenting to getting infected from unsterilized equipment. The state's interest, however, is not based exclusively upon protecting the party consenting to the harmful act; it is also based upon protecting others who might be affected by the act. The Regret Principle and the Harm Principle justify state intervention to ensure that the conditions of consent are fulfilled *and* to prevent an individual's actions from harming others. Even self-regarding activities have the potential to harm others. The use of non-sterile equipment, for example, may spread disease. One study found that there was no evidence of an increased risk of hepatitis C (HCV) when subjects received tattoos and piercings in professional parlors.[572] However, the risk of HCV infection was "significant" when tattoos and piercings were performed in non-professional settings, such as homes, prisons and other nonsterile settings.

Piercings, too, often pose more health and hygiene complications than people assume.[573] One study noted that problems from piercing were common and could be serious and even fatal.[574] Even if someone were willing to get a tattoo or a piercing from a parlor that used non-sterile equipment, the threat to public health is too great to allow an individual's consent to override the potential harm to third parties. The spread of HCV through the use of non-sterile equipment poses a threat to the societal interest in health and safety, which is a greater interest than the individual's autonomy interest in getting a tattoo at a non-licensed parlor. Furthermore, the burden upon society would outweigh the relatively minor burden that licensing poses upon the individual and the tattoo parlor operator. Thus, these types of state regulations on tattoo parlors are justified.[575]

Body modifications which require surgery or implanting devices should be subject to much more rigorous licensure requirements and standards than those modifications, like tattoos, which do not, because of the greater potential long-term harm to the individual. The state should not ignore the demand for extreme body modifications, including body hackings; instead, it should impose regulations to monitor and ensure that the practices are as safe as possible. A failure to recognize and regulate the practices only encourages them to remain underground, increasing the risks to the individual and society.

Gender confirmation/sex reassignment surgery (SRS) for transgender people merits special discussion. Unlike conventional cosmetic surgeries, there is little "advertising" for SRS, and social pressure to undergo the procedure is generally low. However, social and cultural norms regarding what it means to be a "man" or a "woman" and the desire to adapt to these societal preferences may create pressure to undergo SRS.[576] On the other hand, SRS also has the potential to be autonomy-

---

[572] Rania A. Tohme & Scott D. Holmberg, *Transmission of Hepatitis C Virus Infection Through Tattooing and Piercing: A Critical Review*, 54 CLINICAL INFECTIOUS DISEASES 1167 (2012), www.ncbi .nlm.nih.gov/pmc/articles/PMC4613802/pdf/nihms729527.pdf.

[573] Angie Bone et al., *Body Piercing in England: A Survey of Piercing at Sites other Than Earlobe*, BMJ (June 19, 2008), www.bmj.com/content/bmj/336/7658/1426.full.pdf.

[574] *Id.* at 5.

[575] *See, e.g.*, WASH. REV. CODE ANN § 18.300.030 (LexisNexis 2018) (requiring license to engage in the practice of body art, body piercing or tattooing); *see also* WASH. REV. CODE ANN. § 18.300.005 (LexisNexis 2018) (sets forth requirements relating to body art, body piercing and tattooing); *How to Get Your License: Body Art Artists*, WASH. STATE DEP'T OF LICENSING, www.dol.wa.gov/business/ tattoo/bodyartlicense.html (last visited June 10, 2018).

[576] Computer scientist and transgender pioneer and activist Lynn Conway writes about some of these misperceptions and how they are the "wrong" reasons for seeking surgery: "Some examples of 'wrong reasons' and wrong situations for undergoing SRS are (i) efforts to become a center of attention and live a 'sexy life', (ii) thinking it will 'automatically turn oneself into a woman' in others' eyes, (iii) deciding to become a woman on a whim (for example, in the midst of a mid-life crisis), (iv) doing it for autosexual 'thrill', (v) doing it while suffering from preexisting serious mental conditions

enhancing on a profound level, and is generally considered by the medical profession to be therapeutic and not solely cosmetic.[577] The World Professional Association for Transgender Health (WPATH) issued the following statement:

> [G]ender affirming/confirming treatments and surgical procedures, properly indicated and performed as provided by the Standards of Care, have proven to be beneficial and effective in the treatment of individuals with transsexualism and gender dysphoria. Gender affirming/confirming surgery, also known as sex reassignment surgery, plays an undisputed role in contributing toward favorable outcomes.[578]

Significantly, the process and procedures involved for SRS are much more gradual, deliberate and incremental than for conventional cosmetic surgeries, which decreases the likelihood of opportunism on the part of providers and regret on the part of consenters. Generally, experts in the field urge individuals to proceed cautiously before undertaking irreversible treatments.[579] WPATH recommends one year of hormone treatment before the consenter undergoes sex reassignment surgery.[580] The WPATH Standards of Care also recognize that the treatment of adolescents poses particularly complex issues. On one hand, adolescence is an unusually dynamic – often even volatile – period; on the other hand, gender transition is reportedly more likely to be successful if done before the end of adolescence. The WPATH Standards of Care

unrelated to GID (depression, bi-polar conditions . . .), etc." *See A Warning For Those Considering MtF SRS: What If You "Succeed" in Completing a TS Transition, But Did It for the Wrong Reasons?,* U. MICH., http://ai.eecs.umich.edu/people/conway/TS/warning.html (updated Mar. 16, 2007). "SRS" means sex reassignment surgery and "GID" means to gender identity disorder.

577 *See* Tiffiny A. Ainsworth & Jeffrey H. Spiegel, *Quality of Life of Individuals With and Without Facial Feminization Surgery or Gender Reassignment Surgery,* 19 QUALITY LIFE RESEARCH 1019 (2010) (find that the self-reported quality of life of male-to-female transgendered individuals was greater after surgical intervention).

578 See *Position Statement on Medical Necessity of Treatment, Sex Reassignment, and Insurance Coverage in the U.S.A.,* WPATH (Dec. 21, 2016), www.wpath.org/newsroom/medical-necessity-statement.

579 *See* Jane E. Brody, *Being Transgender as a Fact of Nature,* N.Y. TIMES (June 13, 2016), http://well .blogs.nytimes.com/2016/06/13/transsexualism-as-a-fact-of-nature/ ("[E]xperts warn that at any age, and especially in adolescence, great caution must be taken before irreversible treatments are provided."). Brody's article quotes noted endocrinologist Dr. Louis J. Gooren as saying that some people may have "unrealistic expectations about what being a member of the opposite sex entails." *Id.*

580 THE STANDARDS OF CARE: FOR THE HEALTH OF TRANSSEXUAL, TRANSGENDER, AND GENDER NONCONFORMING PEOPLE (7th ver.), www.wpath.org/media/cms/Documents/Web%20Transfer/ SOC/Standards%20of%20Care%20V7%20-%202011%20WPATH.pdf [hereinafter WPATH SOC]; Susan Scutti, *Becoming Transsexual: Getting the Facts on Sex Reassignment Surgery,* MED. DAILY (Nov. 6, 2014), www.medicaldaily.com/becoming-transsexual-getting-facts-sex-reassignment-surgery -309584. It also contains very clear, easily understandable and straightforward descriptions associated with hormone treatment and the risk level associated with each type of hormone. For example, the document contains a table which indicate that there is "[l]ikely increased risk" with "[f]eminizing hormones" of "[g]allstones" and "[w]eight gain." WPATH SOC, *supra,* at 40. There is also a table which contains the "effects and expected time course" of feminizing and masculinizing hormones. *Id.* at 37–39.

contain detailed discussion of the issues associated with children and adolescents (distinguishing between the two), provide guidance for families, and provide a range of possible interventions, including reversible ones.[581] Evidence suggests that as with other types of body modifications, individuals may place too much hope on what SRS might accomplish, so counseling is highly recommended.[582] The WPATH Standards of Care also recognize the role of counseling both to assess mental health and in order for the patient to gain a full understanding of what to expect from treatment.[583] As with any kind of body modification procedure, the requisite robustness levels should vary depending on the threat level to autonomy. Surgeries which limit an individual's future options regarding important personal interests, such as sexual satisfaction or procreation, require more robust consent than consent to receive hormone treatments which are reversible.

Interestingly, while doctors have been willing to perform SRS which results in infertility on teenagers and adults under twenty-five, they have been much less willing to perform sterilization on cisgender women of the same age. The cultural norms and societal expectations of cisgender women may play some role in the refusal of physicians;[584] as perhaps does the troubling history of forced sterilizations upon the mentally disabled, the poor, and minority communities.[585]

Doctors have also generally refused patients' requests for voluntary amputation of healthy limbs, although the reasons patients may have given for wanting the surgery echoed those of patients of sex reassignment and conventional cosmetic surgery.[586]

---

[581] *Id.* at 10–21.

[582] *See generally id.* at 35 ("Obtaining informed consent for hormone therapy is an important task of providers to ensure that patients understand the psychological and physical benefits and risks of hormone therapy, as well as its psychosocial implications. Providers prescribing the hormones or health professionals recommending the hormones should have the knowledge and experience to assess gender dysphoria. They should inform individuals of the particular benefits, limitations, and risks of hormones, given the patient's age, previous experience with hormones, and concurrent physical or mental health concerns."); *see also* Jane E. Brody, *supra* note 579.

[583] *See* WPATH SOC, *supra* note 580, at 36 ("SOC puts greater emphasis on the important role that mental health professionals can play in alleviating gender dysphoria and facilitating changes in gender role and psychosocial adjustment. This may include a comprehensive mental health assessment and psychotherapy, when indicated.").

[584] *See* Cristina Richie, *Voluntary Sterilization for Childfree Women*, 43 HASTINGS CTR. REP. 36, 42 (2013) (Richie notes that "some doctors confronted with voluntary sterilization of women are morally or religiously opposed to sterilization and either do not perform the procedure at all or perform it only selectively, refusing to provide sterilization to some women who are legally eligible for it.").

[585] *Id.* at 41 ("Sterilization was particularly common for those groups 'who are especially vulnerable to abuse – the poor, minors, and the mentally disabled.' Frequently, sterilizations done on women prior to the 1970s were not performed with the woman's consent, and even women who agreed to be sterilized often did so under threat of repercussions or coercion … Forced sterilization done on minority women in America, the mentally challenged and minors in both categories were supported by law") (citing R. Pollack Petchesky, *Reproduction, Ethics and Public Policy: The Federal Sterilization Regulations*, 9 HASTINGS CTR. REP. 29, 32 (1979)).

[586] *See* Peter Brian Barry, *The Ethics of Voluntary Amputation*, 26 PUB. AFF. Q. 1 (Jan. 2012) (explaining how these "would-be amputees" or "wannabes" believe that amputation is "arguably the only available means for relieving their significant suffering.").

Even where a doctor is willing to perform it, the operation will likely be prohibited by the hospital.[587] While doctors must abide by the dictates of their conscience, is their conscience informed by science and sound judgment – or by cultural expectations and prejudice? In the future, will society view these physician refusals to perform voluntary amputations and sterilizations as wise and compassionate, or as inhumane and misguided? Will we wonder why we allowed a physician's personal beliefs and visceral reactions to prolong the unnecessary suffering of a mentally fit adult or will we be grateful for the strength and greater wisdom of the doctor to act in the best long-term interest of her patient – and of society? In assessing consentability, we should consider the ways that society and consent shape, influence and determine each other and think about the values and norms we promote when we permit certain procedures – and forbid others.

Nevertheless, given our human inability to think beyond our current cultural and social environment, the most important consideration should be what the procedures themselves entail and whether they might curtail the future self's autonomy. Consent is a matter of degree, and the degree required to establish valid consent depends upon the act to which one is consenting. It matters why someone is consenting – the mix of socio-cultural factors which shape and influence someone's preferences and desires – but it will always be difficult to disentangle what the heart wants from what it *thinks* it wants. Adaptive preferences can promote aspects of one's well-being even if they diminish or harm other aspects. The relationship between consent and adaptive preferences is complicated. Skilled marketers can manipulate facts and distort the truth, shaping media messages. Media messages, in turn, shape and affect cultural norms and signals. Because culture shapes preferences, the media and skilled marketers are influential in shaping and affecting consent. Consequently, the state should regulate most forms of advertising by providers of body modifications.

Given the seriousness of what is being advertised, providers should not be permitted to condition the public that it "needs" to subject itself to bodily harm in order to conform to an unnatural ideal, nor should it be allowed to solicit "customers" for high-level threat procedures. France has already instituted a complete ban on advertisements for cosmetic surgery in order to make clear that it is a medical, and not commercial, act.[588] Providers should not be able to advertise for *any* type of body modification procedure in media whose primary audience is under-twenty-five years old, nor should they engage in any type of direct marketing, such as social media or direct mail (including electronic mail) which essentially forces the recipient to be a captive audience for the message. Finally, as discussed in Chapter 6, advertisements – if allowed at all – should disclose rather than simply promote. For

---

[587] *Id.* at 1 (discussing how Scottish surgeon Robert Smith's attempt to voluntarily amputate a healthy leg was prevented by the hospital).
[588] Melanie Latham, *"If It Ain't Broke, Don't Fix It?": Scandals, "Risk," and Cosmetic Surgery Regulation in the UK and France*, MED. LAW REV. 384 (2014).

example, advertisements for cosmetic surgeries often show the appealing results in a conspicuous visual display, typically showing the unfortunate (and untouched) "before" and the beautiful (and digitally altered) "after."

If permitted, advertisements for these types of procedures should contain visual images of the risks of treatment, to increase the salience of the warnings to potential patients. An advertisement for Botox which uses images of a wrinkle-free face should also show an image of the droopy eyelid and paralysis that is the not uncommon side-effect of the procedure. While some providers may raise free-speech arguments, many medical professionals are likely to welcome some restrictions, as they understand the harm caused to patients and their profession from unseemly and misleading advertisements. In Britain, plastic surgeons themselves have mobilized to strengthen regulations governing cosmetic surgical procedures, and have urged banning advertisements altogether.[589]

B. BODILY INTEGRITY EXCHANGES

Consent legitimizes an act for as long as it exists. If consent is withdrawn, the act must cease. For example, consent to sexual relations may be withdrawn at any time, and when it is, sexual activity must cease.[590] By contrast, a contract limits a party's freedom by requiring performance even where consent is subsequently destroyed. A contract means that the consenting party *may not* withdraw consent. Consent is only required at the time of contract formation. For this reason, contracts where the subject matter involves the body raise seemingly insurmountable problems. Contract law is ideally suited for commercial transactions because the security of transactions is essential in a credit-based economy.[591] It seems to be an ill fit where the subject matter of the transaction is of an intimate nature, involves the body itself, and is particularly susceptible to internal changes and external pressures. There are compelling reasons to enforce a contract despite later non-consent; *but none of these apply where bodily integrity is involved.* Rules established with commercial transactions in mind have no place where the subject matter of the contract concerns what happens to one's body at the most intimate levels and in the most intrusive ways.

Unlike the other hard cases, bodily integrity exchanges must generally be structured as contracts, as they involve promises to perform in the future. Contract law

---

[589] Jeremy Laurance, *Cosmetic Surgeons Demand Ban on Advertising Their Own Trade*, INDEP., (Nov. 16, 2009), www.independent.co.uk/life-style/health-and-families/health-news/cosmetic-surgeons-demand-ban-on-advertising-their-own-trade-1821247.html; Sarah Boseley, *Cosmetic Surgery Advertising Ban Urged by Leading Surgeon*, GUARDIAN (Jan. 22, 2012), www.theguardian.com/life andstyle/2012/jan/22/ban-advertising-cosmetic-surgery.

[590] *See generally* Matthew R. Lyon, *No Means No?: Withdrawal of Consent During Intercourse and the Continuing Evolution of the Definition of Rape*, 95 J. CRIM. L. & CRIMINOLOGY 277 (2004).

[591] *See* NATHAN B. OMAN, THE DIGNITY OF COMMERCE: MARKETS AND THE MORAL FOUNDATIONS OF CONTRACT LAW (2017) (arguing that the role of contracts in the marketplace provides its moral justification).

constrains the freedom of the parties to change their minds while constitutional law favors protecting freedom, especially in matters involving bodily integrity, as evidenced by the Fifth Amendment protection of due process and the Thirteenth Amendment prohibition against involuntary servitude.[592] Thus, bodily integrity contracts cause the objectives of contract law and constitutional law to clash in a seemingly irreconcilable way.

Contractability is a requisite part of consentability, *especially* in bodily integrity exchanges where there is great potential for exploitation. One of the arguments in favor of legalizing bodily integrity exchanges is that prohibiting such acts actually perpetuates inequality. According to this view, at least certain of these exchanges take place regardless of the law. Consequently, consenters are forced to operate without the protections of the law yet subject to its penalties. Operating outside of the law means that both parties are deprived of the benefits of contract, which include the ability to plan and shape expectations and obligations as well as the power to enforce terms. If society legalizes an activity (i.e. makes it "consentable"), then it must allow contractability to avoid injustice. Someone who has submitted to a procedure or act involving bodily intrusion (e.g. had sex, undergone IVF treatments, become pregnant, had a kidney removed) because she was promised monetary compensation should not be left to appeal to the good nature and decency of the other party who has decided to change his mind about whether to pay.

However, simply having a contract does not guarantee the means to enforce it. The non-breaching party must still grapple with the justice system and the fees and costs associated with pursuing a legal claim. Furthermore, a contract is a gruesome means of enforcement if used to order specific performance against someone who has changed her mind about relinquishing a body part or performing an intrusive activity involving her body. Existing contract doctrines have only limited utility here. For example, the doctrines of fraud and duress would protect the consenting party from having to perform where she was deceived or coerced. However, the situations that give rise to a change of heart would not meet the legal definition of fraud or duress, and it is these situations which are most likely to occur in bodily integrity exchanges. A few contract defenses – notably mutual and unilateral mistake, non-disclosure, and changed circumstances – would permit contract avoidance in the event of a basic assumption error. For example, a surrogate mother could decide to terminate her agreement if she had concerns about the mental health of the future parents or if she discovered that they had a record of child abuse. However, contract defenses typically are not availing where the error was a mistake of one's future preferences. They do not allow avoidance where there was proper consent

---

[592]   In pertinent part, the Fifth Amendment provides, "No person shall . . . be deprived of life, liberty or property without due process of law." U.S. CONST. amend. V. The Thirteenth Amendment states, "Neither slavery nor involuntary servitude, except as a punishment for crime whereof the party shall have been duly convicted, shall exist within the United States, or any place subject to their jurisdiction." U.S. CONST. amend. XIII, § 1.

construction but consent was destroyed due to *foreseeable* external factors (a change in personal circumstances, such as a marriage, divorce, or an inheritance) or internal factors (such as a change of heart, fear or another emotional reaction). Legalizing bodily integrity contracts means that such contracts must be enforceable; yet to specifically enforce them against the recalcitrant consenter is abhorrent and offends our communal sense of what a civilized society should tolerate.

But, one might argue, what about the other party to the transaction who enters into a contract in good faith, relying upon performance? Such a person may suffer greater harm than the victim of a breach in a mere commercial transaction. For example, if X, dying of liver failure, enters into a contract where X will pay Y for a portion of Y's liver, a breach by Y will likely cause X serious injury. X may be unable to find another suitable person for the liver transplantation. How should the law handle such a situation?

The law should determine these situations based upon the relative autonomy interests of the parties. In the scenario above, X should not be permitted to compel Y to undergo the procedure even though the consequence of Y's breach endangers X's life. Y's interest in bodily integrity is greater than X's economic interest in the transaction (even though that economic interest has the effect of protecting X's bodily integrity). Permitting Y to avoid performance is the only humane solution and the only palatable one in a free society. Furthermore, allowing Y to escape the contract provides an incentive to the consent-seekers (X and the intermediaries to the transactions) to act in good faith and in a fiduciary-like manner during both the pre-contractual and performance stages. If Y is allowed to avoid the contract, the consent-seekers are likely to be more forthcoming about the details of the transaction at an early stage as they would not be able to ensnare Y in a transaction simply because a contract was signed. The consent-seekers are also likely to offer better terms, including fair payment and health services. They may treat Y with more sensitivity and care, instead of as an object to be used and discarded. Y is likely to be better prepared mentally and emotionally for the transaction if the consent-seekers provide Y with full information at an early stage. If Y knows what to expect, the terms are fair and reasonable, and X and the intermediaries treat Y with care and concern, Y is less likely to renege on the transaction. Finally, Y would not be able to breach opportunistically, which also minimizes the likelihood of Y acting in bad faith.

The autonomy interests of the parties may change as the transaction progresses. Assume that A enters into a contract with B and C where B and C will pay A to act as a surrogate. What happens if A changes her mind? Using the hierarchy of threats to the autonomy interest as a guide, the appropriate remedy should depend upon the stage of performance at the time of breach and the nature of the performance remaining. If A decides that she no longer wants to be a surrogate after having been impregnated, she should not be compelled to continue with her pregnancy. The consideration/economic interest that B and C have in A's performance does not outweigh A's interest in bodily integrity (or society's interest in freedom/prohibiting involuntary servitude). B and C's remedy would be restitution (the return of money paid to A for unperformed services, which should exclude expenses paid for medical and pregnancy-related tests for which A received no personal benefit).

If, however, A changes her mind *after* pregnancy and childbirth, the analysis differs, because the parties' interests have now changed. A has already performed that portion of her contract which risks her bodily integrity and B and C are *not* seeking to compel A to submit to bodily intrusion. Consequently, the threat to A's autonomy interest is the same as the threat to B and C's autonomy interest (namely, waiver of rights as both are claiming parental rights to the baby). In this scenario, the interests of both sides are equivalent. In a commercial transaction, the societal interest in the security of transactions would tip the balance in favor of enforcing the contract. But here, there are competing societal interests which are independent of the interests of either party. The most important of these is the societal interest in protecting the rights and the autonomy interest of the child. None of the parties has the power to consent to action which would harm a third party under both the Harm Principle and the Opportunism Corollary. The parties' power to contract for surrogacy services does not give them the power to override the state's interest in protecting its citizens from harm (the societal interests of equality/non-discrimination and public safety). After birth, the baby has rights that override any conflicting rights that the parties have created through contract. As between the contracting parties, before birth, the surrogate's right to bodily integrity takes precedence over the rights of B and C; after birth, the legal rights of B and C take precedence over the surrogate's legal rights (although they do not take precedence over the interests of the child or the state's interest in protecting the child). The state should not prioritize A's claim as a birth mother because A has contracted away those rights; rather, it should defer to the contract, unless there are concerns about the parental fitness of B and C.

There are no simple solutions with matters as complex as bodily integrity exchanges. There are, however, guiding principles that help ensure a fair and morally palatable process. As with other contracts, consent should be adequately constructed. However, the consent conditions must be much more robust where bodily integrity and a high degree of threat to the autonomy interest are involved than where the transaction involves merely an economic interest. Furthermore, because those who agree to bodily intrusions in exchange for money presumably have limited financial resources, the voluntariness and knowledge conditions require careful scrutiny to ensure adequate consent and to prevent exploitation.

Many bodily integrity contracts require that contracting parties meet health standards to ensure that they are suitable candidates for the specified procedure. They should also undergo mental and financial counseling so that the implications of the procedures are clear and understandable. Those who are mentally unstable should not be permitted to participate in highly intrusive bodily integrity transactions. Concerns over exploitation of the poor or economically desperate could be alleviated by setting a minimum payment requirement. Rather than imposing a ceiling on these exchanges, regulatory measures should impose minimum pricing to ensure that participants are not getting paid too little.

The rationale underlying ceiling limits, most prominent in the context of egg "donations," is primarily based upon concern that high prices would prove too tempting, and that women who would not otherwise be inclined to sell their eggs would be motivated to do so by the promise of a large payment.[593] The concern reveals an unsettling type of paternalism aimed at limiting women's choices and based upon an idealistic (and unrealistic) view of why women agree to participate in the procedure. Kimberly Krawiec critiques egg donor compensation caps as "an odd-even backwards-response to concerns over the financial coercion of poor women":

> The ability of any sum to coerce action is a direct function of that person's financial need. Egg donor compensation caps, without reference to the potential donor's financial status, do nothing to address financial coercion objections. Ironically, the most likely effect of a ... price cap would be to drive from the market the most highly valued egg donors, who tend to be better-educated and of a higher socio-economic status. These donors should be in a better position to evaluate the risks of egg donation against the monetary benefits and should be less susceptible to the "coercive" effects of monetary compensation, because they are more likely to have other income opportunities from which to choose.[594]

As Krawiec notes, to limit the potential money women can make essentially means that only those women with lower incomes are likely to engage in these transactions. If a procedure is safe enough for some women (i.e. lower-income women) to participate in, it should be safe enough for all women to participate in, even those who are not financially desperate. Exploitation means that someone is being unfairly taken advantage of; women who are tempted to engage in highly lucrative transactions are not being financially exploited by another. Rather, they are making a calculated decision to engage in the exchange based on the expected (financial) benefit.

There are, however, other claims involving *how* women are being exploited which must be addressed. For example, are there adequate disclosures about what the egg extraction process is like? A woman might not realize the degree of pain involved in having an egg removed or the potential long-term health consequences of receiving hormone treatments. She might also misunderstand the financial terms – is the quoted price the amount she will receive free of expenses? How much will she get after taxes? Does it include follow-up medical services?

---

593 Price ceilings in the context of egg donations have been challenged as an antitrust violation. *See* Kamakahi v. Am. Soc'y for Reprod. Med., 305 F.R.D. 164 (N.D. Cal. 2015). The case was subsequently settled and the compensation ceiling guidelines removed as part of the settlement. *See* Kelly Knaub, *Egg Donors Get Pay Limits Axed with Antitrust Settlement*, LAW360 (Feb. 1, 2016), www .law360.com/articles/753389/egg-donors-get-pay-limits-axed-with-antitrust-settlement.

594 Kimberly D. Krawiec, *A Woman's Worth*, 88 N.C. L. Rev. 1739, 1765 (2010).

A knowledge deficit is likely to arise in bodily integrity exchanges because of the uniqueness of the experience. Pregnancy and childbirth, for example, are considered by many women to be emotionally charged experiences. A surrogate may not understand the emotional changes and the attachment she may have to a growing fetus unless she has already had children. If possible, consent-seekers should provide consenters with unbiased information regarding the experiences of others in similar situations. In some cases, limiting the pool of consenters, if practicable, may be effective. For example, to increase the likelihood of a more robust knowledge condition for potential surrogates, regulatory measures should restrict surrogacy to those women who have already undergone pregnancy and childbirth.

Knowledge deficits may also result from false representations or material omissions, cognitive limitations or a combination of the two. For example, studies indicate that people who sold their kidneys on the black market in Bangladesh, India or Pakistan had high levels of regret.[595] Legal scholar I. Glenn Cohen states that the "very high number of kidney sellers" who later regret their decision "likely involve informational deficits, bounded rationality, etc." and is the "strongest argument in favor of legal intervention."[596] Their regret likely stemmed, not from having received payment for their kidney, but from an experience which was not what they expected it to be. They were often lied to about the procedure, their recovery was often rushed, and they did not receive the financial benefits that they were promised. Because the procedure left them in poorer health, they were often unable to work as much as they had before, leaving them worse off financially.[597] The payment was not the source of the regret even though it may have been the motive for engaging in the activity; rather, it was the broken promises and misrepresentations that resulted in the poor outcomes and the subsequent regret.

Their situation highlights the importance of implementing protocols which reduce the need to resort to enforcement mechanisms that depend upon the legal system. The legal system is costly and generally favors those with financial resources. While a contract provides protection on paper, the reality of an expensive and time-consuming litigation or arbitration proceeding means that someone with limited economic resources (which will likely include many of those who are agreeing to provide the "body" in bodily integrity transactions) will not be able to enforce it. Pricing should be transparent, with no hidden fees, and all payments should be made upfront and placed in escrow. Concerns about bad decisions and time-inconsistent preferences could be addressed through required payment mechanisms

---

[595] I. Glenn Cohen, *Transplant Tourism: The Ethics and Regulation of International Markets for Organs*, 41 J. L. MED. & ETHICS 269, 277 (2013) (stating that studies of sellers in Pakistan and India shows that "only 35% and 21% respectively, recommended that a family member or friend sell their kidney; in the Bangladesh study 85% of sellers spoke against the organ market, with many (an exact number is not given) stating they would not sell if given a second chance").

[596] *Id.*

[597] *Id.* at 269–77 (summarizing studies of those who have participated in paid kidney transplants).

and structured payment schedules. For example, rather than receiving a lump sum payment for having a kidney surgically removed, the consenter could request that the money be put in a trust where the consenter would receive a monthly payment for several years. Blockchain contracts, if they prove to be as reliable as their proponents claim, might be a useful solution to the problem of enforcement.

Proposals related to enhancing consent to bodily integrity exchanges need to be tailored to the particular transaction. For example, all exchanges involving payment of money for extraction of human organs or tissues are not the same, and should not be treated similarly. The level of counseling and intervention required should take into account the factors which are used to assess the threat level to autonomy, such as the intrusiveness of the procedure, the long-term health consequences, the permanence, the painfulness of the process, and the particular circumstances of the procedure.[598] Certain procedures are simply so harmful and risky that it would be impossible to meet the requisite conditions of consent. Exchanges involving vital organs should not be permitted unless there is evidence that the procedures are safe and pose no long-term serious detrimental health hazards for the transferor. The transferor should be consenting to the *risk* of serious bodily injury, not the certainty of it. A kidney can be safely extracted and the transferor can live a normal, healthy life. The same cannot be said of someone who gives up his heart or his brain.

Contracts can be a tool of exploitation and the product of uneven bargaining power, but they can also be tools of empowerment which protect and enforce rights and expectations.[599] As previously noted, bodily integrity contracts have been found by some courts to be unenforceable as against public policy. A better approach would be to examine each contract on an individual basis rather than categorizing a particular type of transaction as against public policy. For example, surrogacy transactions should generally be enforceable even if a particular contract term is unenforceable because it is unconscionable or against public policy. Certain provisions might be categorically unenforceable. For example, provisions that require the surrogate to undergo abortion if the fetus has a birth defect might be unenforceable as a matter of policy because they require the surrogate to agree in advance to an intrusive bodily procedure which she may be unwilling to undergo at the time of performance. The conditional nature of the promise and the high level of intrusion create the perfect storm for defective consent. In addition, a provision that deprives a party of a benefit after that party has undergone a bodily intrusion pursuant to the contract also should be unenforceable, as it would undermine the voluntariness

---

[598]   *See supra* Figure 3.5.

[599]   *See* Kellye Y. Testy, *An Unlikely Resurrection*, 90 Nw. U. L. Rev. 219, 219 (1995) ("Lesbian legal theory is resurrecting contract by advocating that lesbians should seek to use contract rather than used by it ... lesbian legal theory recognizes that contract has the potential both to empower women and to oppress them."); Patricia Williams, *Alchemical Notes: Reconstructing Ideals from Deconstructed Rights*, 22 Harv. Civ. Rights-Civ. Lib. L. Rev. 401, 408 (1987).

condition of consent and compel someone to continue with an activity which poses a high-level threat to the autonomy interest with a less than robust voluntariness condition. The risk of forfeiture should be presumed coercive. In each instance, the nature of the competing autonomy interests must be balanced against each other according to the hierarchy of autonomy interests and the corresponding threat level. As with self-harming and self-directed activities, the nature of the activity to which one is consenting matters and the higher the threat level to autonomy, the greater the requisite robustness of the conditions of consent.

Generally, bodily integrity exchanges which are deemed unconsentable have a low expressive value relative to other societal values. For example, prostitution is of low expressive value, since the primary motivation of the prostitute is to earn money, not to express herself sexually. One might argue that the act of sex is an act of autonomous expression, but sex is not the prohibited activity. It is the payment of money for sexual services which is prohibited. But the fact of payment should not minimize or negate the expressive nature of their work.[600]

At the heart of many objections regarding bodily integrity exchanges is that they are potentially exploitative. "Exploitation" can mean different things,[601] but is typically used to refer to a situation where one party takes unfair advantage of another. The meaning of "unfair advantage" is itself context-dependent. There are two broad types of situations where someone (X) takes advantage of another (Y) (although these two types are not mutually exclusive and can even have a symbiotic relationship). The first is where X creates the exploitative situation. X may use information or a relationship with Y to manipulate and take advantage of Y. This first category of exploitation may be understood within the context of consent construction. X takes advantage of Y when X engages in any action that would diminish or dilute a consent condition. For example, if X withholds information in order to obtain Y's consent, X is taking advantage of Y. The extent of that advantage-taking depends upon the type of information (i.e. its materiality) or the situation (i.e. whether she knows the other party has a mistaken belief which could be corrected by the information). Exploitation in this case violates the underlying value of fairness in the consent process and is generally addressed under the doctrines of duress, undue influence or fraud.

---

[600]　As Radin explains, there is a nonmarket aspect to work which is important to personhood. *See* RADIN, CONTESTED COMMODITIES, *supra* note 49, at 106–07 ("Because this is a market society, most people must be paid for their work if they are to live. Yet the kind of work most of us hope to have – I think – is that which we would do anyway, without money, if somehow by other means our necessities of life were taken care of . . . Incomplete commodification can describe a situation in which things are sold but the interaction between the participants in the transaction cannot be fully or perspicaciously described as the sale of things. If many kind of sales retain a personal aspect even though money changes hands, those interactions are not fully described as sales of commodities.").

[601]　*See* JOEL FEINBERG, THE MORAL LIMITS OF THE CRIMINAL LAW: HARMLESS WRONGDOING 176–276 (1990) (discussing the different types of exploitation in great detail).

The second category of exploitation is where the victim finds herself in a difficult situation which is not the fault of the other party. Exploitation in this context typically refers to class or group distinctions; an individual (Y) is a member of an oppressed or subordinated group and the other individual (X) is not. In this context, the exchange is inherently coercive due to preexisting conditions of societal injustice or economic imbalance. X exploits Y when X takes unfair advantage of societal conditions which X did not create. The exchange involves the very essence of subordination. For example, some object to sex work on the grounds that it exploits women.[602] In this second type of exploitative situation, the underlying value of equality has already been violated. It is *because* the playing field is not level that consent is defective. Systemic subordination makes true agency – and thus valid consent – impossible. Consent considers the actors as individual but exploitation in this second type of situation pertains to their social group membership and their subordinated place within the social, cultural or economic system. It is this second type of exploitation which is generally lawful because it does not directly violate the societal value of equality although it may undermine it or perpetuate inequality.

It is this second type of exploitation which is the concern of those who oppose bodily integrity contracts, because it is this type of exploitation which the law is ill-equipped to address. It will almost certainly be the case that very few wealthy people will be selling their organs or agreeing to act as maternal surrogates, and to argue otherwise simply ignores reality. Women who undergo egg extractions for cash will be young and in need of money. Some may argue that these transactions are not necessarily exploitative, and will point to examples to make that point: the suburbanite multiple surrogate who enjoys being pregnant and relishes being able to give the gift of babies to those who are unable to bear them without assistance; the loving husband who donates his kidney to his ailing mother-in-law; the sex worker who feels empowered and lobbies for legalization of prostitution. But these examples are noteworthy *because* they are exceptional, not because they are representative. The reluctance to classify these transactions as potentially exploitative is because there is a countervailing justification for allowing them that is believed greater than the harm created by the exploitative act (e.g. fewer people will die while waiting for an unavailable organ, gay and infertile couples will know the joy of genetic recognition, sex is a fundamental part of being human and access is too limited for some people, etc.). A counterbalancing benefit, however, doesn't mean a party is not being oppressed or exploited, and the benefit from allowing the transaction should not obscure the potential for exploitation. On the other hand, the act should not be prohibited simply because it has the *potential* to be exploitative. In our unequal, market-driven society, acts which perpetuate subordination or which are potentially exploitative are not anomalous. We should, however, carefully regulate them in

---

[602] See BINDEL, *supra* note 102, at vii ("prostitution is a human rights violation against women and girls.").

light of their potential for exploitation. The issue of exploitation concerns whether the practices themselves take unfair advantage of an individual's circumstances, not whether the circumstances creating the inequality are unfair (often they are). The potential for exploitation arises because of the economic disparity between the parties. Consequently, these transactions should not be treated like commercial, arm's-length exchanges involving commodities. Rather, safeguards should be put in place *because* of the potentially exploitative nature of the transaction. If, however, safeguards are unlikely to be effective, and the activity poses a high-level threat to autonomy, then it should not be consentable.

One safeguard might be to carefully regulate the participation of the desperately poor when they engage in bodily integrity transactions which pose a high-level threat to autonomy. Consent requires a choice; the desperately poor often have no real choice but to agree to an exchange for money.[603] If the justification for permitting bodily integrity transactions is consent, it is not accurate to say that those who are driven by dire economic circumstances to undergo major surgery to relinquish their kidney (or other organ) have met the requisite robustness level for the voluntariness condition.[604] In other words, it would be difficult to prove "beyond a reasonable doubt" that the consenter acted voluntarily. The knowledge condition, too, is likely to be deficient (i.e. not provable "beyond a reasonable doubt") as someone in this situation is likely focusing on the immediate monetary benefits and not the later consequences of undergoing the surgery. To use consent to justify these transactions for the desperately poor is to ignore the evidence regarding human cognition and behavior. Humans typically focus on the near term, subject to a slew of cognitive biases which cloud judgment. Desperation only narrows tunnel vision, and poverty drastically reduces options (and weakens the voluntariness condition).

The sale of a kidney or the offering of sexual services is not a panacea for the desperately poor. It may help someone pay off a debt or acquire an asset, but one exchange typically does not fix the condition of poverty for an individual, even if it involves a large payment. As many lottery winners and others who have come into unexpected wealth can attest, economic survival requires more than sudden cash in hand.[605] While a one-time infusion of capital received as part of a bodily integrity

---

[603] For the same reason, drug addicts should be prohibited from engaging in high-level threat exchanges. Presumably, drug addicts would be screened from these exchanges during a counseling session, which is why I do not expressly mention them with the desperately poor.

[604] *See* Sandel, *supra* note 107, at 87, 94 (1998) ("A peasant may agree to sell his kidney or cornea in order to feed his starving family, but his agreement is not truly voluntary. He is coerced, in effect, by the necessities of his situation.").

[605] Michael B. Kelley & Pamela Engel, *21 Lottery Winners Who Blew it All*, Bus. INSIDER (Feb. 11, 2015), www.businessinsider.com/lottery-winners-powerball-jackpot-how-much-2016-7 ("many people's lives became notably worse after they got super rich, and they managed to lose it all quite quickly."); Linda Holmes, *ESPN's "Broke" Looks at the Many Ways Athletes Lose Their Money*, NPR (Oct. 2, 2012), www.npr.org/sections/monkeysee/2012/10/02/162162226/espns-broke-looks-at-the-many-ways-athletes-lose-their-money (discussing a documentary that examines why 78 percent of former NFL players have gone bankrupt or are under financial stress two years after retirement).

exchange might provide immediate relief from financial constraints, it may leave the desperately poor worse off if there is no improvement to the underlying social or personal conditions which led to the dire circumstances in the first place.[606]

Given their vulnerability, the desperately poor are likely to be targeted and misled by those willing to prey upon their desperation. "Get rich schemes" are intended to blind the vulnerable with their own optimism into taking foolish risks. When those "get rich schemes" involve substantial risks to bodily integrity, the state should prohibit them.[607] It might be that a regulated, legal market would minimize such scams, but it is improbable that they would be eliminated, given the lack of resources that the desperately poor have to enforce their legal rights.

To restrict the desperately poor from engaging in bodily integrity transactions is undoubtedly paternalistic, but that does not mean that it is undoubtedly *problematic*. Complaints about paternalism and traditional economic arguments in favor of a free market assume a certain freedom to make choices which ignores the reality of the desperately poor and the ways poverty hinders autonomy-enhancing decision-making. Perhaps the state is not acting paternalistically *enough*, and should put more efforts into assisting the poor in ways that will enhance their autonomy, rather than assuming conditions of equality where none exist.

One might argue that restricting the desperately poor treats them differently from others and that such a policy would be discriminatory. But the reality of the desperately poor is that they *are* in a different position from the non-desperately poor. Their vulnerable status, however, is not an inherent condition or an immutable characteristic, and any exclusion could be temporary, not predetermined or inevitable. Furthermore, some laws *already* discriminate on the basis of income in a paternalistic way. For example, only "accredited" investors may participate in certain private offerings of securities.[608] An "accredited" investor is someone whose "individual net worth, or joint net worth with that person's spouse, exceeds $1,000,000"[609] or a "natural person who had an individual income in excess of $200,000 in each of the two most recent years or joint income with that person's spouse in excess of $300,000 in each of those years and has a reasonable expectation of reaching the same income level in the current year."[610]

---

[606] In one study involving 239 kidney sellers in Pakistan, 85 percent reported that there was no improvement in their lives and that they were still in debt or suffering other financial difficulties. *See* Glenn Cohen, *supra* note 595, at 270 (discussing S. A. Anwar Naqvi et al., *A Socioeconomic Survey of Kidney Vendors in Pakistan*, 20 TRANSPLANT INT'L 934 (2007)).

[607] A study of illegal kidney sales in Bangladesh found that twenty-seven out of the thirty-three sellers did not receive the total amount of money that they were promised. *See* Glenn Cohen, *supra* note 595, at 271 (discussing M. Moniruzzaman, *"Living Cadavers" in Bangladesh: Bioviolence in the Human Organ Bazaar*, 26 MED. ANTRHOPOLOGY Q. 69 (2012).

[608] 17 C.F.R. § 230.500 (LEXIS through June 13, 2018 issue of the Fed. Reg.).

[609] *Id.* at § 230.502(a)(5).

[610] *Id.* at § 230.502(a)(6).

The question might arise whether legalizing bodily integrity transactions is pointless if the group of people most likely to act as providers is restricted from participating. Certainly, that might be the case but if an activity is so distasteful that only the desperately poor are willing to participate in it, perhaps that should not be an activity which is consentable at all. To use consent as a moral justification for an activity which only the financially desperate would undertake provides a balm for society's conscience where none is deserved. As this book has argued throughout, the power to consent does not exist when the requisite conditions are lacking. As Debra Satz notes:

> When people come to the market with widely varying resources or widely different capacities to understand the terms of their transactions, they are unequally vulnerable to one another. In such circumstances the weaker party is at risk of being exploited ... When a person enters a contract from a position of extreme vulnerability he is likely to agree to almost any terms that are offered.[611]

The definition of "desperately poor" is subject to debate; the parameters would need to be specifically defined and may be subject to regional differences, but it would generally include those who are unable to provide for their basic human needs – food, shelter and clothing. A clear cut-off could be those with household incomes at a specified level (e.g. 20 to 50 percent) below the poverty line. (As of 2017, the U.S. poverty threshold for a single person under sixty-five was \$12,752/year; for a family of four, it was \$25,283).[612] Even in countries where social services are offered to the poor, there are people in desperate circumstances who may be susceptible to exploitation. For example, although there are welfare programs to assist the poor in the United States, the programs may be insufficient to meet basic needs, and people may fall through the cracks. The National Poverty Center estimated that there were about 1.46 million U.S. households in 2011 living in "extreme poverty," which was defined as \$2 or less in income per person per day.[613]

It may seem odd to limit the potential for financial gain to those who are most in need of it. But there is no consent without choice because when there is no real choice the voluntariness condition is lacking. Because the very survival of the desperately poor is at risk, they may have no real choice but to agree to bodily integrity contracts. If consent is the justification for bodily integrity transactions, then those with the most constrained choices cannot be understood to have consented to transactions which pose a high degree of threat to their autonomy (e.g. highly intrusive, painful, with permanent consequences). There may be another justification for permitting the desperately poor to participate in these transactions

---

[611] SATZ, *supra* note 49, at 97.
[612] *See Weighted Average Poverty Thresholds for Families of Specified Sizes, Historical Poverty Tables-People 1978–2017*, U.S. CENSUS BUREAU, www.census.gov/data/tables/time-series/demo/income-poverty/historical-poverty-thresholds.html (last visited Apr. 5, 2018).
[613] H. Luke Shaefer & Kathryn Edin, *Extreme Poverty in the United States: 1996 to 2011*, NAT'L POVERTY CTR. (Feb. 2012), at 1, www.npc.umich.edu/publications/policy_briefs/brief28/policybrief28.pdf.

(such as the societal value of fairness or equality, or the utilitarian goal of increasing the supply of organs for transplantation), but that justification cannot be consent and the moral relief that it provides. It is facile as well as inaccurate to claim that someone who is desperately poor "chose" to sell his kidney in order to buy food to survive.

But an outright ban on permitting the desperately poor to participate in bodily integrity exchanges ignores the problem of the "double bind" described by Margaret Jane Radin:

> Those who choose to sell their labor – or their kidneys – under these conditions are poor and oppressed. But even if we think of the exchange as coerced, and not usefully characterized as an exercise of liberty, we are still left with the problem that to the desperate person the desperate exchange must have appeared better than her previous straits, and in banning the exchange we haven't done anything about the straits. It seems to add insult to injury to ban desperate exchanges by deeming them coerced by terrible circumstances, without changing the circumstances.[614]

Yet, to presume that consent is possible in desperate circumstances would mischaracterize the interaction and make it easier to camouflage and justify exploitation using the rhetoric of consent, autonomy and freedom of contract.

An ominous threat also lurks in the shadows if body parts are viewed as "assets" or alternative sources of revenue. A man with two kidneys might be deemed ineligible for public assistance because he has the option of selling one of them. Thus, another reason to prohibit the desperately poor from participating in bodily integrity transactions is to avoid the risk of having public benefits *denied* unless the body is fully exploited.

It may be the case that if only the desperately poor engage in bodily integrity transactions, the governmental agencies charged with regulating those transactions will ignore or overlook abuses and violations as those markets develop. This is particularly troubling, given the way that racial and gender inequality manifests in income inequality, resulting in a compounding of harm.[615] Racial minorities and women (and perhaps hardest hit, women who are racial minorities) might suffer disproportionately from lack of regulatory oversight, exploited for their bodies, and left to suffer the consequences of botched procedures. For example, if organ sales become legalized, state agencies may devote fewer resources to regulating the transactions if the sellers are desperately poor and disempowered members of society. New and risky practices and governmental programs designed to oversee

---

[614] RADIN, CONTESTED COMMODITIES, *supra* note 49, at 49.

[615] This is not to suggest that extreme poverty is limited to racial minorities and women. In 2011, 48 percent of households in extreme poverty were white non-Hispanics, and 37 percent of them were headed by a married couple. *See id.* at 4 (25 percent of households in extreme poverty were headed by African Americans and 22 percent by Hispanics. The study notes that "the percentage growth in extreme poverty" was greatest among African American and Hispanics).

them are likely to be better scrutinized as they develop if those who participate and are affected by them are not the marginalized and disempowered poor.

A possible positive consequence from a prohibition based on economic status might be that those who would otherwise ignore the plight of the desperately poor might make efforts (or encourage the government to do so) to improve their economic condition and to address economic inequality generally. By diminishing the ranks of the desperately poor, the pool of potential providers increases. While I am doubtful that as a consequence there would be a marked increase in organ transplants from those who are *not* desperately poor,[616] the possibility of adequate consent construction increases with economic power (and increased choices), and makes consent viable.

The situation of the desperately poor is ripe for both regret on the part of the consenter, and opportunism on the part of consent-seekers. Until the potential consenter is able to demonstrate the ability to *survive* financially, the option of participating in high-risk, bodily integrity transactions should be restricted because it is likely to perpetuate the conditions of inequality.

Yet, there are also problems with a blanket exclusion. A rule that finds that the desperately poor have no power to consent to high-risk, bodily integrity transactions would mean that those who nonetheless engage in such activities would have less protection and fewer enforcement avenues than the non-desperately poor who engage in the same activities. Even if they are not prosecuted for engaging in prohibited activities, they would not have the power to enforce contracts or to recover for contractual breaches. Rather than empowering the desperately poor, an outright ban on their participation in these high-risk activities would further disempower them, depriving them of rights and remedies available to others. Furthermore, a blanket exclusion or prohibition would violate the fundamental societal value of equality and non-discrimination. As a practical matter, it would likely be difficult to enforce since it may not be easy to distinguish those who are desperately poor from those who are not.

Rather than an outright ban, I propose that a presumption of defective consent be applied to high-risk bodily integrity exchanges which involve the desperately poor. The consent-seeker would have to prove that the desperately poor consenter initiated contact (i.e. that the consent-seeker did not solicit the consenter) and that the terms, economic and otherwise, of the exchange were fair and reasonable. A failure to meet this burden would subject the consent-seeker to punishment depending upon the nature of the harm, including criminal and civil charges. Defective consent would not provide the consent-seeker with the moral or legal assurance that valid consent would provide, although the nature of the charges may be altered or mitigated.

---

[616]   *See* A. Rid et al., *Would You Sell A Kidney in a Regulated Kidney Market? Results of an Exploratory Study*, 35 J. MED. ETHICS 558 (2009) (finding that of 178 high- or upper-middle-class survey participants, forty-eight (27 percent) would consider selling a kidney in a regulated market and of those, thirty-one (66 percent) would only sell under dire financial circumstances).

Restitution (including disgorgement of profits) may be the most appropriate remedy in situations involving defective consent. It is useful to distinguish between two types of consent-seekers in bodily integrity exchanges: the directly affected party and the intermediary. The directly affected party/recipient may not be the wrong-doer in many types of bodily integrity exchanges. Rather, much of the exchange would likely be conducted through intermediaries, such as brokers or clinics. These intermediaries, and not the directly affected party, may be the ones engaging in communications with the consenter. A consenter who is given misinformation about the nature of a kidney extraction operation, for example, may have no claim against a non-breaching recipient. The recipient is not responsible for informing the consenter about the nature and consequences of the experiment and, assuming that the recipient has paid what is owed, has done no wrong. The intermediary, on the other hand, may be subject to liability, given its heightened obligations to the consenter in bodily integrity transactions. The intermediary in bodily integrity transactions should be viewed as being in a confidential relationship with the consenter and subject to a duty equivalent to a fiduciary duty. Where such a duty has been breached, disgorgement of all related profits, and not just what the intermediary has been paid, may be appropriate.[617] Disgorgement is most appropriate where the intermediary has engaged in conduct which is wrongful (e.g. soliciting the consenter or failing to disclose a conflict of interest). The threat of disgorgement disincentivizes bad behavior.[618] It may also be easier to prove disgorgement profits than tort damages.

One safeguard which might reduce exploitation would be to allow only those bodily integrity transactions which are based on necessity rather than mere convenience. There is something fundamentally different about X paying Y to perform the underlying act because X is not capable of performing the act herself, and X paying Y to perform the underlying act because X is *unwilling* to perform the act herself. For example, a woman who is perfectly healthy and physically able to bear children but seeks a surrogate because she does not wish to undergo the inconvenience and pain is closer to exploiting the surrogate and treating her as a commodity than is someone who is unable to bear children. The former is closer to violating the Kantian imperative by treating the surrogate as a means, and thus violating her human dignity. However, it may be difficult to implement this safeguard as it may be difficult to distinguish inability and inconvenience. Furthermore, this safeguard does not account for differences in individual preferences (which are, admittedly, tied to differences in cognitive decision-making ability and socio-economic status).

[617] RESTATEMENT (THIRD) OF RESTITUTION AND UNJUST ENRICHMENT § 43 (AM. LAW INST. 2011) (stating that a person is liable in restitution for breaching a fiduciary duty or "an equivalent duty imposed by a relation of trust and confidence . . . to the person to whom the duty is owed.").

[618] *Id.* § 3 cmt. a ("Liability to disgorge profits is ordinarily limited to cases of what this Restatement calls 'conscious wrongdoing,' because the disincentives that are the object of a disgorgement remedy are not required in dealing either with innocent recipients or with inadvertent tortfeasors such as innocent trespassers and converters.").

A more administrable requirement would be to have the consent-seeker/recipient fully disclose the rationale for the exchange, including whether it is one that the consent-seeker could herself undertake. In some cases, the rationale will be obvious, such as the need for a kidney because the recipient's own have failed or are failing. In other cases, the disclosure will help the consenter see how the recipient perceives her role more clearly and may help guide her behavior through the exchange if she chooses to proceed. Assume, for example, X is able to bear children but wishes to hire Y as a surrogate. The reason for hiring Y may matter to Y and she may wish to enter into the exchange if X's motivation aligns with Y's values, but decline to do so if they do not. If, for example, the reason that X does not want to bear her own children is because her job makes it infeasible for her to do so, Y may be willing to accept the surrogacy arrangement without feeling as though it degrades her or compromises her values. If, however, X's motivation is that the idea of childbirth disgusts her, then Y may be unwilling to act as a surrogate for X because she feels it would be degrading. On the other hand, she may not care what X thinks.

Opportunism and exploitation exist independent of consent. They exist due to a power disparity between the parties, although every transaction between unequally situated parties is not unavoidably exploitative. What makes it exploitative is the intent, knowledge and motivation of the party in the stronger position. Is that party acting in good faith? Is that party offering terms that are fair? Because of the difficulty of ascertaining subjective intent, whether conduct is opportunistic or exploitative is generally judged on external, objective criteria such as the degree of the unfairness and the degree to which the dominant party takes advantage of the subordinate one. Bodily integrity transactions have the potential to be exploitative if the consenter is in desperate need of money and the consent-seeker has money but is not desperate. They are less likely to be exploitative, however, if the party who is the paying party is equally desperate. An otherwise average man offering to pay five hundred dollars in exchange for sex with an unemployed woman with a starving child is engaging in an exploitative act. The woman has no other source of income and is in a desperate situation. Compare that with a scenario involving an elderly, invalid widower living alone and with no romantic prospects who offers to pay his employed, mentally competent neighbor five hundred dollars to have sex. That scenario may be offensive to some, but the act would not be exploitative of the neighbor. The widower has no other way to have his sexual needs met than to pay someone, and the neighbor could decline without repercussion. Exploitation becomes even more obvious if the amount offered in both scenarios was twenty dollars, instead of five hundred. The poor woman would probably still accept even though the price is objectively too low, so low in fact that it seems unbelievable that the neighbor woman in the second scenario would agree to the exchange.

Desperation on the part of both parties diminishes the argument that bodily integrity exchanges are inherently and necessarily exploitative. For example, if the man offering the poor woman money for sex were himself desperately poor and offering his last twenty dollars, there is less of an argument that the exchange is exploitative.

Opportunism is also likely where the consenter is young. Given what we know about brain development, bodily integrity transactions that pose a high-level threat to autonomy ideally should not involve consenters younger than twenty-five. The young generally have fewer resources and lack the experience and perspective to understand the long-term consequences associated with bodily integrity contracts. However, arguments similar to those raised in connection with the desperately poor might be raised with respect to a blanket rule prohibiting adults under twenty-five years of age from engaging in bodily integrity transactions. As an alternative to an outright ban on those 18-25 years of age, a presumption of defective consent could apply to bodily integrity transactions. The consent-seeker could rebut the presumption by providing evidence that the consenter initiated the transaction with the consent-seeker, and that the terms of the transaction were objectively fair and reasonable.

It is important to reiterate that the focus of this book is on consent, but consentability requires evaluation of the social impact of an act. A discussion about the societal impact of each type of bodily integrity transaction is beyond the scope of this book. If negative social consequences cannot be eliminated or reduced through regulatory efforts, then it may very well be that a particular exchange *should* be prohibited. The arguments in this section are not intended to advocate *for* the legalization of all types (or any type) of paid bodily integrity exchange; rather, they seek to parse out the role of consent where consent is relevant.

C. NOVEL/EXPERIMENTAL ACTIVITIES

In May 2012, a private organization named Mars One announced plans to establish a human colony on Mars in 2023.[619] The human settlers would emigrate to Mars and spend the rest of their lives there.[620] Every two years after the initial settlement, the program planned to send another crew on a one-way trip to Mars. To finance the project, Mars One planned to involve "the whole world as the audience of an interactive, televised broadcast of every aspect of this mission, from launch to landing to living on Mars." In short, the Mars One mission would be a reality show capturing every phase of the first human settlers on Mars. In April 2013, Mars One announced the launch of a program to select candidates for the one-way journey to Mars.[621] Unlike the vigorous vetting and training process undergone by NASA

---

[619] *Mars One Will Settle Men on Mars in 2023*, MARS ONE (May 31, 2012), www.mars-one.com/news/press-releases/mars-one-will-settle-men-on-mars-in-2023.

[620] *Id.* ("While sustaining human life on Mars is not trivial, it is far easier and safer than bringing the crew back to Earth.").

[621] *Mars One Starts Its Search for the First Humans on Mars*, MARS ONE (Apr. 22, 2013), www.mars-one.com/news/press-releases/mars-one-starts-its-search-for-the-first-humans-on-mars.

astronauts,[622] the Mars One astronaut-selection process was open to anyone. The organization stated that no particular academic or professional qualifications were required. The participants would go through several screening rounds. In the last stage of the selection process, the final decision for choosing the first four settlers would be decided by an audience vote.[623] Over 200,000 people applied to be one of the members of the first Mars One colony.[624]

Mars One claimed that all components necessary for the mission could be built with existing technologies. Several researchers at MIT, however, concluded that the Mars One mission was not feasible.[625] They determined that new technologies would be required to keep the human settlers alive on Mars, and that technologies for life support, entry, descent and landing were not currently existing or available. They also estimated that the crop growth area described by Mars One was inadequate and that a number of substantial changes and significant technological developments were required to bring the project closer to feasibility.

Human experimentation is an important part of societal progress. Pioneers in science, medicine and technology have advanced civilization, prolonged and improved human lives, and made history by daring to invent and innovate even when outcomes were uncertain and consequences unknown. They may have risked failure, but many of these inventors and innovators did not risk their own health or safety, preferring to have others suffer in the name of science. In too many shameful cases, they coerced, tricked or forced subjects to participate. Progress often entails enormous risks. But who should bear those risks? The question is an important one for a civilized society to ask. It may be easier to rationalize immoral or unethical actions when they are committed in the service of a noble cause. Unfortunately, the distance between the researcher and the subject may make it easier for the researcher to justify exposing the subject to excessively risky, painful and/or harmful experiments. If history is any guide, the subjects who are exploited are often society's disempowered and its most vulnerable.[626] Many of history's most notorious experiments were performed on racial minorities, the poor, the mentally disabled and

---

[622] According to writer Lee Hutchinson, "with one exception, every human being who has walked on another world has been an extremely skilled test pilot or naval aviator (and the one exception, Dr. Harrison Schmidt, was trained and rated on supersonic jets after his acceptance to the astronaut corps) . . . Beyond being incredible pilots, most were also *brilliant* – Buzz Aldrin, for example, holds a PhD from MIT in astronautics and his thesis . . . formed the groundwork for much of NASA's rendezvous procedures during Project Gemini." *See* Lee Hutchinson, *If Mars One Makes You Skeptical, You Might be Dead inside – Like Me*, Ars Technica (May 8, 2013), http://arstechnica .com/staff/2013/05/if-mars-one-makes-you-skeptical-you-might-be-dead-insidelike-me/.

[623] *Id.*

[624] *Mars One Announces Round One Astronaut Selection Results*, Mars One (Dec. 30, 2013), www.mars-one.com/news/press-releases/mars-one-announces-round-2-astronaut-selection-results (last visited Apr. 6, 2018).

[625] Sydney Do et al., *An Independent Assessment of the Technical Feasibility of the Mars One Mission Plan – Updated Analysis*, 120 Acta Astronautica 192 (2016).

[626] *See* Andrews, Future Perfect, *supra* note 152, at 77 (discussing how "past eugenics practices disproportionately disadvantaged women, people of color, and individuals with disabilities.").

those at the bottom of society's caste system, such as prostitutes and the homeless. Slaves were often the subjects of American experimentation.[627] Dr. J. Marion Sims, often referred to as the father of gynecology, perfected his surgical expertise and designed tools used for gynecological examination by experimenting on African American slave women.[628]

But there are others who chose to experiment on themselves before doing so on others. In his book *Who Goes First? The Story of Self-Experimentation in Medicine*, Dr. Lawrence K. Altman writes about doctors, nurses and dentists who engaged in self-experimentation and made significant contributions to scientific knowledge, including the discovery of anesthesia and the development of procedures such as blood transfusions.[629] Altman cites Sir George Pickering, a professor of Medicine at Oxford University, who said that the experimenter has "one golden rule" to help determine whether the proposed experiment is justifiable: "Is he prepared to submit himself to the procedure? If he is, and if the experiment is actually carried out on him, then it is probably justifiable. If he is not, then the experiment should not be done."[630]

Some may argue that self-experimenters lack objectivity, that they are taking undue risks or even that the lives of doctors and researchers are too valuable to risk in an experiment. But, as Dr. Altman explains:

> One man's life is not more valuable than another's . . . The argument advanced by opponents of self-experimentation, that the lives of researchers are too valuable to risk in experiments because of their specialized knowledge, opens up research to elitism of the worst kind. Furthermore, it allows unethical researchers to advance their careers by taking unnecessary risks on patients and volunteers while avoiding them themselves. If there is risk, why should someone other than the scientist himself take it first? If there is no risk, or it is ever so slight, what then is the scientist's objection to going first? When scientists say there is "little risk" to their experiment and do not go first, could it be that the "little risk" looms as a much larger one in their mind, a fear that they are unwilling to express to their subjects, their profes-sional peers, and the public?[631]

Experimenters who are willing to undergo the same risks as their subject are in a more ethically tenable position than those who are unwilling to so. Dr. Altman notes that this "Golden Rule" of medical experimentation has many advantages.[632] It would improve the informed consent process, since the researcher is more familiar with the nature of the experiment and the relevant science and methodology. It may

---

[627] Michele Goodwin, Black Markets: The Supply and Demand of Body Parts 30–32 (2006) (explain-ing that African Americans are "justifiably cautious" of the medical community and government-sponsored medical programs, given their past experience).

[628] Duke, *supra* note 124, at 111.

[629] *Id.*

[630] *Id.* at 313.

[631] *Id.* at 315.

[632] *Id.* at 303–09.

be more convenient. The researcher may be a more reliable participant than one detached from the experiment, especially if the experiment is to take place over a significant period of time or under arduous circumstances. The researcher may also learn more about the experiment from the perspective of a subject, including the nature of any reactions or sensations.[633]

This does not, however, mean that experimenters always should be the first subjects of their own experiments. In some cases, the experimenters may be ill-suited to participate in the experiment.[634] The study may require a particular genetic make-up, or subjects from an ethnic, racial or cultural group different from the researcher's own. The age or health of the researcher may make the experiment particularly risky. The study may require the experimenter to remain outside of it, to ensure the experiment is conducted in an unbiased manner. The study may require that participants are unaware of certain aspects, such as whether they are taking a placebo or an experimental drug. In some cases, a participant may be facing imminent death or suffering from a condition which makes him willing to take a chance on a risky procedure or drug. Nevertheless, an experimenter should always ask herself whether she would be willing to participate in the study if she were eligible to do so. If the answer is no, because the risks are too great or the consequences too dire, she should share that answer – and the reasons for it – with the subject.[635] Full disclosure in this situation would enable the potential subject to assess more clearly the risks involved.

While I have been referring specifically to scientific research, the Golden Rule is equally – and perhaps more – applicable to novel and highly risky business ventures. For example, Elon Musk was explicit about his reasons for not wanting to participate on a SpaceX venture to Mars.[636] Other people may have different preferences than Musk due to their personal circumstances. While Musk has dependents, fame and a company to run, other people may want to volunteer for the Space X trip because they have no dependents and want some measure of fame or recognition – and are willing to risk what they have to participate in something that will give their lives more meaning.

However, businesses which embark on novel endeavors where the potential harm is so high that management is unwilling to participate should not be permitted to proceed simply by claiming that the participants "consented." In all situations

---

[633]   *Id.* at 305–06 ("There is little question that people learn best from reactions they experience firsthand, which is one reason many senior investigators who have experimented on themselves urge their students to do the same ... They chose themselves because humans are the only possible subjects for experiments on sensation and pain.").

[634]   *Id.* at 309–11 (summarizing criticisms of self-experimentation, including that the self-experimenter may be biased or take unnecessary risks, the experiment for technical reasons (such as surgery) cannot be performed on himself, and because the researcher is in poor health or has a condition that would make the experiment particularly risky).

[635]   *Id.* at 314 ("Self-experimentation should become something that every researcher and volunteer considers before undertaking an experiment.").

[636]   *See* discussion *supra* Chapter 2 section C.

involving novel procedures, there is likely to be defective rather than valid consent. Given the complexity of novel and extremely risky endeavors and the limits of human cognition, the provision of information does not necessarily mean that the subject has actually *understood* the potential harm.

Consent requires some information, and the greater the potential harm to autonomy, the more robust must be the conditions of consent. Yet, when there is uncertainty, as there is with novel activities, there is not enough information to assess probability. Blanket consent, or consent to a generic statement regarding "unknown risks" does not constitute valid consent nor does it constitute no-consent. Rather, it should be understood as consent to the risk of foreseeable specific injuries. Assume for example that Subject A agrees to undergo a clinical trial for a pain reliever where the risks are "unknown." Subject A makes certain assumptions about those unknown risks. Subject A understands that she may suffer headaches or that she might get cramps. But if it turns out that a side effect is unbearable pain for the rest of her life, Subject A could not have consented to *that* risk as it was a risk that never entered her mind. It can be assumed that people do not consent to undergo procedures where the risk or outcome would leave them worse off than if they declined the procedure. There is defective consent, meaning that there is consent to proceed (and so the consent-seeker would not be liable for battery), but there is no consent to the risk of injury unless the risk is specified and the probability of the risk occurring is known and disclosed.

Accordingly, experiments – whether in the name of science or technology – should be properly designed and implemented in accordance with industry, professional or social norms.[637] Preliminary trials should be made to gather data and better assess the likely results of the experiment. Even the willingness of researchers and entrepreneurs to "go first" only enhances the ethical nature of the experiment or activity; it does not automatically mean that the experiment or activity itself is ethical or that it should be tried on others.[638] Manifestation of consent to a document disclosing "unknown risks," would constitute defective consent; manifestation of consent to each specifically disclosed risk would constitute valid consent only if there is a reasonably accurate way to estimate the probability of the risk occurring.[639] In cases involving defective consent, whether the consent-seeker is liable for any

---

[637] ALTMAN, *supra* note 156, at 314 ("As science grows in its complexity and sophistication, the public has greater difficulty understanding it. Informed consent does not justify or validate an experiment that is poorly designed or improperly executed, but it forces researchers and volunteers to articulate between the points and principles involved in an experiment.").

[638] *Id.* ("While self-experimentation should ethically precede performing an experiment on other subjects, the fact that a researcher has first tried his experiment on himself does not in itself justify trying it on another.").

[639] *See also* Rebecca Dresser, *The "Right to Try" Investigational Drugs: Science and Stories in the Access Debate*, 93 TEX. L. REV. 1631 (2015) (explaining how stories highlighting patients' experiences with experimental drug trials may better inform policymakers' decisions).

crime or tort would depend upon whether the consent-seeker's actions were reasonable in light of industry, professional and/or social norms.

This approach is consistent with federal law which requires researchers to obtain "informed consent" prior to using any human being in research:

> [N]o investigator may involve a human being as a subject in research covered by this policy unless the investigator has obtained the legally effective informed consent of the subject or the subject's legally authorized representative. An investigator shall seek such consent only under circumstances that provide the prospective subject or the representative sufficient opportunity to consider whether or not to participate and that minimize the possibility of coercion or undue influence. The information that is given to the subject or the representative shall be in language understandable to the subject or the representative. No informed consent, whether oral or written, may include any exculpatory language through which the subject or the representative is made to waive or appear to waive any of the subject's legal rights, or releases or appears to release the investigator, the sponsor, the institution or its agents from liability for negligence.[640]

Federal law also sets forth what information should be provided as part of the informed consent process, including a description of benefits of the research, a disclosure of alternative procedures, an explanation of whether medical treatments and/or compensation are available in the event of injury, and a statement that participation is voluntary.[641]

In the context of consent to medical research, the researcher occupies a position of trust and should act as a fiduciary to the participant. Naomi Duke writes that "trust facilitates one's willingness to contribute to a larger cause or willingness to place oneself in jeopardy on behalf of someone else."[642] She notes that, particularly in the area of medical research, trust creates an opportunity for abuse:

> The goals of research and medicine create or exacerbate conflicts of interests. Indeed, the inherent and opportunistic potential for exploitation of the individual (who may not be a patient or becomes a patient under coercive circumstance) is heightened in medical research, thus necessitating a check on participant motivations. Conflicts of interests in the medical research relationship are difficult to ignore on inspection: research platforms driven by the need to publish, obligations to secure research dollars (i.e., conduct medical research involving human subjects), admonition to teach and train, and the desire for financial gain and public recognition. Physician or medical researcher interests ... may not align with that of the patient. And while this may be expected in some circumstances, contemporary medical research demands may incentivize conduct from medical researchers that

---

[640]   45 C.F.R. § 46.116(a)(6) (LEXIS through June 13, 2018 issue of the Fed. Reg.); 21 C.F.R. § 50.20 (LEXIS through June 13, 2018 issue of the Fed. Reg.).

[641]   45 C.F.R. § 46.116(b).

[642]   The Global Body Market, *supra* note 124, at 112.

deemphasizes the importance of sharing information, building and establishing trust, promoting patient autonomy and preserving integrity and personhood.[643]

The pressure to produce publishable results from experiments may affect the judgment of researchers who may entice others to volunteer for something that they would not agree to themselves.[644] The volunteers, on the other hand, may assume that the scientist is acting without personal conflicts. Subject A, for example, might assume that the researcher would not conduct the trial if the researcher believed it was unreasonably risky or that the risks were greater than the benefits to the participants. Given Subject A's trust, the Opportunism Corollary requires that the researcher exercise care in conducting the experiment, and not expose Subject A to unreasonable harm. Certainly, the researcher should not use Subject A's "consent" as a shield to protect the researcher from liability. A research subject should not be viewed as having consented to an "unknown risk" where the risk of the outcome is worse than the condition which the procedure seeks to ameliorate *unless* that risk is specifically delineated, the probability of the risk occurring disclosed, and the subject manifests consent to that specific risk.

In novel experiments or ventures where there is a high risk of serious bodily injury, the participants may be unable to envision what it would be like to, for example, be trapped in a space shuttle light years from Planet Earth. Given the high-level threat to autonomy and the difficulty of meeting the knowledge condition, valid consent will be unattainable in most situations involving risky, truly novel activities. The rhetoric of "consent" should not provide a green light for businesses to offer products and services that are so risky that the death or serious bodily injury of its customers is probable. Consent to a novel procedure should only be viewed as defective consent, which would mean only consent to proceed, and not consent to the non-specifically disclosed consequences, as there is insufficient information to satisfy the knowledge condition. Accordingly, the participant in a novel venture or experimental study should be permitted to terminate participation at any time during the process. (This may not be feasible in some cases, e.g. where the space shuttle has already ascended into space.) As previously noted, payment for participation in a clinical trial raises concerns of exploitation. During the course of a venture or trial, a participant may have misgivings and may wish to terminate his participation. Because he may fear losing his monetary compensation – and so his participation up to that point would have been in vain – he may feel compelled to continue. Thus, the right to terminate one's participation in a novel activity must include the right to collect compensation for participation up to the time of termination. In the human subject setting, the Food and Drug Administration (FDA) recommends

[643] *Id.*

[644] ALTMAN, *supra* note 156, at 21 ("There are various motivations – sometimes hidden, sometimes overt – to entice other people to volunteer for research projects. Medical researchers may have much to gain personally in terms of career advancement and even monetary profit by doing something to someone else that they would not do to themselves or to family members.").

such an approach, noting that "credit for payment should accrue as the study progresses and not be contingent upon completion of the entire study," and that any amount paid as a "bonus for completion" should not be "so large as to unduly induce subjects to stay in the subject when they would otherwise have withdrawn."[645]

Even unpaid participants might feel pressure to join an experimental trial. A cancer patient, for example, may agree to participate in a novel procedure in a desperate attempt to prolong her life. Given her vulnerability and the difficulty in assessing potential risks involving novel medical procedures, the consent conditions are likely to be defective. This does not mean that she should be prohibited from participating in the trial. It does, however, mean that consent should not justify the procedure. Rather, the actions of the consent-seeker should be subject to scrutiny under existing norms and standards. The FDA's guidance to Institutional Review Boards (IRBs) and Clinical Investigators manifests this approach, stating that IRBs "should determine that the risks to subjects are reasonable in relation to anticipated benefits and that the consent document contains an adequate description of the study procedures" (citations omitted).[646] The duty of care applicable to physicians should apply to researchers.

The FDA states that exculpatory language has the "general effect of freeing or appearing to free an individual or an entity from malpractice, negligence, blame, fault or guilt."[647] Federal law expressly prohibits the use of exculpatory language in the informed consent process:

> No informed consent, whether oral or written, may include any exculpatory lan-guage through which the subject or the representative is made to waive or appear to waive any of the subject's legal rights, or releases or appears to release the investi-gator, the sponsor, the institution, or its agents from liability for negligence.[648]

These rules should also apply to companies engaging in novel ventures. Given the likelihood of defective consent, the terms of the exchange should be fair and reasonable. No waivers of the participant's rights should be permitted. Furthermore, it should be expressly communicated to the participant that the participant retains the right to seek recovery against the researcher/company for injuries.

Although researchers should not be compelled to pay participants if doing so would be prohibitive, there should be some cost-sharing or profit-sharing mechan-ism for the participation of those for whom the voluntariness condition is likely to be

---

[645] *Payment and Reimbursement to Research Subjects – Information Sheet*, FOOD & DRUG ADMIN., www.fda.gov/RegulatoryInformation/Guidances/ucm126429.htm (last updated Jan. 25, 2018).

[646] *Id.*

[647] *Informed Consent Information Sheet, Guidance for IRBs, Clinical Investigators, and Sponsors (Draft Guidance)*, FOOD & DRUG ADMIN. (July 2014), at 5–6, www.fda.gov/downloads/RegulatoryInformation/Guidances/UCM405006.pdf.

[648] 21 C.F.R. § 50.20 (LEXIS through June 13, 2018 issue of the Fed. Reg.).

defective (i.e. the terminally or desperately ill). If, for example, a cancer patient is participating in a drug treatment that is later commercialized, some of the profits might be allocated to a fund to pay for additional cancer research or to make the approved treatment available for free or at a reduced price to low-income patients. A terminally ill patient might feel forced to participate in an experimental trial in order to prolong her life, but knowing that her participation might help other people by making the treatment more accessible, may make her feel better about doing so. Although the original participant may not receive a direct financial benefit from such a fund, the potential public benefit both reduces any opportunistic gain of the researcher and may enhance the voluntariness condition.

This book opened with an account of Kim Suozzi and her decision to be cryopreserved. The procedure involved decapitation and preservation of only her head. Nobody knows whether cryopreservation will be successful and if Ms. Suozzi will ever be revived in the future. Nobody knows what it will be like if she is successfully revived. Ms. Suozzi made her decision to be cryopreserved as she was dying from brain cancer. She was young, only twenty-three years old. She had no way of knowing what it would be like to survive solely as a mind without a body or whether her surviving mind would be like the mind she had. She had no way of knowing whether she would feel pain and, if so, the severity of that pain. She had no way of knowing what the world or her personal circumstances would be like if she survived. Alcor Life Extension Foundation might no longer be in existence, or the management might have different policies or philosophies. Who would protect Ms. Suozzi's rights if she were to survive? Who would look after her interests? The decision she made was under the most difficult circumstances, and she was young with a desperate desire for a future that would not come. The threat to autonomy is unknown but potentially very high. Death could be viewed as the ultimate threat to autonomy, and it could be argued that any attempt to preserve life should be respected. But does death pose a greater threat to autonomy than a condition where one is physically immobile, suffering in excruciating pain, and completely at the mercy of strangers?

Faced with the forced choice of cryopreservation or death, the voluntariness condition is deficient. There are also too many unknown variables and too many unanswered questions to make an informed decision about whether to undergo cryopreservation. The knowledge condition is deficient, given the dearth of information and the difficulty in assessing the risks of such a procedure. There is little known about the outcome, and no ability to control what happens afterward. The knowledge condition requires *some* information. Consent to the unknown cannot constitute valid consent. At most, it is merely consent to proceed which may be withdrawn at any time. The only way that the procedure could be justified on the basis of consent is if someone who was cryopreserved had the option to withdraw consent. If, upon being revived, Kim Suozzi found the circumstances insufferable, she must have the option to terminate her life in order for it to be said that her consent justified Alcor's actions.

D. SUMMARY AND GENERAL GUIDELINES

The careful balancing of the conditions of consent and the threat to autonomy is dynamic, not static. For example, in situations which are novel or rare, the knowledge condition is often weak. Where the threat to autonomy is high, the act should be prohibited for most people.[649] Thus, certain medical trials might be restricted to those who understand the risks of the procedure (perhaps only medical personnel) or to those who have nothing much to lose (because they are suffering from incurable pain, a terminal illness or imminent death). However, as more information becomes available about the potential consequences of an experiment or procedure, the knowledge condition may be more robust for more people with the result being that more people may validly consent to participate. More information may also have the opposite effect on consent. Dr. Altman writes:

> [T]he risks of an experiment must be viewed in the context of the scientific knowledge of the era when it is done. What was considered a major risk only a few years ago may no longer be so because of knowledge gained in the interval. Conversely, the discovery of unexpected hidden dangers from further research may turn what was assumed to be a safe procedure yesterday into something known to be hazardous today.[650]

The same is true of activities outside of the area of scientific and medical experimentation. For example, information about the deleterious long-term effects of American football upon its players means that the sport poses a much greater threat to autonomy than previously assumed. Consequently, much greater robustness of the consent conditions should be required or the sport made much safer.

1. *Examples*

The consentability framework is both complex and obvious. It requires assessing whether consent *really* exists, given who the parties are, what they know, how they act, and the nature of the proposed activity. Although every situation is different, the following examples illustrate how the framework might be applied:

---

[649] For example, Peter Brian Barry writes, with respect to would-be amputees of healthy limbs, "while wannabes may well be autonomous agents capable of autonomous decision making, they are nonetheless bound to lack a certain kind of knowledge necessary to consent to voluntary amputation. So, if the ethical permissibility of voluntary amputation turns on whether or not voluntary amputation is reasonable and proper medical treatment performed with a patient's consent, then proponents of voluntary amputation as therapy for wannabes have not yet made their case." *See* Peter Brian Barry, *The Ethics of Voluntary Amputation*, 26 PUB. AFF. Q. 13, 13–14 (2012).

[650] ALTMAN, *supra* note 156, at 299.

1. An eighteen-year-old woman seeks silicone breasts implants, and her primary motive is to please her boyfriend.

    Breast implant surgery poses a high-level threat to the autonomy interest. Although breast implants may be removed, the surgery itself may leave permanent effects. It may reduce or eliminate breast sensitivity and make it impossible to breast-feed. Breast implants have been linked to cancer.[651] They also need to be replaced approximately every ten years, so that the younger the recipient of the implant, the greater the cost. The youth (and presumed lack of medical training) of the subject and the ubiquity of celebrities and models who have undergone breast implantation surgery indicates that the knowledge condition may be insufficient. The desire to retain her partner indicates that the voluntariness condition may also be less than ideal, given the high-level threat to the autonomy interest. It is unlikely that valid consent can be established. Furthermore, because she is under twenty-five, her consent would be presumed defective *even assuming that the conditions of consent could be sufficiently established,* which is unlikely given the facts. Accordingly, the physician would need to prove that the patient initiated the meeting (and was not responding to a solicitation or advertisement), and that the procedure was medically advisable and performed in accordance with professional norms and standards.

2. A thirty-year-old woman wishes to implant silicone material into her forehead to give the appearance of horns. She is a performance artist with many tattoos and piercings and makes her living creating music videos and art installations.

    Subdermal implants placed on the head pose a high-level threat to the autonomy interest and warrant state regulation. Even if her implants attract more publicity or attendance at her performances, the condition of voluntariness is likely met as she does not seem subject to external pressure to undergo the procedure. The knowledge condition is less than optimal, given the novelty of the procedure and the uncertain outcome. She may be unrealistic about the positive impact the implants might have on her career. She should undergo counseling to ensure adequate information of the risks. She should also be required to undergo a waiting period, given the dangerousness of the procedure. The procedure should be performed only by a trained and licensed medical professional in a sterile environment who has determined that it is medically advisable. Those performing the procedure without a medical license should be subject to penalties and even criminal punishment, as they are posing a high risk of harm to others.

3. A forty-year-old man agrees to participate in a reality show where he will be expected to endure "inhumane and extreme conditions" to test his survival skills.

---

[651] *See* Denise Grady, *More Cases Are Reported of Unusual Cancer Linked to Breast Implants,* N.Y. TIMES (Mar. 21, 2018), www.nytimes.com/2018/03/21/health/breast-implants-lymphoma.html?ribbon-ad-idx=9&rref=health.

He is given no other information about where he will be tested or what the tests will involve. He is made to sign a contract that requires him to complete the tests.

The contract requires the man to agree to circumstance without sufficient knowledge of what they will entail. The knowledge condition is not robust enough, given the potential harm to autonomy, to bind him to the contract. There is, however, sufficient consent to allow the parties to proceed with the activity *provided that* the man is permitted to discontinue the activity at any time. This contract is essentially one with a "terminable at will" clause and is not actually a "contract" at all, but an agreement to proceed, which may be withdrawn at any time. Accordingly, there would be no "breach" and no remedies if the man chose to end his participation.

4. A man with an amputated foot has the opportunity to participate in a trial where he would receive a better functioning prosthetic; however, he would have to amputate part of his leg in order for the new model prosthetic to properly function.

The amputation poses a risk of injury from the surgery and increased pain; ultimately, however, the man will enhance his ability to move (i.e. enhance his autonomy) if the procedure is successful. The requisite level of robustness for the voluntariness condition is likely met as he is not subject to external pressures. However, the knowledge condition might not be robust enough. His doctors must give him all the information that is relevant to his circumstances. For example, if he has hobbies or is engaged in sports or other activities, such as cycling, they should tell him how the procedure will affect his ability to continue them. If the prosthetic will involve maintenance costs or is not fully covered by insurance, they should provide that information. His situation is one involving defective consent, because the robustness level required to consent is impossible, given the novelty of the procedure. Because he has manifested consent, the consent-seekers (the medical personnel performing the procedure) would not be subject to a claim of battery; however, because his consent was defective, they would bear the burden of proving that their conduct was reasonable and the procedure performed in accordance with professional standards.

5. A woman has signed a contract to act as a gestational surrogate for another couple. She becomes pregnant, but because she has received a job offer in another state, she wishes to terminate the pregnancy.

The couple in this case has an economic and emotional interest in the surrogacy contract, but it does not outweigh the woman's interest in bodily integrity. She should be permitted to terminate her pregnancy and rescind the contract. The couple may seek restitution of any prepaid amounts (not including amounts paid for medical expenses already incurred). In addition, the couple may seek damages for mental distress, as emotional distress was foreseeable for this type of breach.

2. General Guidelines

Consent is necessarily a fact-based inquiry, but there are some general guidelines proposed throughout this book which are generated by the consentability framework:

1. Even where there is a manifestation of consent to an act which poses a high-level threat to autonomy, there is a presumption of defective consent where the consenter was under the age of twenty-five.

2. Even where there is a manifestation of consent to a bodily integrity contract which poses a high-level threat to autonomy, if the consenter is "desperately poor," there is a presumption of defective consent.

3. Even where there is a manifestation of consent to a truly novel procedure or to a medically advisable or medically necessary procedure which involves a high-level threat to autonomy, there is a presumption of defective consent.

4. Defective consent makes an executory contract voidable.

5. Where the activity has already been performed, defective consent may provide the basis for a claim in tort, criminal law, or restitution/disgorgement.

6. The presumption of defective consent may be overcome by evidence that the consenter initiated the activity, the terms were fair and reasonable, and the procedures were performed in accordance with professional norms and standards.

7. Acts which pose a high-level threat to autonomy should require a waiting period unless the waiting period itself imposes high-level risks (e.g. such as with certain dynamic health conditions).

8. Counseling and psychiatric evaluation should be a required part of the consent process for acts which pose a high-level threat to autonomy. Special attention should be paid to life-altering events which may affect decision-making, such as the death of a family member or a divorce.

9. Patients should not be permitted to undergo high-level threat acts, such as surgery, during periods of personal trauma or major life changes, unless medically necessary.

10. High-level threat to autonomy acts which are means to an end, rather than ends, should require individual counseling and a waiting period to establish that there is no coercion and that the act is not made impulsively or with unreasonable expectations regarding the result.

11. Distinction should be made between acts which are initiated by the consenter and those which are the result of solicitation by the consent-seeker or a third party. No solicitations or advertising of high-level threat acts should be permitted.

12. The threat level to autonomy should change based upon scientific or technological advances. The effects of a procedure which are currently irreversible might be made reversible, which would lower the threat level to the autonomy

interest.[652] Similarly, a procedure which is currently risky or painful may become much safer and painless. In that case, the threat level to autonomy should be reduced and the requisite robustness of the consent conditions should be adjusted accordingly. The converse is also true. If it is later discovered that an accepted practice or study poses newly-discovered harms, the requisite robustness levels should be much higher.

13. Information should be presented in an interactive manner so that the consenting party is actively, not passively, engaged. The higher the threat level to autonomy, the greater the requisite level of interactivity and engagement.

14. Progressive activities should require additional manifestations of consent. If the activity increases in risk or intrusion, the consent-seeker should obtain an active manifestation of consent and offer the consenter the option to withdraw from the activity at each increased level. If the activity is ongoing, the parties have mutual responsibility for continued consent. The consenter should communicate (verbally or non-verbally) withdrawal of consent, and the consent-seeker should be attentive and receptive to such communication; the consent-seeker should also ensure that the consenter is *able* to communicate withdrawal of consent. In situations where the activity is ongoing over a period of hours or longer, the consent-seeker should offer the consenter the option to withdraw from the activity at regular intervals.

15. The consenter in a high-level threat activity should be permitted to withdraw consent at any time without penalty, notwithstanding a contract or any other agreement between the parties.

16. Mismatched remedies (i.e. restitution where the consenter is the breaching party and expectation damages where the consent-seeker is the breaching party) should apply to bodily integrity contracts. Contracts involving bodily integrity should not be specifically enforced; however, if the consenter is the breaching party, the consent-seeker should be able to seek an injunction to prevent the consenter from breaching opportunistically.

---

[652] For example, tattoos, which were once considered permanent, now can usually be removed, although doing so is painful, costly and time-consuming. One man remarked that getting a tattoo removed "hurts three times more than getting a tattoo." He compared it to "getting cut on your wrist and all around your hand." Victoria St. Martin, *Former Gang Members Remove Tattoos to Break from Past*, WASH. POST (July 10, 2015), www.washingtonpost.com/local/gang-members-remove-tattoos-to-break-from-past/2015/07/10/3bd54ae8-266d-11e5-b72c-2b7d516e1e0e_story.html?noredirect=o n&utm_term=.b170dbd140bc.

Conclusion

At the time of this writing, the #MeToo movement has gripped the nation and raised awareness of the widespread problem of sexual assault and harassment.[653] There has also been a backlash from those who argue that the movement has gone "too far" by lumping together all forms of misconduct.[654] The stories which have come out of the #MeToo movement range from rape and sexual assault to "bad date" scenarios, and some commentators have objected to the breadth of the spectrum.[655] But it is the stories on the margins which illustrate best how deep the divide can be between two people when it comes to issues of consent.

[653] Jessica Bennett, *The #MeToo Moment: When the Blinders Come Off*, N.Y. TIMES (Nov. 30, 2017), www.nytimes.com/2017/11/30/us/the-metoo-moment.html?rref=collection%2Fseriescollection% 2Fmetoo-moment&action=click&contentCollection=us&region=stream&module=stream_unit& version=latest&contentPlacement=8&pgtype=collection (writing about "an ever-growing list of powerful men facing consequences for alleged sexual misconduct at work ... The hashtag #MeToo has exploded on social media as a vehicle for women to share their stories."); Nicola Slawson, *#Metoo Trend Highlights Sexual Harassment in Wake of Weinstein Claims*, GUARDIAN (Oct. 16, 2017), www.theguardian.com/uk-news/2017/oct/16/me-too-social-media-trend-highlights-sexual-harassment-of-women ("The words 'me too' are trending on social media after women were asked to share if they had ever been sexually assaulted or harassed"); Lisa Wang, *#MeToo Whats Next: Why 2018 Is the Year to Take Action*, FORBES (Jan. 2, 2018), www.forbes.com/sites/lisawang/2018/01/02/ metoowhatsnext-why-2018-is-the-year-to-take-action/#56516a89112c ("2017 was the year of the silence breakers. Women's stories of sexual assault, abuse, harassment, and misconduct swept news headlines, and for the first time in history, #MeToo moments could not be ignored.").

[654] Bret Stephens, *Opinion: When #MeToo Goes Too Far*, N.Y. TIMES (Dec. 20, 2017), www.nytimes .com/2017/12/20/opinion/metoo-damon-too-far.html?mtrref=www.google.com&assetType=opinion ("All societies make necessary distinctions between high crimes and misdemeanors, mortal and lesser sins ... the theory that we need a zero-tolerance approach ... may sound admirable, but it's legally unworkable and, in many cases, simply unjust."); Laura Kipnis, *Has #MeToo Gone Too Far or Not Far Enough? The Answer Is Both*, GUARDIAN (Jan. 13, 2017), www.theguardian.com/commentis free/2018/jan/13/has-me-too-catherine-deneuve-laura-kipnis (discussing the "stunningly silly" anti-#MeToo letter signed by Catherine Deneuve and a hundred other French women); Bari Weiss, *Aziz Ansari Is Guilty. Of Not Being a Mind Reader*, N.Y.TIMES, Jan. 15, 2018 (arguing that a failure to differentiate types of behavior "trivializes what #MeToo first stood for.").

[655] Stephanie Zacharek et al., *TIME Person of the Year 2017: The Silence Breakers*, TIME (Dec. 18, 2017), http://time.com/time-person-of-the-year-2017-silence-breakers/ (TIME's interview of men and women from hotel housekeepers to administrative assistants to Hollywood actresses who had been assaulted, harassed and subjected to various forms of male misconduct); Sarah Solemani, *The Aziz*

This book has attempted to get to the essence of consent, and in doing so, to question its role as a way to justify certain dubious, alarming or unconventional behavior on the part of both the consenter and the consent-seeker. The purpose of consent is to empower individuals, to give them a tool with which to exercise autonomy and maximize their self-interest. Too often, the fact of a manifestation of consent is used to substitute for valid consent, and the issue of whether consent in any given case maximizes self-interest or promotes (or diminishes) autonomy is ignored. But tokens of consent should not be used as moral free passes by opportunists to justify acts which harm another. Legal consent is a conclusion, and without understanding how that conclusion was reached, we cannot determine whether it promotes or diminishes autonomy. This book proposes a reconceptualization of legal consent which examines the context in which the manifestation of consent was made, rather than the mere fact that it was made. The burden should not be on the putative consenter to show no-consent, nor should a manifestation of consent alone suffice to establish valid consent for activities which pose a high-level threat to the autonomy interest. This book argues that both the robustness of consent conditions *and* the consent-seeker's responsibility for ensuring valid consent should increase commensurately with the threat to the consenter's autonomy presented by the proposed activity.

Consent is only part of the equation when it comes to consentability. The authority of the consenter only extends to matters within the consenter's purview. Consent is concerned with the autonomy of a particular individual; consentability is concerned with *society's* interest in individual autonomy as a value. Where the proposed activity has disturbing or harmful implications for the consenter or third parties, it has a destabilizing and detrimental effect on social relations and hinders the attainment of individual goals for other members of society.

The future will present many more hard cases because scientists and entrepreneurs will continue to develop new businesses, ideas and experimental treatments which challenge societal values and norms. For example, a company is now testing a novel therapy which might provide significant rejuvenating effects for old people.[656] If successful, this therapy would stall or reverse the progress of age-related diseases and illnesses, such as Alzheimer's Disease.[657] One trial currently being discussed involves having an older person infused with the blood of a younger person. If that trial doesn't prove successful, however, other methods may be tested. The original study involved creating and grafting the wound sites of an older mouse and younger mouse so that they shared the same circulatory system. Should such

Ansari Furor Isn't the End of #MeToo. It's Just the Start, GUARDIAN (Jan. 22, 2018), www.theguardian .com/commentisfree/2018/jan/21/aziz-ansari-metoo-sexual-equality.

[656] *Dana Smith, Blood From Young People May Be a Secret to Fighting Aging*, KQED (June 30, 2017), www.kqed.org/futureofyou/366983/blood-from-young-people-may-be-a-secret-to-fighting-aging.

[657] *Id.; see also* Carl Zimmer, *Young Blood May Hold Key to Reversing Aging*, N.Y. TIMES (May 4, 2014), www.nytimes.com/2014/05/05/science/young-blood-may-hold-key-to-reversing-aging.html.

a procedure be permitted involving consenting humans? Should society permit wealthy, old people to live a few more years, by paying to harm poor, young people? Should they be permitted to do so if it diminishes the longevity of the young and poor participants?

Principles guide us and help us see clearly what might be obscured through rhetoric, prejudice, advertising and other forms of social conditioning. Without an overarching set of principles and a framework which puts practices into perspective, we remain vulnerable to manipulation and social distortion. Practices and norms which we had no part in shaping, which may have originated in a corporation's marketing department or in industries with large financial stakes in manipulating our behavior (Hollywood, Silicon Valley) may cause us to submit to activities and procedures (cosmetic surgery, privacy intrusions) which pose substantial risks to our autonomy. As the proliferation of our personal data and sophisticated data mining techniques allow companies to gain greater insight into human behavior, we become more vulnerable to cultural and social engineering. It is thus vital to remember why consent holds such a sacred position in our society, and to be mindful of how the rhetoric of consent may be used to justify opportunism and undermine autonomy.

The consentability framework provides no easy solutions. It is the antithesis of a magical black box which has well-defined inputs and predictable outputs; to the contrary, it is a "white box" which seeks to render transparent the process by which consent is determined. The objective of the consentability framework is to help guide policymakers and lawmakers through the thicket of issues arising from new technologies and changing social norms. But the state, too, is imperfect. The effectiveness of regulation is subject to the quality and integrity of the implementing and regulating authority. Given the fallibility of the state and its susceptibility to political pressures and special interest groups, determinations of consentability should generally err on the side of moral and value neutrality, to avoid favoring the beliefs and practices of one group over another.

Personal decisions, however, need not – and should not – be similarly value-neutral; rather, personal decisions should be infused with one's own moral beliefs and values. Simply because an activity is consentable does not mean that we should engage in it. In this sense, the consentability framework may be most useful as a tool for better personal decision-making. A structured and systematic framework might help us to recognize our own cognitive blind spots and biases, and help us to better see the self-interest and manipulation of others. The focus of the consentability framework is on the process, not simply the "yes" or "no" output. We might require greater robustness for a consent condition than the state requires and be much less tolerant of opportunistic conduct. We could incorporate some of the safeguards into our own personal decision-making process. For example, before engaging in an appealing activity with risks, we might check for impulsivity and impose on ourselves a "cooling period" even if this is not required by law.

The consentability framework acknowledges that members of a society have a responsibility to each other, and this may help us keep our own opportunism in check when *we* are the consent-seeker. In some cases, a consenter may not be motivated by self-interest; instead, the consenter might be motivated by altruism or a desire to please or accommodate us. We may know that a proposed activity which will benefit us will cause great harm to the consenter. Opportunism can strip consent of its power to morally transform. Our personal standards should be higher than that required by law. Even if we are legally justified in taking advantage of another's compliance, we are not always morally justified in doing so. Consent cannot morally justify harming others or treating them cruelly, even if it is legal to do so.

Cases

AAA Const. of Missoula, L.L.C. v. Choice Land Corp., 264 P.3d 709 (Mont. 2011)
Bankers Trust Co. v. Litton Sys., Inc., 599 F.2d 488 (2d Cir. 1979)
Baxter Healthcare Corp. v. Denton, 120 Cal. App. 4th 333 (2004)
Birchfield v. North Dakota, 136 S. Ct. 2160 (2016)
Cain v. Howorth, 877 So. 2d 566 (Ala. 2003)
Cent. Hudson Gas & Elec. Corp. v. Pub. Serv. Comm'n of New York, 447 U.S. 557 (1980)
Cigar Ass'n. of Am. v. Food & Drug Admin., No. 1:16-cv-01460, 2018 WL 2223653 (D. D.C. May 15, 2018)
Clinton v. Jones, 520 U.S. 681 (1997)
Cobbs v. Grant, 8 Cal. 3d 229 (1972)
Daum v. SpineCare Med. Grp., Inc., 52 Cal. App. 4th 1285 (1997)
Doctors Hosp. of Augusta, L.L.C. v. Alicea, 774 S.E.2d 114 (Ga. Ct. App. 2015)
Embry v. Hargadine, McKittrick Dry Goods Co., 105 S.W. 777 (Mo. Ct. App. 1907)
Erickson v. Garber, 2003 Mass. App. Div. 125 (S.D. 2003)
Flynn v. Holder, 684 F.3d 852 (9th Cir. 2012)
Fumai v. Levy, No. Civ.A. 95–1674, 1998 WL 42297 (E.D. Pa. Jan. 16, 1998)
Geis v. Colina Del Rio, L.P., 362 S.W.3d 100 (Tex. App. 2011)
Greater New Orleans Broad. Ass'n v. United States, 527 U.S. 173 (1999)
Guthman v. Moss, 150 Cal. App. 3d 501 (1984)
Harrington v. Atl. Sounding Co., 602 F.3d 113 (2d Cir. 2010)
Huskey v. Nat'l Broad. Co., 632 F. Supp. 1282 (N.D. Ill. 1986)
In re Marriage of Peters, 52 Cal. App. 4th 1487 (1997)
In re Michael G., 63 Cal. App. 4th 700 (1998)
Kamakahi v. Am. Soc'y for Reprod. Med., 305 F.R.D. 164 (N.D. Cal. 2015).
Larkin v. Saffarans, 15 F. 147 (W.D. Tenn. 1883)
Lawson v. Bloodsworth, 722 S.E.2d 358 (Ga. Ct. App. 2012)
Marseilles Homeowners Condo. Ass'n v. Broadmoor, L.L.C., 111 So. 3d 1099 (La. Ct. App. 2013)

Statutes

15 U.S.C. § 45(a) (2012)
15 U.S.C. §1331–1338) (2012)
17 C.F.R. § 230.500 (2018)
17 C.F.R. § 230.502(a)(5) (2018)
17 C.F.R. § 230.502(a)(6) (2018)
21 C.F.R. § 50.20 (2018)
21 U.S.C. sec. 387a-1 (2012).
27 U.S.C. § 205(f) (2012)
35 U.S.C. § 154(a)(1) (2012)
42 U.S.C. § 274e (2012)
42 U.S.C. § 274e(a) (2012)
42 U.S.C. § 274e(b) (2012)
42 U.S.C. § 247e(c)(2) (2012)
42 U.S.C. § 300gg-14(a) (2012)
42 U.S.C. §1320a-7b (2012)
45 C.F.R. § 46.116(a) (6) (2018)
45 C.F.R. §46.116(b) (2018)
45 C.F.R. § 46.116(b)(8) (2018)
Bus. & Prof. Code § 654.2(a) (2018)
Cal. Bus. & Prof. Code § 17500 (2018)
Cal. Civ. Code § 1542 (2018)
Cal. Civ. Code § 3294(a) (2018)
Cal. Evid. Code § 115 (2014)
Cal. Health & Safety Code § 443.1(q) (2018)
Cal. Health & Safety Code § 443.2 (2018)
Cal. Health & Safety Code § 443.3 (2018)
Cal. Health & Safety Code § 443.17 (2018)
Cal. Health & Safety Code § 443.18 (2018)
Conn. Gen. Stat. § 53a-56(a) (LEXIS through Pub. Acts 18–1 2018)

Bibliography

Aceves, William. *Valuing Life: A Human Rights Perspective.* LAW AND INEQUALITY 36 (2018): 1–66.

Ahmed, Azam, Matt Richtel & Andrew Jacobs. *U.S. Objects to Warnings on Junk Food.* NEW YORK TIMES (March 21, 2018), www.nytimes.com/2018/03/20/world/americas/nafta-food-labels-obesity.html.

Ainsworth, Tiffiny A. & Jeffrey H. Spiegel. *Quality of Life of Individuals with and without Facial Feminization Surgery or Gender Reassignment Surgery.* QUALITY OF LIFE RESEARCH 19 (2010): 1019–24.

Akerlof, George A. *Procrastination and Obedience. Papers and Proceedings of the Hundred and Third Annual Meeting of the American Economic Association,* AMERICAN ECONOMIC REVIEW 81, no. 2 (1991): 1–19.

Albert, Dustin & Laurence Steinberg. *Age Differences in Strategic Planning as Indexed by the Tower of London.* CHILD DEVELOPMENT 82, no.5 (2011): 1501–17.

ALCES, PETER. THE MORAL CONFLICT OF LAW AND NEUROSCIENCE. (Chicago: University of Chicago Press, 2018).

ALTMAN, LAWRENCE K. WHO GOES FIRST?: THE STORY OF SELF-EXPERIMENTATION IN MEDICINE. (California: University of California Press, 1998).

American Academy of Facial Plastic and Reconstructive Surgery. Selfie Trend Increases Demand for Facial Plastic Surgery: Annual AAFPRS Survey Finds "Selfie" Trend Increases Demand for Facial Plastic Surgery Influence on Elective Surgery (March 11, 2014), www.aafprs.org/media/press_release/20140311.html.

American Association of Cosmetology Schools. Hair Braiding Requirements, http://beauty schools.org/hair-braiding-requirements/.

American Psychological Association. Report of the American Psychological Association Task Force on Appropriate Therapeutic Responses to Sexual Orientation (August 2009), http://www.apa.org/pi/lgbt/resources/sexual orientation.aspx.

American Society of Plastic Surgeons. Briefing Paper: Plastic Surgery for Teenagers, www .plasticsurgery.org/news/briefing-papers/briefing-paper-plastic-surgery-for-teenagers.

American Society of Plastic Surgeons. Plastic Surgery Statistics Report (2015), https://d2wirczt3b6wjm.cloudfront.net/News/Statistics/2015/plastic-surgery-statistics-full-report-2015.pdf.

Anderson, Elizabeth S. *Why Commercial Surrogate Motherhood Unethically Commodifies Women and Children: Reply to McLachlan and Swales.* HEALTH CARE ANALYSIS 8, no. 1 (2000): 19–26.

ANDREWS, LORI. FUTURE PERFECT: CONFRONTING DECISIONS ABOUT GENETICS. (New York: Columbia University Press, 2001).

ANDREWS, LORI & DOROTHY NELKIN. BODY BAZAAR: THE MARKET FOR HUMAN TISSUE IN THE BIOTECHNOLOGY AGE. (New York: Crown Publishing Group, 2001).

APTOWICZ, CRISTIN O'KEEFE. DR. MUTTER'S MARVELS. (New York: Avery, 2014).

ARIELY, DAN. PREDICTABLY IRRATIONAL. (New York: HarperCollins Canada, 2008).

Ariely, Dan & George Loewenstein. *The Heat of the Moment: The Effect of Sexual Arousal on Sexual Decision Making.* JOURNAL OF BEHAVIORAL DECISION MAKING. 19, no. 2 (2006): 87–98.

ARROW, KENNETH J. THE LIMITS OF ORGANIZATION. (New York: Norton, 1974).

Associated Press. Artist Has Digital Camera Implanted in Head (November 24, 2010), www.cbsnews.com/news/artist-has-digital-camera-implanted-in-head/.

Astor, Maggie. *Microchip Implants for Employees? One Company Says Yes.* NEW YORK TIMES (July 25, 2017), www.nytimes.com/2017/07/25/technology/microchips-wisconsin-company-employees.html.

Australia Competition and Consumer (Tobacco) Information Standard 2011, https://www.legislation.gov.au/Details/F2011L02766.

Ayres, Ian & Alan Schwartz. *The No-Reading Problem in Consumer Contract Law.* STANFORD LAW REVIEW 66, no.3 (2014): 545–610.

Baenen, Jeff. *Wisconsin Company Holds "Chip Party" to Microchip Workers.* CHICAGO TRIBUNE (August 2, 2017), www.chicagotribune.com/bluesky/technology/ct-wisconsin-com pany-microchips-workers-20170801-story.html.

Barberis, Nicholas, Ming Huang, & Richard H. Thaler. *Individual Preferences, Monetary Gambles, and Stock Market Participation: A Case of Narrow Framing.* AMERICAN ECONOMIC REVIEW 96 (2006): 1069–90.

Barclay, Eliza. Scientists Are Building a Case for How Food Ads Make Us Overeat. (January 29, 2016), www.npr.org/sections/thesalt/2016/01/29/462838153/food-ads-make-us-eat-more-and-should-be-regulated.

Bar-Gill, Oren & Omri Ben-Shahar. *An Information Theory of Willful Breach.* MICHIGAN LAW REVIEW 107 (2009): 1479–99.

Barnett, Randy E. *A Consent Theory of Contract.* COLUMBIA LAW REVIEW 86 (1986): 269–321.

Barnett, Randy E. *Contract is Not Promise; Contract is Consent.* SUFFOLK UNIVERSITY LAW REVIEW 45 (2012): 647–65.

Barry, Peter Brian. *The Ethics of Voluntary Amputation.* PUBLIC AFFAIRS QUARTERLY 26, no.1 (January 2012): 1–18.

Barton, Thomas D., Gerlinde Berger-Walliser & Helena Haapio. *Visualization: Seeing Contracts for What They Are, And What They Could Become.* JOURNAL OF LAW, BUSINESS AND ETHICS 19 (2013): 47–63.

Beauchamp, Tom L. *Autonomy and Consent.* IN THE ETHICS OF CONSENT: THEORY AND PRACTICE, 55–78. (Franklin G. Miller & Alan Wertheimer, eds. Oxford: Oxford University Press, 2010).

Bell, Tom W. *Graduated Consent in Contract and Tort Law: Toward a Theory of Justification.* CASE WESTERN RESERVE LAW REVIEW 61, no.1 (2010): 1–68.

Bennett, Jessica. *The #MeToo Moment: When the Blinders Come Off.* NEW YORK TIMES, November 30, 2017, www.nytimes.com/2017/11/30/us/the-metoo-moment.html?rref=collec tion%2Fseriescollection%2Fmetoo-momentandaction=clickandcontentCollection=usan-dregion=streamandmodule=stream_unitandversion=latestandcontentPlacement=8andpg type=collection.

Ben-Shahar, Omri. *More Failed Nudges: Evidence of Ineffective "Behaviorally Informed" Disclosures.* JOTWELL (August 10, 2017), https://contracts.jotwell.com/more-failed-nudges-evidence-of-ineffective-behaviorally-informed-disclosures/.
BEN-SHAHAR, OMRI & CARL E. SCHNEIDER. MORE THAN YOU WANTED TO KNOW: THE FAILURE OF MANDATED DISCLOSURE. (Princeton NJ: Princeton University Press, 2014).
BERGER, JONAH. INVISIBLE INFLUENCE: THE HIDDEN FORCES THAT SHAPE BEHAVIOR. (New York: Simon & Schuster, 2016).
Bettman, James R., John W. Payne & Richard Staelin. *Cognitive Considerations in Designing Effective Labels for Presenting Risk Information.* JOURNAL OF PUBLIC POLICY AND MARKETING 5 (1986): 1–28.
BINDEL, JULIE. THE PIMPING OF PROSTITUTION: ABOLISHING THE SEX WORK MYTH. (London: Palgrave Macmillan, 2017).
Bix, Brian H. *Contracts.* IN THE ETHICS OF CONSENT: THEORY AND PRACTICE, 251–79. (Franklin G. Miller & Alan Wertheimer, eds. Oxford: Oxford University Press, 2010).
Bone, Angie, Tom Nichols & Norman D. Noah. *Body Piercing in England: A Survey of Piercing at Sites Other Than Earlobe.* BMJ 336 (2018): 1426–28, https://doi.org/10.1136/bmj.39580.497176.25.
Boseley, Sarah. *Cosmetic Surgery Advertising Ban Urged by Leading Surgeon.* THE GUARDIAN (January 22, 2012), www.theguardian.com/lifeandstyle/2012/jan/22/ban-advertising-cosmetic-surgery.
Bourdieu, Pierre. The Forms of Capital. IN HANDBOOK OF THEORY AND RESEARCH FOR THE SOCIOLOGY OF EDUCATION, 241–58. (J.G. Richardson, ed. New York: Greenwood Press, 1986).
Boyd, K. *The Impossibility of Informed Consent.* JOURNAL OF MEDICAL ETHICS 41 (2015): 44–47.
Breuner, Cora C., David A. Levine & The Committee on Adolescence. Adolescent and Young Adult Tattooing, Piercing, and Scarification. (September 18, 2017), http://pediatrics.aappublications.org/content/early/2017/09/14/peds.2017–1962.
Brewer, Noel, Marissa Hall, Seth M. Noar, et al. *Effect of Pictorial Cigarette Pack Warnings on Changes in Smoking Behavior: A Randomized Clinical Trial,* JAMA INTERN MED. 905 (2016), doi:10.1001/jamainternmed.2016.2621.
Brody, Jane E. *Being Transgender as a Fact of Nature.* NEW YORK TIMES (June 13, 2016), https://well.blogs.nytimes.com/2016/06/13/transsexualism-as-a-fact-of-nature/.
Budget. Restrictions and Surcharges for Renters Under Twenty-Five Years of Age. (Accessed June 23, 2018), www.budget.com/budgetWeb/html/en/common/agePopUp.html.
Burton, Scot, Abhijit Biswas & Richard Netemeyer. *Effects of Alternative Nutrition Label Formats and Nutrition Reference Information on Consumer Perceptions, Comprehension and Product Evaluations.* JOURNAL OF PUBLIC POLICY AND MARKETING 13, no. 1 (1994): 36–47.
Butler, Susan. Your Grandmother is a Bodyhacker. (July 27, 2015), https://bodyhackingcon.com/blog/yourgrandmother-is-a-bodyhacker.html.
Buzash, George E. *Comment, The "Rough Sex" Defense.* JOURNAL OF CRIMINAL LAW AND CRIMINOLOGY 80, no. 2 (1989): 557–84.
Calabresi, Guido & A. Douglas Melamed. *Property Rules, Liability Rules, and Inalienability: One View of the Cathedral.* HARVARD LAW REVIEW 85 (1972): 1089–1128.
Californians Against Assisted Suicide. Organizations that Oppose Assisted Suicide. (Accessed April 2, 2018), http://noassistedsuicideca.org/about/organizations-that-oppose-assisted-suicide-legalization.
Californians Against Assisted Suicide. Why We Oppose SB 128: California's Assisted Suicide Bill. (May 6, 2015), http://noassistedsuicideca.org/images/CAASCoalitionLetterto-CASenatev2.pdf.

Camargo da Rosa, Marco Aurélio. Overlap Between Food Addiction and DSM-5 Eating Disorders in a Treatment Seeking Sample. (Accessed June 23, 2018), www.drugabuse.gov/international/abstracts/overlap-between-food-addiction-dsm-5-eating-disorders-in-treatment-seeking-sample.

Camerer, Colin F. & George Loewenstein. *Behavioral Economics: Past, Present and Future.* IN ADVANCES IN BEHAVIORAL ECONOMICS. (Colin F. Camerer, George Loewenstein & Matthew Rabin, eds. Princeton NJ: Princeton University Press, 2004).

Carey, Benedict. *Brain Implant Enhanced Memory, Raising Hope for Treatments, Scientists Say.* NEW YORK TIMES (February 7, 2018), www.nytimes.com/2018/02/06/health/brain-implant-memory.html.

Cary, David. *Pressure Mounts to Curtail Surgery on Intersex Children.* CHICAGO TRIBUNE (July 25, 2017), www.chicagotribune.com/lifestyles/health/ct-surgery-intersex-children-20170725-story.html.

Centers for Disease Control and Prevention. Health Effects of Cigarette Smoking. (Accessed June 20, 2018), www.cdc.gov/tobacco/data_statistics/fact_sheets/health_effects/effects_cig_smoking/index.htm.

Centers for Disease Control and Prevention. U.S. Public Health Service Syphilis Study at Tuskegee: How Tuskegee Changed Research Practices. (Accessed February 22, 2017), www.cdc.gov/tuskegee/after.htm.

Chemerinsky, Erwin & Michele Goodwin. *Compulsory Vaccination Laws are Constitutional.* NORTHWESTERN LAW REVIEW 110, no. 3 (2016): 589–615.

Christman, John. *Constructing the Inner Citadel: Recent Work on The Concept Of Autonomy.* ETHICS 99, no. 1 (1988): 109–24.

Coffey, Rebecca. *The Colorful Modern History of Gay Conversion Therapy.* PSYCHOLOGY TODAY (July 25, 2014), www.psychologytoday.com/blog/the-bejeezus-out-me/201407/the-colorful-modern-history-gay-conversion-therapy.

Cohen, I. Glenn. *Transplant Tourism: The Ethics and Regulation of International Markets for Organs.* JOURNAL OF LAW, MEDICINE AND ETHICS 41, no. 1 (2013): 269–85.

Cohen, Jon. *Memory Implants: A Maverick Neuroscientist Believes He Has Deciphered the Code By Which the Brain Forms Long-Term Memories.* TECHNOLOGY REVIEW (Accessed June 21, 2018), www.technologyreview.com/s/513681/memory-implants/.

Cohen, Morris. *The Basis of Contract.* HARVARD LAW REVIEW 46, no. 4 (1933): 553–92.

Conway, Lynn. A Warning For Those Considering MtF SRS: What If You "Succeed" in Completing a TS Transition, but Did it for the Wrong Reasons? (Accessed June 21, 2018), http://ai.eecs.umich.edu/people/conway/TS/warning.html.

Cook, Philip J. & Kimberly D. Krawiec. *A Primer on Kidney Transplantation: Anatomy of the Shortage.* LAW AND CONTEMPORARY PROBLEMS 77, no. 3 (2014): 1–23.

Cook, Phillip J. & Kimberly D. Krawiec. If We Pay Football Players, Why Not Kidney Donors? (Spring 2018), https://object.cato.org/sites/cato.org/files/serials/files/regulation/2018/3/regulation-v41n1-4.pdf.

CORBIN, ARTHUR LINTON. CORBIN ON CONTRACTS. (St. Paul MN: West Publishing Company, 1952).

CORRIGANN OONAGH, ET AL (eds.) THE LIMITS OF CONSENT: A SOCIO-ETHICAL APPROACH TO HUMAN SUBJECT RESEARCH IN MEDICINE. (Oxford: Oxford University Press, 2009).

Creative Research. Regulation of Cosmetic Interventions: Research Among the General Public and Practitioners (March 28, 2013), www.gov.uk/government/uploads/system/uploads/attachment_data/file/192029/Regulation_of_Cosmetic_Interventions_Research_Report.pdf.

Creative Research. Regulation of Cosmetic Interventions: Research Among Teenage Girls (March 11, 2013), https://assets.publishing.service.gov.uk/government/uploads/system/uploads/attachment_data/file/192030/Report_on_research_among_teenage_girls.pdf.

Davey, Monica. *Online Talk, Suicides, and a Thorny Court Case.* N.Y. TIMES (May 13, 2010), www.nytimes.com/2010/05/14/us/14suicide.html?action=clickandcontentCollection=U.S.andmodule=RelatedCoverageandregion=EndOfArticleandpgtype=article.

DeAngelis, Tori. Fighting Food Addiction (2011), www.apa.org/gradpsych/2011/11/food-addiction.aspx.

DellaVigna, Stefana. *Psychology and Economics: Evidence from the Field.* JOURNAL OF ECONOMIC LITERATURE 42, no. 2 (2009): 315–72, https://eml.berkeley.edu/~sdellavi/wp/01-DellaVigna-4721.pdf.

Dellinger, A. J. Majority of Three Square Market Employees 'Excited' to Insert Biochip in Hand (July 26, 2017), www.ibtimes.com/majority-three-square-market-employees-excited-insert-biochip-hand-2570669.

Demierre, Marie-France, Daniel Brooks, Howard K. Koh & Alan C. Geller. *Public Knowledge, Awareness, and Perceptions of the Association Between Skin Aging and Smoking.* JOURNAL OF THE AMERICAN ACADEMY OF DERMATOLOGY 41, no. 1 (1999): 27–30.

Do, Sydney, et al. *An Independent Assessment of the Technical Feasibility of the Mars One Mission Plan – Updated Analysis.* ACTA ASTRONAUTICA 120 (2016): 192–228.

Dolan, Laura. *New York Professor Installs Camera in Head.* CNN (December 2, 2010), www.cnn.com/2010/US/12/02/new.york.camera.head/index.html.

Dresser, Rebecca. *Life, Death and Incompetent Patients: Conceptual Infirmities and Hidden Values.* ARIZONA LAW REVIEW 28, no. 3 (1986): 373–405.

Dresser, Rebecca. *The "Right to Try" Investigational Drugs: Science and Stories in the Access Debate.* TEXAS LAW REVIEW 93, no. 7 (2015): 1631–57.

Duke, Naomi N. *Situated Bodies in Medicine and Research: Altruism versus Compelled Sacrifice.* In THE GLOBAL BODY MARKET: ALTRUISM'S LIMITS, 107–24. (Michele Goodwin, ed. Cambridge: Cambridge University Press, 2013).

Dvorsky, George. 23-Year-Old Kim Suozzi Undergoes Cryonic Preservation After Successful Fundraising Campaign (January 21, 2013), https://io9.gizmodo.com/5977640/23-year-old-kim-suozzi-undergoes-cryonic-preservation-after-successful-fundraising-campaign.

Editorial Board. Egg Donor Wanted, "B" Students Need Not Apply (May 30, 2012), www.stanforddaily.com/2012/05/30/egg-donor-wanted-b-students-need-not-apply/.

Eisenberg, Melvin Aron. *The Emergence of Dynamic Contract Law.* CALIFORNIA LAW REVIEW 88, no. 6 (2000): 1743–1814.

Ehrenreich, Nancy. & Mark Barr. *Intersex Surgery, Female Genital Cutting, and the Selective Condemnation of "Cultural Practices."* HARVARD CIVIL RIGHTS – CIVIL LIBERTIES LAW REVIEW 40 (2005): 71–140.

ERTMAN, MARTHA M. & JOAN C. WILLIAMS (eds.) RETHINKING COMMODIFICATION: CASES AND READINGS IN LAW AND CULTURE. (New York: New York University Press, 2005).

ERTMAN, MARTHA M. LOVE'S PROMISES: HOW FORMAL AND INFORMAL CONTRACTS SHAPE ALL KINDS OF FAMILIES. (Boston MA: Beacon Press, 2015).

Eveleth, Rose. The Half Life of Body Hacking (June 25, 2015), http://motherboard.vice.com/read/the-half-life-of-body-hacking.

Eyeborg. About the Project.(Accessed on June 23, 2018), http://eyeborgproject.com/.

Fallon, Jr., Richard H. *Two Senses of Autonomy.* STANFORD LAW REVIEW 46, no. 4 (1994): 875–905.

FARNSWORTH, E. ALLAN. CHANGING YOUR MIND: THE LAW OF REGRETTED DECISIONS. (New Haven CT: Yale University Press, 1998).

FARNSWORTH, E. ALLAN. CONTRACTS. (Netherlands: Wolters Kluwer Legal & Regulatory, 2004).

Fechner, Holly B. *Three Stories of Prostitution in the West: Prostitutes' Groups, Law and Feminist Truth.* COLUMBIA JOURNAL OF GENDER AND LAW 4, no.1 (1994): 26–72.

Federal Drug Administration. Informed Consent Information Sheet, Guidance for IRBs, Clinical Investigators, and Sponsors, (Draft Guidance) (July 2014), www.fda.gov/down loads/RegulatoryInformation/Guidances/UCM405006.pdf: 5–6.

Fehr, Ernst & Klaus M. Schmidt. *A Theory of Fairness, Competition and Cooperation. In* ADVANCES IN BEHAVIORAL ECONOMICS, 271–296. (Colin F. Camerer, et al., eds. Princeton NJ: Princeton University Press, 2004).

Fehr, Ernst, Georg Kirchsteiger & Arno Riedl. *Does Fairness Prevent Market Clearing?: An Experimental Investigation.*QUARTERLY JOURNAL OF ECONOMICS 108, no. 2 (1993): 437–59.

FEINBERG, JOEL. HARM TO SELF: THE MORAL LIMITS OF THE CRIMINAL LAW. (Oxford: Oxford University Press, 1986).

FEINBERG, JOEL. HARMLESS WRONGDOING: THE MORAL LIMITS OF THE CRIMINAL LAW. (Oxford: Oxford University Press, 1990).

Fischhoff, Baruch & Julie Downs. *Accentuate the Relevant.* PSYCHOLOGICAL SCIENCE 8, no. 3 (1997): 154–58.

Fiss, Owen M. *The Autonomy of Law.* YALE JOURNAL OF INTERNATIONAL LAW 26 (2001): 517–26.

Frederick, Shane, George Loewenstein & Ted O'Donoghue. *Time Discounting and Time Preference: A Critical Review.* JOURNAL OF ECONOMIC LITERATURE 40 (2002): 351–401.

FRIED, CHARLES. CONTRACT AS PROMISE: A THEORY OF CONTRACTUAL OBLIGATIONS. (Cambridge MA: Harvard University Press, 1981).

Friend, Tad. *Jumpers: The Fatal Grandeur of the Golden Gate Bridge.* THE NEW YORKER (October 13, 2003), www.newyorker.com/magazine/2003/10/13/jumpers.

Fritscher, Lisa. *Age Requirement to Rent a Car.* USA TODAY (Last updated March 13, 2018), http://traveltips.usatoday.com/age-requirement-rent-a-car-62294.html.

Fukuyama, Francis. Special Report: Transhumanism (October 23, 2009), http://foreignpolicy .com/2009/10/23/transhumanism/.

Fuller, Lon L. *Consideration and Form.* COLUMBIA LAW REVIEW 41, no. 5 (1941): 799–824.

Gan, Orit. *The Many Faces of Contractual Consent.* DRAKE LAW REVIEW 65, no. 3 (2017): 615–61.

Ginsberg, Marc. *Informed Consent: No Longer Just What the Doctor Ordered? The Contributions of Medical Associations and Courts to a More Patient Friendly Doctrine.* MICHIGAN STATE UNIVERSITY JOURNAL OF MEDICINE & LAW 15 (2010): 17–69.

Goldstein, Jacob. *So You Think You Can be a Hair Braider?* NEW YORK TIMES (June 12, 2012), www.nytimes.com/2012/06/17/magazine/so-you-think-you-can-be-a-hair-braider.html? _r=1andref=magazineandpagewanted=all.

Good, Nathaniel S., Jens Grossklags, Deirdre K. Mulligan, & Joseph A. Konstan. Noticing Notice: A Large-Scale Experiment on The Timing of Software License Agreements. (Paper presented at the Conference on Human Factors in Computing Systems. April 28–May 3, 2007, San Jose, CA, USA).

Goodwin, Michele. *Compelled Body Part Donations. In* THE GLOBAL BODY MARKET: ALTRUISM'S LIMITS, 67–86. (Michele Goodwin, ed. Cambridge: Cambridge University Press, 2013).

GOODWIN, MICHELE. BLACK MARKETS: THE SUPPLY AND DEMAND OF BODY PARTS. (Cambridge: Cambridge University Press, 2006).

GOODWIN, MICHELE. THE GLOBAL BODY MARKET: ALTRUISM'S LIMITS. (Cambridge: Cambridge University Press, 2013).

Gorman, James. *Scientists Trace Memories of Things That Never Happened.* NEW YORK TIMES (July 25, 2013), www.nytimes.com/2013/07/26/science/false-memory-planted-in-a-mouse-brain-study-shows.html.

Goudreau, Jenna. *The Hidden Dangers of Cosmetic Surgery.* FORBES (June 16, 2011), www.forbes.com/sites/jennagoudreau/2011/06/16/hidden-dangers-of-cosmetic-surgery/#122afa7d8805.

Grady, Christine. *Payment of Clinical Research Subjects.* JOURNAL OF CLINICAL INVESTIGATION 115, no. 7 (2005): 1681–87, www.jci.org/articles/view/25694/pdf.

Grady, Denise. *More Cases are Reported of Unusual Cancer Linked to Breast Implants.* NEW YORK TIMES (March 21, 2018), www.nytimes.com/2018/03/21/health/breast-implants-lymphoma.html?ribbon-ad-idx=9andrref=health.

GREENFIELD, LAUREN. GENERATION WEALTH. (New York: Phaidon, 2017).

Hall, Greg. *Tattoos Affect Your Health: Long-Term Side Effects Ink Has on Your Immune System and Disease Risk.* MEDICAL DAILY (November 15, 2016), www.medicaldaily.com/tattoos-affect-your-health-long-term-side-effects-ink-has-your-immune-system-404404.

HALPERN, DAVID. SOCIAL CAPITAL. (Cambridge: Polity Press, 2005).

Hamzelou, Jessica. *Artificial Womb Helps Premature Lamb Fetuses Grow for 4 Weeks.* NEW SCIENTIST (April 25, 2017), www.newscientist.com/article/2128851-artificial-womb-helps-premature-lamb-fetuses-grow-for-4-weeks/.

Hardin, Garrett. The Tragedy of the Commons. SCIENCE 162, no. 3859 (1968): 1243–48.

Harmon, Amy. A Dying Young Woman's Hope in Cryonics and a Future. NEW YORK TIMES, September 12, 2015. www.nytimes.com/2015/09/13/us/cancer-immortality-cryogenics.html.

Hartman, Kurt M. & Bryan A. Liang. *Exceptions to Informed Consent in Emergency Medicine.* HOSPITAL PHYSICIAN (March 1999): 53–59.

Hernstein, R. J., George F. Loewenstein, Drazen Prelec & William Vaughan, Jr. *Utility Maximization and Melioration: Internalities in Individual Choice.* JOURNAL OF BEHAVIORAL DECISION MAKING 6, no. 3 (1993): 149–85.

Hirschman, Elizabeth C. *The Effect of Verbal and Pictorial Advertising Stimuli on Aesthetic, Utilitarian, and Familiarity Perceptions.* JOURNAL OF ADVERTISING 15, no. 2 (1986): 27–34.

Hirshleifer, David A. & Tyler Shumway. *Good Day Sunshine: Stock Returns and the Weather.* JOURNAL OF FINANCE 58, no. 3 (2003): 1009–32.

Holmes, Linda. ESPN's 'Broke' Looks at the Many Ways Athletes Lose Their Money (October 2, 2012), www.npr.org/sections/monkeysee/2012/10/02/162162226/espns-broke-looks-at-the-many-ways-athletes-lose-their-money.

Hull, Dana. *Musk Seeks Mars Explorers with $200,000, Guts to Risk Death.* BLOOMBERG (September 27, 2016), www.bloomberg.com/news/articles/2016-09-27/musk-seeks-mars-explorers-with-200-000-gumption-to-risk-death.

Human Rights Watch & InterACT Advocates for Intersex Youth Report. A Changing Paradigm: US Medical Provider Discomfort With Intersex Care Practices. www.hrw.org/report/2017/10/26/changing-paradigm/us-medical-provider-discomfort-intersex-care-practices.

Hurd, Heidi M. *The Normative Force of Consent.* In THE ROUTLEDGE HANDBOOK OF THE ETHICS OF CONSENT. (Peter Schaber, ed. Abingdon: Routledge Press, 2018).

Hutchinson, Lee. If Mars One Makes You Skeptical, You Might Be Dead Inside – Like Me. (May 8, 2013), http://arstechnica.com/staff/2013/05/if-mars-one-makes-you-skeptical-you-might-be-dead-insidelike-me/.

Jacobs, Andrew. *In Sweeping War on Obesity, Chile Slays Tony the Tiger.* NEW YORK TIMES, February 7, 2018. www.nytimes.com/2018/02/07/health/obesity-chile-sugar-regulations.html.

Jefferson-Jones, Jamila. *Quid Pro Quo Altruisim. In* THE GLOBAL BODY MARKET: ALTRUISM'S LIMITS, 87–106. (Michele Goodwin, ed. Cambridge: Cambridge University Press, 2013).

Johnson, Sara B., Robert W. Blum & Jay N. Giedd. *Adolescent Maturity and the Brain: The Promise and Pitfalls of Neuroscience Research in Adolescent Health Policy.* JOURNAL OF ADOLESCENT HEALTH 45, no. 3 (2009): 216–21.

Jolls, Christine, Cass R. Sunstein & Richard Thaler. *A Behavioral Approach to Law and Economics.* STANFORD LAW REVIEW 50, no. 3 (1998): 1471–1550.

KAHNEMAN, DANIEL. THINKING, FAST AND SLOW. (New York: Farrar, Straus & Giroux, 2011).

Kahneman, Daniel, Jack L. Knetsch & Richard H. Thaler. *Fairness as a Constraint on Profit Seeking: Entitlements in the Market.* In ADVANCES IN BEHAVIORAL ECONOMICS, 728–41 (Colin F. Camerer, et al., eds. Princeton NJ: Princeton University Press, 2004).

Kar, Robin. *The Art of Promise and Power of Contract.* JOTWELL (June 13, 2016), http://juris.jotwell.com/the-art-of-promise-and-power-of-contract/.

Karlamangla, Soumya. *Riverside Judge Overturns California's Doctor-Assisted Suicide Law.* LOS ANGELES TIMES (May 15, 2018).

Kay, Matthew & Matthew Terry. Textured Agreements: Re-envisioning Electronic Consent. (Paper presented at the Symposium on Usable Privacy and Security (SOUPS), July 14–16, 2010, Redmond, WA, USA), www.mjskay.com/papers/soups_2010_textured.pdf.

Kees, Jeremy, Scot Burton, J. Craig Andrews & John Kozup. *Tests of Graphic Visuals and Cigarette Package Warning Combinations: Implications for the Framework Convention on Tobacco Control.* JOURNAL OF PUBLIC POLICY & MARKETING 25, no. 2 (2006): 212–23.

Kelley, Michael B. & Pamela Engel. *21 Lottery Winners Who Blew It All.* BUSINESS INSIDER (February 11, 2015), www.businessinsider.com/lottery-winners-powerball-jackpot-how-much-2016-7.

KHADER, SERENE J. ADAPTIVE PREFERENCES AND WOMEN'S EMPOWERMENT. (Oxford: Oxford University Press, 2011).

Khazan, Olga. *Babies Floating in Fluid-Filled Bags.* THE ATLANTIC (April 25, 2017), www.theatlantic.com/health/archive/2017/04/preemies-floating-in-fluid-filled-bags/524181/.

KIM, NANCY S. WRAP CONTRACTS: FOUNDATIONS AND RAMIFICATIONS. (Oxford: Oxford University Press, 2013).

Kim, Nancy S. *Wrap Contracting and the Online Environment: Causes and Cures.* In RESEARCH HANDBOOK ON ELECTRONIC COMMERCE, 11–36. (John A. Rothchild, ed. Cheltenham: Edward Elgar Publishing, 2015).

Kim, Nancy S. *Online Contracting.* BUSINESS LAWYER 72, no. 1 (Winter 2016–2017): 243–53.

Kim, Nancy S. *Relative Consent and Contract Law.* NEVADA LAW JOURNAL 18, no. 1 (2017): 165–219.

Kipnis, Laura. *Has #MeToo Gone Too Far or Not Far Enough? The Answer Is Both.* THE GUARDIAN (January 13, 2017), www.theguardian.com/commentisfree/2018/jan/13/has-me-too-catherine-deneuve-laura-kipnis.

Klein, Gary. *Performing a Project Premortem.* HARVARD BUSINESS REVIEW (September 2007), https://hbr.org/2007/09/performing-a-project-premortem.

Kleinig, John. *The Nature of Consent. In* THE ETHICS OF CONSENT: THEORY AND PRACTICE, 3–24. (Franklin G. Miller & Alan Wertheimer, eds. Oxford: Oxford University Press, 2010).

Knapp, Charles L. *Is There a "Duty to Read"?. In* REVISITING THE CONTRACTS SCHOLARSHIP OF STEWART MACAULAY: ON THE EMPIRICAL AND THE LYRICAL, 315–343. (Jean Braucher, John Kidwell & William C. Whitford, eds. Portland: Hart Publishing, 2013).

Knaub, Kelly. *Egg Donors Get Pay Limits Axed with Antitrust Settlement.* LAW 360 (February 1, 2016), www.law360.com/articles/753389/egg-donors-get-pay-limits-axed-with-antitrust-settlement.

Kolata, Gina. $50,000 *Offered to Tall, Smart Egg Donor.* NEW YORK TIMES (March 3, 1999), www.nytimes.com/1999/03/03/us/50000-offered-to-tall-smart-egg-donor.html.

Kolata, Gina. *With Liposuction, the Belly Finds What the Thighs Lose.* NEW YORK TIMES (April 30, 2011), www.nytimes.com/2011/05/01/weekinreview/01kolata.html?_r=1andref=health.

Kolata, Gina. *Birth of Baby with Three Parents' DNA Marks Success for Banned Technique.* NEW YORK TIMES (September 27, 2016), www.nytimes.com/2016/09/28/health/birth-of-3-parent-baby-a-success-for-controversial-procedure.html.

Krawiec, Kimberly D. *A Woman's Worth.* NORTH CAROLINA LAW REVIEW 88 (2010): 1739–69.

Krawiec, Kim. Gift Cards for Blood! (February 7, 2017), www.thefacultylounge.org/2017/02/gift-cards-for-blood.html.

Kronman, Anthony Townsend. *Paternalism and the Law of Contracts.* YALE LAW JOURNAL 92, no. 5 (1983): 763–98.

Latham, Melanie. *"If It Ain't Broke, Don't Fix It?": Scandals, "Risk," and Cosmetic Surgery Regulation in the UK and France.* MEDICAL LAW REVIEW 22, no. 3 (2014): 384–408.

Laurance, Jeremy. *Cosmetic Surgeons Demand Ban on Advertising Their Own Trade.* THE INDEPENDENT (November 16, 2009), www.independent.co.uk/life-style/health-and-families/health-news/cosmetic-surgeons-demand-ban-on-advertising-their-own-trade-1821247.html.

Leff, Arthur Allen. *Unconscionability and the Code – The Emperor's New Clause.* UNIVERSITY OF PENNSYLVANIA LAW REVIEW 115 (1967): 485–559.

Leonhard, Chunlin. *The Unbearable Lightness of Consent in Contract Law.* CASE WESTERN RESERVE LAW REVIEW 63, no. 1 (2012): 57–90.

Leonhard, Chunlin. *Illegal Agreements and the Lesser Evil Principle.* CATHOLIC UNIVERSITY LAW REVIEW 64, no. 4 (2015): 833–66.

Lerner, Barron H. *When Lobotomy Was Seen as Advanced.* NEW YORK TIMES (December 19, 2011) www.nytimes.com/2011/12/20/health/report-on-eva-peron-recalls-time-when-lobotomy-was-embraced.html.

LEVITIN, DANIEL J. THE ORGANIZED MIND: THINKING STRAIGHT IN THE AGE OF INFORMATION OVERLOAD. (London: Penguin, 2014).

Levy, Alan S., Sara B. Fein & Raymond E. Schucker. *Performance Characteristics of Seven Nutrition Label Formats.* JOURNAL OF PUBLIC POLICY AND MARKETING 15, no. 1 (1996): 1–15.

LIN, NAN. SOCIAL CAPITAL: A THEORY OF SOCIAL STRUCTURE AND ACTION. (Cambridge: Cambridge University Press, 2001).

Loewenstein, George. *Out of Control: Visceral Influences on Behavior.* ORGANIZATIONAL BEHAVIOR AND HUMAN DECISION PROCESSES 65, no. 3 (1996): 272–92.

Luke, Shaefer, H. & Kathryn Edin. Extreme Poverty in the United States, 1996 to 2011. (February 2012), www.npc.umich.edu/publications/policy_briefs/brief28/policybrief28.pdf.

Lunt, Neil, Richard Smith, Mark Exworthy, Stephen T. Green, Daniel Horsfall & Russell Mannion. Medical Tourism: Treatments, Markets and Health System Implications: A Scoping Review (September 20, 2011), www.oecd.org/els/health-systems/48723982.pdf.

Lyon, Matthew R. *No Means No?: Withdrawal of Consent During Intercourse and the Continuing Evolution of the Definition of Rape.* JOURNAL OF CRIMINAL LAW AND CRIMINOLOGY 95, (2004): 277–314.

MACKINNON, CATHARINE A. WOMEN'S LIVES MEN'S LAWS. (Cambridge MA: Harvard University Press, 2005).

MACLEAN, ALASDAIR. AUTONOMY, INFORMED CONSENT AND MEDICAL LAW: A RELATIONAL CHALLENGE. (Cambridge: Cambridge University Press, 2009).

Magat, Wesley A., John W. Payne, Peter F. Brucato, Jr. *How Important is Information Format? An Experimental Study of Home Energy Audit Programs.* JOURNAL OF POLICY ANALYSIS AND MANAGEMENT 6, no. 1 (1986): 20–34.

Maheshwari, Sapna. *Why Tobacco Companies Are Paying to Tell You Smoking Kills.* NEW YORK TIMES, (November 24, 2017), www.nytimes.com/2017/11/24/business/media/tobacco-companies-ads.html.

Malhotra, Naresh K. *Information Load and Consumer Decision Making.* JOURNAL OF CONSUMER RESEARCH 8, no. 4 (1982): 419–30.

Malmendier, Ulrike & Devin Shanthikumar. *Are Small Investors Naïve About Incentives?* JOURNAL OF FINANCIAL ECONOMICS 85, (2007): 457–89.

Mandhai, Shafik. *Finding Organ Donors among Qatar's Muslim Community.* AL JAZEERA, July 13, 2015. www.aljazeera.com/news/2015/07/finding-organ-donors-qatar-muslim-commu nity-150713090541298.html.

Mann, Traci. *Informed Consent for Psychological Research: Do Subjects Comprehend Consent Forms and Understand Their Legal Rights?* PSYCHOLOGICAL SCIENCE 5, no. 3 (May 1994): 140–43.

Mars One Press Release. Mars One Will Settle Men on Mars in 2023. (March 31, 2012), www .mars-one.com/news/press-releases/mars-one-will-settle-men-on-mars-in-2023.

Mars One Press Release. Mars One Starts its Search for the First Humans on Mars. (April 22, 2013), www.mars-one.com/news/press-releases/mars-one-starts-its-search-for-the-first-humans-on-mars.

Mars One Press Release. Mars One Announces Round One Astronaut Selection Results. (December 30, 2013), www.mars-one.com/news/press-releases/mars-one-announces-round-2-astronaut-selection-results.

Masunaga, Samantha. *A Quick Guide to Elon Musk's New Brain-Implant Company, Neuralink.* LOS ANGELES TIMES (April 21, 2017), www.latimes.com/business/technology/la-fi-tn-elon-musk-neuralink-20170421-htmlstory.html.

Matsumura, Kaiponanea T. *Binding Future Selves.* LOUISIANA LAW REVIEW 75, (2014): 71–125.

Matsumura, Kaiponanea T. *Consent to Intimate Regulation.* NORTH CAROLINA LAW REVIEW 96, no. 4 (2018): 1014–84.

Matsumura, Kaiponanea T. *Public Policing of Intimate Agreements.* YALE JOURNAL OF LAW AND FEMINISM 25, (2013): 159–116.

Max, D.T. *Beyond Human.* NATIONAL GEOGRAPHIC MAGAZINE 231, no. 4, (April 2017): 40.

McNeil, Jr., Donald G. *How to Get Smokers to Quit? Enlist World's Ugliest Color.* NEW YORK TIMES (June 21, 2016), www.nytimes.com/2016/06/21/health/cigarette-packaging-ugliest-color.html.

Metcalfe, Janet & Walter Mischel. *A Hot/Cool System Analysis of Delay of Gratification: Dynamics of Willpower.* PSYCHOLOGICAL REVIEW 106, (1999): 3–19.

Michigan State Police. Myths and Facts About Seat Belts. www.michigan.gov/msp/0,4643,7-123-72297_64773_22760-13689-,00.html.

Milgram, Stanley. *Behavioral Study of Obedience.* JOURNAL OF ABNORMAL AND SOCIAL PSYCHOLOGY 67, (1963): 371–78.

Milgram, Stanley. OBEDIENCE TO AUTHORITY: AN EXPERIMENTAL VIEW. New York: Harper Collins, 1974.

MILL, JOHN STUART. ON LIBERTY. (New York: Barnes & Noble Publishing, 2004).

Miller, Franklin G. & Alan Wertheimer. *Preface to A Theory of Consent Transactions: Beyond Valid Consent.* In THE ETHICS OF CONSENT: THEORY AND PRACTICE, 79–106. (Franklin G. Miller & Alan Wertheimer, eds. Oxford: Oxford University Press, 2009).

Morin, Rich. For Many Injured Veterans, a Lifetime of Consequences. (Pew Research Center, November 8, 2011), www.pewsocialtrends.org/2011/11/08/for-many-injured-veter ans-a-lifetime-of-consequences/.

National Center for Health Research. (Accessed June 18, 2018), www.center4research.org/.

National Conference of State Legislatures. Dependent Health Coverage and Age for Healthcare Benefits. (November 1, 2016), www.ncsl.org/research/health/dependent-health-coverage-state-implementation.aspx.

National Conference of State Legislatures. Tattooing and Body Piercing. (August 1, 2017), www.ncsl.org/programs/health/bodyart-1.htm.

NATIONAL INSTITUTES OF HEALTH: NATIONAL CANCER INSTITUTE. TAKING PART IN CANCER TREATMENT RESEARCH STUDIES. (Maryland: National Institute of Health, 2016).

National POLST Paradigm. About the National POLST Paradigm. (Accessed June 20, 2018), www.polst.org/about-the-national-polst-paradigm.

National POLST Paradigm, Patient FAQs: Does a POLST Form Limit the Type of Treatment I Can Get? What if I Develop a Simple Infection?, http://polst.org/faq/.

Nemeroff, Charles. *Suicide. Ask an Expert*, KPBS, www.pbs.org/wgbh/takeonestep/depres sion/ask-suicide_1.html.

New York State Department of Health. Article 4A Regulation of Body Piercing and Tattooing. (Accessed March 31, 2018), www.health.ny.gov/community/body_art/article_4a.htm.

New York State Department of Health. Body Art – Tattooing and Body Piercing. (Accessed March 30, 2018), www.health.ny.gov/community/body_art/.

Nickerson, Raymond S. *Confirmation Bias: A Ubiquitous Phenomenon in Many Guises.* REVIEW OF GENERAL PSYCHOLOGY 2, no. 2 (1998): 175–220.

Noonan, David. *Meet the Two Scientists who Implanted a False Memory into a Mouse.* SMITHSONIAN MAGAZINE (November 2014), www.smithsonianmag.com/innovation/meet-two-scientists-who-implanted-false-memory-mouse-180953045/?page=2.

NUSSBAUM, MARTHA C. HIDING FROM HUMANITY: DISGUST, SHAME, AND THE LAW. (Princeton NJ: Princeton University Press, 2004).

O'Hegarty, Michelle, Linda Peterson, Gayanne Yenokyan, David Nelson, & Pascale Wortley. Young Adults' Perceptions of Cigarette Warning Labels in the United States and Canada. April 2007. www.cdc.gov/pcd/issues/2007/apr/06_0024.htm.

Olson, Elizabeth. *The Benefits of a Trust.* NEW YORK TIMES, March 25, 2018. www.nytimes .com/2018/03/22/your-money/trust-wills-inheritance.html.

OMAN, NATHAN B. THE DIGNITY OF COMMERCE: MARKETS AND THE MORAL FOUNDATIONS OF CONTRACT LAW. (Chicago IL: University of Chicago Press, 2017).

ORENSTEIN, PEGGY. GIRLS AND SEX: NAVIGATING THE COMPLICATED NEW LANDSCAPE. (New York: Harper Collins, 2016).

Ostrom, Elinor. *A Behavioral Approach to the Rational Choice Theory of Collective Action.* AMERICAN POLITICAL SCIENCE REVIEW 92, no. 1 (1998): 1–22.

Ostrom, Elinor. *Polycentricity, Complexity and the Common.* THE GOOD SOCIETY 9, (1999): 37–41.

Parfit, Derek. *Personal Identity.* THE PHILOSOPHICAL REVIEW 80, no. 1 (1971): 3–27.

Peralta, Eyder. *"Body Hacking" Movement Rises Ahead of Moral Answers.* NATIONAL PUBLIC RADIO (March 10, 2016), www.npr.org/sections/alltechconsidered/2016/03/10/468556420/ body-hacking-movement-rises-ahead-of-moral-answers.

PERILLO, JOSEPH M. CONTRACTS. (St. Paul's MN: West Academic, 2014).

Pollack, Andrew. *Is Money Tainting the Plasma Supply?* NEW YORK TIMES (December 5, 2009), www.nytimes.com/2009/12/06/business/06plasma.html.

Porat, Ariel & Stephen Sugarman. *Limited Inalienability Rules.* GEORGETOWN LAW JOURNAL 107, (forthcoming 2018).

Posner, Eric A. & Cass R. Sunstein. *Moral Commitments in Cost-Benefit Analysis.* VIRGINIA LAW REVIEW 103, (2017): 1809–60.

Post Implementation Review of Tobacco Plain Packaging, Australian Government. (February 26, 2016), http://ris.pmc.gov.au/2016/02/26/tobacco-plain-packaging.

Presten, Elizabeth, Why You Get Paid to Donate Plasma, but not Blood. (January 22, 2016), www.statnews.com/2016/01/22/paid-plasma-not-blood/.

Purshouse, Craig & Kate Bracegirdle. *The Problem of Unenforceable Surrogacy Contracts: Can Unjust Enrichment Provide a Solution?* MEDICAL LAW REVIEW (February 7, 2018), https://academic.oup.com/medlaw/advance-article/doi/10.1093/medlaw/fwy001/4841967? searchresult=1.

Putnam, Robert D. *Tuning In, Tuning Out: The Strange Disappearance of Social Capital in America.* PS: POLITICAL SCIENCE AND POLITICS 28, no. 4 (1995) 664–83.

R. R. Kishore. *Human Organs, Scarcities, and Sale: Morality Revisited.* JOURNAL OF MEDICAL ETHICS 31, no. 6 (2005) 362–65.

Rabin, Roni Caryn. *"Going Flat" After Breast Cancer.* NEW YORK TIMES. (October 31, 2016), www.nytimes.com/2016/11/01/well/live/going-flat-after-breast-cancer.html.

Radin, Margaret Jane. *Property and Personhood.* STANFORD LAW REVIEW 34, no. 5 (1982): 957–1015.

RADIN, MARGARET JANE. BOILERPLATE: THE FINE PRINT, VANISHING RIGHTS, AND THE RULE OF LAW. (Princeton NJ: Princeton University Press, 2013).

RADIN, MARGARET JANE. CONTESTED COMMODITIES: THE TROUBLE WITH TRADE IN SEX, CHILDREN, BODY PARTS, AND OTHER THINGS. (Cambridge MA: Harvard University Press, 1996).

Raymond, E. G. & D. A. Grimes. *The Comparative Safety of Legal Induced Abortion and Childbirth in the United States.* OBSTETRICS AND GYNECOLOGY 119, (2012): 215–19.

Reilly, Michael. *A Three-Parent Child Was Conceived in Mexico, Because the U.S. Won't Allow It.* MASSACHUSETTS INSTITUTE OF TECHNOLOGY REVIEW (September 28, 2016), www.technologyreview.com/s/602499/a-three-parent-child-was-conceived-in-mexico-because-the-us-wont-allow-it/.

Reproductive Health Matters. *Round Up: Cosmetic Surgery.* REPRODUCTIVE HEALTH MATTERS 18, (2010): 175–81.

Richie, Cristina. *Voluntary Sterilization for Childfree Women.* HASTINGS CENTER REPORT 43, no. 6 (2013): 36–44.

Rid, A., L. M. Bachmann, V. Wettstein & N. Biller-Andorno. *Would You Sell A Kidney in a Regulated Kidney Market? Results of an Exploratory Study.* JOURNAL OF MEDICAL ETHICS 35, (2009): 558–64.

Rind, Bruce. *Effect of Beliefs about Weather Conditions on Tipping.* JOURNAL OF APPLIED SOCIAL PSYCHOLOGY 26, no. 2 (1996): 137–47.

Robinson, Lisa A., W. Kip Viscusi & Richard Zeckhauser. *Consumer Warning Labels Aren't Working.* HARVARD BUSINESS REVIEW (November 30, 2016), https://hbr.org/2016/11/consu mer-warning-labels-arent-working.

Romm, Cari. The Life of a Professional Guinea Pig. ATLANTIC (September 23, 2015), www .theatlantic.com/science/archive/2015/09/life-of-a-professional-guinea-pig/406018/.

Ross, Lee & Richard E. Njisbett. THE PERSON AND THE SITUATION: PERSPECTIVES OF SOCIAL PSYCHOLOGY. (London: Printer & Martin Publishers, 2011).

Sabini, John, Michael Siepmann & Julia Stein. *The Really Fundamental Attribution Error in Social Psychological Research.* PSYCHOLOGICAL INQUIRY 12, no. 1 (2001): 1–15.

SALES, NANCY JO. AMERICAN GIRLS: SOCIAL MEDIA AND THE SECRET LIVES OF TEENAGERS. (New York: Knopf Doubleday Publishing Group, 2016).

SANDEL, MICHAEL J. WHAT MONEY CAN'T BUY: THE MORAL LIMITS OF MARKETS. (Basingstoke: Macmillan, 2012).

SANE Australia. Lessons for Life: The Experiences of People Who Attempt Suicide. (2015), www.sane.org/images/PDFs/lessons-for-life.pdf.

SATZ, DEBRA. WHY SOME THINGS SHOULD NOT BE FOR SALE: THE MORAL LIMITS OF MARKETS. (Oxford: Oxford University Press, 2010).

Saunders, Jr., Edward M. *Stock Prices and Wall Street Weather.* AMERICAN ECONOMIC REVIEW 83, no. 5 (1993): 1337–45.

Sawicki, Nadia N. *Modernizing Informed Consent: Expanding the Boundaries of Materiality.* UNIVERSITY OF ILLINOIS LAW REVIEW (2016): 821–72.

Sax, Joanna. *Dietary Supplements Are Not All Safe and Not All Food: How the Low Cost of Dietary Supplements Preys on the Consumer.* AMERICAN JOURNAL OF LAW AND MEDICINE 41, (May 2015): 374–94.

Sax, Joanna. *Financial Conflicts of Interest in Science.* ANNALS OF HEALTH LAW 21, (2012): 291–329.

Schaefer, Jesse A. *Beyond a Definition: Understanding the Nature of Void and Voidable Contracts.* CAMPBELL LAW REVIEW 33, no. 1 (2010): 193–210.

Schwarz, Norbert & Gerald L. Clore. *Mood, Misattribution, and Judgments of Well-Being: Informative and Directive Functions of Affective States.* JOURNAL OF PERSONALITY AND SOCIAL PSYCHOLOGY 45, no. 3 (1983): 513–23.

Scutti, Susan. *Becoming Transsexual: Getting the Facts on Sex Reassignment Surgery.* MEDICAL DAILY (November 6, 2014), www.medicaldaily.com/becoming-transsexual-getting-facts-sex-reassignment-surgery-309584.

Seelye, Katharine Q. & Jess Bidgood. *Teenager Who Urged Friend to Kill Himself Is Guilty of Manslaughter.* NEW YORK TIMES, (June 16, 2017), www.nytimes.com/2017/06/16/us/suicide-texting-trial-michelle-carter-conrad-roy.html.

Seira, Enrique, Alan Elizondo & Eduardo Laguna-Müggenburg. *Are Information Disclosures Effective? Evidence from the Credit Card Market.* AMERICAN ECONOMIC JOURNAL: ECONOMIC POLICY 9, no. 1 (2017): 227–307.

Shaefer, H. Luke & Kathryn Edin. Extreme Poverty in the United States, 1996 to 2011. (February 2012), www.npc.umich.edu/publications/policy_briefs/brief28/policybrief28.pdf.

Shannon-Missal, Larry. Tattoo Takeover: Three in Ten Americans Have Tattoos, and Most Don't Stop at Just One. (February 10, 2016), https://theharrispoll.com/tattoos-can-take-any-number-of-forms-from-animals-to-quotes-to-cryptic-symbols-and-appear-in-all-sorts-of-spots-on-our-bodies-some-visible-in-everyday-life-others-not-so-much-but-one-thi/.

Sharma, Sujit. *Are Fast Food Ads Killing Us?* CNN (April 27, 2017), www.cnn.com/2017/04/27/opinions/overeating-the-new-tobacco-opinion-sharma/index.html.

SHAROT, TALI. THE OPTIMISM BIAS: A TOUR OF THE IRRATIONALLY POSITIVE BRAIN. (New York: Knopf Doubleday Publishing Group, 2011).

Shavell, Steven. *Is Breach of Contract Immoral?* EMORY LAW JOURNAL 56, no. 2 (2006): 439–60.

Shiffrin, Seana Valentine. *The Divergence of Contract and Promise.* HARVARD LAW REVIEW 120, (2007): 708–53.

Simon, Herbert A. *A Behavioral Model of Rational Choice.* QUARTERLY JOURNAL OF ECONOMICS 69, no. 1 (February 1955): 99–118.

Simon, Herbert A. *Rational Decision-Making in Business Organizations.* AMERICAN ECONOMIC REVIEW 69, no. 4 (1979): 493–513.

Slawson, Nicola. *#Metoo Trend Highlights Sexual Harassment in Wake of Weinstein Claims.* GUARDIAN (October 16, 2017), www.theguardian.com/uk-news/2017/oct/16/me-too-social-media-trend-highlights-sexual-harassment-of-women.

Smith, Dana. Blood From Young People May Be a Secret to Fighting Aging. (June 30, 2017), www.kqed.org/futureofyou/366983/blood-from-young-people-may-be-a-secret-to-fighting-aging.

SMITH, STEPHEN A. CONTRACT THEORY. (Oxford: Oxford University Press, 2004).

Solemani, Sarah. *The Aziz Ansari Furore Isn't the End of #MeToo. It's Just the Start.* GUARDIAN (January 22, 2018), www.theguardian.com/commentisfree/2018/jan/21/aziz-ansari-metoo-sex ual-equality.

Span, Paula. *The Patients Were Saved. That's Why the Families Are Suing.* NEW YORK TIMES (April 10, 2017), www.nytimes.com/2017/04/10/health/wrongful-life-lawsuit-dnr.html.

SPAR, DEBORA L. THE BABY BUSINESS: HOW MONEY, SCIENCE, AND POLITICS DRIVE THE COMMERCE OF CONCEPTION. (Cambridge MA: Harvard Business School Press, 2006).

SPAR, DEBORA L. WONDER WOMEN: SEX, POWER, AND THE QUESTION FOR PERFECTION. (New York: Farrar, Straus & Giroux, 2013).

Spar, Deborah L. *Aging and My Beauty Dilemma.* NEW YORK TIMES (September 24, 2016), www.nytimes.com/2016/09/25/fashion/aging-plastic-surgery-feminism.html.

St. Martin, Victoria. *Former Gang Members Remove Tattoos to Break from Past.* WASHINGTON POST (July 10, 2015), www.washingtonpost.com/local/gang-members-remove-tattoos-to-break-from-past/2015/07/10/3bd54ae8-266d-11e5-b72c-2b7d516e1e0e_story.html?noredirec t=onandutm_term=.b170dbd140bc.

Stanley, Chuck. *Tobacco Companies Settle Long-Running Health Warning Dispute.* LAW360 (April 25, 2018), www.law360.com/consumerprotection/articles/1037281/tobacco-cos-settle-long-running-health-warning-dispute?nl_pk=0f3b3b3b-80ff-46e8-a41c-.

Steinberg, Laurence, Sandra Graham, Lia O'Brien, Jennifer Woolard, Elizabeth Cauffman & Marie Banich. *Age Differences in Future Orientation and Delay Discounting.* CHILD DEVELOPMENT 80, (2009): 28–44.

Stephens, Bret. *Opinion: When #MeToo Goes Too Far.* NEW YORK TIMES (December 20, 2017), www.nytimes.com/2017/12/20/opinion/metoo-damon-too-far.html?mtrref=www .google.comandassetType=opinion.

SUNSTEIN, CASS R. WHY NUDGE: THE POLITICS OF LIBERTARIAN PATERNALISM. (Yale CT: Yale University Press, 2014).

Tavernise, Sabrina. *FDA Sets 2018 Deadline to Rid Foods of Trans Fats.* NEW YORK TIMES (June 16, 2015), www.nytimes.com/2015/06/17/health/fda-gives-food-industry-three-years-eliminate-trans-fats.html.

Testy, Kellye Y. *An Unlikely Resurrection.* NORTHWESTERN UNIVERSITY LAW REVIEW 90, (1995): 219–35.

The Dept. of Health, Australian Government. Evaluation of Tobacco Plain Packaging in Australia. (Last updated October 23, 2017), www.health.gov.au/internet/main/publishing .nsf/Content/tobacco-plain-packaging-evaluation.

The Medical Board of California. Frequently Asked Questions—Cosmetic Treatments. (Accessed March 30, 2018), www.mbc.ca.gov/Licensees/Cosmetic_Treatments_FAQ.aspx.

The Modern Religion. Is Organ Donation Permissible? (Accessed June 20, 2018), www .themodernreligion.com/misc/hh/organ-transplant.html.

Thomas, Morgen L. *Sick/Beautiful/Freak: Nonmainstream Body Modification and the Social Construction of Deviance.* SAGE OPEN, (October–December 2012): 1–12, http://journals .sagepub.com/doi/pdf/10.1177/2158244012467787.

Thusi, I. India. *Radical Feminist Harms on Sex Workers.* LEWIS AND CLARK LAW REVIEW 22 (2018):185.

Tohme, Rania A. & Scott D. Holmberg. *Transmission of Hepatitis C Virus Infection Through Tattooing and Piercing: A Critical Review.* CLINICAL INFECTIOUS DISEASES 54, (2012): 1167–78, www.ncbi.nlm.nih.gov/pmc/articles/PMC4613802/pdf/nihms729527.pdf.

TREBILCOCK, MICHAEL J. THE LIMITS OF FREEDOM OF CONTRACTS. (Cambridge MA: Harvard University Press, 1996).

Tversky, Amos & Daniel Kahneman. *Judgment Under Uncertainty: Heuristics and Biases.* SCIENCE 185, (1974): 1124–31.

U.S. Census Bureau, Weighted Average Poverty Thresholds for Families of Specified Sizes, Historical Poverty Tables-People 1978–2017. (Accessed April 5, 2018), www.census.gov/data/tables/time-series/demo/income-poverty/historical-poverty-thresholds.html.

U.S. Department of Health and Human Services. Surgeon General's Report: How Tobacco Smoke Causes Diseases … What It Means For You. (2010), www.cdc.gov/tobacco/data_statistics/sgr/2010/consumer_booklet/pdfs/consumer.pdf.

U.S. Food and Drug Administration. Background on Drug Advertising. (Last updated June 19, 2015), www.fda.gov/Drugs/ResourcesForYou/Consumers/PrescriptionDrugAdvertising/ucm071964.htm#authority.

U.S. Food and Drug Administration. Payment to Research Subjects – Information Sheet. (Last updated January 25, 2018), www.fda.gov/RegulatoryInformation/Guidances/ucm126429.htm.

VanEpps, Eric M., Julie S. Downs & George Loewenstein. *Calorie Label Formats: Using Numeric and Traffic Light Calorie Labels to Reduce Lunch Calories.* JOURNAL OF PUBLIC POLICY AND MARKETING 35, (2016): 26–36.

Vider, Stephen & David S. Byers. *A Half-Century of Conflict Over Attempts to "Cure" Gay People.* TIME (February 12, 2015), http://time.com/3705745/history-therapy-hadden/.

Vollmann, Jochen & Rolf Winau. *Informed Consent in Human Experimentation Before the Nuremberg Code.* BRITISH MEDICAL JOURNAL 313, (1996): 1445–49.

Wang, Lisa. *#MeTooWhatsNext: Why 2018 Is the Year to Take Action.* FORBES (January 2, 2018), www.forbes.com/sites/lisawang/2018/01/02/metoowhatsnext-why-2018-is-the-year-to-take-action/#56516a89112c .

Washington State Department of Licensing. How to Get Your License: Body Art Artists. (Accessed June 12, 2018), www.dol.wa.gov/business/tattoo/bodyartlicense.html.

Weinstein, Neil D. *Unrealistic Optimism about Future Life Events.* JOURNAL OF PERSONALITY AND SOCIAL PSYCHOLOGY 39, (1980): 806–19.

Weiss, Bari. *Aziz Ansari Is Guilty. Of Not Being a Mind Reader.* NEW YORK TIMES (January 15, 2018), www.nytimes.com/2018/01/15/opinion/aziz-ansari-babe-sexual-harassment.html

West, Robin. *Authority, Autonomy, and Choice: The Role of Consent in the Moral and Political Visions of Franz Kafka and Richard Posner.* HARVARD LAW REVIEW 99, (1985): 384–428.

WESTPHAL, JONATHAN. THE MIND-BODY PROBLEM. (Cambridge MA: Massachusetts Institute of Technology, 2016).

Willens, Michele. *No More Stigma Against Plastic Surgery, Please.* ATLANTIC (July 1, 2013), www.theatlantic.com/sexes/archive/2013/07/no-more-stigma-against-plastic-surgery-please/277427/.

Williams, Patricia. *Alchemical Notes: Reconstructing Ideals from Deconstructed Rights.* HARVARD CIVIL RIGHTS – CIVIL LIABILITIES LAW REVIEW 22, (1987): 401–33.

WILLISTON, SAMUEL. A TREATISE ON THE LAW OF CONTRACTS. (New York: Lawyers Cooperative Publishing, 1990).

WINKLER, ADAM. WE THE CORPORATIONS: HOW AMERICAN CORPORATIONS WON THEIR CIVIL RIGHTS. (New York: W.W. Norton & Company, Inc., 2018).

WORLD PROFESSIONAL ASSOCIATION FOR TRANSGENDER HEALTH. THE STANDARDS OF CARE 7TH VERSION. (2011), www.wpath.org/publications/soc.

World Professional Association for Transgender Health. Position Statement on Medical Necessity of Treatment, Sex Reassignment, and Insurance Coverage in the U.S.A. (December 21, 2016), www.wpath.org/site_page.cfm?pk_association_webpage_menu= 1352andpk_association_webpage=3947.

Youn, Dr. Anthony. *Body Modification – or Mutilation?* CNN (November 7, 2013), https:// edition.cnn.com/2013/11/07/health/youn-body-modification/.

Youn, Anthony. *Plastic Surgery: "Wild West" of Medicine.* CNN (July 25, 2012), www.cnn .com/2012/07/25/health/youn-wild-west-medicine/index.html.

Youn, Anthony. *Suffering from "Tattoo Regret."* CNN (April 8, 2013), www.cnn.com/2013/04/ 08/health/youn-tattoo-regret/index.html.

Zacharek, Stephanie, Eliana Dockterman & Haley Sweetland Edwards. *TIME Person of the Year 2017: The Silence Breakers,* TIME (December 18, 2017), http://time.com/time-person-of-the-year-2017-silence-breakers/.

Zakowicz, Halina. How to Make Extra Money by Participating in Clinical Trials (April 9, 2012), https://ivetriedthat.com/2012/04/09/how-to-make-extra-money-by-participating-in-clinical-trials/.

Zalesne, Deborah. *The Intersection of Contract law, Reproductive Technology, and the Market: Families in the Age of Art.* UNIVERSITY OF RICHMOND LAW REVIEW 51, (2017): 419–87.

Zimmer, Carl. *Young Blood May Hold Key to Reversing Aging.* NEW YORK TIMES (May 4, 2014), www.nytimes.com/2014/05/05/science/young-blood-may-hold-key-to-reversing-aging.html.

Zuckerman, Diana. *Teenagers and Cosmetic Surgery.* ETHICS JOURNAL AMERICAN MEDICAL ASSOCIATION 7, no. 3 (March 2005): 1–4.

Index